AS FAR AS I REMEMBER

As Far As I Remember

MICHAEL KERR

FIRST INDIAN REPRINT 2008

Universal
Law Publishing Co. Pvt. Ltd.

First published 2002
Reprinted-hardback 2006
1st paperback print-2006
First Indian Reprint 2008

Published by
UNIVERSAL LAW PUBLISHING CO. PVT. LTD.
C-FF-1A, Dilkhush Industrial Estate, (Opp. Hans Cinema, Azadpur)
G.T. Karnal Road, Delhi-110033
Tel: 011-27215334,27438103,42381334
Fax: 011-27458529
e-mail *(For sales inquiries):* sales@unilawbooks.com
Website: www.unilawbooks.com

Under Special arrangement with
HART PUBLISHING, UK

Licensed for sale in Indian Sub-continent only

British Library Cataloguing in Publication Data
Data Available

ISBN: 978-81-7534-662-8

Typeset by John Saunders Design & Production

Printed in India at Glorious Printers, New Delhi

Contents

Illustrations

TEXT

PLATES

Between pages 22–23

Between pages 238–239

BACK PANEL OF COVER

In memory of my parents.

For Diana.

And Candy, Jo and Tim, and Lucy and Alexander.

And my sister Judy, who saw it all.

Preface

100 copies of an earlier version of the first 58 chapters were published privately under this title in 1994, but written at the beginning of the nineties. I only have three left in my possession which have found their way back. An incomplete version of part of the remainder was then also in draft. Both have now been greatly revised, extended and brought up to 2002.

My thanks for their great help with this book go to my wife Diana, my sister Judy, my old friend Geoffrey Lewis for his encouragement, to Johnny Veeder, and to Ailsa Mackillop in Chambers for solving all the word processor problems, to Mark and Marguerite Littman and to Martin Kramer for their support throughout as well as to many others and to Richard Hart and his team for publishing it.

Michael Kerr
London
April 2002

PUBLISHER'S NOTE

Michael Kerr's book was to all intents and purposes completed before he became seriously ill. During his final illness, determined to see the book published, he spent much of his time re-writing passages with which he was not entirely happy, always striving to "tell the truth". Sadly he died before the book was published, although it was finished by the time of his death, so that he was able to visualise how it would finally look.

In many ways a modest and private man, Michael nevertheless cherished the belief that his and his family's story deserved to be re-told. Those who were privileged to know him, and those who will only ever know him through this book, will surely agree.

As my father used to say:

"A quelque chose malheur est bon."

French proverb, after Voltaire.

1 · The Beginning

I LISTENED to the first of many rows between my parents – who had a happy marriage, despite everything – in the early morning of Sunday, 1 March 1921, in the Charlottenburg Hospital, Berlin. Since I was then less than an hour old I have to rely on my mother's numerous descriptions of this row, which evidently remained their biggest ever. Admittedly, she tended to overstate and simplify, whereas my father was reserved and deeply private. He would never admit to having had a row with anyone, let alone with my mother, other than on points of principle, ethics, literary merit, or politics, when he relished their necessity. But he never denied her accounts of this row.

The subject was my middle name or names, if any. Both were agreed on Michael, and my father wanted no more. Multiple forenames were not usual in Germany, and throughout his life my father was renowned for his brevity and staccato style. But my mother insisted that I should also be called Robert, after her father, whom she greatly admired. My father had no respect for him, to put it mildly. But she was as persistent as she could sometimes be. She pointed out to my father – and reminded me countless times, as though it had been my fault – that she had just undergone a horrific labour extending over two days, at a time when medical conditions in Germany were still suffering from the aftermath of the first world war. Knowing her, and despite her harrowing experience, as it had undoubtedly been, she would nevertheless have recovered quite sufficiently to make an overwhelming case for the right to name the end-product as she wished. By mid- morning her insistence had become irresistible and worn my father down. Their compromise was what neither wanted. I was named after both their fathers, Robert and Emanuel, as well as Michael, and MREK much later at school in England.

Although distinctive and something of a joke, my third forename has always caused me trouble. In English it is spelled with two m's, and everyone sniggered and looked at me in chapel when we sang "Our Lord Emmanuel." I had changed to spell it with two m's, because for most of my life I wanted to be as English as possible. I didn't want people to know that I was really German and had only begun to acquire a respectable history at the age of fifteen. But as I got older and more secure – much older – I finally reached the stage of 'to thine own self be true.' One of its manifestations was that I again spelt Emanuel with one

m. But on an application to renew my driving licence – in my fifties, I think – this produced a refusal from the Vehicle Licensing Centre in Swansea, pointing out the discrepancy in my third forename from my previous licence. The implication was that I was giving a false description with criminal intent. I wrote and explained that recent research had revealed that the spelling with one m was a better interpretation of the original Hebrew and Greek sources. I never had a considered reply. But I got my licence; and as in my recent passports, the single m was restored. *On retourne toujours à ses premiers amours* may be an oversimplification. But certainly to one's origins.

I cannot claim that this row between my parents is my earliest actual memory, although it is presumably still stored somewhere in my mind. But it is certainly the earliest event of my life of which I have been made aware since. However, is it true? As I am writing this, eighty years later, I do not know; nor does anyone else who is still alive. One gets used to this as one gets older; that there is no one left to ask. As a lawyer, one instinctively reaches out for a book to look it up. But there is also no book. My sister has a phenomenal memory, as shown by her books about our childhood. But she is two years younger and was not there. So, as with many other things in these memoirs, there is no one to consult about the truth.

But since this account is intended to be entirely truthful, and only truthful, if it ever gets written, I must explain in what sense I use this word. As a committed lawyer who has never had any respect for politicians I have nevertheless always liked the aphorism that truth is a matter of opinion. But that is not what I mean. Nor do I mean truth which is as near absolute as it can be; the truth of eye-witnesses or documents. Even that, of course, is never absolute. If four people stand at different corners of a cross-road and see two cars collide, their truthful eye-witness versions will invariably differ. So, in comparison with the most accurate version of actual events, one's lifetime recollections are inevitably highly inaccurate. (The first of many clichés).

However – and I must make this clear at the outset – I am not even trying to be as accurate as I could be. With some effort and research I could be much more accurate. Indeed, there are no doubt many details which are simply wrong and could be shown to be so, even now. For this I am sorry. But I am not going to do the research necessary to get more closely from the perceived truth (to use this awful adjective) towards detailed accuracy. Otherwise this book would never get written. I have many large box files containing hundreds of letters and other papers about my family and career, extending over the whole of my life, which are there if anyone wants to look at them. Perhaps someone will one day, if only to demonstrate how recollections can differ from documented history. But for me the actual events are not necessarily more interesting than my recollection of them. After all, writing memoirs is only writing about oneself; setting down impressions of what one's life was, or appears to have been, and how one saw other people's lives. To the writer this is much more interesting than what 'really' happened. Most happenings are purely fortuitous and have little to do with oneself. But the way one remembers them has everything to do with oneself.

So that will be the way of this account. Anyway, it is mainly for my children. The grown up ones, Candy, Jo and Tim, now in their middle forties, encouraged me to write about my family and my life. They want to know where they come from, before all is lost and forgotten. And Lucy and Alexander, now 17 and 14, will also read it and one day understand many things which I can't explain to them in any other way. That is my excuse.

But most of all I want to write this in memory of my parents. That is the strongest reason. They were remarkable people who led remarkable lives. Their names will survive through my father's works. But not their lives.

And ultimately I am of course writing this for myself. Because I feel I must. Not because of the law or the administration of justice, or anything to do with my work, though that is bound to figure. But mainly to set down what happened to my family and to me, before my life in the law. Most of the events worth writing about involved my parents, and all of them happened before I was thirty. After that, except for what happened to my mother, the story becomes more commonplace and is largely telescoped. With the exception of Diana, who will be my last, abiding memory.

None of it is meant as more than a chronicle of facts and events. With as little emotion as possible. And no philosophy.

My sister, now a literary celebrity in the world of children's books, will certainly find many inaccuracies, because her memory is amazing. She kept closer to her childhood and to the essentials of our family, because she did not let her mind be cluttered up with unimportant facts and information, such as sixty years of law. But at least I can say that everything is as true as I can remember, or remember being told. And that will have to do.

2 · My Father and his Family

THE ROW on 1 March 1921 about my names was part of a long war between my father, the dramatic critic who was renowned – and feared – throughout Germany in his time, and my grandfather, soon to become Secretary of State for Prussia in the Weimar Republic. They disliked each other heartily; professionally, temperamentally and – in my father's case – aesthetically. The unfortunate battlefield was mainly my poor mother, whom both wanted to possess and who loved them both. My advent, and the need to name me, was no more than a skirmish in what was already a long war.

My father was the older of the two, which is of course unusual, but typical of my complex family. He was born in what was then Breslau in Silesia on 25 December 1867, three years after his elder sister Annchen, 135 years ago as I write this. So he was already 53 when I was born. For three generations, back to his great-grandfather Jacob Henschel, born in 1795, the family had been wine merchants importing Tokay and other wines in horse-drawn carts from various parts of the Austro-Hungarian empire. His father served his apprenticeship with a wine merchant in Berlin and saved one of his employer's carts from being used as part of a barricade during the 1848 revolution, which earned him promotion. But Emanuel's heart was not in wine, nor in any other form of business. He had always wanted to paint. In the end he sold the business and used all his capital to set up a factory to produce 'chrome-lithographic' pictures. This soon went bankrupt, and thereafter he and my grandmother lived quietly in their house in Breslau, with few resources, devoted to painting, music and reading. The home influence was French, as it was in nearby Poland and Russia. My grandmother's family, born Calé, had emigrated from France, and my father had a succession of French governesses. All his life he spoke and wrote French as fluently as German. But never English; and that became his tragedy.

He was born Alfred Kempner. But even as a schoolboy in Breslau he told his teachers and friends that when he grew up and became a writer in Berlin he would shorten his name to Kerr. This was to avoid any association with Friederike Kempner, the 'Silesian Swan,' whose dreadful and unmistakable poetry resembled the style of William MacGonagall of the same period, and who is now similarly treasured. Throughout his life my father found himself pursued by assertions that she was his aunt, which she was not, though I have seen many articles claiming that she was, without a shred of evidence. But it may have hastened his decision to call himself Kerr from an early age. Later on he got permission to change his name officially – a difficult thing in those days – from the Prussian Minister von Moltke in about 1909. I have the original document somewhere, countersigned with many flourishes by Kaiser Wilhelm. And so his *nom de plume* was finally legalised as Alfred Kerr, still a household name in Germany today.

The change of name meant more to him than escaping from the association with the poetry of Friederike Kempner. The contraction reflected his literary style. Brevity, ringing staccato phrases, coined words and sounds, these were a major part of his stylised craft. He would have had no idea, nor cared, that Kerr was a Scottish name. And he could not possibly have foreseen that his son, to be born over a decade later, would spend much of his life fending off enquiries about his Scottish ancestry. Nor could he foresee the problems of pronunciation from which I would suffer. In German, Kerr is 'care,' with a very hard double r; it rhymes with Herr. In Scotland and England it may be 'care' or 'cur' or 'car.' Of these 'cur' is obviously the most natural and probably the most common, though not a pleasant sound or association; and 'cur' is what I was at school. One of my great mistakes was not to insist on 'care' from the beginning. And then, for some reason which I can no longer remember, 'cur' became 'car;' I think during the war. And my sister, writing her famous children's books under her name Judith Kerr, followed the same course.

There was a similar transformation in my father's early life on the subject of religion. His parents, and their parents for generations, had been Jewish. This was something of which he was always proud. But any form of structured faith, religion, or ritual was abhorrent to him. He recognised nothing and no one as having any authority over the human mind. Perhaps he was an existentialist, though he would never acknowledge any kind of group or school of thought which included him, except socialist in politics. He was a committed individualist, an artist in words, a writer and a poet. So he abandoned his ancestral religion in his early youth. And I still remember clearly, on first being taken to school by my mother at the age of six, my father's parting words, not of advice but as a command:

"If you are asked about your religion, you are a 'Dissident'."

In German this term is not as confrontational as it sounds in English. It means an atheist or agnostic. But my father meant the former, the positive rejection of any superior being. He would have no truck with

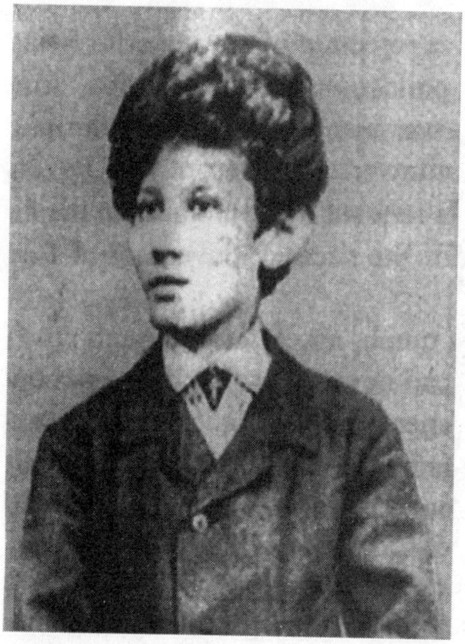

My father at 15, 1882.

any philosophy of 'don't know.' And so, when he died at the age of 81, it was by his wish, again in the nature of a command, that no priest was allowed to be present; and no reference to anything religious. His sole request for something in the nature of a spiritual celebration was for the second movement of Beethoven's seventh symphony.

But that was much, much later, though now already more than half a century ago. Yet I can never hear that deep, sad opening note of this infinitely gentle funeral march without a *frisson*.

In 1918 my father married, being then already over fifty. She was a young, blonde Pomeranian, Inge von Thormaehlen. One picture and some descriptions of her have survived in writings about my father. My mother, then 19, knew them both before their marriage. She told me that she had tried to help them find a taxi from the Grunewald at the start of their honeymoon. Later on he told her – and much later they both told us – that he had first seen her in a tram in her late 'teens and thought that he would have liked to have married her if he had not been going to marry Inge. It was one of our mother's favourite stories.

But then Inge died during the Spanish flu epidemic, pregnant, six months after their wedding. For some time my father seemed heartbroken. But ultimately they married, though that comes later. About 25 years ago I came across my mother's wedding ring, engraved 'Julia 21.4.20.' I had it enlarged, and for some reason I have worn it ever since my second wedding.

But before I come to my mother, let alone myself and what followed, I must go to her parents.

3 · My Grandparents

MY FATHER and my grandfather, Robert Weismann, could not have been more different. My father was slight, old-fashioned in his dress, fastidious in his habits and reserved in his manner. He was a very private person; vivacious, but full of gentleness and charm. My younger grandfather was the opposite in everything. He was tall, immensely good-looking at every stage of his life, and a great extrovert and socialite. His charisma and success with women were legendary. We have a large portrait of him on the children's landing in our house, and there's a photo of him on a horse smoking a big cigar under a bristling up-turned moustache, a bit reminiscent of the Kaiser. I have always been told that I resemble him, but unfortunately without his stature, figure or panache.

His father had been a well-to-do businessman who had emigrated to Manchester, where my grandfather was born; a fact which never ceased to surprise me. But the family returned to Germany when he was quite young and settled in Frankfurt. He had three sisters. One of them married and moved to St. Gallen and Paris, where she was to help many years later. The others stayed together in Frankfurt and taught bridge for a living. In 1938, in their seventies, when the Nazi pogroms started, they took an overdose and died together.

At the age of twenty-one my grandfather had the option of retaining his British nationality of birth or of becoming German. Inevitably he chose the latter. Although surprisingly English in his looks, he never spoke the language without a strong accent. He studied law and rapidly did well. As a young man he became a *Staatsanwalt*, something of a cross between a Queen's Counsel and a Public Prosecutor. He was a great ladies' man. But – unlike my father, who was one too, but privately – everything my grandfather did was reflected in a glare of society gossip, and later on in the press. His ways and habits did not change in any way after his marriage to my grandmother.

She was a considerable catch, coming from a much older and immensely rich family, the Reichenheims. Their wealth had been founded on textile mills in Silesia. That may have been part of the reason for my father's antagonism to my mother's family. He was a close friend and admirer of Gerhart Hauptmann, and both came from Silesia. Hauptmann owed much of his early success to my father's total support, such as he rarely gave, and Die Weber was his first masterpiece, a heart-rending play about the misery and oppression of weavers and spinners in Silesia.

My grandmother, Gertrud, was the oldest of seven Reichenheim children, ruled throughout her life by my majestically beautiful great-grandmother Anna, an archetypal matriarch. She and my great-grandfather Adolf produced Gertrud. When he died a year or so later, after a fall from a horse, she married his younger brother Julius, and they had six more children. Throughout my life I was unable to master the complexities of their names, nicknames and those of their innumerable progeny. When Anna's second husband followed his brother she reigned as a resplendent widow over her vast family, and over most of Berlin society, from her palatial mansion in the Tiergarten. I only remember her as a white-haired old lady, but still a stately beauty. Those of her descendants who know my youngest daughter Lucy often see a resemblance to her great-great-grandmother Anna. My sister and I were regularly taken by our mother to be shown off and inspected at her house on special occasions. Each seemed like an audience at court. Maids in black dresses, white aprons and caps, served unforgettable cakes in frightening surroundings of family portraits, antique furniture, deep carpets, heavy silver and transparent china, all of which cut our appetite and rendered us speechless with shyness.

My father never accompanied us on these visits. He had no time for people whom he regarded as socialites, if not Philistines. When my mother reminded him that they were his relations, he always said that he alone decided to whom he was related. Throughout his life he only acknowledged two relations apart from the three of us, his beloved older widowed sister 'Annchen,' Anna Ollendorf, and one of her children, Käthe, who became a doctor like her father. Both lived in Silesia, in Wüstegiersdorf, where we visited them one Christmas, tobogganing on their local mountain, the '*Grosse Kamm*,' because it was shaped like a comb. After the war the whole of the region, including Breslau, would become part of Poland. But fortunately they were spared the war and the worst of Hitler. Both would ultimately emigrate to Israel and end their lives there.

There were no other relations on my father's side. But on my mother's side the family was numberless. Their forebears had all been Jewish, like my father's. But for at least two generations, they had become converts to Christianity for social and political reasons. My mother was christened at birth, as had been her parents and grandparents, at any rate on her mother's side. This was yet another aspect of the

My Grandfather

Reichenheims and Weismanns which did not endear them to my father.

The only occasion on which I met all of the Reichenheims together was at the reception in the Tiergarten which followed Anna's funeral. I must have been about ten. But I still remember it vividly, particularly since there was a great row because my sister was considered too young to go. This infuriated her; she pointed out that she had already missed the circus because she had been sick. But it pleased me. However, I was taken to have a haircut on the way, which I hated and therefore pleased her, although my mother said that I was always impossible after haircuts.

On that evening the vast staircase and salons of the Tiergarten mansion were crowded with generations of Reichenheims and their satellites. I had never seen such chandeliers and pictures; nor any vaster buffet. There was no getting near it through the jostling multitude. Since it was all one family, no one held back, and all shouted at the top of their voices. But above the confusion, dominating all the jewellery, the stiff collars, and the thunderous cacophony of a family tribe released from a funeral service into an enormous champagne party, there was the famous portrait of my great-grandmother Anna. It hung over the row of buffet tables, still presiding over the Reichenheim generations exactly as before. No one could then foresee that, within a few years, except for some non-survivors, nearly everyone present would be dispersed across the world to live in varying degrees of poverty, a family diaspora.

Invitation to my grandparent's wedding, 1897.

Diez, Gert (Nucki) and my mother, 1910.

For decades, on my travels after the war, I would see reproductions of Anna's famous portrait in many countries in the homes of distant relations. They all had copies of it. And they all tried to explain my maternal family tree to me. But it had too many branches and endless twigs. I never mastered the names and the innumerable nicknames, nor the relationships.

Although none realised it at the time, Anna's funeral was a landmark for my mother's entire family. Within a year it would be followed by the end of an era, as my father already foresaw and feared. But he did not accompany us to this last great family gathering. It was not his scene. He was arrogantly selective in his acquaintances. In years to come this would make his life much harder, and bring infinite unhappiness for my mother, despite her love for him.

4 · My Mother

WE MUST NOW go back to the eighteen-nineties. When the brilliant young *Staatsanwalt* Robert Weismann married the wealthy Gertrud Reichenheim, his legal practice was centred in Frankfurt. But they lived in another typical Reichenheim mansion, bought with Reichenheim money, in nearby Wiesbaden. One of my innumerable Reichenheim cousins showed it to me quite recently from the outside, a minor marble palazzo like those around the Borghese in Rome. Although her family was the provider of all this wealth, my grandmother was completely overshadowed by the personality, looks and charm of her husband, whose word was law. Her features were kind and engaging rather than pretty, and she developed a homely plumpness soon after they were married. Her task in life was simply to organise the many categories of servants to run their household, to act as a social hostess to help her husband's career, and to produce their children.

There were three. My mother, Julia Anna Franzeska, was the oldest, born in 1898. She had a romantic, simple nature, with an instinctive, endearing belief that the world was good and that she was bound to be successful and happy. This brought her great suffering in the years to come. In her features she had inherited the good looks of her father: a snub nose, very blue eyes, dark hair and a radiant smile. But in her figure she tended towards her mother's stockiness in later years, which she also passed on to her son. She had a great aptitude for mathematics and a talent for musical composition, which she studied with a teacher, Herr Klatte. I only remember the name and his beard. Both my parents played the piano; there was a Bechstein grand. My father would strum the classics with more feeling than accomplishment; above all Schumann; the march of the *Davidsbündler*. But my mother would play for hours, humming her melodies, experimenting, always writing a score in pencil. Two or three of her tunes still come back to me. Because of her music she always had a special interest in my son, Jo, who also composed from childhood. Apart from music she had a passion for games and sports throughout her life, in particular tennis and bridge, and she always wanted to win. Later on she would add springboard diving, turning over and over in what she proudly called a *salto mortale*; and then learning to ski late in life when she could afford it. For a young girl in a wealthy family of that time she was surprisingly ambitious. She always wanted to be seen to excel. Her nature needed success and recognition. And just when she might have achieved it in her own right, not through her father or her husband, all was taken from her.

From the age of 32 until her death at 67 her life would never cease to be a struggle, at first against real poverty and having no home, and then against loneliness and the feeling of not belonging anywhere. But in those golden years in Wiesbaden before the first world war nothing could have seemed more improbable to her than her future life.

She had two younger brothers, my uncles Diez and Gert, always known as Nucki. They were totally different from each other, but both had something in common with my mother. Diez was a gawky boy, tallish, but without his father's good looks. As soon as I learned the expression I thought of him as a *beau-laid* all my life, and my younger son Tim looks astonishingly like him. His passion was the violin. Although he had no great talent, his father's money and influence helped his ambition to become a soloist. He actually performed with Berlin orchestras on several occasions, but there was never any pretence that he was capable of more than reasonable competence. It was a well known story in the family that after one of these arranged concerts, a friend, while muttering some muted praise, felt bound to point out some errors in a difficult coda. This produced the famous riposte from Diez, which was not seen as the mark of a future prodigy: "Spiel's du 'mal!" ("Well, you try and play it!") But in his love for music, with a limited talent, and his romantic idealism and lack of any ability to cope with practical problems – even when he had to – he resembled my mother, and for many years they were very close.

Diez would later emigrate to New York via Mexico, marry twice, have one stockbroker son who rejected him for most of his life, and he would always have to fight against poverty. For many years he earned his living in Stamford, Connecticut, by working in a radio components factory and giving violin lessons. He had to look to his younger brother Nucki for regular help. Ultimately he would survive him by many years, but suffer a huge final financial disappointment at his death. All that comes later. Meanwhile his salvation was Ruth, a nice American widow whom he married in his fifties and who was devoted to him.

The third, the darling of the family and great favourite of his father, was Nucki, born in 1903, a year after Diez and five years younger than my mother. Although not tall like his father, he had his astonishing good looks and the same charisma. Alexander, my youngest son, reminds me of him and of my grandfather. Nucki and he were much alike. To women Nucki was irresistible all his life, but he was also greatly liked by men. And unlike my mother and Diez, he was born as a man of the world, with all his father's practical talents, in his case in finance. He was a natural merchant banker, and later became one, although the term was hardly known in his youth. When Hjalmar Schacht became the German Finance Minister, Nucki became his personal assistant at the age of 18, at first through his father's influence, but later because he was a natural. Of the three children he was the only one who would never really have to struggle, who would never be poor, and who would in fact die quite wealthy. He was an accomplished rider and polo player, and like his father and sister outstanding at tennis and bridge. Later on he would have to help his elder sister and brother in their times of great hardship. But they always felt uncomfortably in his debt. He was more generous to his parents, whom he helped for many years.

He and I finally became close friends towards the end of his life because he liked people who were successful in their careers. But I never got over the feeling that, to him, all members of our widespread family with whom he was in contact were in the category of poor relations. He married Gretchen, now approaching ninety. They had no children. She says that the reason was : 'because Nucki had to help your family!'

But meanwhile we are still back in Wiesbaden, when the three of them were children. My grandfather's career and reputation flourished. In about 1912 the family moved to Berlin, into a huge villa in the Grunewald, in the Niersteinerstrasse just north of the Königsallee. It was a few hundred yards from the spot where Walter Rathenau, the Foreign Minister and a life-long friend of my father, was to be murdered some ten years later. His colleagues in the Weimar Republic erected a small cast-iron pillar to him at the place where he was shot, which I was to pass every day on my way to school. Later, in our exile, after the monument had been removed by the Nazis, my father wrote a book about him. The opening chapter, *Der Kinderwagen*, records their last conversation shortly before Rathenau's assassination, as they were pushing me in my pram around the Grunewald in 1922. And when my school, originally named after Kaiser-Wilhelm and then the Grunewald Gymnasium, became the Walter-Rathenau-Schule after the war, and made me an honorary Old Boy, I sent the chapter for publication in its magazine. Another case of '*on retourne*.'

However, the time is still before 1914, before the first world war. It had little impact on the Weismann family or their lifestyle. My grandfather was too old to fight, and the boys too young. But then came defeat, unimaginable inflation, a Spanish flu epidemic which took Inge, my father's first wife; and ultimately the Weimar Republic, with Hindenburg, briefly Rathenau, then Stresemann and Brüning. And with it came promotion for my grandfather, as Secretary of State for Prussia. And a passionate love affair for my mother.

5 · My father's work

MY FATHER and mother had already met before the war. He also lived in the Grunewald. This was hardly a coincidence, since it was the favourite and prettiest residential district of Berlin – and still is, leading out to woods and lakes. He had a bachelor flat a few streets away from the house of my grandparents. He was already a celebrity as a dramatic critic, writer and poet. During the twenties and early thirties his reviews were all-powerful and regarded as infallible. Berlin was then the greatest theatrical centre of the world, and success or failure was largely determined by my father. For over twenty years he went to every first night, sat in the middle of the third row, and made – and destroyed – authors, producers and actors by his reviews. These always appeared on the following day, for most years in the *Berliner Tageblatt.* They could be spotted at a glance, divided into paragraphed sections headed by Roman numerals. In a recent article in *Die Welt* on the occasion of the re-publication of his collected works he was described as an 'incorruptible witness of his time,' and as a critic who was celebrated and feared '*wie ein Papst*,' like a Pope.

What was it that made his words and opinions so all-important? What makes any dramatic critic important? Culture, scholarship, and great experience of the theatre, of course. But, in addition, a critic's own style and personality, which make people want to read *him* as much as to hear his views. I have often been asked with whom my father could be compared in this country during the past century. The answer is: nobody since Bernard Shaw. The nearest would be a combination of James Agate and Harold Hobson of fifty years ago, Bernard Levin over the last thirty years, with a dash of Milton Shulman in his heyday, all rolled into one. The reason for his influence and fame lay mainly in his inimitable staccato style, in the pure, seductive quality of his writing. My father was a *Sprachkünstler*, a wordsmith, a virtuoso of the German language, of its infinitely rich vocabulary, which lent itself to the combination of words and the creation of new words, which could express more than ordinary speech. His sentences were always short, and he could somehow convey his feelings in prose and verse which sang or blasted in a few lines. Much of his work would make and unmake plays, productions and reputations. These writings were his reviews and articles in the press, which later became the five volumes of *Die Welt im*

Drama. But there were also two volumes of *Die Welt im Licht* and many others about his travels, his contemporaries, and his everyday life, all interspersed with poetry, lyrical, polemic and humorous. His style and presentation were unique and instantly recognisable. But unfortunately they made him untranslatable, and far less well known abroad than his translatable contemporaries, over whom he sat in judgement.

Although I speak and read German quite fluently, I find some of his vocabulary difficult. I sense the meaning from the sound and punctuation without knowing all the words. But his prose is like a painting in words, and his poetry for me the best of all. His collected poems now fill a whole volume. Many are political, many *Berlinerisch* and very funny; and there are also some unforgettably moving poems to the loves of his life; his first wife Inge, my mother, his elder sister Annchen, and Judy, his daughter Puppi.

His style was irresistible, because it was the direct opposite of conventional German, with its never-ending sentences, which he always derided. He disliked Thomas Mann, whose style he would parody mercilessly. I remember him saying that instead of writing that a stone had been thrown through a window, Mann would say that the window had been shattered by means of a propulsion of a mineral fragment. (*Das Fenster wurde zumittelst des Steinwurfs zertrümmert*). He said that Mann's endless sentences only kept one awake because to follow the sense of what he was saying one had to wait for the final verb, with or without an unforeseeable negative. But the dislike was mutual, throughout their lives. Thomas Mann claimed that my father's attitude to him had nothing to do with his views on literary style. He said that it stemmed from the fact that my father had once proposed to Thomas Mann's wife shortly before their marriage and had been rejected, and that is what she later wrote in her husband's biography. For all I know, this may well have happened. But that my father despised the turgid and endless convolutions of the writings of Thomas Mann, and of many others like him, is not open to doubt. It was one of the tenets whereby he lived. I don't need to read his books to know this. He was preaching to the virtue of brevity as the soul of wit, in every sense, to me from my earliest youth.

Because of his radically new way of writing he had already become a celebrity as a young man, within a few years of his arrival in Berlin from Breslau. His full-length portrait was painted by Corinth and exhibited when he was still in his thirties, and many later paintings and cartoons have survived, at least in books. Alfred Kerr was a household word, not only in Berlin but throughout Germany. At least one new play would open in Berlin more or less every week, and many people have told me that his column would be the first thing to which they would turn the following morning, not for the sake of the plays, which they would never see, but because it made irresistible reading. People read him in the local papers all over Germany, living the first nights of the Berlin stage through his words, even though they would never go to see a play.

However, he was not universally liked, except by those who knew and treasured him as a person. He was too powerful, and he had many enemies. He was proud of this and courted controversy. The battles between Kerr in Berlin and Kraus in Vienna were legendary, and today Kraus is seen as the victor, because he has been translated and is known abroad. That is the price which my father had to pay for his idiosyncratic shaping of the German language. It is a loss for posterity, not merely for the style of his writings, but also for the historical content of what he wrote about. Although so gentle and quiet-spoken at home and among his friends, he never tried to avoid rows in the press, in the courts, or in any form of print. On the contrary he relished them. They gave him the opportunity of saying what he believed, and that was everything. Believing passionately in what one wrote went without saying. But that was not enough. If one believed something, then it had to be said and published. Whether it hurt or not. And sometimes particularly if it hurt.

He was once asked to list the things he liked best. He said, "Sea voyages. To make music. To say goodnight to children. To breathe. To master sentences. And rows." ("Krach," in the sense of polemics).

My father as a bachelor, aged 40 and 50

6 · My Parents together

My mother was about 17 when they first met, in about 1915, and he must have seemed a legendary figure to her even then. He was a tireless traveller, writing wherever he went. In 1896, before she was born, he had travelled to London for the Second Socialist International Congress and probably met Lenin and Trotsky. He had been a pupil of Fontane; he had interviewed Zola and spoken at Ibsen's funeral. Gerhart Hauptmann, Einstein, H.G. Wells and Bernard Shaw were among his countless friends. He founded a literary journal, *Pan*, and had written the libretto for a song-cycle with Richard Strauss (*Der Krämerspiegel*) and had given expert evidence in defence of Schnitzler's *Der Reigen* (*La Ronde*) at a *cause célèbre de scandale* when the public prosecutor sought, unsuccessfully, to ban the play for obscenity. The transcript of the evidence appeared in the press and survives to this day.

He met my mother again at a party in 1919 to which her parents had also been invited, and it seems that there was an instant attraction. On the way home my grandfather is reported to have said that, "*der grosse Kerr*" only talked to *Jula*, as my mother was always called in German. That encounter may have been the excuse for my grandparents to begin to invite him to the soirees at their house. Their daughter was certainly not the reason' and they had bitter regrets about these invitations later on. The reason for inviting him was to show him off to their socialite friends. Not merely because he was a celebrity. He was also something of a social curiosity. Throughout his life he always dressed severely, in an old-fashioned way. I cannot remember him without a waistcoat, and he wore high, small collars and cravats; never a normal tie. He must have looked old-fashioned and timeless even before the first world war, and he hardly changed his style of dress during his life, wearing the same suits throughout the twenty- seven years I knew him; increasingly worn, but never shabby. When my mother met him he still had a full beard, until she made him take it off before their marriage. But he always kept his small and somehow delicate moustache.

Apart from slightly eccentric looks he also had eccentric interests. With his passion for travel he collected and brought home curiosities, carpets, opium pipes, skins and pictures; and – strangely enough – animals. He was entirely unpractical, and I cannot imagine him picking up a cat or a dog, let alone knowing how to look after them. But when he

My Father, 1941.

was young – in his thirties and forties – he must have been different. On one holiday he went out with seal-hunters in the North Sea, something which now seems wholly out of character. An adult was shot from his boat, and he discovered to his horror that it was a female with a cub. So he brought both home. He had the mother stuffed, and tried for several weeks to rear the cub on his balcony. It was surrounded by a wall, and he managed to plug the drain-holes and to fill it with water. Apparently the cub took bottled milk for some time, but then became too big and needed fish. He tried to give it to the Zoo, but they had insufficient food for their existing animals. So the baby had to be put to sleep as well and it was stuffed alongside its mother.

I remember both seals in the drawing room. They joined his favourite cat, a white male called Kater Miezeslaus. All his memorabilia from his travels were in the *rotes Zimmer*, with red wallpaper and curtains, which was out of bounds to us. Judy says that she remembers that Miezeslaus had to be destroyed because he had been stuffed during the war and had begun to smell. So he may only have been a legend to us in our father's bedtime stories. But he survives in German literature, where I later came across his faint, and perhaps smelly, memory. Our father adored cats and often wrote about them; there is now a book of his collected essays about animals. We also had two dogs during my childhood in Berlin, a German shepherd called Ecco and a shaggy Old Irish sheepdog called Bello, with whom he was often photographed. But his interest in animals was a side of him I hardly knew. My mother never shared it, and it had no place in exile.

So he was known as something of an eccentric, and he was wholly impractical in day-to-day affairs. When my mother got to know him she discovered that he had never had a bank account, but kept money and cheques stuffed down the sides of his sofa and armchairs. All he cared about were wandering travels with his typewriter, staying in simple places, the sun, wine, good food, unsophisticated girls and women, and – above all – his work. In those days money meant nothing to him, and to my mother's great despair later on it never meant much. He had no sense for money or interest in financial success, and although he could ride a bicycle, and taught me, I cannot imagine that he would ever have learned to drive a car. His needs and wants were so modest that he never realised how much it cost to live, to pay for rent and food, and to bring up a family. All those cares fell on my poor mother and largely ruined her life.

How then did my unworldly, deeply cultured father become involved with the household of my grandfather, a wealthy, worldly and highly social lawyer-politician, or perhaps by then already a politician-lawyer? It was not that he was a recluse. On the contrary, he went out into *die Gesellschaft*, to parties, in evening dress nearly every night. His routine was to work every morning, to relax in the afternoon and to enjoy Berlin in the evening, with a large circle of girlfriends. Why then did he become something of a habitue, though never a friend, at the house of my grandparents? The answer must be that, apart from being an eccentric

My father by Lovis Corinth, 1907.

The Reichenheims, with matriarch Anna and my mother, aged about 16, 1914.

The Weismanns (Gert – later Whitman – Robert and Diez) and MK in the Wilhelmstrasse, about 1930.

My father with Bello, Grunewald, 1927.

PLATE IV

My mother in Venice on their honeymoon, 1920.

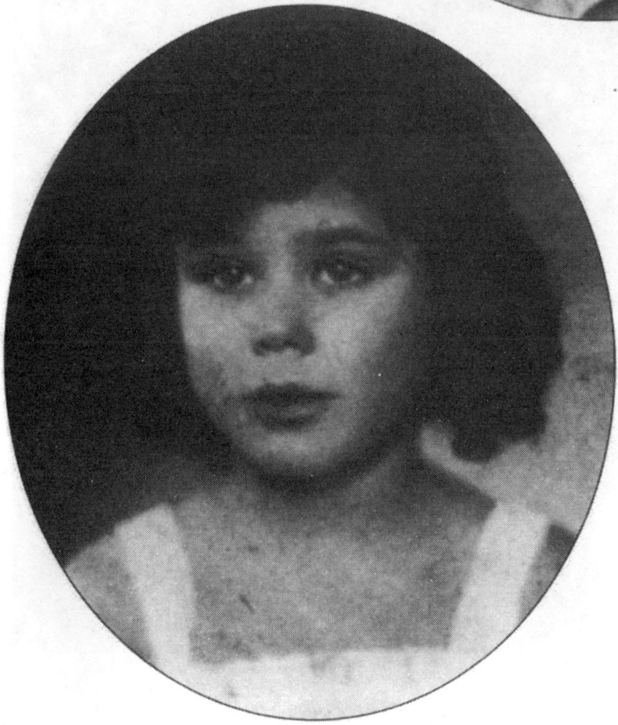

Michael and Judy, about 1928.

PLATE VI

My grandparents' Silver Wedding, about 1921.

Painting of my grandmother, Gertrude Reichenheim, by Passini, 1896.

PLATE VIII

My Grandfather, on his terrace in Nice, 1934.

celebrity, a polemic conversationalist and a great catch at dinner parties, my father was still a bachelor, although over fifty. That must have been an additional attraction for my grandparents' parties and regular 'at home' *salons*, pronounced zalongg in Berlin, as by Marlene Dietrich. And he lived just round the corner. So, gradually, as the ice was broken, the relationship developed into a degree of familiarity, something quite unusual for my father, who would never be part of a crowd, or even a group, and who was no admirer of my grandfather. The reason was my mother. Originally he had met her in her mid-teens. She was pretty, vivacious, highly intelligent, part of an interesting family living in a beautiful house only a *Katzensprung* away on his way into town. So, because of her, he must have made an exception in his reluctance to become involved with groups or families.

That was the origin of what turned into a *coup de foudre* for them both, and a life-long love on his side. There were more than 30 years between them, and when they met she was only old enough to be called a Backfisch, a teenager. But, already fascinated by the attentions of this extraordinary personality, she went from adolescent admiration and infatuation into a great open love affair, against every kind of parental opposition. And to him her youth and spirit must have been irresistible.

When their affair and intentions became public there was a family uproar from the Weismanns, especially her mother, and from the serried ranks of Reichenheims. My mother was threatened with everything they could think of, including the high probability that she would have no children. But she thought she knew better. They had no allies, but they

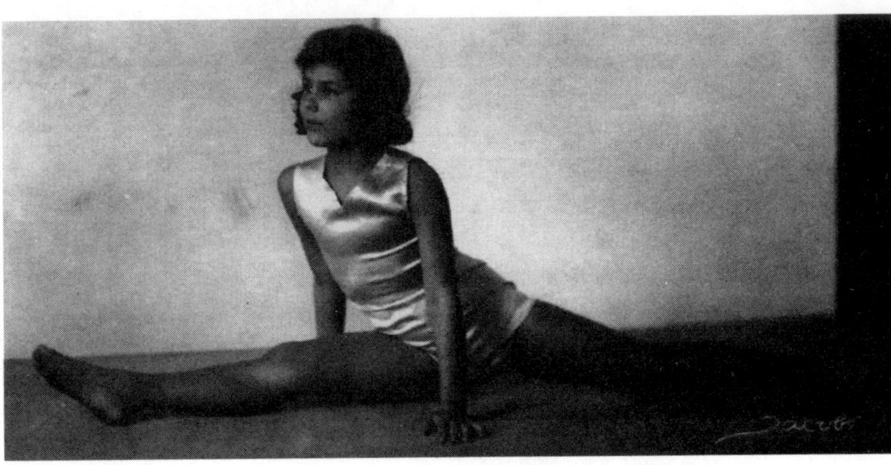

Judy aged about 7.

had total passion and determination. In the end they won; no parental or social opposition could ever have had a chance against their combined personalities. But my grandfather never forgave my father, and my father never forgot. My grandmother was a little more forgiving and liked my father personally. But her loyalty had to lie with her husband, who ruled her life.

And so my parents were married, on 21 April 1920. He was 52 and she was 21. My father had meanwhile moved into a flat further out into the Grunewald, in the Höhmannstrasse past Hundekehle, and after the wedding my mother moved in with him. I joined them there after barely 10 months, on 1 March 1921.

7 · My Sister

SHE arrived two years later, on 14 June 1923. There must have been more discussions about names, because the end-product was amazing, Anna Judith Gertrud Helene. But apparently there was no row this time; resistance to the ancestral barrier had been broken. Having commemorated my grandfathers through me, it was presumably taken for granted that my sister should have the same treatment with her grandmothers Gertrud and Helene. My mother's family again came first. But, in addition, my sister was named after her maternal great-grandmother, the matriarchal Anna, who fortunately had the same name as my father's sister Annchen. My father consented because he liked the sound of Anna-Judith, with a hyphen. The only name he cared about in this selection was Judith; the biblical heroine who treacherously decapitated Holofernes in bed. He really thought of my sister as Judith all his life; not Anna. But neither of us were called by our proper names. Michael was Michel, the German popular version, and it remained the same later on in Switzerland, and then again in France, although pronounced differently. My sister was always Puppi; perhaps I was responsible for that, because originally she looked like a pretty little doll. Then, when we came to England, I became Michael for the first time, and she became Judy, as she still is; but always Puppi to our parents.

Until I went away to boarding-school in England, when I was 15, we were more or less inseparable. So, whenever I say 'we' I usually mean my sister and myself. Our parents were 'they.'

Judy was dark, pretty in a small-featured way, with a natural talent for drawing, then painting, and finally writing. My mother was convinced that she would become an actress, but that proved to be her ambition for Judy, not Judy's own. She was always private, self-sufficient and very reserved; exactly like her father, except that he had no graphic talent. It was only much later that I realised how close they must have been throughout the remainder of his life. He wrote poems to her, of how it felt when she came to see him in his seedy little room in the boarding-house in Putney, in her teens. That was when she and my parents lived there in poverty, which was far from 'genteel,' although they did their utmost to conceal it. Judy must have been everything to my father then, and he to her, but she never spoke of it. Taking the family as a whole, they were a couple. And my mother and I were another one: fair-haired,

Michael, Judy and Bello.

blue eyed, sporting, practical, sociable and extrovert; superficial in comparison with the other two. My mother paraded her pride and love for me to all who would listen, and they usually had little choice. The feelings between my father and Judy were kept to themselves.

As I grew up, which took me an unusually long time, I gradually realised how much I had dominated Judy throughout our childhood. Since then, it has been more the other way round, because she has an infinitely stronger personality. But, as a child, she believed everything I said, and she did whatever I told her. Throughout our time in Berlin we shared a bedroom, even when we moved into a house in the Douglasstrasse soon after she was born. Lying in our beds in the darkness, along opposite walls with the room between us, I used to tell her that we were not at home, but in a train. Of course she said that she didn't believe it. But I told her to be silent and listen, for the wheels. And after a while she heard them, and became satisfyingly frightened. She probably suffered a lot from me. Her desperation was greatest when I got in some friends and we played football with her favourite toy, the woolly pink rabbit that was to acquire literary fame forty years later. But she believed and followed me implicitly in everything, and I took full advantage of it. We stole the apples off the only fruit tree in the garden and I made her lie about it, finally confessing that we might have taken one or two "halves." I taught her how to ride a bike by putting her on mine, which was too big, and sending her down the paved incline from the garage to crash into the wooden gate at the bottom. But she never questioned my methods. She helped me to steal a rowing boat, designed to rescue people, which was tied up in one of the small lakes on our way to school, and to moor it, hidden under a bridge, for future use. And she helped me make a fire with stolen candles in the loft of the garage and to deny all knowledge of it. When she was on her own she was always drawing, painting or writing, or dancing and doing minor acrobatics, like handstands and the splits. But when I called, she came and followed, faithfully and adoringly – until she grew up and got wise.

8 · The early years

WHEN JUDY was born my parents rented a timbered house in the Grunewald, a bit further into town, Douglasstrasse 10. It looked like a large Swiss chalet, with a garden back and front and a garage with huge doors beside it at the top of a steep asphalt drive .We never had a car, and neither of my parents ever learned to drive, but the garage was invaluable for hitting tennisballs against, for hours on end, with a chalk line for a net. When I went to see the house with Diana and our children about sixty years later, all that remained of it was a blue plaque on a non-descript apartment building with my father's name and dates, 25. 12. 1867 – 12. 10. 1948.

Based in this house during the twenties, our childhood was full of variety. Our parents travelled – to Corsica, Italy, France and all over America, a long journey in those days, and my father wrote about everywhere they went, as he had done for decades on his earlier travels. They met President Coolidge in Washington who arranged for them to visit Yellowstone Park, although it was still closed for the winter. My father claimed to have thrown his hat on a porcupine, and he brought it back with the spikes in it, to prove it to us.

Sometimes we travelled with them, always with one of our succession of governesses. Only few memories remain. A brilliant day in Levanto near Pisa. A monastery and lines of laden mules at the top of a steep white stone staircase curving down towards the sea. And my mother in a white dress, holding Judy as a baby, falling and tumbling over and over again, with my father and me at the bottom, and everyone screaming. Blood on the stones; but my mother only bruised and battered, and Judy quite unhurt.

Then a train, our first sleeper. It stops somewhere in Germany or France, and there is our father, joining us in the middle of the night; where I never knew. But I still remember the window of the compartment being opened, a noisy platform at a time of night when I had never been awake and thought everyone slept; and there he stood and laughed, so happy to see us.

It may have been on the way to Biarritz. It has a long straight beach and a horseshoe-shaped small one, with a big rock at the entrance towards the sea. My mother insisted on swimming out to it during a storm warning, with guards blowing whistles and waving flags. And my father pale and apologetic, polite as ever:

"Excusez nous! J'ai tout fait pour l'arrêter. Il faut l'aider, la sauver!" But she came back, proud and dripping, and said it was nothing. And my father was embarrassed and apologised for her youth. He was also angry, but in a different way, when he found out that our governess had struck up a friendship with a chauffeur who used to take the three of us for drives. He and Fräulein Gottingen would then leave Judy and me in the car while they disappeared into the woods. My father said that such conduct was doubly wrong, but I couldn't see why. It was only years later that I understood what he meant.

Then Paris on the way home. A hotel overlooking the Tuileries, and a huge merry-go-round with horses. Also my first words of French, the only ones with which I was to return to Paris some eight years later:

Mademoiselle, mademoiselle
Donnez moi un peu de sel.

Back home, the Grunewald was a lovely place for children. It adjoined a real huge forest, with lakes for swimming, and blackberries and red (not grey) squirrels in profusion. In the winters it always snowed and froze. We skated on the lakes, and for a while I was a proficient ice hockey player. There were also toboggan runs in the woods, some quite steep. Once when I was eight, I was careering down out of control, straight for a tree, when I decided to throw myself off to save myself. But I slammed my right leg hard against the trunk, and when my mother scrambled up I said that it was broken and that I couldn't stand up.

She said: "Rubbish. Of course you can. Stand up at once." So I did. "Told you so – of course it's not broken," she said. But I said I couldn't walk, and she had to pull me all the way home, muttering threatened punishment if there was nothing wrong. The doctor was called out reluctantly and I then heard, with the greatest satisfaction, that it was a clean break across both bones. But when he set them in plaster on the dining-room table I passed out.

I never let my mother forget this episode, whenever she claimed infallibility, as she often did.

During the summer of every year we went for a month to Neuhaus near Rostock in Mecklenburg. A solitary large white hotel on an endless beach, with the pier of Warnemünde jutting out to sea in the shimmering distance to the west. The hotel was surrounded by woods full of blueberries and wild strawberries in the dense undergrowth, and once we saw a wild boar.

The hotel was always full of children. I used to wrestle with a boy called Horst. My father was unimpressed. "There are only two variations. *Er liegt oben – oder du liegst unten.*"

There were regular races and competitions on the beach. I could sprint, but never won. And when I had been eliminated from the final of the 100 metres, the organisers discovered that they couldn't start it as usual with the hotel gong, which they used to bring out on the beach. I had pulled off the woolly ball from the baton and thrown it into the sea. No one suspected me. But it was all in vain; they started it with a whistle, and left me feeling foolish as well as guilty.

A few years ago I went to Neuhaus for a holiday with Diana and our teenage children, by ferry to Hamburg to see my parents' graves, and then by car along the Baltic through what used to be East Germany. It was all a huge disappointment, except for a few well-nourished topless elderly ladies who amazed Alexander. The beach and the hotel were small and scruffy, but nothing like my memories of them. But these have remained exactly as before. Whereas our visit is already a blur, the childhood picture of Neuhaus is as fresh as ever.

Back in the twenties in Berlin, my influence over Judy enabled me to carry out some joint escapades, which would spread the responsibility if we were caught. The most daring nearly ended in disaster and in weeks of fear of discovery. Neither of us ever forgot it, and we still talk of it with awe. Every other week we were given money to go to the swimming pool in Halensee, a *Wellenbad* which produced waves for five minutes in every twenty. It involved going by tram for about half an hour from Hundekehle, and in retrospect it seems surprising that two children, then probably ten and eight, were allowed to do this on their own. But child kidnappings only started later, with the Lindbergh baby.

We had got bored with these outings and longed to go to the Lunapark, a large fairground in a different part of Halensee, which had a new Giant Dipper. I had discovered that one could go there by the *Stadtbahn* from the Grunewald station near our gang's football field, and that the fare was less than half the tram fare. So, after weeks of planning and saving, we had what we thought was enough money. Having ostensibly departed towards Hundekehle one morning, and waving goodbye with our towels, we ducked back below the garden wall and ran to the railway. All went perfectly, and an hour later we were in the *Lunapark*, approaching the Dipper. To our surprise we were welcomed by several people as though we had been expected. We were ushered into the front row of the Dipper in which a silent crowd was already waiting. When I proffered our money, it was refused. When I tried to insist, having calculated the amount for weeks, it was waved aside as unnecessary, and we were told we were there as guests. They were making a news-reel of the Giant Dipper!

Only then did we see the camera crews all round, and fear gripped us at once, without the need for any words. We knew that our parents regularly went to the cinemas as well as theatres. They were bound to see us, in the front row, and all would come out. I remember nothing of the ride; I think there were several. All we wanted was to get home and forget. But forget we could not, and for weeks we lived in daily fear of discovery. It never came, but the memory of the fear is still there. We never told our parents.

Altogether I was a pretty unpleasant and surprisingly lawless person in those days. Soon after we had to flee from Berlin the *Völkischer Beobachter*, one of the main Nazi papers, published a front-page article about me, then just twelve years old. It said that I was a member of a gang of well-to-do children who behaved like vandals, a '*Früchtchen*,' a nasty brat, of whom the Grunewald was well rid. My mother saw the cutting in Switzerland and stormed about it. But in fact it was quite true, though I didn't tell her. We used to operate in a gang of about seven boys. I can now only remember three of them. One was killed on the Russian Front. Another, my closest friend in those days, emigrated with his family to New York and we have never met again. But Judy was still in touch with his sister after fifty years, including a break of twenty. The third used to wear a swastika; he wrote to me out of the blue only about fifteen years ago. He had become a successful lawyer whose career had obviously not suffered from the Nazis or the war, and he had seen my name somewhere. I replied politely, expressing the formal hope that we might meet one day, as one always says, but fortunately rarely does. And not in this case.

In our nicer moments our gang was a highly successful local football team, seven or nine a- side. We played in the streets or on the waste ground near the Grunewald station, with myself in goal, whistling the Radetzky March to keep up the side's morale, although I was never the captain or leader. But our main activities were vandalistic. We rang innumerable bells and ran away. We broke into empty houses and enjoyed ourselves in a moderately destructive way, mostly to show off. The high point came with a house due to be converted into flats, in which sacks of plaster were stacked on the top landing. We emptied them all down the stairwell and emerged terrified, looking like snowmen, and rushed home. We then heard that the owner of the house was a senior police officer, and my fear became desperate, waiting for the knock on the door. But although the story about the vandalised house appeared in the papers, the knock never came.

Since we did everything as a gang, showing off to each other, the main feeling of shame in retrospect is not so much about individual deeds, but to have been such a thoughtless and weak part of a herd. It was a fairly lawless time, however, with an atmosphere of constant crime, political vandalism and violence, and we all felt part of it. But one episode, which has haunted me for decades, was much more trivial, in class at the Gymnasium. One day, when our teacher was writing on the blackboard, I threw a large squib at him; why, I don't know. There was a loud bang and quite a lot of smoke. Most of the boys must have seen me throw it. But for some reason I insisted that it was the boy next to me who had thrown it, and nothing could move me from this total invention. Why, I cannot think; probably initial panic, followed by the fear of being found out to have been a liar and false witness. So I solemnly persisted in my story, without the slightest reason. My neighbour was a nice boy called Litvinov, and I had nothing against him whatever. His father had been the Russian Foreign Secretary or ambassador to Germany. He denied the accusation with dignity, and I cannot remember how it all ended. But the memory of this deed has always stayed with me. Years later I saw from press reports that Litvinov had also joined the Russian Ministry of Foreign Affairs or diplomatic service. I followed his career in the press and always hoped – though without real belief – that he might have forgotten the incident.

9 · The twenties

Most of my memories of Berlin in the last two or three years before we left are unpleasant. But not the earlier years, until the end of the twenties. They still seem like a golden time, as they were for all of us. Hitler was merely a name, a small cloud on the political horizon. My parents lived in a whirl of social and professional success. They were out at the theatre or parties nearly every night. But my father never went backstage or to any functions connected with the world of entertainment. It was his strict rule never to mix with actors, producers or directors, in case his judgement might be influenced or his integrity called into question. He was an early admirer of Marlene Dietrich and the first to write about her. The review was of a play which he slated, except for the spectacle of a girl's perfect bare back, turned towards the audience during a dinner party on the stage, who never spoke. That was Marlene's first review. Many years later I sensed that he may always have had some inner emotional involvement with her. But he never allowed himself the weakness of getting to know her, as would have been so easy. When she did a solo show in London in the seventies, long after his death, I went backstage and talked to her about him. She said how much his reviews had helped her in her early days and that she had admired him all her life. She had always regretted that they knew so much of each other, but had never met.

My father's friends were legion, from everywhere except the stage, and they all came to the house. I distinctly remember Einstein, Gerhart Hauptmann and Schnitzler (because of his beard), and my sister sat on all their laps. We knew that they were famous and that our father was famous, and we took it all for granted. Our mother, who had done advanced mathematics, used to boast that Einstein had explained relativity to her and that she thought she could understand it. My father obviously couldn't and wouldn't even try. But Einstein was also interested in all the same things as my father, in everything that went on in Berlin, then an immensely exciting city; not merely in mathematics. Although so different, they were close friends. My sister still has a drawing of Einstein by Struck which Einstein gave to my father, and which he carried with him into exile, among his few remaining possessions, together with Orlik's drawing of him.

As our father's children we were also publicly involved with his life.

We were photographed with him whenever he was interviewed at home, and one of my earliest memories is sitting on the rostrum with my mother and little Judy when he unveiled the Heinrich Heine statue in the centre of Hamburg in about 1926. It was pulled down in 1933, when all Heine's poetry – which could not be killed even by the Nazis – was published as 'Anon.' But recently, in the eighties, another Heine statue was erected, and the Senate of the City of Hamburg invited Judy and me for its unveiling. We were honoured. But once was enough.

Being older than Judy, I was sometimes allowed to go out with my father without her, which was always a double pleasure. One special occasion was a short film which was being produced to demonstrate the newly invented 'talkies.' A crew came to our house to film my father making a speech or giving a reading, and I was made to recite '*Mit dem Pfeil, dem Bogen . . .*', from Schiller's 'Wilhelm Tell', which I had learned at school. One morning I then went with him to a private showing in a cinema and can still remember how I looked and what I wore in my first and only appearance on a large screen. But the most memorable part was a short film beforehand, a strip-tease with singing and music, ending in unforgettable total female nudity. My father and I were sitting in a box and they had placed some screens or curtains around me. But then they all watched the film and paid no attention to me. I can still remember one bit of it, but nothing of my father's speech, although I have an old '78' record of it somewhere. One can just hear his crackling voice greeting the advent of the talkies.

My mother also had her own career and quite a lot of success. She had composed an opera, *Die schöne Lau*, based on a text by Möricke, a tale about a mermaid. It was performed, perhaps mainly because of her name, and we were taken to the first night at the Opera House in Schwerin in Mecklenburg. This must have been about 1929. I only remember that it all took place on the bottom of the sea and I couldn't understand how they stopped the water from flowing into the auditorium or how the people could sing under water. I was not very musical at that time. When I was taken to my first real opera, *The Flying Dutchman*, I said that the story seemed good but that the music got in the way. And, asked what I liked best, I said "*die blonde Senta.*" I don't remember this, of course, but it appears somewhere in my father's books.

Die Schöne Lau only ran for a week and never came to Berlin; I don't think that it has ever surfaced again. But in the early thirties my father and mother wrote an opera together, which might well have succeeded if there had been time. It was called *Der Chronoplan.* A physicist, obviously Einstein, has invented a time machine and invites a group of his friends –

The Family, three generations, but not my father.

a writer, a painter, a critic and a musician – to travel back in time to ancient Rome. But they break down in the second Act after reaching the beginning of the nineteenth century. There they find a young poet, mourning by a lake in England because his love has rejected him. He turns out to be the young Byron, and in his unhappiness he accepts their offer to travel forward by returning with them to the present time. The third Act then takes place at a golf club, which has meanwhile been built on the same lake. Byron meets the great-granddaughter of his love, a look-alike. But he is shocked to find that she is perfectly happy to go to bed with him more or less at once. So he decides to go back to his own more romantic age, and again takes off in the Chronoplan, this time on his own and presumably from a fairway.

The story sounds horribly corny, as nearly all operas are. But I can still hear some of the tunes which my mother used to hum and play incessantly on the Bluthner. The *Chronoplan* was due to be staged, but then we had to leave. For years the handwritten score, mostly in pencil, travelled with us in old suitcases. Later, after the war, people in Germany remembered it, and it was performed a few times on radio, and there has been talk of a revival. But never on stage.

A separate side of our family life, but only for my mother and us children, were her parents and other innumerable relations. This was a totally different world with which my father would have nothing to do. My grandparents lived in state in the Wilhelmstrasse, in the Ministry for Prussia, over my grandfather's 'shop.' They were called Opapa and Omama, except by my father. We usually went there for lunch on Sundays, fetched in Opapa's – or the Ministry's? – Cadillac, driven by Herr Schindler. Before lunch – which was always a formal affair – my sister and I were allowed to play in the empty conference rooms of the Ministry. I only remember that they were huge and dark, with red velvet on the walls. The most interesting places were the spaces between the double doors around the Cabinet Room, pitch dark when closed, soundproof, and perfect for hiding.

There were always guests for lunch, Reichenheims or visitors, and we had to be on our best behaviour. The speciality was artichokes with Hollandaise sauce; we never got these at home, and they would not reappear in our lives for about forty years. But they were difficult to eat, and maids and butlers were always standing around watching. From time to time we also had to visit our great-grandmother Anna for tea and to go to formal grown-up parties, where we had to bow or curtsey to everyone in turn. I only remember two children's occasions. One was a huge fancy dress dance at the French Embassy given by François Poncet mainly for the children of Jewish or prominently anti-Nazi families, as a gesture against the rising wave of Nazism. We met the children of friends of my parents, the MacFadyeans, whose father was dealing with German reparations and the Dawes plan. Forty years later, though not as a result of this meeting, Colin MacFadyean, then a senior partner at Slaughter & May, sent me some of my early work at the Bar and then a promising young pupil called Michael Mustill, later to become a Law Lord and then to return to Chambers with me again as an arbitrator – about all of which much later.... The other party was a charity for children, with Charlie Chaplin as the star; somewhere I still have a photograph of myself aged eight or so, sitting on his knees and trying to snatch something from him, which appeared on the cover of the *Berliner Illustrierte*.

All our meetings with our grandparents and their relations lay in their own moneyed social world, which had nothing in common with our way of life. It included a large crewed motorboat on the Wannsee, with

My Grandfather 1930

hampers of food and *Sekt*, where my mother was able to show off her expertise in being towed at speed behind her parents' boat. But in those days one was still towed on a board, not on a pair of skis, let alone a single ski; water-skiing had not yet been invented. On other occasions we were taken to tennis clubs and riding stables; our uncle Nucki played polo and my grandfather had horses which performed in trotting races.

But my father would have nothing to do with any part of this world. He greatly disliked our contacts with it, and our regular visits to the Wilhelmstrasse always produced rows between our parents. To a large extent it was jealousy over my mother, and then about us as well. But that was only part of it. The main reason was that my father and grandfather disliked each other, heartily and openly. They had nothing in common. My grandfather was a politician and a wealthy socialite. His love affairs were legion and common knowledge, particularly with young actresses. When my father reviewed the first night of a play for which my grandfather had put up money so that one of his latest acquisitions could star in it, he wrote that she might well excel at certain things, but not on the stage. This produced great hilarity and a row which assumed public proportions and even greater private hostility. One day, when my father was walking in the woods in the Grunewald, he was politely accosted by two men. He told me this story much later, in Paris, as a warning against his (younger) father-in-law. We were then being sent to our grandparents in Nice, when our parents could no longer afford to keep us with them while they were searching for a future in England. The men removed their caps and informed the Herr Doktor, with a measure of sadness, that they had been commissioned by my grandfather to beat him up. But their heart was clearly not in it. My father had little difficulty in persuading them to discuss it all over a beer in the Jagdhaus Grunewald, which they did, before departing peaceably and with mutual respect.

For Berlin society this enmity was a good story and a joke. But for my mother it was a tragedy. She loved my father deeply, but she had always worshipped her father. And now the two most important men in her life hated each other and fought over her and her children. She felt that she belonged to both of them and could not give up either. This poisoned the happiest years of her marriage. Even my sister and I were fully aware of the tensions with the Wilhelmstrasse and between our parents. We knew that we were in the middle, together with our mother. And for me it was also not a simple choice. I adored and admired our father, and understood that he was very special. But he was reserved, old-fashioned, endlessly typing in his study, and often remote. My grandfather was younger; he spoiled us with presents and I thought he was a lot of fun. Like our mother, I wanted to be loyal to both. Judy saw him through my father's eyes and never really liked or trusted him. But this division in the family was not a tragedy for either of us; merely an irritant in what was then still a glittering childhood.

10 · Clouds

By about 1931, when we were ten and eight, the atmosphere had begun to change, and even we could feel it. There was a general sense of threat and insecurity, not specifically directed at us, but everywhere. Perhaps it had been there earlier and we had been too young to notice it. Now we became part of it. Fear and a feeling of potential upheaval were in the air. My 'gang' broke up, because some were communists and others were Nazis, depending on their father's background. We could no longer go around together, and most of us wore political badges. I had the "three arrows" of the Social Democrats. I think I may have got them from my father; I certainly wore them with his total approval. There were now only about four of us, from adjoining streets, who walked to school together in convoy, in fear of other gangs. We were regularly ambushed on the way and beaten up several times. I have a vivid memory of being pinned against a high stone wall by three bigger boys. The reasons were not directly political, and I never encountered any anti-semitism. It was more like a class war. There was a great deal of unemployment, and the differences between the relatively rich and what were then still called the working classes were enormous. I remember that one boy, the son of a porter in a Grunewald house, who had been a member of our gang, had meals at home with each of us in turn because his parents could not afford to feed him properly. But then he departed too, whether to be a communist or Nazi I cannot remember. I began to dread the walk to and from school, and by then there were only two or three of us left. But we were ultimately saved from our regular attackers by a strange and surprisingly civilised form of ransom.

This takes a bit of explaining. There was a prolific German writer of adventure stories called Karl May: At any rate, that is what he called himself, he was probably a bit mad and may have resembled, and certainly worshipped, Wagner. He had never travelled outside Germany. But his stories were about many parts of the world, pitched in the 19th century. Mainly about the Wild West, with Indians and superior cowboys; but also about Africa and the Middle East, the Tuaregs, the Dervishes, the Mullahs, the Bedouins and the Afghans. The same blond German hero appeared in all of them. He always cultivated the local colour and speech, or what he thought it was. Thus, the Wild West hero was known as 'Old Shatterhand,' his nickname among the

Apaches. He wielded a faithful Winchester repeater that never missed. He pledged blood-brotherhood with a young Indian chief called Winnetou, whom he had freed from white baddies by untying him at night from a totem pole uncomfortably close to a camp fire. Old Shatterhand also had a Sancho Panza called Hawkins, who actually rode a mule. His favourite expression when threatened was, "Pshaw, sir!" There was an abundance of other idiomatic English – or Arabic – snippets throughout the books, of which there were over forty, each of about 300 pages.

Karl May was by far my favourite author. One day, when my father was being interviewed by some reporters, they saw me on the stairs and asked me what I read. So I told them. And when this interview appeared in the papers, the delighted publishers of Karl May sent me the whole of his works, and proudly announced that they had done so.

And so it became known amongst the gangs around the Grunewald that I was the possessor of a unique collection of every boy's favourite books; all hardbacks, since paperbacks had not been invented. This proved to be the ransom, for two gangs in turn, one book every week, to be returned and renewed the following week, like a library. It worked, because forty books is many weeks, when you add in the holidays. In fact, Hitler arrived, and we departed, long before there was any fear that the ransom might run out. Unfortunately, however, the Nazis – the SS, not the SA, which was unusual – ultimately got all the Karl Mays, together with everything else.

That must still have been some way off. But meanwhile the tensions heightened all round. During the breaks at school we now had regular pitched battles between the Nazis on one side and Communists and Social Democrats on the other. The school yard was full of stones, from medium-sized cobbles to large pebbles, which were put into paper bags to be hurled and explode like shells. It was vicious and fun rather than dangerous, and the politics were still little more than a good excuse for a fight. But there was violence in the air. Brown uniforms began to appear in the streets and many of the boys at school were joining the Hitler Youth. The papers were full of clashes in the eastern parts of Berlin, the stronghold of the communists. Slogans threatening death and destruction to the opposition were scrawled on every wall. But the Grunewald remained relatively quiet, apart from occasional warfare among gangs of boys. My only confrontation with violence was entirely non-political, but it made a deep impression on me. One day during our last winter, on the way to school, I found a dead blonde woman on the ice under one of the bridges. I used to walk across some of the small lakes although it was dangerous and forbidden, but they were not deep. She was naked, with a bright red evening dress around her feet and a black revolver beside her. I scrambled up the bank and ran to a police station nearby, and was shocked and disappointed when they displayed a mixture of disbelief and a considerable lack of interest. In the end one of them said that he would go and have a look. I wanted to have another good look too and wished I had been in less of a hurry. But it was time for school and he refused to let me go back. For days I looked in the papers, but there was nothing. Perhaps a private murder was already no longer newsworthy.

My father's life also changed. He now had a regular half hour every week on the radio, I think on Monday evenings. His topics were generally political – the menace of the Nazis and of any form of political dictatorship. He was now collected and brought back with a police escort; the talks were all live, because pre-recording was not yet known. Sometimes we listened to him, sitting with our mother, understanding very little, but waiting for him to come back. Once he wrote a farewell letter to my mother before he left, to say that he had loved her more than anything in his life, and that he wanted to tell her this before someone shot him. During the last six months before Hitler and our flight, Berlin Radio no longer dared to let him speak. Of course, I only learned all this much later.

By the summer of 1932 even Neuhaus in deepest Mecklenburg had changed. It was to be our last time there. Coming down early one morning to the terrace facing the sea I found a huge red swastika chalked across the stones. When the police came later on, I tried to stimulate their obvious lack of interest by claiming that I had seen the men who did it, even describing them vaguely, which was quite untrue. But the two policemen remained uninterested and hardly expressed any regret, let alone promise for action.

"PGs," one of the guests said to me and shrugged.

I had to ask my father what it meant. He looked angry. *Parteigenossen*, party colleagues. Then we went inside, and later people tried to scrub it off. But it was still visible when we went home at the end of the holidays.

11 · Flight

I CAN REMEMBER nothing about Christmas 1932; presumably it was as lavish and happy as ever. It was always on the evening of the 24th and remained like that for me all my life. But it was the lull before the storm, and by January 1933 the political atmosphere had changed dramatically. It finally became clear that the old President, General Hindenburg, was losing control and that Hitler could no longer be left out of government. The political manoeuvring lurched from crisis to crisis, until the inevitable happened: on 30 January Hitler was nominated Chancellor. But victory for the Nazis was still not certain. They were nowhere near to having an overall majority in the Reichstag. So Hitler called for elections on 5 March.

I must briefly pause at this point, early February 1933. I think that my father foresaw most of what was going to happen; he had warned and warned about it for years. But most people did not. And if my father had been asked whether he thought that we would all have to flee within a few weeks, never to return, even he would have found this hard to believe. After all, the Weimar constitution was still in place. Hindenburg was still the President and the Chancellor was merely the head of the cabinet. The Nazis only had three members in a cabinet of eleven, and apart from Hitler none of them held any key posts. Göring was made Minister without Portfolio, because there was too much opposition to giving him any power in the services or the police. Legislative power lay in the Reichstag, and it seemed highly unlikely that the National Socialists would obtain a majority. So, although there was fear and great uncertainty, there was no panic.

There was certainly no talk of joining my grandparents, who were by then living in retirement in Nice. After my grandfather had reached the retiring age of sixty in 1931 they decided to live on his pension in the South of France, but not for any reason connected with politics; merely for the climate. My grandfather never claimed to have foreseen what was to come, the collapse of his government. As Secretary of State for Prussia he had also been a bitter opponent of the Nazis, and was soon to appear on the same 'black list' of enemies of the Reich as my father. But my grandfather was a politician; he preferred to operate behind the scenes. He felt that my father's polemic warnings were exaggerated and harmful, and that he should leave politics to politicians. But anything my father did or said would have been anathema to him anyway.

During the second week of February my father was in bed with 'flu and a high temperature. There was a phone call from a friend in the police or some ministry: people were coming to take away his passport. My mother took the call and told him. He immediately got up and left the house with a rucksack, to catch a train to Prague, the nearest frontier. He was there that evening, back in bed in a hotel. My mother went to see him two days later and brought him his portable typewriter. They must have faced a very difficult decision. I cannot remember ever speaking to them about the details; it was not a time about which we often spoke. And of course, at the time, I knew nothing of what was going on. It was not exceptional for my father to be ill in bed; he had had a long – and nearly fatal – illness two years before. And his life in the house was largely separate from ours. We did not often go into our parents' bedroom, and hardly ever into my father's study, where he had his own small bed, desk, huge old typewriter, and papers and books everywhere.

So his sudden departure did not alert us; nor our mother's. But when she came back and explained, we were astounded. To be taken out of school and to travel to Switzerland in the middle of term was amazing enough. But that the house was to be emptied and all the furniture packed up, together with all the books, carpets, the piano and all our toys – that must have been incomprehensible. I say 'must have been,' since I have no recollection of how it was put to us or how we reacted. Only two things showed the full extent of what was clearly a disaster: Heimpi would not be coming with us, and my twelfth birthday party would be cancelled.

Heimpi, Fräulein Alice Heimpel, was the last and most important in our long line of governesses. She was probably in her early thirties when she came to us, but she seemed a lot older. I know nothing about her except that she was born in India of distantly mixed parentage and had lived there for some years, so she spoke some English. How much, I cannot remember. That was her task, to speak English to us, at any rate on Fridays. She was not a happy person and I think that she had few friends. Every morning she would come into our room and draw the curtains with a sigh, saying: "*Gott, lass' Abend werden*," except on Fridays, when she said: "Lord, let evening come." Meals on Fridays were always silent except for requests to pass the salt. But Heimpi was enormously important in our lives and we had never travelled with our parents alone. They were too important and a bit distant. We could not imagine the family without someone else, and Heimpi had been there for several years. The fact that she was not coming with us must have made it a bit easier for my mother to persuade us that it was only a journey, and that we were coming back. But for her it must have been the end of an era. As indeed it was, for all of us and millions who did not yet know. Most of them were to stay on for several years. The rest for too long.

What my mother must have gone through during the last two weeks of February 1933 is hard to imagine. People came and packed up all our possessions around us. I don't remember whether there was a last day at school or whether we just stopped going. I only heard much later that, like the *Völkischer Beobachter*, the headmaster of the Grunewald Gymnasium made an announcement that the school was well rid of me and others like me. However, fifty-six years later I learnt something of the circumstances of my departure, more or less by chance. In 1989 I became an honorary life member of the prestigious *Juristische Gesellschaft zu Berlin* and read a paper for the occasion. There were a number of people at a reception afterwards who said they had known me as a boy, but none that I could remember. Then an elderly man introduced himself as a recently retired headmaster of the Gymnasium. He said that when he heard I was coming to Berlin he had looked in the archives and copied two documents, which he gave me. The first was my last term's report, Christmas 1932. Like all the others, the keynote was: 'Could do much better if he worked.' By then I had seen earlier examples of similar reports among my parents' papers in the Akademie der Künste and was not surprised. But I had never known of the other document and found it strangely moving. It was a short letter, unmistakably in my mother's handwriting, dated 28 February 1933, addressed to the headmaster:

> *'Sehr geehrter Herr Direktor,*
> *I regret to have to inform you that we have to take our son Michael out of school as from tomorrow. Due to the state of my husband's health we have to undertake a long journey.'*

When I saw this letter for the first time the journey had already lasted fifty-six years. And my poor mother must have had to write another similar letter for my sister, amidst everything else.

The following day, 1 March 1933, was my twelfth birthday. I was only allowed one friend, and the three of us played hide and seek among innumerable packing cases. Everything had to be packed up and stored; the house was rented and had to be emptied to save the rent, even if we might come back. My mother had to deal with everything alone. My father was in Prague and her parents in Nice. She was thirty-four. Until then she had had little to cope with or to do for herself. No cooking or a single day's housework. But the rest of her life was to be all hardship, struggle, failure, and much loneliness at the end.

On 3 March, four days after the Reichstag fire and two days before the elections, we left. There must have been agonising decisions about what to take and what to leave behind, but I have no recollection of any of them, except that I was not allowed to take my football, full size and real leather. Judy was evidently persuaded to take a small new toy dog in preference to her favourite old pink rabbit, on the ground that it would not be for long. We were told that we were going to come back. I have a vague recollection of a small farewell party at the station, Heimpi and two or three members of the latest gang, and there are one or two goodbye letters somewhere in the files. Then the train pulled out with the three of us. Heimpi was the only important person who was left behind, and although we were told that she would follow when the furniture had been stored, we never saw her again.

But about thirty years later Heimpi read something about my sister or me in the papers and wrote to her. She had survived the war and the bombing of Berlin, and had worked for years as a labourer, clearing debris and then shovelling coal. By then she must have been well into her seventies. But she lived in the East, and there was then no way out. My sister sent her letters and food parcels for many years until her death. And when she gave a lecture in Berlin a few years ago, she told the audience about Heimpi and her life. It has now been published, and so Heimpi survives.

What Judy said and wrote was mainly a tribute to Heimpi's memory. But there was more. There was also a message of sorrowful remembrance of an unforgivable past. I had a similar feeling when I was presented with the *Grosse Verdienstkreuz*, the Order of Merit, of the Bundesrepublik in Berlin in 1991, ostensibly for furthering relations between the two countries as President of the British-German Jurists Association. In reality I had done nothing to deserve this. But I was not embarrassed, because our hosts rightly felt that something was due: not to me, but to my parents, to our family and to millions of others like us. So the theme of my thanks was low-key: 'The wheel has come full circle.' *On retourne toujours*. But let us not forget . . .

However, I must return to 3 March 1933, to a compartment in an express train with my mother and Judy. She was nine and I was two days over twelve. Strangely enough, I remember the day because it was a beautiful journey through a Germany I hardly knew. We spent the night in a hotel in Stuttgart. On the next day there was another train and then the excitement, and by now the fear, of the Swiss frontier. But nothing happened. Finally we arrived in Zürich, and there was our father on the platform. Looking a little frail, pale and anxious, after his journey from

Prague via Vienna. But there he was, and I remember a sense of confused relief.

I have no direct memory of our luggage on this journey. But since we lived with it for several decades it is easy to reconstitute. There was a black cabin trunk, huge and heavy, the kind that no longer exists, with rows of round metal studs, which had gone with my parents to America and contained all my mother's clothes. You could stand it up and it opened in two halves, hanging space in one and drawers in the other. Then there were three, or perhaps four, suitcases which became familiar companions, above all the '*blonde Koffer*' containing my father's papers. Possibly there were five of them, but certainly no more. Two or three of them survive in the Akademie der Künste in the Alfred Kerr Archiv in Berlin, on top of the rows of shelves. Then there was my father's rucksack and his portable typewriter, his *alter ego*. He used it every day for the rest of his life, and we kept it for years, until it succumbed to his grandchildren long after his death.

We spent a few days in Zürich, but there is only one thing about them which I remember. It also makes me realise that I could hardly have known any English. What I noticed was that there were many signs in Zürich proclaiming what appeared to be a woman's name. Transcribed from English, the German pronunciation would be 'Thea Rohm.' But 'Tea Room' obviously meant nothing to me. However it must have

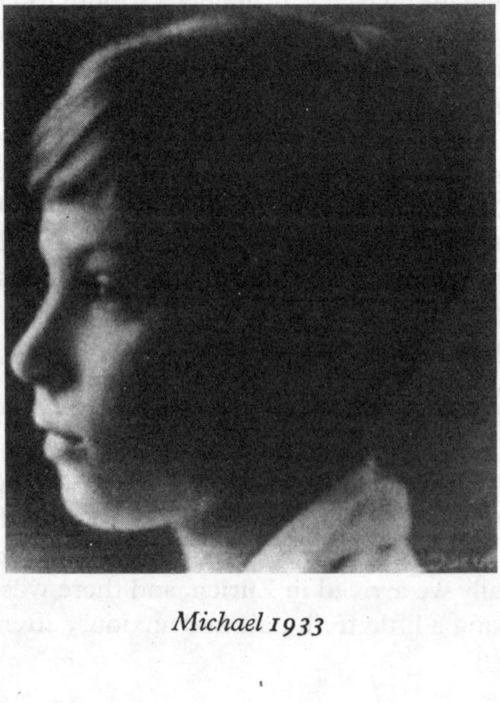

Michael 1933

meant something to the burghers of Zürich, because there were many such tributes to English influence and taste in the thirties. Even my father's non-existent English was good enough to explain to me what, not who, 'Tea Room' was.

My parents must have decided that it was a time for thought and consolidation, and presumably they still had access to some cash. So we went to a small hotel on the outskirts of Lugano, a town which my father must have known from his travels. I remember being with him at the counter of a travel agency in Zürich and begging him to reconsider his choice. The agent and he were discussing a hotel in a place called Cassarate. But they had previously discussed a hotel in another nearby place called Castagnola, the most beautiful sound I had ever heard. So that was where I wanted to go, knowing nothing about either. But Cassarate it was, because of the cost. Both became familiar, the only difference being that one was a bit higher up the Monte Bré. Cassarate was right on the lake, at the end of a tramline from the centre of town. It should all have been magical, and when I went back many years later, I realised that it was. But at the age of twelve it was only the tram terminal which fascinated me, in the same way as Hundekehle in the Grunewald. Tram terminals seem to do for me what his childhood *madeleine* did for Proust.

Here I must again go back in time, about four years earlier. The only occasion on which my father ever struck me, or even touched me in anger, was when I put my gym shoes on the unused off-side running board of a tram. He would never have remembered this incident and would have been filled with horror if he had. But the memory has remained with me for ever. My sister and I were walking home from school along the Königsallee, approaching Hundekehle. I was carrying my gym shoes when the tram stopped beside us. We had no money for the tram and were not supposed to go on it anyway. But I thought that it might as well carry my gym shoes and that I would pick them up at the terminus in Hundekehle, where it was due to stop at a station with a kiosk, for at least ten minutes. I had often done this before with books and unwanted clothing. So I put them on the steps on the side that was closed to passengers. But something must have gone wrong with the timetable, because it left just as we were approaching Hundekehle. It then departed on a long, leisurely loop via Roseneck and the Hubertusallee, more or less parallel to the Königsallee but a mile or so south, back to Halensee and the Kurfürstendamm. So it was an awkward moment. I hurriedly told Judy to go home to explain, so far as she could, and started running south, taking a short cut. Unfortunately I just missed the tram again, having misjudged the streets leading to the nearest point of interception. I could see my gym shoes departing again, this time east, towards the centre of Berlin. So there was nothing to do but to walk home in the hope that Judy had explained. But I was astonished to find my father waiting for me in the hall, obviously in a state of great anger. He said nothing at all but gave me a surprisingly strong *Ohrfeige*, or box on the ear; both expressions are ridiculous. I cannot say what had come over him; the incident was never mentioned again and was totally out of character. A more non-violent person than my father would be hard to imagine, and it was also quite unlike him to be so involved with anything at children's level. It could not have been the gym shoes. It must have been a bad day, with some bad news, when he needed my mother, who now had to go to the other end of Berlin to try to get them back from the Lost Property Office, when she had more important things to do. But she did, and got them back, triumphantly, though only so far as she and I were concerned. My father wanted to hear no more about it.

I have often thought that if I had reminded him of this episode he would have denied all knowledge of it. Truthfully, because he was not himself that day. He was under some great strain, much more upset than I, and that is why I have always remembered it.

However, that was some years earlier. We had meanwhile reached Lugano in March 1933, and the tram terminal in Cassarate, about two miles out of town, along the lake. But this terminal was nothing like as interesting as Hundekehle in the Grunewald. There was no station, no kiosk, and the trams went straight back into the city. However, they also had an unused running board on the side which was closed to passengers.

I cannot remember precisely what articles I sent forth in this case, like casting bread upon the waters. Certainly nothing precious, as gym shoes by then were, since money had suddenly assumed a new dimension in our lives. But brown paper parcels containing rubbish or bricks were sent off regularly, many times a day, towards the centre of Lugano. They nearly always returned safely, as I could see from our bedroom in the hotel when I could not be present, which overlooked the terminal. I felt like a transport manager.

That is one of my memories of Lugano. They other is Renate, the daughter of the owner of the garage immediately behind the terminal. She only spoke Italian, but we knew each other by sight and gestures. She used to appear in silhouette before she went to bed, knowing that I was watching, and then we would meet again the next day, self-

Judy 1930

consciously and not really knowing what to do next. But the relationship, such as it was, went on, and it was fairly typical of other similar encounters during those years. I was never particularly precocious.

These are my main memories of about a month or so in Lugano, our first month away. I have been back since, also to Castagnola, and not very much has changed. It is still very beautiful. San Salvatore, the more spectacular mountain near the city, and Monte Bré still face each other. My mother claimed later on that I had worn out my best pair of trousers sliding down Monte Bré, which I vaguely remember. But the most important event of that time, which I do not remember at all, is that Judy became extremely ill and that her life was thought to be in danger. It was a streptococcal infection, now easily curable with antibiotics, but life-threatening then. In the end she recovered slowly, and the next decision had to be made. This must have been in early May 1933. What my parents must have decided is that it was too soon to make any real decision, except to stay in Switzerland for the time being. To see what could be salvaged.

Judy and I still hoped we might go back. But our parents did not tell us what they had meanwhile heard from Heimpi. On the day after our flight, at eight o'clock in the morning, the police had come for all our passports. If we had delayed by one more day all our lives would have been different – and much shorter.

So there was no way back. And although they could fortunately not foresee it, for the rest of their lives my parents would never again have a home of their own.

12 · Switzerland

STAYING in Switzerland obviously meant moving to Zürich. Zürich was the capital, German-speaking and the cultural centre. The Züricher Zeitung, then not yet the Neue Züricher, had a world-wide reputation and an important literary section. So that was where my father obviously had to be, and there were many who claimed to be clamouring for him. But my parents were too depressed and – I suspect – insecure to want to live in the city. It was also always my father's nature to want to write in peace, to keep apart from people, and to let them come to him if they wanted. My mother was generally quite different; she was a natural mixer and longed to be in the midst of things. But I think that on this occasion they both felt the same way. They must have been bewildered by what had happened so quickly, and bewildered to know what to do next. And Zürich was nothing like Berlin. So they found a small family hotel on the north shore of the lake, in Küsnacht, about twenty miles outside the city. The hotel was 'Die Sonne.' It had been run by the Guggenbühl family for generations, and still was when I called in for a drink about fifty years later.

For us, my sister and me, Die Sonne was ideal. It was right on the lake, adjoining the landing stage for the steamers in both directions and across to the south side. There was a large gravelled yard enclosed by an annex and outhouses, with two trees and a contraption for beating carpets which more or less faced each other at a distance of about thirty yards. The contraption consisted of two iron stanchions with a bar across. So we had two perfect goals for playing football. Which we did, more or less endlessly, with Werner and Rosemarie, the Guggenbühl children, and others from the village; my sister less enthusiastically than I. Then, going inland away from the hotel one had to cross the main road to Zürich, still relatively free from traffic, to get to the railway station. The trains ran between Zürich and Rapperswil at the far end of the lake, and beyond. Although most of them were local, they were still pulled by enormous steam locomotives, a constant attraction. Beyond the station was the *Dorfschule*, and adjoining it the ground of the Küsnacht football club, with real goals with nets and a few wooden seats. All within walking distance, and all like paradise.

The problem, surprisingly enough, was the language. Everyone spoke *Schwyzerdütsch*. Although *Hochdeutsch* was the official language at school, at any rate for the older classes, the children would laugh at us when we spoke it. To them it seemed pompous and affected. We, on the other hand, could not understand a word of what they were saying. It seemed much more than a dialect, it was really a different language. For instance, if you wanted to say that you had been somewhere, we would say "*Ich bin da gewesen.*" But they would say something like: "*I bin doh gsi.*" Every vowel tended to be given an Umlaut or a sub-vowel in the middle, and nouns were turned into diminutives ending in i. It was quite impossible for us to follow what they said until they said it again in stilted high German, roaring with laughter.

But of course we learnt, and after two months we spoke it more or less perfectly and understood everything. But now, when I am with friends in Switzerland who speak *Schwyzerdütsch* to each other, I am again quite lost. Unlike my German and French, which remain fluent and even seem to get better with reminiscent old age, *Schwyzerdütsch* has again become an unknown language.

It was clear that we were going to live in Switzerland for the time being. It was a place which had provided a refuge for many cultural refugees from Germany. And, being German-speaking, I think that it made my parents feel that all bridges back to Berlin might not necessarily be destroyed. So they tried to make some sort of life there, and above all to survive financially.

But in this they were quite unsuccessful, both in salvaging anything from Germany and in earning any money in Switzerland. We soon heard that everything we had left behind had been confiscated. Our possessions in store had been taken over by the Waffen SS, Hitler's elite black-shirted bodyguard. Where it all went, we never knew. My father's publishers, who owed him what was then a lot of money, said that they were unable to remit anything, because 'it would be against the law.' Of course they had assets outside Germany and could easily have paid what they owed. But they swam with the tide. I will not mention the name of the owners or of the firm, though both, and their connection with my father, are of course well known in Germany. The owner and his wife had been close friends of my parents. But they seemed to have no shame or feeling, although they must have known of their plight. Many years later they wrote to my sister and me, after the death of our parents, and asked to meet us, but we refused.

When the famous burning of the books took place on 10 May 1933, all my father's works were among them. Some years ago I saw the square in east Berlin where the burning took place, between the Opera and the Library. The brown-shirted SA threw tens of thousands of books out of the Library windows until the pile reached the first storey and covered much of the square. They then set fire to the pile, which burned for several weeks. There can have been nothing like it since the burning of the great library in Alexandria. My father had taken one set of his works, with some duplicates, perhaps twenty volumes, in the *blonde Koffer*, which my sister and I later shared out between us. And from time to time I have been given some further copies by friends who had saved them or found them in odd places, as the originals have become rarities. I once found one of my father's books in a shop in Jerusalem or Tel Aviv and another one on a stall market in Long Island. He did not live to see them reprinted though my mother did, to some extent; and since then collections of his works have been republished several times.

But my father was always proud to be singled out by the Nazis as a public enemy. He was put on the first short 'black list' published in the *Völkischer Beobachter* as early as 1932 of people who would be shot as enemies of the Reich which had been drawn up by Göbbels. Then there was a second list of 33 in July 1933 of refugees who were being deprived of their nationality. *The Times* printed this, including my father, Lion Feuchtwanger and Heinrich Mann, on 26 August 1933, under the heading 'New Act of Nazi Persecution' and re-printed it sixty years later on 26 August 1992 in the serial feature 'On this Day' when I happened to see it. But between 1933 and 1939 *The Times* became a shamefully silent, and then outspoken, supporter of 'appeasement,' and my parents probably never learned of the publication of the 1933 list in England when they had to deal with the Home Office later. Meanwhile Judy and I had been told in Switzerland that a price of 1,000 Marks had been put on our father's head. I was not sure whether it was price or prize and Judy had nightmares about him. He said that he was proud of the distinction, but that the amount was an insult.

So my parents were deprived of their nationality in July 1933 and we all became stateless. This caused endless problems later on, when our passports ran out, and I remember that we had great difficulty in obtaining some kind of travel document from an unsympathetic Home Office which seemed to have little idea of what was happening in Germany.

There was nothing to be saved from there; neither national status nor possessions other than the contents of our luggage. And fairly soon it also became clear that my father could not make a living in Zürich. The *Neue Zürcher Zeitung* and other publications were frightened of alienating their powerful German neighbours. Austria was rapidly adopting Nazism, and with the murder of Dollfus it was clear which way the country was going. I still remember the despair of my parents when they heard about it when we halted at a station on a train journey in Switzerland. The *Anschluss* was obviously just round the corner. So it gradually became clear that my father would no longer be able to earn his living in the German-speaking world, and that he would lose the thing he valued most and which had been his whole working life, the German language. It was to be like a pianist losing most of his fingers. So he began to think of Paris, and my mother of London.

But we knew little or nothing of any of this and had meanwhile been sent to school. I went to the *Kantonsschule* in Zürich by train. It took about half an hour and then a walk from the station. I cannot remember whether this caused any anxiety to my parents or any discussion about it. Switzerland was of course an unusually peaceful and orderly country, as it largely still is. But I felt grown-up, catching a real train, and some of them were expresses.

I can remember virtually nothing of the school except learning some Swiss and Central European history in stilted high German. I also had a few first lessons in Latin, which I had not done in Berlin but which the other boys had already started. So I think that I was fairly lost, but not at all unhappy. On the train I was gradually accepted as a member of the schoolboy commuter gang from stations up and down the line, and as I began to speak *Schwyzerdütsch* I felt quite at home. Werner Guggenbühl and I played incessant football in the yard of the hotel, and when it rained we played it in the ballroom of the main building, which never seemed to be used, and in long musty passages upstairs. There was also an unofficial village children's football team, which was allowed to practise on the Küsnacht Club ground with the real goals. I was the goalkeeper, as usual. But unfortunately, when my parents once came to watch and I had little to do, they saw me eating a pear during a match, leaning against a goalpost and watching the action at the other end. I was never allowed to forget it; goalkeepers were people who had time for snacks during matches.

My sister meanwhile made friends with the children at the *Dorfschule* beyond the railway station, where she went every day and gradually we were accepted by the locals as curiosities. The successor to the dark Renate was a blonde, also about two years older than I, Ruth Felder, inevitably called *die Felderi*. We never held hands, went for a walk or even had a conversation, but we knew that we were a couple, and so did everyone else. It was all done by looks. I would go and stand below her window in the evenings, and I still have a vivid picture of her silhouette against the light, not undressing, but ironing. I used to throw apples at the window, and at her when our paths crossed; this was evidently a traditional local symbol of a special relationship. In return she would deride me as a *Teigaffe*, a dough monkey, to show that she was unimpressed and could resist this foreign stranger. But there was some magnetism between us. When my sister's school went up into the mountains for a long weekend to a *Ferienkolonie*, and I was invited to go along, Felderi and I inevitably sat next to each other in the bus. We and everyone else arranged this. But we only exchanged looks, not words; she would only talk to the girls and I only to boys. Romance nevertheless ran high. All of us, some fifty children and a few teachers, spent the night in a barn on an *Alm* somewhere in the high meadows of the Engadin, and we slept in the hay, self-consciously, not far apart. Then we all got up in what seemed like the middle of the night and walked up a mountain to watch the sun rise. It was one of the great days of my life. In retrospect it all seems rather like Heidi.

Meanwhile my parents were treading water, wondering what to do. They had quite a number of visitors, friends, relations, advisers and – I think – a few helpers. My father decided to make one more attempt to retrieve our possessions. He had made friends with Herr Guggenbühl, the landlord of Die Sonne; they liked and respected each other's different backgrounds. Neither had any talent for business. But they were proud of the stratagem which they had devised over wine one evening. My father executed a document, drafted by both of them, whereby he transferred all his assets in Germany to Herr Guggenbühl. Whether there was any mention of a price or other consideration I do not know. Herr Guggenbühl then wrote a letter on the notepaper of Die Sonne to the furniture store where all our possessions had been taken, giving instructions, as their owner, to have them forwarded to Küsnacht. I think that both of them were so honest and simplistic that they couldn't see how it could fail to work. But of course there was never any response; the Gestapo must have roared with laughter.

Among the visitors was my grandmother, Omama. She had left her husband in Nice in order to comfort her daughter and grandchildren, while my father was on a reconnaissance trip to Paris. Otherwise she would not have come. She brought her ancient Dachshund, Pams, whom we had known for years in the Wilhelmstrasse. The sadness of the emigration must have got to him, because one morning he was found dead by the edge of the water, having fallen off the low parapet of the hotel garden onto the shingle below. My grandmother was convinced it was suicide; she was inconsolable and cried for days. To cheer her up Herr Guggenbühl drove her, my mother and us on an excursion into the mountains. But when the sight of someone else's black *Dackel* provoked a fresh outburst of sobs, he was suddenly heard to say reflectively: "Ach ja, I quite forgot to make out a bill for *den Verblichenen*," the one who has paled away. This provoked an attack of grandmotherly hysterics to such an extent that we had to stop. But fortunately it turned into a frenzy of laughter. My sister and I have never forgotten the '*Verblichener*;' the ch is pronounced hard, as in loch. It was the apogee of an epitaph, in meticulous high Swiss-German, to a dead Dachshund.

My parents had meanwhile decided that further action and emigration were unavoidable, as had indeed been obvious for some time. For the very reason that Zürich was German- speaking, and therefore culturally in the German orbit, Switzerland could not provide any basis for my father's future career. He was an outlaw. The question was where to go.

With hindsight, and perhaps even at the time, the obvious answer was America. Many German refugees who had played a cultural role in the Weimar Republic, often far less prominent than my father, had found it relatively easy to make a living in America; at universities, with the assistance of foundations or institutes, or in many cases in the Hollywood of those days. In retrospect it seems clear, from the point of view of my parents' careers and happiness during the rest of their lives, that the most sensible solution would have been for us all to have gone to New York, where many people would have helped us. My parents would certainly have been spared much deprivation and misery, and this thought must often have crossed their minds in later years. In 1933 it would still have been relatively easy for them to have obtained residence in the States, which was soon to become more and more difficult.

They may have regretted it later, even my father, who set no store by money. But they clearly did not see it in that way at the time. And although for many years Judy's and my lives were also not easy, neither of us has ever regretted the decision which our parents must then have made.

However, abandoning any idea of trying to get to America did not solve any problems. On the contrary, it created them. Both my parents were Europeans who wanted to stay in Europe. But their tastes and inclinations diverged strongly as between Paris and London. My father spoke and wrote French fluently since his childhood, and France was like a second home to him. England, on the other hand, was foreign. He had enormous respect for its traditions of freedom, and as an asylum for refugees. But in all other respects it was alien. Much of this was due to the language, the climate and the food. But most of it was due to the feeling that the English were not European in the same way as the

Continentals, either in their own eyes or through eyes like my father's. He liked them, but they also seemed a little comic to him. He could never forget the two English spinsters whom he had met in Italy and who had raved about 'Ammelfi,' on the Naples peninsula. The mutilation of beautiful sounds like Amalfi made him quote Kaiser Wilhelm's '*Gott strafe England.*' He also made fun of the English addiction to games, which he regarded as supremely unimportant. When he was in England in 1896 for the Socialist International Congress he had stayed with some friends or acquaintances in Suffolk and had been made to play tennis. He was always telling us how he had been gravely admonished for never getting his service in, with his hosts pointing to the service area, time and time again, saying: "You must put it here!" It was one of his favourite phrases. And he had found the food atrocious, wine virtually non-existent, and the language quite difficult. When he went into a tobacconist to buy a pipe, he said that they had failed to understand him when he said perfectly clearly: "Goodbye, have you a whistle?"

For my mother the choice between Paris and London was exactly the opposite. She had nothing in common with France, although she could understand and speak French. But England was her ideal, her promised land. She had spoken English since she was a child, loved English books, the English sense of humour and their love for sport and games. Her mother had gone to an English finishing school in Wimbledon. And my mother had won the family argument by getting an English-speaking governess for us, even though it meant little more than having meals on Fridays in English, more or less in silence.

These were the battle lines, but it was a battle which my father would obviously win. His fame and career had to come first; in fact they were everything. He wrote fluently in French, and had already often written for publications like the *Nouvelles Littéraires*, which he could hope to do again. In addition, there was already an active German émigré nucleus in Paris. They had founded the *Pariser Tageblatt* and were urging my father to come. So Paris was obviously the first choice; possibly with the thought of New York as a fall-back alternative.

He went on a preliminary reconnaissance trip and came back full of hope and enthusiasm. Paris it was to be. My parents decided that they would have to go ahead to find us somewhere to live while Judy and I were to remain at Die Sonne in Küsnacht. My mother was frightened to leave us, but we were not at all worried. On the contrary, we felt quite secure with our school lives, the village and the Guggenbühls. Berlin had become a past world of which we no longer thought. We now knew that we would never go back. But not where we would end up.

13 · An interlude, 'fast forward'

We must have been on our own in Küsnacht for quite a while, because I vaguely remember that our parents visited us during a short holiday. But we were perfectly happy and as assimilated to being Swiss as two Berliners of twelve and ten can become in a period of a few months. We must have moved to Küsnacht after Lugano in March, and started school in May. The holiday for which my parents came was probably the half-term for the harvest in the autumn. By then our *Schwyzerdütsch* was fluent, although we still spoke *Hochdeutsch* to each other. Altogether we must have spent about seven months linguistically in *Schwyzerdütsch*, with Die Sonne as our home, and the hotel yard in which we played football as my particular spiritual patch.

Before parting from it I must briefly digress again, this time into the future, to an event which remains extraordinary in my life. A coincidence of millions to one.

We had met many other children while we were at Die Sonne, not only locals, but also tourists who stayed there with their parents on holidays. In one case the children were German, and we got on well with them until we heard their parents forbid them to play with us, because we were 'unsuitable.' This inevitably provoked a blazing row between them and my mother. They were the only other children in the hotel of whom I have some recollection, because it was our first – and only – experience of knowing that we had become outcasts. Something which we had not realised before. My father never spoke to the German couple, but told the Guggenbühls that their children could either play with us or the Germans.

The scene then shifts, like the *Chronoplan*, from another child in Küsnacht in 1933 to Prague fourteen years later, in November 1947. I was then 26 and had returned to Cambridge after the war and met Lord McNair, then still Sir Arnold McNair, later to become President of the International Court of Justice at the Hague. He was an eminent Old Aldenhamian, and I a recent one, who had to make a speech at some post-war OA Dinner in his honour. At that time he was Whewell Professor of International Law at Cambridge and also temporarily President of the prestigious Institut de Droit International which used to meet every other year. After the war the conferences were revived and the first was to be in Prague. I was reading law at Clare, and he invited me to the conference as his assistant. Since my expenses were paid I was of course delighted to go.

Of the conference itself I can remember little except the opening reception in the famous castle overlooking the city and river. The host of the conference on behalf of the Czech government was 'young' Masaryk, and I shook hands with him in the reception line in the magnificent room from which he was to be defenestrated about five months later. My only other memory is a dark-haired Czech girl in her early twenties, a few years younger than I, one of the interpreters at the conference. If not infatuation, it was certainly attraction at first sight, and we became inseparable for the week of the conference. I had never been to Prague before, and the reason why I don't remember the conference is probably that I didn't go to any of the sessions. We just looked at the city and went out to dinner every night. But then came the official banquet on the Friday, before our departure on Sunday, to which I failed to get her invited. I had to go. She said that she would go to a party, and we arranged to meet on the Saturday as usual, our last day.

When we met in a bar on the next morning she said that she had a surprise for me. She gave me six snapshots, which I still have. Five of them were of three children playing football, and one of three children and two grown-ups. I immediately recognised my sister and myself and the yard in Die Sonne, with the structure for carpet-beating which we used as a goal. I also vaguely recognised the third child, a girl of about our age. She was kicking a half-size football which I clearly remembered because it belonged to Werner Gugenbühl. But of course, when I showed the photos to Judy on my return to London, she remembered the little girl perfectly, including her name. She had been eleven and on holiday with her parents from Czechoslovakia, who had taken the pictures. The one of the three of them with Judy and me, all looking relaxed and happy, must have been taken by someone else.

I was naturally astounded to be handed these photos by this new friend in Prague, fourteen years and a world war later. I had only been there for a few days and was due to leave on the following morning. She told me how it happened. She had gone to the party on the Friday night but had got bored, and had begun to look through a photograph album which was lying on a table. In it she saw these pictures. She said that she instantly recognised me, but I suppose that there must have been captions with our names. So she went to her host and told him that "this boy is in Prague tonight and leaving on Sunday." He took the photos out of the album and asked her to give them to me, and to tell me the story. The girl in the pictures had been his fiancee. They were going to get married, but she was Jewish. When she knew that she would be taken away she gave him her photograph album to look after, together with her other possessions. She was taken to Theresienstadt together with her parents. It must have happened three or four years earlier, during the war. None of them survived; and for Judy and me only these pictures.

I have often wondered about the statistical odds of this extraordinary series of coincidences. A distance in time of fourteen years and in space between Zürich and Prague, where I only happened to be for four days for the first and only time. And then the chance of these photos being seen and recognised by this girl, who hardly knew me, on that Friday evening in the house of someone I never knew. And his giving them to her to give to me on the Saturday, to take them back with me to London. As I did.

I left on the Sunday. The girl – whose name I have long forgotten – had hoped to come to England, and I tried to help her. For some months we wrote a lot of letters. But then came the Soviet-organised coup of February 1948. It killed Jan Masaryk and brought down the Iron Curtain. After that I never heard from her again.

Judy and Michael with the girl from Prague, Die Sonne, *1936.*

14 · To France

OUR MOTHER came from Paris to fetch us for the next migration. It was the beginning of winter, in early December 1933. By then Berlin was only a memory, and even letters from Heimpi could not bring it back as a reality. We had both grown up and were no longer the same children.

It was a sad farewell from Küsnacht and Die Sonne. In many ways we felt it more than leaving Berlin, when we had been rushed and bewildered and could hardly take in what was happening. By now we felt that we were wanderers, and we knew that we were wandering on, not to return. And except for an unforeseen holiday during the following summer, neither of us did, for decades. But little had changed when I called in some years ago. Werner was running Die Sonne. His sister, who lived in the village with her family, had won a prize in the local paper for writing about Judy, who was by then quite famous for her books. And both mentioned Felderi, still treating us as a couple fifty years later, although we had never spent five minutes alone. Apparently she had never married. However there must have been some better reason than the romance of our public courtship of hurling apples and insults.

So when we left Die Sonne it was a real farewell, the first time in my life that I felt that '*dire adieu est un peu mourir*,' which I have often felt since. We were on our way to Paris, where my parents had found a small furnished flat. But we were not keen to move on again. And I still knew no French, apart from asking Mademoiselle for *un peu de sel*, which I had learnt in Biarritz when I was six.

We were very careful changing trains in Basle because our mother told us what had happened when our father had set off for Paris in the autumn. He got on a train standing on a wrong platform which would have taken him to Stuttgart and Frankfurt. He only just got off in time and then had a terrible rush to find the platform with the Paris train, and just caught it. It was only then that he really realised what might have happened. So we took great care on this occasion. It was a great relief when we saw from the names of the stations that we were in France, although we didn't know how to pronounce them.

I remember our arrival at our new home in Paris. After the Grunewald and Die Sonne it was very depressing, although my mother kept saying that it was in one of the best parts of Paris, the *16ème Arrondissement*. It was a furnished flat on the fourth floor of an old dirty building in a narrow street off the Avenue Kléber, quite near the Arc de Triomphe. The street was then called Rue de Villejuste, but when I tried to find it after the war the name had changed, as many Paris street and metro names have, to Rue Paul Valery.

Our father was there when we arrived. We hadn't seen him for several weeks, and he again looked pale and a little shrunken. There was also a concierge, a rather forbidding woman who naturally only spoke French, so we couldn't understand a word of what she was saying. But we realised immediately that our father understood perfectly and spoke it in the same way as she, whereas our mother sounded more like her usual self and less French. But it was she who had to do most of the talking, since it was all about practical things.

There was a tiny lift, with a white door like a concertina which had to be slammed hard before the lift would go, and when it did, it groaned. My sister and I immediately called it "*Stöhni*," which would be German or *Schwyzerdütsch* for something like 'Groany.' It took several trips to ferry up the luggage, and there seemed to be not much room for it in the flat. There were two bedrooms with two beds in each, much smaller than we had known before, a sitting room with a table for eating, and a small kitchen, bathroom and loo. I remember wondering how we could all fit in. The view outside was of other dark houses and roofs.

15 · Paris – the beginning

I HAVE LITTLE recollection of our life in our flat. My mother had some help from an Austrian girl who was in Paris to learn French, but she found it quite impossible to cope with the language or anything else. Most of the work was done by my mother. She had never cooked before in her life, but she now had to do it, and gradually got quite good at it. My main memory is of her ironing in the sitting room, which she seemed to be doing whenever I came home. My father always complained about her ironing our pyjamas and underwear, which he considered to be a total waste of time and effort.

Since Paris was to be our home, the first thing was of course that we had to learn French. Judy had had one term of French at her school in Berlin, but I had done English and knew literally nothing. So we had a crash course with a Mademoiselle who came three or four times a week, and in between we had to write little pieces for her with the aid of a dictionary. Somehow we developed a small vocabulary of nouns and learnt a few verbs. After about a month I still felt I knew nothing and could not read anything in a newspaper. But our parents thought that it was time for us to go to school and that we would learn much faster if we did. My school was to be the Lycée Michelet on the southern outskirts of Paris. It had nothing to commend it for proximity or any particular scholarly reputation. The reason for the choice was that my mother had been told that it was the only Lycée in Paris which had playing fields, including a football ground. So that was the school for me.

I vaguely remember being taken there by my parents and meeting the headmaster. I could not understand much of what was being said, but there was evidently no problem about my being accepted, and the education was entirely free. One only paid for lunches and extras. My parents could hardly afford those, though I did not yet know how marginal our existence was. All I knew was that our journey by Metro there and back seemed endless, and I could not visualise doing it every day.

But I did, and ultimately got used to about fifteen stations each way with one change. Many of the names are still with me, though some have altered in the last sixty years. I got on at Kléber or Boissière, in the Avenue Kléber, which was no distance. Then Trocadéro, Passy and Champ de Mars, where it emerged from the ground and one saw the

Eiffel Tower. Then further on to La Motte-Picquet, Grenelle and Cambronne, named after the General who is supposed to have coined '*le mot du général*,' *merde*, or shit, both of which I learnt later. Further on was Pasteur and then – so far as I remember – Réaumur-Sébastopol, if that is the right name; I still don't know what it means, probably a battle. It is now called Montparnasse Bienvenue. There I had to change. And then four more stations before the Porte de Vanves, which was then right on the outskirts of Paris, so that one could see fields. Finally a walk to the school, set in its own grounds.

But getting there and back, with a very cheap schoolboy's season ticket every day except Thursdays – for some reason *le jeudi* was always free – was the least of my problems. The two overwhelming ones were my clothes and satchel, and secondly the language.

Surprisingly, the foreignness of my appearance worried me more than anything else. Even more than my French, because it was noticeable at once, and at a glance. At that time, and for many, many years, probably into my forties, I wanted to conceal my foreign origins, first in France and then in England. In part it was of course a personal characteristic and a weakness of character. But one must also remember that the thirties were quite different from the post-war times. Everything was more formal and *comme il faut*. People conformed. Even 'casual' clothes – a term which had not yet been invented – would be studiedly formal. It was a stigma to be different. At any rate, that is how it appeared to a child, and later to a young man. My sister never suffered from this like I did, which is a tribute to her independence and strength of character. She had no ambitions which depended on success within a particular framework, whereas I was always overconscious of my working and social environment. I always wanted to excel. But I felt this could only be done within the system, whatever it might be, and in conformity with it. Being different necessarily involved ostracism and failure. It took me decades to discover how wrong this often was, at any rate at the highest levels. But by then my nature and path had been set.

Being foreign had not seemed to matter so much in Zürich. It was clearly only a staging post, and I was still a child. Of course, I was also only still a child in France, just thirteen. But an adult child. I now knew that there was no way back and that everything in the future was going to be a battle.

The immediate problem, which I found acutely embarrassing, was that my parents could not afford to buy me proper clothes, as for an ordinary French schoolboy. My appearance therefore marked me out as a foreigner, and therefore as a freak, even before I opened my mouth.

At that time German boys wore shorts until they were about fifteen. In France none of them did after the age of about ten. Apart from shorts, I only had one pair of trousers which someone had given me, a mixture of knickerbockers and old-fashioned golfing trousers which you stuffed into woollen socks. And my main pair of shorts had built-in square braces, rather like *Lederhosen.* Then the final ignominy was my satchel. French schoolboys had briefcases which they carried under their arm, like little businessmen. I only had my old *Tornister*, like a square stiff rucksack. But my parents could not afford anything else. So that is how I had to go to school, braving those fifteen Metro stations for the first time on my own and dressed like a freak.

16 · Lycée Michelet

I WAS AGAIN taken to the headmaster, the proviseur as the directeur of a lycée is called, but still understood very little of what he said. He ushered me into a classroom in the middle of a lesson. I was faced with a stunned silence of many boys. The teacher indicated a desk near the front. This had evidently been kept for me and made it worse. I sat down and looked nowhere. The lesson was Latin, which the boys had done for several terms, and I only had a few weeks in Switzerland. And it was in French, of which I could only speak a few sentences. I felt like a stranger from outer space.

I remember nothing of the rest of the day, but the following weeks were among the worst of my life. Somehow they passed, in a sort of daze. I gradually understood more and more of what the teacher and the boys were saying, and started to speak myself, almost without noticing. It was Parisian slang, not French. A boy was "*un type*," and every sentence bristled with "*merde*," "*ta gueule!*" (an emphatic version of shut up) and "*vâchement*," which, like "*oh la vâche!*", served as a universal pejorative superlative. It seemed to be derived from posters and advertising a soft cheese spread, which covered Paris, like the Metro advertisements for Dubonnet. In every tunnel between stations the interminable illuminated signs would flash past: 'Dubo - Dubon - Dubonnet.' But no longer now.

French children are worked extremely hard. In comparison with Berlin, Zürich and England later on the atmosphere was like a crammer. I worked and worked, for the first time in my life, because I had to if I wanted to belong and to understand what was going on around me. We started at 8.30 in the morning and stopped for lunch, which deserves a special mention when I got used to it later. Then an hour's play in the yard. Then more lessons until about 4.30. Then another break, with a snack, *le goûter*. And then 'prep,' *les devoirs*, in our classroom until about 6.30 or 7.00. This was a period of concentrated silence, rigorously enforced by part-time student teachers called *pions*. Then home on the Metro, and often more work after supper, cooked by my mother, who was learning fast. I knew that my coming home would be the best moment of the day for her. But I was usually too tired to talk. And this new French world was soon becoming difficult to describe to her in German.

A great deal of the work consisted of learning things by heart. I knew all the French *départements*, the *rivières* and the *fleuves* and could draw them on a map. I learnt much anglophobe French history, a little English, a lot of Latin, and a vast amount of French literature. Of the English, I only remember 'John Gilpin was a citizen of credit and renown..' But I could recite the first twelve chapters of Caesar's '*De Bello Gallico*' ('*Gallia omnia divisa est in partes tres* ...'), the first two acts of Corneille's *Cid* and Racine's *Athalie*, some Voltaire, Diderot and Rousseau and many fables of *La Fontaine*. At the end of each term, and again at the end of the year, there were exams called *compositions* which covered all subjects. In the *composition de récitation* the opening lines of passages from all the pieces learnt during the term, and then the year, were put on slips of paper, which were mixed up in our form master's hat. Each boy was then called forward in turn and had to draw two slips and recite. Mostly in French, quite a bit of Latin, and a few also got John Gilpin *et al.*

However, all three languages sounded much the same, because the intonation did not vary. The stress was inevitably put on the last syllable of every word. I am always surprised that English speakers, however Francophone, are quite unable to acquire the simple hallmark of French speech: the accentuation of the last syllable. So it was '*Jean Jilpàin vas a citizèn.*' And the intonation was particularly marked in Latin. In Swiss-German, French and English, Latin is pronounced similarly, as though there were three similar dialects, though there is also another older school in England which pronounces Amalfi as 'Ammelfi.' The Germans claim that they pronounce Latin like the Romans did, and this is also claimed by the more sensible of the English Latins. The word '*fuerunt*,' for example, "they were," is pronounced similarly in all three countries, except for a hard and soft r. But in French it is '*fühérrònt*' with an accent on the 'ont,' which only Romans from Marseille might possibly have recognised as Latin. It sounds like a different language. My pronunciation naturally followed the French. So later on I had to relearn my Latin in England.

One of the reasons why I found it easy to work so hard is that I had virtually no friends out of school. Within the school, and especially within my class, I began to be accepted. I was tall for my age, and there was never any question of bullying, although I was a curiosity. We played proper football on one afternoon a week, and I soon played in goal for my class. But the real test of being accepted came in the daily five- or seven-a-side games with a tennis ball in the yard, when each class had its break at different times, with jackets for goalposts. It was on one such occasion, as I still remember, that I suddenly realised that I had become an accepted member of the crowd and almost felt at home.

But this did not mean that I had friends outside school hours. France is – or certainly was – quite different from what I later found in England, and from what I would also have found in Berlin if I had gone on living there. In both countries schoolchildren have a social life after and outside school. But not in France, at any rate before the war. One of the things always said about France is that people do not invite friends to their homes, or – if they do – that visits are highly formal. I found the first to be true, and never experienced the second. I had friends at the Lycée Michelet in Paris and later at the Lycée de Nice; they were close friends, every day at school. There was a Castallani in Paris and an Avignon and a Rastier in Nice and many others whom I have forgotten. We were soulmates during the day. But outside school and at weekends their friends were their relations and neighbours. I never saw any of my school friends out of school. And Judy and I only had our parents and each other; no neighbours or relatives.

17 · The Fizaines (and others)

BUT UNEXPECTEDLY the whole family found a miraculous exception to this French tradition, which transformed all our lives. Fernand Fizaine and his wife 'Maggie' came from Lorraine. Although fervently French, and with loathing for the Nazis and even les boches, their culture was Franco-German. He had a high position in the Agence Havas, the French equivalent of Reuters, and had been an admirer of my father since his youth. They had got to know each other a little before we moved to Paris. Thereafter Fernand and Maggie Fizaine adopted the Kerr family and became our spiritual salvation, together with their tall blonde daughter, Michèle, twelve, halfway between Judy and me.

Uncharacteristically for France, we became inseparable households and family friends. They lived in a flat near the Porte Maillot and we spent most of our weekends together. Maggie taught my mother how to cook, how to sew, how to knit, and how and where to shop. She was brilliant at all these things, and I never hear the word '*ménagère*' without thinking of her. She was dark, irresistibly vivacious and more or less exactly the same age as my mother. But very French. My father and she clearly had a great flirtatious attraction for each other, which added something to the family relationship, apparently without upsetting anyone. Fernand was vast in girth, with a nose like Cyrano, cultured, and a *bon viveur* who revered my father. As a native of Lorraine he understood and disliked the Germans, but he spoke the language fluently. Later on he was to write a competent life of Frederick I of Prussia, the father of Frederick the Great. He and my father had many common interests; from literature, language and history to wine and women. They talked interminably, in both languages, over endless bottles. But Fernand was infinitely more practical, and he knew the literary and journalist circles in Paris. He educated my father in the ways of the émigré factions and helped him in his negotiations with the *Pariser Tageblatt* and other publications. He tried to make my father worldly-wise. Looking back on it all, I don't think our family could have survived in Paris without the Fizaines, at any rate spiritually.

The only other support for the family of which Judy and I were aware came from an old aunt on my mother's side, Lucy, one of her father's three sisters. She had left Frankfurt for her native St. Gallen to marry a wealthy Swiss, Emile Reichenbach, whose family owned *Uniprix*, and apparently still does. She was to survive her other sisters, who jointly committed suicide in Frankfurt. For years Lucy and Emile had lived in St. Gallen. Then they moved to Paris, bringing their awful *schwyzerdütsch* French accent with them. They lived in a sumptuous apartment with servants on the Avenue Foch, reminiscently of our grandparents in Berlin. She was vast, quite old, extremely deaf and talked incessantly. He had a small pointed beard, always wore a frock coat, and rarely said anything. She overflowed with garrulous kindness, shouting at the top of her voice, as very deaf people do. How he stood it, I could not think. I have an irrational, and admittedly pedantic, aversion to badly spoken French, even when people speak it fluently. I can't come to terms with an accent which will not put the stress on the last syllable. This is crucial for the elegance of the language, and so simple. The everyday English sound of the Champs Élysées is painful. But nothing is as awful as French spoken with a Swiss-German accent. It is a linguistic atrocity. They don't only put the stress on the first syllable, like the English, but they do it with a gutteral German accent. I used to shudder when Aunt Lucy shouted at Emile, having been briefed by my mother: "*Il était premier en latin.*" And I have never forgotten her braying refrain, whenever the tea trolley was rolled in by a maid in white cap and apron: "*Mais il est méchant - il n'aura pas de gaaateau!!*" I would then offer my apologies for whatever had caused her to pretend to be upset, shouting into the wide opening of her vast ear-trumpet. This was renowned among the members of my mother's family. It was said to be Emile's nightly task to retrieve any lost dentures which might be found in its recesses at the end of the day.

But Emile and Lucy were not to be underestimated. Their son had married the former wife of Léon Blum, the socialist politician. We were presented to him and his current mistress and paraded before some important and interesting people, as even we realised. They all knew of my father. But he would not go to Aunt Lucy's salons or meet any of Emile's friends, although my mother begged him.

The importance of Aunt Lucy for Judy and me, and so for our mother, was that she was on the committee of an organisation which collected and distributed clothes to poor children. Of course, my father would have nothing to do with the possibility of his son and daughter being clothed by any form of charity. He hated the thought of it and there were many rows. He would not visit them with us after her offer to help any more than before. But she knew of the Kerr-Weismann feud and accepted it. I got long trousers and normal jackets and a briefcase as a satchel; and Judy got dresses. I recently found a photograph of my mother and myself of the time, arms around each other's shoulders and not looking terribly different in age. When I showed it to Judy she immediately remembered when I was given the suit that I was wearing, and that Maggie Fizaine had made my mother's dress and hat.

By the time of the summer holidays in 1934 we were to some extent settled. With the help of Aunt Lucy, Judy had at first been sent to a fashionable private school in our neighbourhood, the Cours Suchet. But she did not really like it, and the fees were going to double when she would move up in the autumn. So she announced that it was a waste of anyone's money, and went happily to the *Ecole Communale*. There, she too, gradually became a Parisian child.

But then the summer came and school stopped. The problem was where we would be for the long summer holidays. We had no money to stay in a hotel. The Fizaines had a small house in the Oise north of Paris, close to Auvers, where Van Gogh ended his days in a lunatic asylum. But an extension of our friendship in Paris into the *campagne en vacances* would have been a different dimension, and they also knew that my father would never stay with anyone. We feared that we would just have to stay in our flat, in a hot empty city. But then salvation came from the Guggenbühls in Küsnacht. They must have known how we were placed, because they invited us all to stay at their beloved Sonne for the whole of August. My parents only had to find the fare, which they did, somehow. Before leaving, we celebrated the 14th of July with the Fizaines until dawn, eating and drinking, and dancing in the streets. We saw Paris from the Sacré Coeur on Montmartre as the sun came up. It was the only 'party' with my father which I can remember. Then we said goodbye for the summer, and went home to bed. The Fizaines *à la campagne*, and we to Küsnacht.

I remember virtually nothing about that August. In fact, I had forgotten all about it until I recently asked Judy to take me through the history. The reason why it is a blank is that it must have been a blank at that stage of my life. I was becoming half assimilated in Paris, but still belonged nowhere, and certainly not back in Switzerland. All that now remains of Die Sonne is the memory of a family like the Guggenbühls, and what they did for a family like us, who could not have been more different. I vaguely remember that I again took up with the Felderi in a slightly more sophisticated way, which meant more frequent evenings throwing apples at her bedroom window, where she always seemed to be ironing, at least in my memory. There were also more sophisticated tribal encounters between the sexes during the day, but always in separate giggling groups, with exchanges of projectiles and invective; typical of Swiss mid-teen courtship during the thirties. The rest was football, watching the Küsnacht Wanderers and the mighty Zürich Grasshoppers. And fishing from the landing stage in the lake, though Judy said I was only bathing worms. By September I was restless, and ready to go back to Paris and school.

18 · Paris – the second year

WHEN WE returned it seemed like coming home, at any rate more like home than anywhere else. By now I was used to the routine of the long school days, and even the daily lunches. I clearly remember the tremendous noise of about two hundred boys rattling away in French in a vast dining room with wooden tables for ten, with unlabelled bottles of red wine and carafes of water on each. Everyone drank wine, but all in their early 'teens, like myself, added water. Of course, I had never tasted wine before and could hardly believe it at first. But it was important not to be different. So I drank watered red wine at lunch every day when I was thirteen, and then hardly ever again until after the war, though not with water. I didn't really like wine at thirteen, and I could see why my mother always said that it tasted like red ink.

The tumult at lunch and during breaks was in total contrast with the boys' behaviour at work. All the classes were large, about 35 to 40 boys. But there was total discipline; I cannot now understand why, because I remember no sanctions. We were frightened of the young pions who supervised the evening session of l*es devoirs*, though there were no beatings, as later in England. But in any case I had totally changed from the rowdy schoolboy of Berlin. I was now more or less *un élève modèle*, who worked and worked in order to survive. There was nothing else for me.

I suppose that it was by about Christmas 1934, when we had been in Paris about a year, that I suddenly realised that I could speak and even think in French like German. Of course, my vocabulary was limited, as that of any boy of fourteen, although it helped that I was reading a great deal of French literature. But I had no accent. I don't think I ever had one, because I learnt French at school from the teachers and the other boys, and never heard French spoken with a German accent. Judy's French developed just like mine; she had even had a small start from her school in Berlin. So we began to talk French, almost without realising it, and only talked German to our parents.

Apart from school, our parents and the Fizaines, I remember very little of Paris. Sometimes we were given money to go to a cinema in the Champs Elysées on Thursday or Sunday mornings to see cartoons and newsreels. At weekends we played with Michèle, usually football in the Bois de Boulogne. She was a natural athlete and ball player, nearly as tall as I, although a year younger, and Judy often felt left out.

Meanwhile the grown-ups went on as before. My father would talk and drink wine with Fernand, and Maggie would teach my mother the French domestic arts, which she could have learned in no other way, and made dresses for her. The two families remained inseparable, and they seemed like our salvation.

Occasionally there were also still echoes of society and money, as in Berlin. We were often paraded at the Swiss great-aunt's flat in the Avenue de Foch and had to shout our school successes into her ear trumpet, to hear them repeated in her braying Swiss-French to her friends.

But although our parents must have known many people, I cannot recall any others. Their desperate money worries were now part of our life too; they no longer kept anything from us, and they could no longer talk French when they didn't want us to understand. We shared their occasional bouts of optimism, for a series of articles, perhaps a book, or even a film. But mostly we shared our mother's fears and depressions. Not our father's. If he had them, he never let on. And his creed was to be positive, because it was wonderful just to be alive and to live in Paris. In fact, what he achieved was amazing in the circumstances. His book on *Rathenau* was published in Amsterdam in 1935, and also another in paperback in Brussels about Hitler, *Die Diktatur des Hausknechts* (*The Dictatorship of the Varlet*) an appeal to the great powers to intervene in Germany. But, as he himself wrote to a friend, this had little prospect of success. "They appear to be satisfied with treaties – and are being taken for a ride. It is a time of blindness". (With four more years of "appeasement" to go!).

He also wrote many articles for the *Pariser Tageblatt* and some French papers, including his famous denunciation execrating Gerhart Hauptmann, his life-long friend, for having thrown in his lot with the Nazis. And Richard Strauss was not far behind, and also jettisoned as a friend. So he still had a voice, even in exile, and he must have toiled incessantly, refusing to admit defeat. But try as he would, he could not earn enough to support his family, and I think we sensed that there must have been helpers of whom we did not know.

My last memory of Paris is of the exams in July 1935, at the end of the school year. To my amazement I came top of the class and won the *Prix d'excellence*, which probably remains my greatest achievement ever. It was presented by the *proviseur* in a crowded hall full of boys and parents, including mine. For them, and particularly for my father, it was a very special day for another reason. A large visiting group of Hitler Youth boys had for some reason been invited for the occasion, and the gallery was crowded with brown shirts, black belts and swastikas. For my father this was a triumph, that they had been compelled to witness his son's accolade in France. He was convinced that they would know his name, and therefore realise what Germany had lost. Although my parents knew no one there, he tried to explain this to other parents around them. I felt embarrassed, and also sad for him, because I realised the emptiness and futility of his moment of pride.

But it would not be honest for me to claim that my academic achievements at the Lycée Michelet were entirely excellent. I had a distinct setback in Arts. For some reason I did not hit it off with the master who taught us to draw, or rather supervised what we drew. We had a prolonged argument, spanning several early lessons, about the usefulness of his class and craft, in which I found myself driven into increasingly indefensible positions. But I felt that I didn't really deserve his contribution to my first term's report: '*Aucun goût*,' no taste, or appreciation. So I protested gently, and there was then a studied truce and total silence in the reports for the following terms. But he had the last word. At the end of my year's report, which got the *Prix d'excellence*, my Arts report was '*Reste sans goût*.' It still rankles. La Rochefoucauld said most things: '*Tout le monde se plaint de sa mémoire, mais personne de son jugement*.' Or *son goût*.'

For my parents my *Prix d'excellence* was the only ray of light at a time which had reached despair. There was no money, no prospect of any income or way forward. France had been hit by a deep depression and the little pockets of refugee earnings were drying up. There was no way of paying the rent for the flat. I now realise that it must have been one of the darkest times in the lives of both my parents.

How dark, I only realised a few years ago. My sister had a letter from a Frenchman who was writing Einstein's biography and had found correspondence with our father among his papers. Extracts from heartrending letters from my father in Paris had been translated embarrassingly into French. Then recently we got copies of the originals from the *Alfred Kerr Archiv* in the *Akademie der Künste* in Berlin. For my father to have to implore for help from anyone must have been an even greater tragedy than what he was going through, but of course we knew nothing of this. There had evidently been the possibility of an invitation to lecture in America, including his fare to New York. But this would have meant leaving us behind and provided no future, so it was not an option. All he wanted was to save his family, nothing for himself. But, as he wrote to Einstein in May 1934, after trying everything and coming to the end of the small advances for the two books, "we will be on the street in the middle of June".

Michael and Mother, Paris, 1934.

Einstein wrote that he was *erschüttert,* devastated, as we would now (too readily) say. He could do nothing directly, but he appears to have sent a friend. His name was Rudolf Kommer, and he is often referred to in their correspondence. Until recently he was something of a mystery to my sister and me, and we thought of him merely as a wealthy businessman who had emigrated to the States and was a friend of Einstein. But Judy always maintained that she had heard that he was a spy, and recent discoveries in the *Exilliteratur* through the *Goethe Institute* in London certainly support the conclusion that he must have been in, or close to, the CIA of those days. Perhaps a cultured double agent. There is nothing else to explain why a former Austrian journalist and film agent from Czernowitz, with largely unfulfilled literary ambitions, should have had such a lavish life-style on both sides of the Atlantic, with large funds at his disposal without any visible source of income, and extraordinary contacts in high places in America and Europe as a *confidant* of writers, artists, politicians and a few tycoons. In one of his many letters to my father, in 1937 after we had come to England, he wrote that he had discussed my father's plight with Winston Churchill, Duff Cooper and Somerset Maugham. Kommer was hoping somehow to secure a small regular stipend for him, to free him from his destructive daily money worries, with a plan that my father should write a book about Disraeli and Marx, two prominent Jews of their period, who lived in London at the same time but never met. (Though why that should have been a surprise to any reader is not at all clear to me. It would have been extraordinary if they had).

My father had originally met Kommer in Berlin, and they had met again in Zurich in 1934, probably orchestrated by Einstein, when their long correspondence began.. They soon became friends, with Kommer a great friend in need, and in the following year my father dedicated his *Rathenau* book to him. Then after we had moved to England, when a collection of his poems, *Melodien,* was published in Paris in 1938, my father again dedicated this to Kommer as "the best friend whom I encountered in my life".

It must have been Rudolf Kommer who got us through the summer of 1934. But by Christmas (of which I have no recollection whatever, if it happened) things were even more desperate. In a long letter to Kommer of 20 December 1934 my father thanked him "from his heart, again and again" , mentioning a telegram which he had recently sent him "only in the direst situation". He wrote: "We have gone through a terrible time. I have had to react against the despairing madness of my wife, constantly in my ears, to put an end to the trauma of this precarious existence by a joint overdose, also for the children. Such stuff is anathema to me, but it is difficult to watch over her". He had kept us going for a few weeks by "*Versatz*", pawning, "but indispensable articles in everyday use, considered in the context of their redemption, immediately turn into debts". This is the only businesslike "commercial" statement I have ever heard from my father.

Rudolf Kommer evidently saved us in Paris and went on helping my parents with what may have been quite small, but probably fairly regular, sums over many years, though at the time we knew nothing of this. According to the *Exilliteratur* about Kommer and my father, some payments may have continued until Kommer's death in New York in

1943, about which my father wrote a long sorrowful poem, *Epilog*, to be published in his collected works many years later.

My father's correspondence with Einstein also went on for some years after we had come to England. Einstein wrote in 1938 that Judy and I should be sent to America as soon as we were old enough, but by then this was not to be taken seriously. The last letter from my father to him which has survived was dated 30 August 1940, during the battle of Britain. My father wrote that he had heard of a man making enquiries about him in connection with a plan with which Einstein's name was associated "to rescue anti-Nazi writers whose lives would be threatened in the event of a German invasion, by taking them to America " and that, if true, "I would certainly be deeply grateful to you for prolonging my life". The irony seems to have been lost on Einstein, who replied on 19 September 1940 that there was "no doubt that this was Roosevelt's initiative to bring endangered persons temporarily to the United States without regard to the political [immigration] Quota". Fortunately for all in this country, the truth or invention of the existence of such a plan never fell to be tested. And this is where their known correspondence ended.

But I am going far ahead. All this had stemmed from our time in Paris, years earlier, and that is where I was in this chapter. So back to 1935. All that Judy and I were told at the time was that we were leaving our flat in the Rue de Villejuste, that we would spend the summer at the seaside in Belgium, and that later on we might go to England. What we did not know was that the flat had been given up because there was no way of paying the rent and that England was no more than a faint hope, though now the only one left.

This hope rested on a film script which my father had also written in Paris, about the life of Letitia, Napoleon's mother. He knew Corsica well from his travels and had visited her house. He was always quoting what she said whenever she heard of her son's triumphs, in her harsh southern accent: "*Pourrvou que ça dourre,*" "*Pourvu que ça dure,*" so long as it lasts! He sent the script to Alexander Korda in London, the Hungarian film director, whom he knew, and who was fluent in German. And so my parents were now waiting for a miracle, an answer from him. Meanwhile we moved to a small boarding house in Coxyde, on the Belgian coast just south of Ostende. The sand dunes with their sharp blades of tall grass were like Neuhaus in Mecklenburg, but the North Sea was not like the Baltic. We were still there in early October of 1935, when all the people had gone and the autumn storms had begun, because there was nowhere else to go. But there was no sign from England. Perhaps my parents were also still hoping for a sign from America, without telling us. But with the need for visas and the fares this could by then have been no more than a dream.

In the end they felt that they must somehow go forward, since there was no way back and nothing in France. So it was decided that they would go to London and that Judy and I would be sent to our grandparents in Nice, because there was no money to keep us anywhere else. It must have been my father's bitterest moment, having to face a second forced separation from his children, and to have to be grateful to his scorned father-in-law for taking them in. I think that even Judy and I realised something of what it meant for him, and for our family. But there was no alternative left.

19 · To Nice

SO THE next chapter was Nice. I would have remembered nothing about getting there if I hadn't happened to mention it to Judy. Generally speaking, I have not discussed these recollections with my sister, because her memory is so much more precise than I can cope with. I am not aiming at total precision. Otherwise I would never get anything written, or – to be precise – dictated. In case it is of any interest, the original version of this book was dictated on a small dictaphone, mostly walking about at weekends and in the holidays, and then revising the typescript for shorter sentences, improvements and greater accuracy when I happened to talk to Judy. She also made corrections to the final text.

Anyway, Judy reminded me about that drawn-out strange summer in Coxyde. It was drawn out because my parents did not know when or where to go next. When she reminded me about it I also remembered a sophisticated Belgian or French teenager with a square *Bubikopf*, a typical thirties haircut for which I never learned the English word. She was dark, as were most of my memorable transient acquaintances. We used to meet regularly along the front, on the edge of the dunes, ogle each other meaningfully and exchange a few shy words. But she was not important like the Felderi in Küsnacht, where our so-called relationship only existed because the village insisted that it should. Nor was it anything like my relationship with Michèle Fizaine, who was then still only a footballer and a friend, but who might as well – at that time – have been a boy. The girl in Coxyde and I never really spoke, but only looked and parted self-consciously. I cannot remember her name, but she is the most vivid memory of this empty, insecure summer in Belgium. All of which I would have forgotten if I hadn't happened to ask Judy about how we got to Nice.

She reminded me of the journey. It began with a night and a day for all of us in a really dingy hotel in Paris, near the Gare du Nord, before Judy and I were to take the train to Nice and our parents hoped to travel to England sometime later on. England had become the main family topic of conversation, a mixture of despair, hope and mainly indecision.

Judy reminded me about the day in Paris. There was some sort of spirit lamp in our parents' room in the hotel. My mother must have bought some eggs, because Judy clearly remembers – and I do vaguely –

that our father tried to boil them over this spirit lamp so that we would have hard-boiled eggs for the journey. But whether he gave up, or thought he had succeeded, I do not know. All that Judy remembers is that they were ultimately more or less raw.

There was no money for my mother to accompany us, but by then we were fourteen and twelve, so we could go alone, and Opapa would meet us in Nice. Our recollections differ about the journey, but whether it was the raw eggs or some other trigger of memory, I do remember it. Our parents put us on the late night train from the Gare de Lyons. It stopped somewhere during the night and I got out to spend a bit of our money on ham rolls. I remember a total sense of freedom, because it was the middle of a warm night in a strange place, and the first time on a train that our parents were not with us. But I also remember that the train began to move before I jumped on, and the consequent feeling of fear and guilt, because I might have let my small sister disappear on her own into the darkness. I remember walking through a great part of the train, full of sleeping people, before I found her.

Our grandparents Opapa and Omama lived in a spacious ground-floor maisonette of a beautiful villa, La Roseraie, with a large garden, in Cimiez, on a hill above Nice. They had a living-in Italian girl, Fernande, a *bonne* and cook, whose complex love life was only explained to me later on, and they were comfortable and happy. They liked the climate, the food and the wine, and they could live quite cheaply, even with some style. My grandfather, then in his mid-sixties, went down to town every day and had a regular routine which he cherished. It all revolved around the Promenade des Anglais along the sea, where it runs into the main square with the Casino. A tall, good-looking man, in a lightweight grey or white suit and a Panama hat, he was a familiar figure for many years. First, he went to his barber to have himself shaved and spruced up. Then he did some errands in the neighbourhood, including the English Library once a week. German books were not easy to get, and my grand-parents found it easier and much more relaxing to read English than French. He also belonged to an English bridge club, and if it had occurred to them to go to church, then it would have been the English church. Nice was very English in those times. Then he would swim at the first 'beach' establishment along the Promenade, though this is a euphemism since the entire length, past what is now the airport, consists of stones. Finally he would go and have coffee and cake at his usual cafe in the square and gossip with his acquaintances, before catching the tram back to Cimiez for lunch. Over lunch, if we were there, we would be taken through the morning's events, having to guess what he did next, and whom he had met. Many of the names became familiar. '*Ein Wolf*' was a member of the family Theodor Wolf, an old friend and former publisher of my father's. He and his family stayed on, even when the German army occupied the south of France in 1942; and they were all deported and killed. Judy told me about them, because she was always the one to remember '*ein Wolf*' when we had to guess at lunch.

My grandfather was delighted with his life and dominated the household. My grandmother was also quite content, but she loved her flat and the garden and did not often go into town. They did not have much money, because my grandfather's state pension had been stopped soon after the Nazis came into power. They were effectively kept by their youngest child, my uncle Nucki, who had emigrated to London and was doing well in the City.

Our arrival in October 1935 must have put quite a strain on the even tenor of this elderly household. But they seemed delighted to have us. They arranged for us to go to school, for me to the Lycée de Nice and another *Ecole Communale* for Judy. This meant going to town every day, down the long, steep Avenue de Cimiez, broad but winding, with double tram tracks in the middle. I volunteered to go down by bicycle and to take Judy on the crossbar. To my amazement this absurd suggestion was accepted. I was presented with a second-hand racing bike with gears, which I was allowed to choose from a local shop, and Judy and I got down into Nice about twice, clutching briefcases, in this perilous way. Certainly no more than twice, for two good reasons. First, our means of descent was obviously dangerous to the point of foolhardiness, and probably illegal even then. We were soon reported and stopped. Secondly, and perhaps of even greater weight, there was no way in which we could have got back up that hill. Both should have been obvious from the beginning. Fortunately my grandparents hadn't thought of either problem. Perhaps the attraction of saving two daily tram fares was too great. But when they did, I had the bicycle, which became one of the joys of my life, the biggest thing I had ever owned; almost as important as football.

The Lycée de Nice posed no real problems, although it was embarrassing to arrive again after the term had started, in about mid-October. I went into the next form up from where I would have been in the Lycée Michelet. And since it was near the beginning of the school year, I was just a boy who had been living in Paris and who had now moved to Nice. No one knew that I was not French, and I told no one. And since the custom of keeping home and family apart from school applied just as much to Nice as to Paris, this caused no problems and no one found out.

In retrospect I naturally find it surprising that throughout my youth, and even later on, I should always have been so anxious to conceal my past. Judy never had the same instinct or tendency. But to a large extent I can still understand why I felt so strongly about this. I had been uprooted and become a refugee, a wanderer, and I wanted desperately to belong. I was not an individualist or artistic like my sister. I instinctively felt that my life and career would have to find their way in a down-to-earth practical male society in which – at any rate in those days – security and acceptance depended upon being a recognisably conventional member of the community. Being different seemed fatal. If one was, one would not fit into the system and be accepted by it, and one could therefore not make a career within it in the same way as other men. That, at any rate, is how it seemed to me. But of course, I never tried to analyse these feelings or to come to grips with them; it was all instinctive. Security, and perhaps ultimate success, for a boy with no particular originality or personality, could only lie in conformist conventionality. Being different meant not belonging.

If the emigration had taken us to America, in particular New York or Hollywood, these feelings might have been quite different, because America would have been a naturally mixed society in which a large proportion were recent immigrants. But this was not so in old countries like Switzerland, France and England, with closed conventional middle-class societies.

Later on, during the war, this feeling of the need for concealment took on different proportions, and even Judy had to accept it for a time. But that was still four years away.

I was quite happy in Nice, although I knew of course that it was only another interlude. It could not be, or lead to, a home or any settled future. But, so far as it went, I felt that I was having quite a good time. I made friends at school, learnt a lot about girls, and became the regular goal-keeper of a school team. I also went for bicycle rides, and three friends and I went off for a long weekend along the coast as far as Toulon, sleeping in a tent on the beach and in fields. I had been quite surprised that my grand-parents allowed me to go without knowing the other boys, *les types* or *copains*. But they probably felt that they had little control over me, though they had more than they realised, since I had no security elsewhere.

I got on extremely well with them. Both played bridge; my grandfather extremely well, terrorising my grandmother whenever she was his partner. They taught us both, and I became a fanatic, and ultimately quite a good player; all my life. I also played endless *bézique* with both of them in turn. But Judy was much less happy. For many years she was to

Visit to La Roseraie, 1992.

have a much more difficult life than I, and this was when it began. For some reason she did not get on well with my grandparents, particularly Omama. They liked me because I was so much like their daughter, gregarious and keen on games. But Judy was like the cat that walked by herself. She reminded them of my father, and she saw them through her father's eyes. I did not realise how miserable she was. And of course, she was two years younger, and needed her parents more. Although we did not speak about it much, both of us were beginning to wonder if they would be able to keep us and what would ultimately become of us. But Judy thought about these things more than I, because she was unhappy and more thoughtful, whereas I was always reasonably happy and lived for the moment.

There was only one crisis which I can remember. It now seems like a joke, but not at the time. I had a friend at school; I think he was called Avignon. One of the things we had in common, apart from football, bicycling and talk of girls, was a loathing of Geology as one of our compulsory subjects. Even now I feel faintly nauseated by any reference to the Jurassic, Pleistocene, etc. So we decided at an early stage that we would just opt out of any attempt to understand geology. We would ignore it and cheat in the exam. After that we only concentrated on how to do it. There was no photocopying in those days, but we tore out the important pages from our text-book and stuck them up our sleeves. We might have got away with it if we had sat apart. But both sitting together, pulling up our sleeves and ogling sideways, proved to be *trop voyant*. We were both hauled before the class, stripped of our cribs, and told that – apart from some other punishment which I have forgotten – our papers would be marked *zéro*, and that *le zéro* would appear in our Christmas reports and speak for itself. Or, more realistically, pose obvious questions at home when the reports were opened. It was apparently not intended to state explicitly that we had been caught *tricher*.

The crisis was that the reports were sent by post, in my case addressed to my grandfather, of whom I was much more in awe than he probably realised. We had to have another plan and we only had two weeks before Christmas. There were agonising early mornings of sneaking down to the front door of the Roseraie to intercept the post, often being nearly intercepted myself. But one morning the envelope was there, and after school Avignon and I met in the kitchen of a café run by one of his cousins. He had his envelope too and we steamed them both open, quite easily. There were our marks for every subject, marked out of 10, all in red ink; and there were *les zéros*, "*sautant aux yeux*," as Avignon elegantly pointed out. To have added an *un* in front and turned them into *dix* would have been equally conspicuous and compounded our crime to an unacceptable degree. To turn them into a *neuf* or *huit* was considered, but thought to be unworkable. So it had to be ink eraser, which we used at school. But this contained acid and could cause holes. In my case it did. But Avignon somehow patched it beautifully and minutely, and drew an exquisite and modest *sept* over the patch.

Judy, Deal, 1936

The next morning the envelope was replaced and arrived formally. There was more anguished waiting. But my grandfather noticed nothing; the report was good; and he seems to have had as little interest in geology as I.

20 · Our parents in London

WE HAD heard very little from our parents during that autumn. They had gone on staying in the dingy hotel near the Gare du Nord where we had spent that one night with them, between Coxyde and Nice. They had no money to go anywhere else, and there was no reply from Korda about the script of the life of Letitia. My mother said that she only kept her sanity, and some of her spirit, by reading the Forsyte Saga from beginning to end. It made her long for England even more. My father wanted to go to London to see Korda to convince him about the script's prospects as a film. Since they had no money for the fare they had been forced to apply for help to some refugee organisation in Paris, something which my father hated. The members treated him with respect approaching veneration, but the organisation was highly ineffective and the relevant committee never seemed to decide anything. Ultimately, as our mother told us, my father asked for a meeting. When there were more polite words but no clear action, he must have got near to breaking point. He banged the table and said that he had never asked anyone for anything, but he was now asking for their fares to London. This produced the money, and in late October or early November 1935 they travelled to England.

They lived in a room in a small boarding house in Greencroft Gardens, off the Finchley Road. My father must have besieged Korda, and they also met other friends who had gone direct to England. Among them were Janos and Melanie Plesch. Of Hungarian origin, like Korda, he had been a fashionable doctor in Berlin who now practised equally successfully off Park Lane. They were old friends of my parents, and they and their children, whom we knew from Berlin, were to become important in our lives for years.

For the Pleschs, like so many others, England was the only realistic hope of a future home in Europe. The language was reasonably close to German, much easier and somehow more natural than French. England seemed solid and secure, despite the depression, whereas France already seemed weak and fragmented. I think that it must soon have become clear, even to my father, that his literary excursion to Paris had been a wild goose chase which could never have led to anything solid. In retrospect it must have seemed as though we had wasted nearly three years in our battle to build a new existence. This loss of time was to have serious consequences for us later on. The war came before we could be naturalised and overtook any prospect that my parents might have had of earning some money and setting up a proper home. But Judy and I never regretted our time in France, because we learned to speak French like natives. I have loved the language ever since. And although it must have seemed to our parents that they were among the last to arrive, they were in fact among the first. The main waves of German refugees came two years later, after the pogroms in 1938. But most left it too late.

I don't know what happened between my father and Korda. But just before Christmas we got electrifying news in Nice. Korda had bought the script for £1,000. One thousand pounds! A lot of money in those days when one thinks that my first term at school was to cost less than £40. Although at one stage removed from us, since its direct effect was far more important for our parents, it must have been the greatest *deus ex machina* stroke of good fortune for Judy and me during the whole of our lives. We had played no part in it at all. But I cannot think what would have happened to us, but for *Letitia.* It was like a miracle, a fairy-tale. The first success in nearly three years since Hitler, which was to transform our lives.

I never asked my father, and my father never told me, what had passed between him and Korda. I felt instinctively that this was not a subject to be discussed. Perhaps I suspected that it was a business deal mixed with charity. Sympathy and friendship, if not charity, no doubt played a part in it. But this was a time when Alexander Korda was still on a 'high' and the collapse of the British film industry not yet in sight. So he may have been profligate and optimistic. Or perhaps I am doing an injustice to my father, since I know nothing of the qualities of the script. A copy is now in the *Archiv* in the Akademie in Berlin, read by students working on dissertations. But I am ashamed to say that I have never read it. Although it changed our lives. All I did, years later, was to visit Letitia's house on a holiday in Corsica with my children.

21 · The end of the Lycée de Nice

THE NEWS about the film script came too late to enable our parents to join us for Christmas. A contract had to be drafted and signed before they got the cheque. So we spent Christmas with our grandparents in Nice and I remember nothing about it except the beginning of the realisation that we would be going to England.

My mother arrived about the middle of January, totally exhausted. Judy remembers that she had new hair brushes, so presumably they had got the money. She came home to her parents, to recover from months of fear and uncertainty, and to build up enough strength for the next stage, our transfer to England. But since we were happily at school and there was no deadline, all she wanted was to be with her parents and children, and to collapse and forget, for a time.

Of course we realised none of this, except that we were overjoyed to see her after three months of separation, when we had wondered if we would ever be reunited. We were now sure that we would be going to England, and I was keen to go before the next geology exam at Easter. We listened endlessly to her descriptions of London. I only remember one thing clearly, because my mother talked about it more than anything else. This was about Lyons tea shops in general and the three 'Corner Houses' in particular. (I think they were called 'teashops,' although there is no such word now). My mother enthused about them; they were everywhere, cheap, and the cakes were wonderful. The Tea Rooms in Zürich had made no impression on me, and I mistook them for some lady's name. But Lyons tea shops was my first overwhelming impression of London, even before we got there. They became the promised land.

But we were not there yet. The next great event, slightly dreaded by all in different ways, was to be the arrival of my father, who had stayed behind. My mother had come to be with her parents and children as soon as possible. He had stayed behind to tie up loose ends and in the hope of building a bit more. But, above all, he was in no hurry to have to thank his parents-in-law for having looked after his children for several months, when there was no one else to whom my parents could have turned. The whole of that time must have been bitterness and humiliation for him, which he was quite unfitted to face by anything in his previous long life. He was now sixty-eight, and it was only in the last three years that he had known anything except success and acclaim.

He arrived in Nice some weeks after our mother. Of course there was no question of his staying with us. He would never live in other people's houses in any event, let alone my grandparents'. He had not spoken to either of them for many years, nor they to him. There was never even any perfunctory conveyance of greetings via my mother. There was simply open and mutual dislike. So he arranged to stay at a nearby rustic hostelry, the Pré Catalan just above the *Arènes*, the Roman amphitheatre which is the tourist sight of Cimiez. It was simple and a bit dilapidated, but he loved it because he was back in France, out of the alien ugly stresses of London. And he never minded simplicity; on the contrary, he greatly preferred it; one thing which he and I have always had in common.

Then came the dreaded moment when he had unpacked and a walk round to us at *La Roseraie* could no longer be postponed.

I remember that it was a fine warm evening, although it must have been late in January or early February, because we were all out on the terrace. In fact, the weather is the only subject of conversation which I remember. First there had been polite, but distant, handshakes. Then a few formal sentences from my father, on behalf of himself and his wife, to thank my grandparents for looking after their children at a difficult time. Then a pause, then the weather, and then I realised that this wasn't going to work at all. The weather was never discussed in our family, not even after we went to England, where it is of course the main subject of conversation. To us the weather is simply there, one takes it for granted, it is the same for everyone and therefore nothing to talk about. I remember that after the war in Cambridge, when I first noticed the weather and mentioned it like everyone else, I felt I was beginning to get old. So when I heard my father refer to the weather I knew that this was not going to be a forgiving family reunion, letting bygones be bygones. The past had been too long and bitter, and the rift would never be healed.

And so it proved, although we managed, because we had to. My father stayed to dinner, briefly, and once or twice came to tea later on, always with other people. On one occasion I remember a heated argument about politics with recriminations which nearly got out of hand. But then there was more polite small talk, before it could turn into a row. We saw our father mostly in the Pré Catalan, where he was writing and typing, perfectly happy. So was I, because there were two tennis courts in front of the old building, which I had eyed for a long time. They were neglected and a bit overgrown, but they had lines and a net. I mostly played with my mother, and for the first time I beat her. It was becoming a second passion in my life, only exceeded by football. It was all self-taught by countless hours of rallies against the door of the empty garage in the Douglasstrasse. But gradually I was becoming quite a good player.

Since I was close to my grandfather and liked him, I tried to convince my father that he had got him wrong and that they should become friendlier, at least for my mother's sake. But it was no good. When I mentioned my grandfather's afternoons at the bridge club my father laughed and said that he obviously had some girl in the town. When I mentioned his political career, my father said that he had no principles, that he was as corrupt as other politicians, and that he had always been a playboy. Part of this may have been true, and my grandfather had certainly succeeded more with his charm and good looks than his other qualities. But he was undoubtedly a kind and loving man, and he also had some honest scruples. When I began to understand my grandparents' financial difficulties, although nothing in comparison with our own, my uncle Nucki, the banker, told me a story which went some way to prove it. In the summer of 1931, just before my grandfather was due to retire, they were on one of their usual holidays in the South of France. He was a keen gambler and regularly played baccarat and roulette in the casino at Monte Carlo. That summer he had a series of amazing wins approaching £20,000, an enormous sum in those days. He could easily have tucked the money away in a French bank, knowing that he was shortly due to retire and planned to live in Nice. But his duty as Secretary of State, and under German law, was of course to bring it back to Berlin. And this he decided to do. When he ultimately left he was unable to bring it out again and it was all lost. But the point of the story is not that my uncle Nucki wanted to demonstrate his father's honesty and public spirit. The point is that Nucki had strongly advised him to leave the money in France. He felt bitter that his advice had been ignored and that he now had to help his parents even more. It was the first of many complaints which I was to hear from my successful uncle Nucki about the financial problems and lack of success of all his relatives, including my mother.

Judy has a different picture of my grandfather from mine, perhaps because he and I had a lot in common, including books, and he had a great *penchant* for me. She remembers that he did have a girl in town, and even brought her to the *Roseraie*, overruling the feeble protests of our grandmother, '*Trudchen*,' Gertrud. And all this on Nucki's money, for our grandfather had and earned nothing, while our father, his older son-in-law, never stopped working and trying to find a way to keep the four of us.

That is her perspective, and the true one, as I realised later.

By the end of February my parents had had a sufficient rest to face the next stage. This must have loomed increasingly large in our minds for a long time. But apart from my mother's passionate accounts of Lyons Corner Houses I don't think that Judy and I saw London as the promised land. We knew our mother's enthusiasms and that England had always been her objective. But to us it was again the unknown, with new battles, and we were getting used to France. However, it was now clear that France, our father's choice, could not support us. So England it had to be. And this time we felt that there was a greater chance of permanence than at any time since leaving Berlin. So we decided that we had to make another effort and feel positive about the land of Lyons tea shops and cakes.

22 · The Promised Land

I REMEMBER nothing of the journey except that we spent a night in Paris and inevitably had an evening's celebration with the Fizaines. But this was not seen as a farewell. My father still regarded France as his new spiritual home, and Judy and I now had a standing holiday invitation to our grandparents at La Roseraie. And Michèle and I were close friends, a bit like a brother and sister, but different. At the end of the evening, and perhaps under the spirit of celebration, the Fizaines said that they would do something which they had never done in their lives, spend a holiday in England. No doubt the main reason was for Michèle to learn some English, since there was nothing in the climate, food or lifestyle of the England of the thirties to attract viveurs like Fernand and Maggie. But it was a bit of a joke to them, as it was a more painful joke to our father and only a Mecca to our mother. So we agreed to meet in England in August, and somehow that made everything easier.

I have a faint recollection of a cold foreboding Channel crossing. It was either just before or just after my 15th birthday on 1 March 1936. But my first clear memory of England was the view of endless ugly terraced houses beginning long before London. This was something quite different from Berlin and Zürich, and even from Paris; more solid, but also more forbidding.

I remember nothing of our arrival or whether there was anyone to meet us. Probably not, because there were no relations or close friends. We were to live in a Swiss pension, the Foyer Suisse, in Bedford Way, off Russell Square. The whole of that side of the street was later to be destroyed in the Blitz and to be rebuilt as part of London University. Charles Clore House would fill the corner, to house the British Institute of International and Comparative Law and the Institute of Advanced Legal Studies, on whose Councils of Management I was to spend many years. But meanwhile there was only the small dark Foyer Suisse. It was run by an elderly spinster and had some semi-official status with the Swiss Embassy. Someone must have recommended it to our parents, and we were given demi-pension terms on a long-term basis. Between us we had three rooms, but I cannot remember who shared with whom. It was in any event only to be a temporary arrangement so far as I was concerned, for I was to go to boarding school, to give me the best chance of becoming English as soon as possible. Poor Judy was seen as a secondary consideration. For the first time we were to lead different lives.

My parents had offers of free places for me from two excellent schools. That is certainly what they became in the fullness of time. The first was Gordonstoun, a British version of Salem, the only well-known boarding school in Germany, created by its founder, Kurt Hahn. It has of course acquired a great reputation since the war, with royal connections and a reputation for toughness which I am glad to have escaped. But the offer was firmly, and I fear perhaps ungraciously, rejected by my mother, who was now wholly in charge. Her boy was going to go to an English school, not to the Scottish branch of a German school. The second offer came from Bryanston, a recently founded boarding school in Dorset with a reputation for being progressive. I think that I would have been perfectly happy there, and of course it also acquired a high reputation after the war. But my mother saw it as an experimental, not traditionally English, which is what she wanted. So she accepted the recommendation in favour of his own old school of the Rt. Hon. Hastings Bertrand Lees-Smith, a former Postmaster General in the Government of Ramsay Macdonald. How my parents came to know him I can no longer remember; presumably through the ubiquitous Janos Plesch, whose patients included the famous and fashionable, though mostly women. But I remember that I was taken to meet him somewhere in Westminster, a small kindly man, and that for the first time I had to speak English to a stranger. His old school was Aldenham, a small boarding school which then had about 250 boys, between Elstree and Radlett in Hertfordshire.

My parents and Judy in Deal, 1936.

23 · Aldenham

ALDENHAM WAS of course far from being a major public school. But there were fewer schools in those days, and it was probably better known before the war than now. Its playing fields were famous. And it was a soccer school, not rugger, which I regarded as essential. It was also clearly old enough to meet my mother's requirements, having been founded in 1597 by a Master Brewer, Richard Platt. His portrait hung in the Hall, holding a tankard of beer for the first three hundred years, before it was overpainted and replaced with a Prayer Book in Victorian times.

Mr Lees-Smith took us out to the school in his chauffeur-driven car to meet the headmaster; he must really have been extraordinarily kind. The headmaster, George Riding, was an exceptional person, in some ways almost a great man. He was very large, with a strong face, and would stand out in any crowd. Proud to have come from a humble North Country background, he was an outstanding product of Manchester Grammar School, followed by a Second Class in French and German after a scholarship to Oxford. Aldenham was his first headship and was unfortunately to be his only one, perhaps partly because of the war. His problem was that the school was too small and not sufficiently important for his personality and ambitions, which he was never able to disguise. Like all headmasters, he had to deal with four constituencies with divergent views and interests, the boys, the staff, the parents and the old boys. Different headmasters would give different emphasis to these in their orders of importance. George Riding succeeded only with the parents, mostly the mothers. With the other three he was more or less universally unpopular throughout his career, sometimes undeservedly, but often not. The reason was partly that he always wanted things for the school which were in advance of the time and unpopular with the traditionalists who then tended to shape the atmosphere of public schools. In this case he was right in principle, even though it was always obvious that he used his vision for the school as a projection of his own personality and ambition. But his main failing was that in trying to push through the necessary reforms, he was overbearing, upsetting and alienating everyone who worked or lived in his shadow. It was not merely that he was tactless; he could be cruel. His treatment of a gentle elderly music master, whom he forced to retire and then prohibited from playing a farewell 'voluntary' in chapel, was worthy of the best traditions of Mr Chips and is remembered by all my diminishing contemporaries. Of course he would say that he had his reasons. He saw himself in Olympian terms, with a mission, surrounded by smallness and mediocrity.

But the need for his vision was justified. The school had sunk to a low ebb in discipline and morals before his arrival in 1932. He undoubtedly brought a wind of change and put the school on the map of the thirties. When he retired nearly twenty years later he was a well-known name among headmasters, though never popular. He never received the recognition which he thought he deserved. After his reluctant retirement to Cornwall in the fifties his son amazed me by asking if I could get him some sort of honour. My reaction was not that I felt that it would have been out of place to give him an OBE, or whatever. But I was amazed that it should be thought that I, one of his former schoolboys, could possibly have some influence to promote my former headmaster. He had been a great figure in my life. Not a hero or someone whom I liked. But someone of whom I was too much in awe, and to whom I owed too much, to dislike freely.

However, like all the strong personalities in small settings, George Riding relished having to respond to unusual situations. He was flattered by the recommendation of this former Cabinet Minister, one of the most distinguished OAs of the time. And he was impressed by what he was told about my father and our history, and perhaps by what my mother told him about me, since she did the talking. So he saw me as something of a catch.

While George Riding might possibly not make a crisis out of every drama, he certainly enjoyed the dramatic. It was then only about ten days before the Easter holidays. But, in case I should disappear, he ordained that I should come on the following day, to "play myself in." In retrospect, he was probably quite right. Although it meant again being thrown in at the deep end, it also meant that during the holidays I would know what I would be going back to, instead of wondering and worrying. But, once again, the experience was a bit of a shock. And it was different from Paris, because there was no going home at night. It was like entering a different life and a strange new world.

Like all old-established public schools before the war, whether major or minor, Aldenham was steeped in hierarchical customs and rules, always called traditions. Although it is an old joke, I really believe that I have seen the House Captain put up a notice on the board saying that, from tomorrow, something or other would be a tradition. We wore grey trousers and white shirts with stiff round collars all the year, with black jackets and ties in winter and blazers, blue ties and straw hats in the summer. Only school and house preposters, 'praes,' were allowed to have all their buttons undone. After the war this was extended to sixth formers generally, in recognition of the growing influence of academia. Other privileges, as they were called, were similarly restricted, such as being allowed to 'brew up' in the 'houses' by making tea or toast or heating baked beans, or to cross the huge cricket field during school hours, which divided two of the five houses from the rest of the school. There were particularly strict rules for boys in their first year, before they sank into the limbo of the *laissez-faire* of the second and third years, perhaps to attain privileges thereafter. New boys always had to have all three buttons of their jacket or blazer done up. They were not allowed to carry books under their arm, but always had to carry them like trays. And of course they were not allowed to speak to anyone senior to them unless spoken to first.

There were also strict rules about beatings, but these were not quite as frequent as the matrix of rules suggests. Praes, but not ordinary sixth-formers, were allowed to beat other boys freely, originally with a cricket bat, but later with a cane. House praes could only do so with the permission of their housemaster, and school praes also had to get permission to beat boys above a certain seniority. Housemasters often beat boys, but other masters only rarely. It was a school rule that no boy was allowed to receive more than six strokes in one day, unless it was proved that he had padded himself with notebooks or newspaper.

This is the world into which I was plunged shortly before Easter 1936. But I was just fifteen and tall, which was of course exceptional for a new boy, and that helped, though I had no school uniform and again felt very foreign.

The most important factor at that time must of course have been the quality of my English. But, strangely enough, I cannot remember this at all, unlike my French in Paris. I had done some English at school in Berlin and Paris, and perhaps also in Zürich and Nice. I knew *Alice in Wonderland*, *Three Men in a Boat* and *Tom Sawyer*, but I cannot now remember if I had read them in English or German. I could certainly read a lot of English and understood virtually anything that was said to me, if people spoke slowly. But I cannot remember how well I spoke it.

I do not think that I ever had a German accent. If I had had one, then I would never have lost it. That, at any rate, is what I find universally among people who have come from Germany. Indeed, the older they get, the worse their accents become. The reason why I have no German accent in either French or English is that I did not learn either language from people with German accents. While I was picking them up I only heard both languages spoken by other boys and teachers. My mother had a slight German accent in English and a fairly strong one in French, but at that time we still only spoke German at home. So there was no linguistic contamination while I was learning, and after that it just fixed itself. I now have an English accent when I speak French and German. But at the same time, as I get old, I sense the undertones of a German accent in English for the first time. "*On retourne toujours à ses premiers .... origines*" (*et quelquefois à ses amours*).

I must have survived those days before Easter because I have no unpleasant recollection of them. During the holidays I was then kitted out with the vast list of clothes and equipment which had to be bought from the school Tuck Shop. Although we cut it down as much as possible I remember how horrified my mother and I were about the hole which all this was making in the precious £1,000. But of course, fees and prices were entirely different in those days. I have a faint recollection that the cost of the first term's fees and of kitting me out was something of the order of £40. Whatever it was, it turned out to be the last amount that my parents ever had to spend on my education. From then on it was scholarships topped up by grants of one kind or another. Apart from my pocket money – 1/s 6d a week – they were free of the burden of me. But without my father's *Life of Letitia* none of it would have happened. It – and Alexander Korda – had given me the start.

24 · The first year

I HAD NO trouble settling in during the summer term and was soon quite happy. Cricket was a mystery for a time, since I only knew the word as a kind of grasshopper. But I learnt to bowl a bit and to play serious tennis. I made a close friend, John Fleetwood-May, known as Fleeters, since one did not use Christian names. He had been a new boy at the beginning of the Easter term and was therefore also not a member of the great intake during the previous autumn, which ruled our generation. He was unorthodox in his views, left wing and never popular with masters. So we were both different from most of the others and soon teamed up, although he was not interested in games or in going to university. His father was in Reuters and he wanted to follow him into Fleet Street and journalism as soon as he could leave.

O Levels and A Levels were then called School and Higher Certificate, but they were not as exacting or competitive. I did a set of School Cert papers internally at the end of the summer term for a test and was told that I would have passed although I had only had the Easter holidays and one term to get up the set books. I suppose it was all that learning by heart in France. Exams were never a problem to me; they only require memory and technique, not real knowledge. I got a Double First in Law at Cambridge merely by summarising textbooks and lecture notes without ever having opened a Law Report; in fact I would not have known how to find them. The technique is then to summarise the summaries by a process of increasing refinement, and at the end you cannot help knowing it all. The rest is merely the additional technique of displaying knowledge by seeing the points which the questions are designed to elicit and then feeding them into the answer, bit by bit, in an articulate way, letting the examiner find them one by one. It never fails, but proves nothing except an aptitude for exams. The technique of getting a judge on your side by advocacy in instalments is a bit similar.

After the School Cert test in the summer my parents received no demand for the autumn term's fees. Instead they got a letter from George Riding, who was delighted to tell them that I had been awarded the top internal scholarship together with a grant from the Brewers' Company which would cover my fees for the next three years. From then on, until the end of their lives – and I cannot remember who died first – George Riding was my mother's greatest hero and the epitome of

'Fleeters' and Michael, Aldenham

everything that was wonderful about England. Even my father succumbed. He wrote him a letter which Riding preserved and proudly showed me after his retirement to Cornwall many years later. And there is a fulsome reference, by my father's standards, to George Riding in his last book, *Ich kam nach England.*

There is no doubt that I owe a great deal to George Riding, perhaps more than to anyone else. Why is it then that I feel no real gratitude, as I do to so many others later on in the law, whose fleeting contacts were so much less important but somehow meant so much more? The reason was something which I could see even at fifteen, but not my parents. I could see that I served as an exhibit for Riding and the school, and therefore effectively for him. He was a collector of human trophies and he could see me as one of them. So I have never felt the gratitude which his help to me and my parents really deserved. However, I have always felt grateful to Aldenham, and later on served as a governor of the school for more than 25 years.

But I am going much too far ahead. The news of my scholarship with the consequent enormous relief for my parents' financial worries so far as I was concerned, did not come until September, shortly before I was due to go back to school. Meanwhile there had been the long-planned summer holiday with the Fizaines in England. The choice had fallen on Deal, on the south coast. I thought the reason was that Fernand and Maggie wished to remain as close to France as possible. Since the purpose, apart from joining up with us, was for Michèle to learn some English, they may have felt that there was no need to go further than the language barrier required. But Judy remembers the real reason: the fare. My mother longed for the rockpools of Cornwall, of which she had heard since her childhood. But it would take nearly another 30 years, and three grandchildren, before she would get there. The cost to Deal was less than one-tenth of the fare to Penzance.

Although we loved being with the Fizaines as always, as a holiday it was not really a success for any of us. We were effectively all foreigners in England, and Deal was not a place to rave about in comparison with all the other places we knew. It was really a curiosity, and to Fernand and my father something of a bad joke. It was the age of Wodehouse, whom my mother adored and whose style even they could appreciate insofar as they could understand it. So the two men played Wooster and Jeeves and Fernand addressed everyone as "Old'orrsse" or other idiomatic endearments. They went to pubs and dutifully drank beer *à l'anglaise*. But their jokes ran out at meal times in our little hotel because they simply could not believe what they saw and tasted. It must be remembered that the food and drink of the thirties was entirely different from now. The variety of restaurants which we now take for granted simply did not exist. There were no cafes or bars, and no one drank coffee, which was virtually unobtainable, as was wine, quite apart from the price. It was meat and two veg with gravy, sausages and mash, fish and chips or beans on toast, and beer, lemonade or tea for drinks. That is why Lyons and ABC tea shops seemed so imaginative and were so popular.

Michèle had no reason to like England any more than her parents and I think that she also sensed that I was changing. For to me this was now home, however strange, and I insisted on defending it against all comers. She and I were always drawn to each other and exploded into brief emotional entanglements much later on. But we were really incompatible, and for her the main reason was that I had become too English and conventional, and therefore boring.

The Fizaines did not stay long and returned to their country house in the Oise with undisguised relief. But we stayed on; it cost no more than the Foyer Suisse and it was nice not to be in London. My main memory of the remainder of the holiday was of a ravishing dark girl from Paris, Jacqueline, a little older than I. She was also there to learn English and therefore of course delighted to be able to speak French. We swore eternal love and that we would meet again in Paris just before Christmas, when we would be passing through on our way to Nice for the holidays. As we parted, fervently and with some tears on her side, she gave me a photo of her with a remarkable inscription on the back, in elegant French: 'To Michel, the only boy to whom I have not lied when I told him I loved him.' We promised to write regularly, and in fact we did throughout the autumn term.

This was a happy time for me. My scholarship, but to my relief, not the additional grant, was announced on the school noticeboard. More important for my reputation, however, was the beginning of the football season. Within a few weeks I was playing in goal for the school for the under-16s, the Colts. But then came a great opportunity and fame. Something happened to the regular First XI goalkeeper. I cannot remember what, except that it was welcome, and I also cannot remember what happened to his substitute in the Second XI. But suddenly I was drafted in by the great Bowman, the Captain of my house and Captain of Football, to play for the first XI against another school, I think Westminster, in a match which both schools watched. We won 2:0 and I was lucky enough to make some saves in an unnecessarily flamboyant continental style, but which created a lot of *éclat*. After the general applause the most moving moment came in the changing room, a mixture of Mr Chips, Tom Brown's Schooldays and the meeting between Stanley and Livingstone. I was sitting shyly in a bath in the midst of a crowd of bigger boys, cavorting and celebrating, all naked. It was to be a long time before I got used to communal nudity; I never did entirely. Then suddenly a silence fell. The great Bowman came in from a shower. Stark naked he advanced towards me and gravely said, "Well done!" I didn't know what to do. It was obviously wrong to remain seated in the water. So I got up, standing in my bath and he on some duckboards. I remembered not to bow, but unfortunately I forgot that I was no longer in France. So I extended my hand, and he shook it, slightly nonplussed, because in those days one did not shake hands in England. Least of all in full-frontal nudity. I realised I had made a mistake after all.

But the moment passed and I never looked back again. I played in every match and got my 'colours' just before Christmas. Although I still felt like a stranger, the ice was truly broken.

At Christmas we all travelled to Nice, stopping off in Paris on the way.

I had looked forward to this moment throughout the autumn because I was finally to be reunited with Jacqueline, the girl from Paris with the unforgettable and unforgotten photograph and inscription whom I had met at Deal. In her letters she had told me all about her home and her school, and – above all - the route from one to the other. For we soon decided that we would have to start by my intercepting her on the way. She took it for granted, and I accepted, that my existence must be kept secret from her family and friends at school. So I had numerous maps and timetables of arrival and departure at both ends for different days. I didn't know when we would get to Paris. But I wrote that she should expect me any time, any day, shortly before Christmas. She wrote that she would always try to walk on her own and look for me. Our letters were getting more and more tense and excited.

But I had counted on having about a week in Paris. Why, I have no idea, unless it was pure wishful thinking. When the time finally came we were only going to be there for one night. The evening was inevitably spent with the Fizaines and there was no possibility of getting anywhere near Jacqueline on her way back from school. The Fizaines were near the Port Maillot; we were staying in a small hotel near the Gare du Nord, and Jacqueline was somewhere near the Bastille.

But our train to Nice on the next day was not until a little after 10, and Jacqueline left for school at 7.30. So I insisted that there was plenty of time. My mother and Maggie were dead against the idea. My father was amused but Fernand won the day for me.

"You could object if at his age he left girls at 7.00 in the morning, but hardly if he goes to meet them."

And so it was settled. It was her last day at school before Christmas and I stole out of the hotel in darkness soon after 6.00, promising to be back by 9.00 at the latest. I found her street and then the house where she lived on the third floor. Then I waited round the corner. And waited and waited. It was cold and I had my school coat on. Then suddenly, the magic moment. I nearly missed her. She had gone past me on the opposite side from where I was lurking and was walking away quickly. I ran after her, and finally she heard me and turned. But she only stopped long enough to utter a sentence which has always stayed in my mind, one of the greatest anti-climaxes of my life.

"*Tiens, Michel, tu es là!*"

Then she walked on, more or less at the same pace, and I had to keep up with her. Neither of us found much to say. She explained that she was going to school for the last time before Christmas, which I knew, and I explained that I was about to catch a train to Nice, which did not appear to interest her greatly, since she knew it from endless letters of detailed planning. She seemed a different person, very grown-up, and I felt like a schoolboy, which is what I was.

We parted some distance before her school. She asked me to come no further, and we solemnly shook hands, glad to go our separate ways and not to have to try to live up to our torrid correspondence.

I went back to my parents and Judy to catch the train to Nice and felt that another sub-chapter of my life was over. It was a relief to be able to stop worrying about how to handle the situation. 'Fresh pastures new' seemed a better idea; I was reading Milton for School Cert.

25 · 1937

I HAVE NO real recollection of that Christmas in Nice except that I wanted to get back to Aldenham. But I still felt like a stranger, and to some extent this feeling never stopped. The reason was that there was no 'at home.' My parents and Judy continued to live at the Foyer Suisse. Their lives were quite unsettled and without promise of any future. Fortunately the problem of Judy's school had been solved after a fashion. There was not enough money for two and it would then have been unheard of to send her to a state school. The solution came through American friends of my uncle Nucki, Freddy and Jebbie Bate. He represented CBS or some other American radio corporation, and they lived in style with their two daughters in a grand house on Campden Hill Square. Jackie and Judy had been sent to join us for a week in Deal with their governess during the summer. They were about the same age as my sister, and they had all their lessons from tutors at home. So it was arranged that Judy should join them, ostensibly to teach them German, but in reality to help her and my parents. So her life was spent between the Bates on Campden Hill and the community of refugees in the Foyer Suisse.

Although Judy survived it all, and ultimately with great success and happiness, her youth was infinitely harder than mine. She had to share my parents' daily money worries and unhappiness, and there was little in her own life to distract her. I was away and only re-entered this world reluctantly during school *exeats* and the holidays. My worry was that I had no home to which I could ask boys to stay, as they began to ask me to stay, and that I felt embarrassed to introduce them to my foreign parents. I did not really like my parents to come to visit me at school, because they were so different. And my father said how different I was, too. I was continuously worrying about breaking 'traditions', keeping my parents out of the way of others and making sure that we behaved correctly. My father said that it was hardly worth visiting me, since I 'wore my soul in a trouser crease.' But they still sent me the more or less obligatory pocket-money of 1/6d per week. I kept accounts, and my diaries have many entries recording the purchase of pots of jam at 6½d each, though few others.

During the short holidays such as Easter the whole family was usually invited by the Pleschs. Janos had an enormously fashionable practice, and Melanie had been a Gans, one of a number of sisters who were heirs to the I.G. Farben fortune. There was money beyond our imagination. Apart from their sumptuous house off Park Lane, from which he practised, they had rented from one of the Rothschilds a charming manor house on a substantial estate near Aylesbury, 'The Pavilion.' This became something like a holiday home for us. The Plesch children, Peter, Honoria and Odilo, were about 17, 16 and 14, and collectively older than Judy and I. Again we felt inevitably like poor relations, which was effectively what we were. But Melanie was kind to my mother and Janos admired my father. And being able to store their clothes in the cellar of the Foyer Suisse and not having to pay for their rooms saved a significant amount of money. So from time to time my father had to overcome his distaste of staying in other people's houses. There was always a large crowd at The Pavilion, which Janos made something like a salon, since he knew a lot of people. My main memory is of Kokoshka, who was a regular visitor and old friend from Berlin, who drew both Janos and my father. Judy and I were never happy there, but there was no alternative. She began to draw and paint, and I again took refuge in work for the official School Certificate in the summer.

But by the summer of 1937 this fragile family existence again fell to pieces. The famous £1,000 had virtually run out, and nothing more was in sight. Janos Plesch spread the story of my parents' plight among his patients, and one of them, Gladys Gardner, took pity. She was a tall, kind but slightly vague willowy figure in her fifties, looking a little like Virginia Woolf, and was married to Charlie, ex-Indian Army, whom I never saw without a topee. They lived in a charming house in Sussex near Herstmonceux with their tall 15-year-old daughter Melissa. It was decided that my mother and we would spend the summer holidays with them, the excuse being that my mother would teach Melissa German. This was our first real contact with England and English people in their home, and again we felt like strangers. But Summertree, their old house, had a tennis court, and that was my salvation. I played endlessly with my mother and Melissa, and there were local tennis parties, and I played well enough to feel less like an object of charity.

Meanwhile my father was sent off to France on his own. Obviously nothing would have induced him to come with us and he really had to get out of England, back to sunshine and wine. I think Janos gave him the money.

When he came back he could not believe that we had spent nearly two months in a small country house with total strangers. For him this would have been unbearable. I still remember his question: "Did you have a lot of rows?" Rows were something which he could understand. That was perhaps one of the reasons why he could just about stand the idea of staying with the Pleschs. Theirs was like a central European household in which Balkan wars constantly appeared to be waged among the family, the countless affluent visiting relations and a constant stream of servants presided over by Frau Lemke, the old cook imported from Berlin who was never known to leave the house or to speak a single word of English.

By the autumn there was no longer any question of my parents being able to afford the Foyer Suisse for my mother and Judy. For a while they shared my uncle Nucki's guest room in his house off Sloane Avenue, an arrangement which was equally disliked by all of them. It was also greatly disliked by his ravishing blonde girlfriend, always known as Wuzi, *der Betthase*. Occasionally I also stayed there and was once amazed to find her sitting on the edge of Nucki's bath when he was relaxing in it. I hadn't realised that people behaved like that.

The arrangement with Nucki could not last. In desperation my mother went back to her parents in Nice, taking Judy, more or less like a piece of luggage for which there was nowhere else. Their board and lodging in *La Roseraie* were free, but our family was now separated, with my mother and Judy exiled back to France It was a desperate time for my mother, and she returned to her earlier thoughts of a final solution. In a letter which has survived she wrote to my father: "I had no idea that one can suffer so much.....I have <u>no</u> hope. Have you any, honestly? And Alf, if (without it being my fault) it becomes impossible to provide for the children, is it not better to put an end to such a shameful existence, instead of being a drain on other people's pockets? If strangers have to keep us, is it not better if there were only two and not four? For the little ones someone may perhaps come forward to pay for their school until they're grown up, but no one would easily decide to take on a whole family. I hardly know anymore what I am writing, with this endless waiting, and never, never any news....... But I must tell you frankly, I would have made an end of it long ago, but I cannot impose the funeral expenses on my parents (8000 frs), and unfortunately there is no possibility simply to dissolve into nothing. Also, I cannot leave Puppi here alone; my mother, however kind, is now quite unfitted to look after a child......But soon I'll be no use to her either. Sleeping pills every night for 3 weeks, and when I try to stop, terrible palpitations......"

Judy, then 14, knew of our mother's state of mind, but says that she found ways of not being really unhappy herself. She did a lot of drawing, which became her main interest, and let our mother teach her School Cert Maths to take their mind off things.

Meanwhile I was happily at school, in my second football term and something of a rising star. I got credits in all my School Cert subjects and it was decided that I should go for Higher Cert in one instead of the usual two years, taking French and German as main subjects and English and Latin as subsidiaries. So I had no worries and regrettably little thought for 'home.' I avoided the thought, and anyway there was nothing I could do. My only comfort was that I cost my parents virtually nothing.

My father stayed alone in the Foyer Suisse, constantly writing, trying to sell articles and to interest people in his ideas for films or books or broadcasts to Germany. Although none of us knew it, he was also keeping a diary, *Ich kam nach England*, which was ultimately published in Germany in 1979, more than thirty years after his death. But the depression had come to England as well, and there was now no chance of *Letitia* ever being filmed and producing more money. My father and I visited each other from time to time in a melancholy sort of a way, neither really understanding the other's life, and too depressed about our family circumstances to talk much. He must have felt very lonely all on his own. His beloved sister Annchen and her daughter Käthe had emigrated to Israel in 1935 when we were still living in Paris and he knew he would never see them again. So he had had to say goodbye to them. I don't know how he found the money, but he had travelled to Marseille to spend one last day with them and to see them off on their boat. He had been to Israel on his travels in the twenties and written a famous piece about the country's beauty, beginning with the first sight of the promised land from the sea, which I have on a *Deutsche Grammophon* record of readings from his works. By now he was nearly seventy, and perhaps part of him would have wanted to sail to Israel instead of having to plan to travel on to England's dark satanic mills. But that would have been flight, which was not his way. So they said farewell, and never met again. But Annchen lived on in his mind, and in his poems and letters, even in England, until her death in 1948, a few weeks after his.

26 · 1938–1939

FOR CHRISTMAS 1937 I joined my mother and Judy again in Nice, and my father also came. For me it was like a piece of déjà vu . My bicycle was still there and the tennis court at the Pré Catalan where my father stayed as usual. Also my friends from school. I remember arriving late at night and rushing to the phone at La Roseraie to announce my arrival with a sentence which has remained part of family history: "Il faut convoquer les types!" But my main memory is of my grandfather telling me that after a journey I must shave, not just wash a bit. Even though it was not morning and I only shaved about once a week.

On our return to London in January 1938 Judy at last got something of a life of her own. She had outgrown being taught with the Bates at home and there was no way that my parents could afford to go on keeping her at the Foyer Suisse. So something like a committee must have been organised to pay for her education. Honoria Plesch had been at a girls' boarding school in Kent, Hayes Court. It was a society school, something like the Cours Suchet in the Avenue Foch which she had disliked because it always reminded her of *Les petites filles modèles* by the Comtesse de Ségur, which we had tried to read with our teacher when we first arrived in Paris. But it seemed a natural choice if Melanie Plesch was going to provide the bulk of the money, as she did. Gladys Gardner – bless her memory – evidently provided some more, as well as a friend of hers, purely on hearsay. They all rightly felt that there was no point in trying to go on paying for Judy's room at the Foyer Suisse. They might as well pay for her board and lodging, as well as an education, at a school.

So Judy went to boarding school in Kent, in the wake of the memory of Honoria which made things no easier for her. It was not her scene, and she hated it. But she had to be somewhere, and it gave her an English education, though she did not need it all that much, being an individualist. She made no secret of disliking it intensely and having to pretend to be grateful. But she had to admit that it made sense to send her there. I remember going over to see her with my parents on a few occasions and even meeting the headmistress, who never went anywhere without being dragged along by four Irish wolfhounds. It was that sort of school. Judy was a witch in the school performance of Purcell's *Dido and Aeneas*. I remember feeling sorry for her and for myself for having to sit through it. But she had also played Nerissa in the school production of *The Merchant of Venice*, directed by the young Alec Guiness. It was his praise for her acting that led to her being sent to a number of auditions and screen tests later on, one with Elisabeth Bergner, in the hope that she might become a film star and solve all our problems. But these were our mother's ambitions for her, which gave her no peace and destroyed her confidence. My mother even pointed out to her that I was a prefect at Aldenham and that she must become one too! Which she never did or wanted. Her real interests already lay in drawing and writing.

She had liked her lessons with the Bates girls, and Hayes Court at least gave her an escape from the daily worries of my parents' existence at the Foyer Suisse, although she disliked it greatly. In the end it was only to be another unhappy interlude for her, until the beginning of the war. . .

For me all this time passed happily and – as I now see it – unthinkingly. I got Higher Cert with distinctions in everything, though this was obviously not particularly difficult for me in French and German. (I always think of them in that order, because that was the school order, though not mine). But fluency in the languages was in fact relatively unimportant. True, there was an 'unseen,' a translation of a piece into English. But I remember no 'prose' paper, as there was in Latin, of translating English into a foreign language. The emphasis was on the set books and plays, and writing critical essays about them in English. Of course I could read faster than anyone else, and therefore far more, and I was sometimes ahead of the teaching. My housemaster was the senior French master, married to a gentle, unhappy French wife from the Savoie, where they spent all their holidays with her relations. He was understandably proud of his French and I was unforgivably rude when I smiled at some solecism in class. I was sent out. But I could hear the diatribe which resounded through the door. "He is getting too big for his *boots!*"

Later he called me in to his study and said that he was going to beat me. I was in the Sixth Form, which should have presented a moral impediment, though nothing could be relied upon as being constitutionally *ultra vires*. But I demurred when he said that he was going to give me six. For some reason why I cannot remember, although I was hardly ever beaten, I had already had three from another housemaster that morning. When I pointed this out he gave me the choice of three at once or six tomorrow, and so we both got it over there and then.

Neither of us enjoyed it, for we had a sneaking feeling of respect for each other, though no affection. Apart from football, I now also had my 'colours' as goalkeeper for the Hockey XI and was due to be Captain of

Tennis. So I was an asset to his House, about which he cared more than anything else. I had even begun to play cricket, but without any real promise except as a medium-paced bowler. At this Fred English – for that was his name – coached me for many afternoons, in his private garden, trying to get me to maintain a length. But I never made any school cricket team and only went to the 'away' matches as scorer, because the Captain, T.G. Argile, was a special friend. My only other memory of Fred English, who was strict and very old-fashioned, was of his hobnailed boots. The stairs in our House were all made of stone, and the floorboards of the dormitories reverberated with every step. Long after 'Lights Out' we could hear the sound of Fred patrolling the House, and even praes and heads of dormitories held their breath.

1938 was the year when Austria had been annexed, the Sudetenland was menaced, and the peace was 'saved' – or a respite was gained – by Munich and Chamberlain. I cannot pretend that any of us at school had clear views about anything. But my father only spoke of Churchill and what he saw as the infamy and blindness of Chamberlain. At school our contribution to history was assembling gas masks and the modernisation of the OTC, the Officers' Training Corps. I had joined this in preference to gymnastics or long-distance running. A radical break with the army drill of the past came in 1938 when we no longer formed 'fours' but operated in more loosely-knit 'threes.' A forerunner of the SAS. We also had one Sten gun and learnt to take it to pieces and assemble it. But the target orientation by the clock ("Enemy Post – 2 o'clock – aim – rapid fire") remained as before. There were 'camps,' tough weeks under canvas in Yorkshire and near Aldershot, and annual inspections by a Brigadier sent by the War Office. There was also some sort of exam which I passed and therefore got a commission. It was all part of school life. But in my case it may have made a difference later on, though I never knew for sure.

Assembling gas masks was boring, but we did it, night after night, in the class room. Fire drills and anti-aircraft exercises, like lying flat in ditches in the dark, were perfunctory and clearly ridiculous, but we did them as well. There was a feeling of waiting for something to happen, but hoping that it wouldn't, except to get over the feeling of waiting, like treading water.

But most of the rumours of war were on the sidelines of our lives, and still only in the papers. The important things were work and games and promotion at school. The autumn term of 1938 would be my third season in the Football XI and I was now senior to all the others. Logically I should become Captain of Football. But I feared that as a goalkeeper I would be passed over. I worried and worried about it all summer, imagining high ranking discussions among the masters about this epoch-making decision. In those days reports about school teams and matches were far more in the national news than today. *The Times* reported school matches extensively; there were regional matches between Southern and Northern Public Schools; and the Corinthians and Casuals were prestigious amateur clubs which existed side by side with the Old Boy Teams of the soccer schools who competed annually for the Arthur Dunn Cup. So being Captain of Football really mattered. However, my worst fears were realised; I became Secretary and Argile was made Captain of Football as well as Cricket and (I think) Fives. Fortunately we were close friends. But off-hand I cannot remember a greater disappointment throughout my life, including my failure to get promoted from the Court of Appeal to the House of Lords.

In my school work I had now achieved something like senior citizen status. One could take Spanish as an additional subject in the Higher Cert exam, and I decided to take it during the following summer, for fun. For the rest I worked more or less full-time in the school library, since it had been decided that I should try for an open scholarship to Cambridge in Modern Languages and then to read Law. Why Law? Not because I had a burning passion to go to the Bar; indeed, I hardly knew what it was. But because I could think of nothing else that I wanted to do. Certainly nothing academic, like History; and Economics seemed a bit feeble and generalised. So Law it was. But I must have been quite clear about it in my mind, and must even have found out something about the syllabus, because I recently found Buckland's *Manual of Roman Law* among my books in Chambers, and the plate on the inside cover shows that I got it as a school prize while I was still at Aldenham.

With Judy also away at Hayes Court my parents continued to live in two small rooms in the Foyer Suisse off Russell Square. They were now largely kept by my mother, who had found a series of social secretarial and p.a. jobs. Or, more precisely, they were found for her among Janos' patients. There was a Lady Wimborne who owned the whole of Arlington House next to the Ritz, where she had a flat. And there was a retired Army officer with a slight scientific background and considerable private means, Colonel Grenfell, who had the extraordinary idea that food could be kept fresh by freezing it. There were evidently not many who shared his belief, and the technology was not yet good enough to establish the possibilities either way. I think that there were also other figures, now shadowy, for whom my poor mother worked from time to time, trying to keep her and my father in the Foyer Suisse, to find a little pocket money for Judy and me, and to save up the fare for the annual long family holiday with her parents in Nice and my father's stay at the Pré Catalan.

He had meanwhile never stopped writing, and never lost heart. One or two of his articles were published, occasionally even in English, and I recently came across one in the *Daily Telegraph* which must have given him great joy and a little encouragement. His main contact with the literary world was now through the German P.E.N. Club, of which he had been elected President soon after our arrival in England. But there was no market for his work. Apart from the support of a few wealthy friends, in particular the Pleschs, and occasional contributions from my mother's brother Nucki, made with ill grace from his office in the City, he was entirely dependent on my mother.

Sadly for both of them, especially my mother, my parents led fairly isolated lives. This need not have been necessary. It was largely their choice, although it made them unhappy. My father shunned the society of German refugees, among whom he would have been greatly welcomed and who now formed a highly cultured and closely-knit community around Hampstead and Finchley. For him this was an aesthetic choice; he had to remain aloof. For my mother there was no such feeling; her great passions were bridge and tennis, and anyone who shared them was her friend. But she also inclined away from the society of refugees because her ambition was to be as English as possible. She spoke more or less perfect English and felt English, just as I did. But all this made things still more difficult for them. Long after their death a close friend of mine, Dr F. A. Mann, told me that their isolation was well known. His father had been a friend of my father's, and he himself knew all his works. He told me that when my parents lived in Putney during and after the war, Francis Mann and his wife sometimes saw them walking arm in arm on Putney Common, looking sad and forlorn, but also unapproachable. He said that he never had the courage to get in touch with them, but that they both knew how much their community and friends could have done for my parents if they had not kept themselves apart.

Unfortunately it was also only when Richard Wilberforce, the retired Law Lord and by then an old friend, read the earlier text of this book some years ago that he realised that he had been a frequent visitor in my grandparents' house in the Wilhelmstrasse before 1933, where he got to know many members of the family and must have met my mother. When he wrote and told me this, by now in his 90's, I took him and Judy out for a nostalgic lunch, with all of us thinking what a wonderful friend and ally he would have been for my parents during all those cruel years.

I have only known one occasion in his life when my father gave in and compromised about anything to do with his work. It must have been in 1939. Janos Plesch had written his memoirs, *The Story of a Doctor*, and he asked my father to revise them. My father said that they were unprintably bad and refused adamantly. But my mother wept and wept, explaining how desperately they needed the £25 which went with the request, to pay for their rooms for some weeks. In the end he surrendered and made some suggestions and alterations, on condition that there was to be no acknowledgement or mention of his name. Even then he made no secret of his views, least of all to Janos, and said that no one could possibly dream of publishing it. But of course his standards were too high, and Janos got it published, though soon to be remaindered. I found a copy on a stall in the Portobello Road some years later, when Judy and I lived in Notting Hill.

Apart from school I remember few details of the last 18 months before the war. Holidays were spent with the Pleschs at The Pavilion, occasionally still with the Gardners in Sussex, whose refugee protégés we now were, to be shown off among their friends. My life at school was idyllic, because I was now on top of the heap. There had only been one incident of bullying which I can remember, soon after I got my football Colours for the first time, when the senior generation in my House felt that I was getting too cocky. So there was a kind of formalised pushing-around and minor beating-up in the Houseroom before prayers. This was a rare event, but the process had official status, with a now forgotten name, and Fred English delayed the evening assembly to give the 30 boys of my generation a good chance of having a go at me. I was not really frightened, nor hurt. But it taught me a lesson, to put on the brakes; to assume what would now be called a lower profile.

But in my last year all this was forgotten. There were four of us, close friends, sharing the praes' study, and running the House, though none of us would ever beat anyone. Tom Argile was Captain of the House, then myself, then my first friend Fleeters, John Fleetwood-May, and Ian Mclean, a scientist and sprinter. It was a glorious last year for all of us. Although none of us knew it, and I don't even remember ever talking about the coming war, within two years we would all be pilots in the RAF. And by the end of the war I would be the sole survivor. Argile would crash and be killed on a training flight with his instructor in Rhodesia. Fleeters would be shot down in a Lancaster over Cologne, soon after I got his last letter, about his horror of the war. And Ian Maclean was to become a night fighter pilot and win the DFC, only to be shot in a jeep by an Indonesian sniper during the war in Borneo, after V

Day and VJ Day, when all should have been over. In a way, his was the greatest tragedy. I still have letters from all of them somewhere, and from their parents.

I duly scraped through my Spanish exam, and then there was the frightening week of scholarship papers in Cambridge. One chose a group of colleges which set the same papers and then put down an order of preference within the group. How I came to choose Clare I can no longer remember, but presumably some OA had managed to get in there. I must have been well taught, or well directed in my reading, because I remember that there were no unpleasant surprises. The main paper was an essay on a modern languages subject, and the question was: 'Can you be surer of your own existence than of the bread you eat?' I happened to have read a bit of condensed Descartes, and somehow I managed to dole out '*Cogito, ergo sum*' over several pages. In the result I felt that I had satisfied any reader that there was a good argument for answering the question in the affirmative, unless a loaf of bread could think as well. This was of course not to be excluded, and so I added a vague reference to some Christian Science nonsense which may also have appeared impressive. One way and another I felt reasonably confident, although my neighbour's interpretation of the Latin Unseen was worryingly different from mine.

I knew that if I got an award I had to hear by a certain date, at latest two days before the end of term, the night of the House Plays. The last Speech Day and the final OTC inspection came and went, with scratching khaki puttees in the heat. But nothing from Cambridge. And then the day of the House Plays, and still nothing. It was a terribly important occasion for me since there was no question of going to university unless I won a scholarship, in which case I could expect the same sort of supplementary grants as at school. My parents arrived for the House Plays and we sat in grim and tactful silence in the School Hall waiting disconsolately for the beginning, for by now it was too late to hear. Then George Riding, in a dinner jacket, mounted the stage to greet the assembly, his favourite kind of moment. I then heard him say that one boy, me, had won a major Open Scholarship to Cambridge. My mother burst into tears. But all I could think of was what a bastard he was, even though I quite admired and liked him. He had known for more than 48 hours and kept it to himself, in order to sensationalise the announcement. The thought of what I must have been going through probably never crossed his mind. Admittedly, I owed him a great deal. But I had no illusions about him and never forgave him.

27 · The final end of Nice

THAT WAS the end of Aldenham and the long summer holidays of 1939 lay ahead. Apart from my three great friends in my House I had made friends with a man (as we used to say) called John Butler, the Captain of another House, and a little older than I. He was remarkable for looking like a mixture of Gary Cooper and Gregory Peck, only better, and for having little wordly ambition. He was due to be Captain of Cricket that summer term, but he shocked everyone, his parents and Housemaster, and above all Riding, by saying that he wanted to leave at Easter and travel around in France. Nowadays that sounds perfectly normal, but it wasn't then. He was also due to go up to Cambridge in the autumn, to Christ's to read English. So we agreed to meet in France in early September, after August with the grandparents in Nice, to tour Britanny on bicycles.

But that was not to happen. By mid-August, when we had only been in Nice for about three weeks, the threat of war at last seemed imminent. We talked and thought of nothing else, and I went down to town every day to read the English papers in the Library. My grandfather's daily trips to his barber, the café and *la plage* were suddenly absurdly trivial. Finally I could stand it no longer and announced that I was going back to England. I had nowhere to go since Cambridge was not due to start until mid-September, and I had no way of getting hold of John Butler, cycling somewhere in France. But I was not going to take the risk of being unable to get back.

This produced the biggest family row that I can remember, mainly between my mother and me. Our return tickets were valid for a further month, and we could live free with my grandparents until then. There was nowhere for me to go, nor any money to keep me. It followed, according to my mother's logic, which always saw the world as she hoped it would be, that there was no imminent danger of war. And even if there was, there would be no problem about getting back. And so on and so forth. But all of us knew, all the time, that what was breaking her heart was the thought of a wasted month covered by the return tickets.

In the end something must have happened to make her give in. I think that my father was on my side. But he was not in control. She was supporting the family, as she constantly – and rightly – reminded us. Perhaps there was one day of a particularly menacing forecast. And there must have been some communication with the Pleschs. At any

Grandparents and Nucki in Nice, 1939.

rate, within a few days of my ultimatum (about which I was not all that confident) my mother capitulated. I would return at once and the rest of the family a few days later, and we would then spend the rest of the holidays with the Pleschs at The Pavilion. It was not a thought that any of us relished, but for me it was salvation. None of the others, not even my father, felt this need to get back like I did.

So I packed up and left during the second week of August, and remember spending some aimless time at The Pavilion. My parents and Judy followed, and my mother began to relent when the German-Russian pact was announced on the 24th. The writing was now on the wall. It was almost a relief to hear Chamberlain announce the outbreak of war at 11 a.m. on 3rd September, a momentous day in the history of the world. But I doubt if anyone was more relieved than my mother. The tickets had not been wasted after all.

And "Endlich!", at last, was the entry in my father's diary *"Ich kam nach England"* for September 1939 under the heading *"Dank an England"*. He wrote: "At last! War! To think that one can wish for a disaster to happen, because another would be even more terrible . . . . Meanwhile England goes to work. For the great battle of all humanity. For deliverance. When I came to England I thought it possible that the world would be saved by this country, and I let it be printed, in 1935. Then Chamberlain had to be overcome with all those crushing nightmares, by faith in England. Today I know: I was not wrong. Gratitude goes out to this island —— which no words can express!"

⋆ ⋆ ⋆

That was the end of Nice, and I never saw my grandfather again. They both stayed there, fearfully, throughout the German invasion, the fall of Paris and the occupation of northern France in the summer of 1940. The Italians occupied the Cote d'Azur and renewed their ancient claim to Nice, but evidently left them alone, perhaps because my grandfather had received a high decoration from the Pope when he had been Nuncio in Berlin. But by 1943 it had become clear that the Germans would move south and occupy the rest of France to forestall an allied attack from North Africa. So they knew they had to flee. Their son Nucki had emigrated to New York just before the outbreak of war, leaving the Wuzi, the *Betthase* behind. He knew a lot of people, some in Washington, and got permission for his parents to come to the States, if they could. Somehow they made their way by train through southern France and Spain to Lisbon and onto a boat. I know no details of their journey, but it cannot have been easy. They were both in their seventies and I don't know what papers or money they had. But they got to New York, while all others like them, who stayed behind, were caught by the Germans and sent to their death in the camps. But my grandfather only survived a few months. Nucki found them a small flat somewhere in Manhattan. But after a decade in Nice and the journey he must have found it unbearable. I was told that he had a heart attack while washing up. My grandmother found him dead in their kitchen.

But she survived for another 12 years or so, well into her eighties, and in many ways she took on a new lease of life. She lived out the war in the States, for some time teaching German at some minor college in the south, to supplement the allowance which she got from Nucki. After the war she came back to Europe and lived near one of her sisters in Garmisch-Partenkirchen, on the large pension which had been due to her husband and which the new German government restored at once. My mother was then working in Nürnberg and later in Berlin and often visited her. She once came to London to see me and my family, and we also all once went to see her in Germany. Having lived in the shadow of my grandfather for so long, it was as though she had attained her independence towards the very end of her life. She wrote some reminiscences, both in German and English, of what it was like to be a '*deutsche*

Frau' in the twenties and of life in the Wilhelmstrasse. I have them in her spiky old-fashioned writing somewhere, but never got to the end of them. In Garmisch she played a lot of bridge, walked and was known to everyone as *Frau Staatssekretär* in the German way, as though nothing had intervened since 1932. In 1958 she went to live in a home in Merano, one of her favourite places. My mother went to see her there, but her mind had given way and she no longer recognised her and died a few months later. Many of my grandfather's papers came to us from her via my mother, and I think that he now also has some memorial in Berlin.

Gertrud Weismann was a good and patient woman who deserved the relative contentment of her last years. I had been closer to the overpowering personality of my grandfather, despite my father's hostility. He taught me bridge, which I have never forgotten, and in my mind I still have this sunny picture of his beloved routine morning excursions from Cimiez down to Nice, which I had shared so often. And the last memory was his. About thirty years after my last time in Nice, sometime in the late sixties, I was flying from North Africa to Paris on some case; why I cannot remember. I had a day to spare, and the plane was due to stop in Nice. So I decided to spend it there and fly on in the evening. I went all the way up to Cimiez, where La Roseraie and the Arènes were quite unchanged, but buses had replaced the trams. Coming back into town I remembered that I needed a haircut and went to see if the barber's shop was still there, corner Place Messéna and Promenade des Anglais. It was and looked exactly as before. Inside was an old man whom I did not recognise, nor he me. But when I was settled in the chair, I asked him if he had known my grandfather who had fled more than 20 years ago. He remembered him well and talked and talked about him. He described him perfectly, his daily visits, and his own visits to the Roseraie to shave him every Sunday. Then we talked about the war and the German occupation, and I told him about the end of my grandparents' lives. When I left I asked him if he still had customers who had themselves shaved everyday. He said there were none, not since the war. I muttered something like: "People no longer have the time." He looked at me and said: "They have exactly the same amount of time as people have always had. But they don't know how to use it. *Ils ne savent pas s'en servir. Il ne savent pas vivre.*"

That was about thirty years ago. About fifteen years ago I was again in Nice, for a legal Conference, with Diana. We went up to Cimiez, past the Arènes, and I showed her La Roseraie. Nothing had changed about the house or the garden. But my poor father's Pré Catalan had become a supermarket, though under the same name. And the tennis courts had gone.

28 · The phoney war – Cambridge

BUT I MUST go back to September 1939, the 'phoney war' and my first year at Cambridge. John Butler had returned from France, and as neither of us was due to live in College we decided to share digs. We each had a small bedroom and a common sitting room in Portugal Place near St John's, in a good position for Clare and Christ's and the places where we had lectures. Neither of us had any money; I lived more or less entirely on my scholarship and an additional college grant. Our landlady was a proverbial horror. We had gas fires and thought she overcharged us, but she denied it passionately. When I said that I was only in for about three hours a day she looked at me archly and said: "Oh, Mr Kerr, I do think you underexaggerate there!" It is strange how one never forgets some remarks, however unimportant. The bane of her life, and a never-ending subject of conversation, was her old mother, who was dying. When I returned after the Christmas vacation, lugging my suitcase upstairs, I enquired, a little anxiously, how she was. She stopped and glared at me: "Still lingering on! Isn't it marvellous!!" After that I kept off the subject.

From the autumn of 1939 until May 1940 the war was hardly noticed, at any rate not directly. I played football and tennis for the College, went to all the lectures and supervisions and spent a lot of time discussing girls with John and going to coffee and sherry parties in Girton and Newnham. The Law of that year was mostly Roman Law, Constitutional History and Jackson's *The English Legal System*. There may also have been some elementary Public International Law. It was all very general; the English part was mostly Mediaeval, and of no practical use whatever. But the excuse was that Law was supposed to be a cultural and educational subject, at any rate in the early stages. The concepts of arbitration and other methods of dispute resolution, which were to dominate my later working life, were then unknown in any law syllabus.

The effect of the war was felt indirectly. We read about the Maginot Line, and the radio was constantly telling everyone that their washing would soon be hanging on it. Then there was a flare-up in Norway. The Germans occupied it and we launched an expedition which was obviously going wrong, but no one would admit it. Then there was the gallant interception of the *Altmark* in Norwegian territorial waters, freeing a lot of our prisoners and making Norway seem like a victory, whereas it was the first of many defeats. The writing was again on the wall. But few saw it, and no one wanted to see it.

For the Cambridge community these were only things of which we read in the papers and occasionally heard on the radio when we were not at so-called parties. They never stopped. Most supervisions (or tutorials, as they are at Oxford) began with a statement by the supervisor that he did not expect to be there the following week. We should therefore combine the study of the Roman Law or feudal land tenure with a small celebration and each bring a bottle. On the other hand, if he should still be there, it would have to be an occasion for a super bottle party, because that would definitely be the last time when he would be able to discuss our essays. And so it went on, week after week. Between lectures one met for coffee at the Whim opposite Trinity, or the posher K.P. establishment in King's Parade. In the afternoons there were games, and parties in the evenings, in the men's colleges or Girton and Newnham, where one was less pleased to see one's friends. I remember climbing into, or out of, Girton, but I remember nothing of what happened inside the establishment except that nothing happened. Most of the time I was working, because I had no money. It was always a struggle to keep up with others, and my heart was not really in Varsity life.

But I was taken up by Peter Plesch, then in his second or third year at Trinity, and admitted to the outskirts of his circle of friends. As I got to know them, I realised that quite a few of them were sleeping together, in a sense, during the afternoons. Their 'oaks were sported,' a strange phrase for the closing of the double doors in all college rooms, generally only for one purpose.

I also gradually realised that some of the girls within his circle, all about two years older, were considering my educational admission to it. But I was not ready for that and could not keep up with the style and pace of their Varsity lives. I preferred John Butler, who had little more money than I, and a small crowd of Clare men who were also reading Law. As it turned out, though I had not realised it before, this was not a subject for which Clare was particularly suitable. Its strength lay in science and medicine, and for many years the College would not elect a Law Fellow. So we had our supervisions in other colleges, from Cecil Turner in Trinity Hall and old Charlie Ziegler in Pembroke, with microphones hanging round wires in his room because he was so deaf. I made a great new friend, Bill Simpson from near Liverpool, who was also reading Law and determined to go into practice. Although he appeared to come from a wealthy background and had plenty of money, we became fairly inseparable in early 1940. I told him nothing about my background or my parents. But he met Judy when she came up to stay with me for a weekend and was a great success with all my friends.

Her life had not become more cheerful while I was having a good time at Cambridge, and I felt guilty about it. She had finished at Hayes Court when I finished at Aldenham, but there was no money for her to go back to the Foyer Suisse, where my mother kept herself and our father, together with some help from others at which I can only guess. Nucki had emigrated to become a stockbroker in New York; for once in his life he was also experiencing some money difficulties. So Judy was sent first to the Plesch's at Aylesbury until the spring of 1940 and then stayed with the Bates in Campden Hill Square, doing a term's Art at the Polytechnic in Oxford Street.

But then the war came closer. The losses at sea were horrendous and England felt like a beleaguered island, which is what it was. Food and clothes rationing had been introduced. Those who were too old for the services joined the ARP, Air Raid Precautions, and the Home Guard. Air raid shelters were built in London and all iron park railings were taken down to be melted for munitions. That strange phrase, the war effort, which became a cliché, had taken off in earnest. And although there was not yet any fighting nearer than Norway and Denmark, which had been overrun by the Germans without resistance, everyone began to realise that it was going to take a long time. But no one foresaw how bad it would be.

The Bates fled back to the States. So Judy had to go back to the Foyer Suisse. She was coming up to 17 and living in a boarding house, sharing a room with my mother for six years, until she was 23. She had to get a job, and so she had to train for something. She decided on a secretarial course near Holborn, where she learnt stenotyping, touch-typing by phonetic syllables, which was then beginning to take over from shorthand. I was impressed, having tried in vain to learn shorthand with several of George Riding's secretaries at Aldenham. A refugee organisation paid for her course. At last, when she finished it and had her own machine, and could type fluently in three languages, everything appeared to be open to her, from the Foreign Office downwards. But then she realised, as I was to realise, that officially we were enemy aliens. Although we had lost our German nationality seven years ago and my father had been declared a public enemy of the Reich, for all bureaucratic purposes we still counted as German, since we were nothing else. Naturalisations were only granted after five years' residence. But we had spent three years in Switzerland and France and had only arrived in the spring of 1936. Many friends and acquaintances, like the Pleschs, were

Bill Simpson 1940

in time to be naturalised before the war, although their English was atrocious or non- existent. But there was no hope for us. My father tried, supported by his sponsors, Bernard Shaw and H.G. Wells. But five years' residence was the law, or at least a rule which was hardly ever waived. Then the Home Office shut up shop on the outbreak of war and there were to be no more naturalisations 'for the duration,' another phrase of the times. Exceptions to that rule were then only made in a few individual cases much later during the war, which were kept secret, when atomic physicists were needed.

I cannot remember what I expected or even hoped to happen to me. I was just 19. As a student of that age I would have been exempt from being called up even if I had been eligible. Bill Simpson had had polio as a child and had a slight limp which disqualified him from the services. So he never talked about joining up and that made it easier for me to keep silent about it as well, since I did not want him to know that I couldn't have gone away. Only John Butler, 6'6" and looking every inch an old-fashioned officer, spoke lazily about the temptation of joining up and the futility of lectures and supervisions. He knew my parents and I could talk to him about the future. But I never did, because there was nothing to say and no one knew what would happen. We just all somehow hoped that the war might go away. Perhaps the Americans would come in, like last time, and meanwhile there were the French and the Maginot Line.

My only immediate interest was to get a First in the Law Qualifying Exam at the end of my first year and perhaps the special prize in Roman Law. With a few others I went to Professor Buckland's last term of lectures, the famous author of the Manual, and my supervisor was Kurt Lipstein, also a refugee from Germany, who then already occupied a small room in the Squire Law Library. Both said they had high hopes of me.

29 · The real war starts

DURING THE first week of May 1940 the German army attacked. Although the news flashes of the attack went up and down and no one knew much, it soon became clear that Holland and Belgium would be overrun, and there were disturbing rumours of some Panzer units having rounded the northern unfinished end of the magic Maginot Line. Rotterdam was destroyed by fire bombs.

In Cambridge life had meanwhile gone on much as before, except that the post-graduate community had largely disappeared. For me it was a particularly busy time. I was due to play in the Varsity tennis trials, and the exam was only two weeks away.

On Friday, 10 May, I went to a bridge party. A second cousin, Peter Reichenheim, about four years older than I and already a friend from London, was a brilliant medical student at Bart's. After the outbreak of war its medical school and research staff had been evacuated to Cambridge and he lived in digs with his wife, Elizabeth, who was the same age. They had known each other since childhood and married when they came to England in 1938. I felt closer to him than to any other of my innumerable relations on my mother's side, perhaps because we were both training for a profession. In the fullness of time, with his name changed to Rickham, he was to achieve virtually every medical honour, including many honorary degrees and the *Légion d'honneur*, for his services to paediatric surgery, in which he would become the foremost pioneer and a lasting name. He always said that he only failed to get the Chair at Great Ormond Street because of his German accent, and because he always spoke his mind in it. Which he certainly did. His unbelievably atrocious accent, which he did nothing to tone down, and his contempt for authority, increased endearingly throughout his life. Unlike me, he was no respecter of anyone, but respected by all who knew him.

The medical community in Cambridge during the first year of the war was very different from my circle of friends. To them the war not an interruption but a professional challenge and opportunity. And, being medical students, they were much more adult. Even playing bridge with them was different.

On the Friday of that week Peter's younger brother, Klaus, was also there. He was shy, under the shadow of his ebullient brother, and worked in a bank in London. For this weekend he had at last succeeded in persuading Peggy, his girlfriend, or as he hoped she would become, to go away with him to Cambridge, to stay at the Blue Boar. The presence of his brother and sister-in-law somewhere in digs was to confer the necessary measure of propriety or excuse for the occasion. In fact, as I learnt later, at the last moment Peggy had cold feet, or whatever, and invented a monthly impediment.

That was Friday night, a lot of bridge and drink, and very late. For Saturday I also had a modest first initiation, by taking a girl out to supper, more or less at her suggestion. 'Dinner' would hardly be appropriate for the café of the cinema in the High Street, or whatever the prolongation of Station Road is called. But it was a place which I knew from outings with John Butler, and Pru, one of the girls in Peter Plesch's affluent circle, didn't seem to mind. In fact, she told me that she also found it difficult to keep up with some of her friends, as I obviously did. I thought that was why she had singled me out, but I realised later that she had merely been clever and tactful. It was a memorable evening, full of promise of a new relationship and real 'pastures new.' The news of the German attack over-shadowed the evening. But it did not seem directly relevant to the immediate future.

What I overlooked was that I had become an enemy alien.

30 · Internment

THE NEXT DAY, Sunday, 12 May 1940, is one of the few dates in my life that I have never forgotten. It was a perfect day and very hot. I had played tennis in some College game early in the morning and was going back to Portugal Place at about 11.00 to do some revision before meeting Pru in the afternoon. There was a policeman at the door. He verified my name from a list and said that I should go with him to the Guildhall. I asked him why, and he said that it was just a formality and that I would be back in half an hour. Our landlady was out and John Butler was playing cricket. So I left him a quick note and went along as I was, in white tennis shorts, gym shoes and a sports shirt. On an impulse I picked up my games pullover with the Aldenham Colours. This was lucky, because I was to have nothing else to wear until September. Fortunately it turned into a very hot summer. But that was also to be good for the Luftwaffe in the coming Battle of Britain.

The Guildhall was quite close, off Petty Cury. I had only been there once to watch a Magistrates Court. My name and address were checked and I was taken into the main hall. To my amazement there were about 150 men there, of all ages, from undergraduates to old men. There were some chairs, but most of them were sitting on the floor or standing around in groups, looking baffled. I couldn't really take it in. Then the policeman said that Cambridge was in a Defence Area and that all enemy aliens were being rounded up for checking. But someone else said that we were all going to be interned.

Gradually I met some of the people I knew. First was my Roman Law supervisor, Kurt Lipstein, who was upset. I tried to comfort him and said that I was sure we would soon be out, but he only shook his head. He had been following the legal preparations for this possibility since the beginning of the war. But until then only non-refugee Germans and known Nazi supporters, including Moseleyites, had been brought before tribunals and interned. This was clearly something on an altogether different scale, and totally unexpected. It was probably one of the best-kept secrets of the war, including D-Day.

Gradually I met many others. My cousins Peter and Klaus Reichenheim were there, and Klaus predictably said that he wished that he had stayed in London, which was not a Defence Area. He had had a frustrating night and a frightening morning. I also met two students whom I recognised from Law lectures, though I did not know them then. Konrad Goldschmidt was in his last year, about to take Part II, and expected to get his Tennis Blue for the match against Oxford in three weeks. Hans Wilmersdoerfer was in his second year and also determined to go to the Bar. Anyone of my generation in the law will know them under the names of Brian Grant, later to become H. H. Judge H. B. Grant, and John Wilmers, QC, and both became life-long friends. Brian is still living happily in retirement in Cumbria, though minus the leg which he was to lose in Italy three years later. Strangely enough, my cousin Peter's wife Elizabeth had known Brian when they were in Berlin as children and they had also recently met in Cambridge. So a bit of a group began to form, and we tried to cheer up Kurt Lipstein, who was known to every law student in Cambridge. He still is. I had to miss an invitation to speak at his 80th birthday, but recently saw him at a Clare dinner, now turned 93 and still cycling around Cambridge, but no longer at night.

Nothing happened at the Guildhall until late afternoon except that everyone got very hungry. Then we were taken outside to a fleet of coaches and headed east, towards Suffolk. All road signs and place names had been removed to confuse the Germans, and when we stopped outside what looked like a warehouse on the outskirts of a town, we did not know that it was Bury St Edmunds. The building was an empty Walls ice cream factory, as we discovered inside. It was entirely bare, with vast concrete floors, except for some piles of blankets and about 30 soldiers with fixed bayonets.

Unfortunately these had been the only preparations for our arrival. There was nothing to eat or drink. So we wrapped ourselves in the blankets and went to sleep on the floor. My last memory was of a soldier standing 'at ease' near my feet, holding his rifle with the bayonet. The heat outside had not touched the concrete floors, and the night was very cold. When I woke up in the morning there was another soldier there, stamping his feet. But later there was bread and margarine and urns of sweet, hot army tea.

We spent the next day sitting on piles of bricks and stones in a yard of the factory in which a building had been demolished, surrounded by a high wall. Everyone got very hungry until there was more bread, margarine and tea during the afternoon. By that time we had begun to get to know the soldiers and convinced them that we were not prisoners of war who had been captured in the fighting, as they had thought at first. Some papers were smuggled in and we heard confused news of what was thought to be going on in France. But there was nothing about the interment of enemy aliens. We discovered that we were in Bury St Edmunds. But that meant little to us, and there was no way of contacting anyone outside or of knowing whether they knew where we were.

We stayed in this factory for a week. The soldiers standing guard over us disappeared on the third night, and those that remained now kept their bayonets in their scabbards. I had nothing but a handkerchief in my shorts, but most of the others had some money and persuaded the soldiers to buy them chocolate and papers. The round-up of enemy aliens in Defence Areas – but without saying which these were – had by now been reported as a short news item. But there was no reason to think that any of our families knew where we were. They didn't, for nearly two months. And it was to be over three months before we could write or receive censored letters and parcels.

The hope of getting out in time for our exams faded quickly. Kurt Lipstein set me one of the Roman Law papers from memory. I did it with a borrowed pen on some lavatory paper to pass the time, and he said I would have got a First in that one. Meanwhile poor Brian Grant knew that he would miss the Varsity match and his Tennis Blue, as well as Part II of the Tripos.

We were moved early one morning, on the day when the exams were due to start. We were marched to the station, where there was a train with a lot of other people, already waiting. As we walked along the platform to two empty carriages at the back they told us through the windows that they had come from London. So it had started there as well, and many wondered about our families. But it was difficult to find out anything; there were soldiers on the train and we were not allowed to move about.

We travelled slowly all day, going north-west through the Midlands where the names of the stations had not been removed. Somewhere we were given some bread, margarine and tea and about 6 o'clock in the evening we arrived in what we found to be Liverpool.

It was again a Sunday, a week since we had left Cambridge behind us in what seemed like another world. The next two hours were among the worst I can remember. We were marched through Liverpool, about four abreast, in what seemed like an endless procession. Many of the people from London had suitcases with them, especially the old ones, but there was no one to help them. It looked as though the whole of Liverpool had turned out to see us. They stood silently, watching us go by, neither friendly nor hostile, with no reaction when a few tried to explain who we were. We just went on and on, and it was very hot. In the end we stopped and filed into a low building, but vast inside. It turned out to be a huge empty underground car park, somewhere in Liverpool or on the outskirts.

We went there for about 10 days; I more or less lost count. There was now some regular hot food ladled out from Army containers like barrels, but we were always hungry. Food and news from the outside were to be our main preoccupations for a long time. But there was no maltreatment, no bullying, and no longer any real hostility. We were now hearing some news about the war. The soldiers – now units of the Home Guard – brought in some papers, and a few of the people from London had brought radios. They had had more time to get ready and had realised that they were being interned.

We slept on the floor, but I think there were now more blankets. I certainly remember no real discomfort, but was terribly glad I had taken that school pullover. My shorts and shirt were filthy, but so was everyone else, and few tried to shave. I spent virtually all the time playing bridge and occasional games of poker for matches or imaginary money. Apart from food, cigarettes were a craving for most of us. In Switzerland, when we were 10 and 12, my sister and I, and our father, had solemnly signed a piece of paper in which he promised to pay each of us £100 if we didn't smoke or drink until we were 21. Judy voluntarily added a clause proscribing make-up, in her case. But I broke the smoking prohibition as soon as I was interned and then became a regular smoker for more than 40 years. It didn't matter, because our father probably never again had £100 to give anyone.

I managed to get a few cigarettes every day. How, I cannot remember; presumably I won them at cards. I remember working out that I had played over 600 hands of bridge in that underground car park. My only other recollection is when we were all called together for an announcement by the Camp Commander, as he was called. He was a timber merchant who had been a Captain in the First World War. He said that although we were not supposed to receive news from outside he was happy to be able to tell us that the British Expeditionary Force had retaken Amiens. Or perhaps it was Arras; one of the well-known First World War names. He told us that he had fought there himself and that it had been the strategic hinge of the Front. So, he said, it would soon be over. There was polite clapping and expressions of thanks and appreciation. But mainly fear for the competence of the British Army, if that exposition was representative of its approach to the war.

We did not see him again, and on the following day the evacuation from Dunkirk began.

Around 1st June we were moved again, marching to a vast camp surrounded by barbed wire. It was known as Huyton, which was later to be Harold Wilson's constituency. But I am not sure that it was in Huyton, since we were told that it was on part of the Aintree race course, the annual home of the Grand National, which does not nowadays appear to be part of Huyton. There were many hundreds of people in the camp; it seemed like over 2,000. About 250 were all in black, figures like I had never seen before, Hasidic Jews with beards, black curls down their cheeks and skull caps. They were all from the East End of London and spoke Yiddish, English and Hebrew, in that order, but no German. Many of them had been born in this country of Jews who had emigrated from Germany in the twenties or earlier but had never bothered to acquire British nationality. I never discovered why they had been interned or when they were ultimately released. Most of them had no idea why they were there, or where they were.

We now lived in huts with bunks, and we ate in larger huts. Everyone got a tin plate and mug and a knife, fork and spoon, which we carried to meals and then back to our bunks. But this produced an insuperable problem on the first Saturday. The orthodox Jews refused to eat because their religion did not allow them to carry anything outside their home on the Sabbath. But some rabbi or lawyer found an answer, and the Camp Commandant, whom I never met but who must have been an imaginative person, co-operated in the solution. It was agreed that the senior rabbi should buy the entire barbed wire around the camp for a shilling, thus making the whole camp into their home. When that had been done and explained they were happy to carry their utensils like everyone else.

We still knew or felt that we were in a state of transit, and there were more and more references to the Isle of Man. So we lived from day to day and there was little attempt to organise anything. But one or two people were mysteriously released. They included my cousin Peter Reichenheim because the Dean of the Medical School of Bart's said that he was his most brilliant student and the country needed doctors. He simply disappeared from one day to the next and it was only later that Klaus told me to my amazement that he had gone. He was to have a remarkable war, which he thoroughly enjoyed, ending up as a full Colonel in the Medical Corps. He said that one of his more arduous duties was to travel on a slow boat around the Cape to India and then to Burma, with 10 other doctors and 300 nurses, one of the most enjoyable journeys of his life. After D-Day he commanded a mobile hospital in France and traded American food and drink for condoms, which his unit had for distribution to the allied forces.

It was lonelier without him and I had days of real depression. I had no idea what had happened to my family, and they did not know where or how I was and had no way of communicating with me.

It was only months later that I was to hear what had happened in Cambridge and at home. When John Butler found my note he rang my parents in London. Needless to say my mother was beside herself with rage that anyone could do this to her son, who in her eyes was by now not only completely English but more English than most. And after everything that my father and grandfather had done against Hitler, etc., etc., and all his scholarships! She stormed and phoned, and tried to see and write to everyone she could think of. She could not grasp that anyone who might have had some power or influence at that time had more important things on their mind. As usual, my father tried to restrain and calm her. He was more philosophical. "*C'est la guerre – à la guerre comme à la guerre.*" And to my mother's disappointment John Butler, my closest friend, shared my father's view. They both said that it was terrible, but only for a time; and anyway, what could anyone do for me? They did not even know where I was.

My mother begged John to get on to someone in the Law Faculty. But he knew none of my teachers and could see no point in it anyway. However, he knew that Bill Simpson was a friend who also read Law, so he phoned him the next day. At first Bill couldn't understand what John was talking about, except that he wondered why I hadn't turned up at lectures. Then John realised that Bill knew nothing about me, and told him some of my story. Bill's reaction was totally different. At first he was amazed, and then outraged at what had happened. The thought that, in a way, I had deceived him for several months, when we were such close friends and constantly discussing our attitude to the war, never seems to have crossed his mind. He got the number of the Foyer Suisse from John and rang up my mother. She did not know him, had only vaguely heard his name. But he immediately seemed like a kindred spirit and a voice from heaven. Although the exams were so close, he took the next train to London to see my parents to have everything explained to him, and then announced that he would go into action. My mother told me what he did, but I can only remember that he went to see old Dr Thirkill, the Master of Clare, whom we called the Plumber, and the Vice-Chancellor of the University. I think that he also wrote to his MP in Cheshire and people in the government.

If I had known about all this at the time I would have felt flattered and a bit embarrassed. But also amazed at the friend that Bill was to me, although I had only known him for a few months, when he really knew nothing about me. He was quiet spoken, good-looking, with strong principles which I had hardly sensed, and probably much more aware of his slight limp than anyone who knew him. Thinking back about him I realise that he may have been one of the most outstanding people I ever knew. Certainly my mother thought that, and she only met him twice. He planned to be a solicitor and would have been a life-long friend, but I never saw him again. He kept on volunteering for the Army, and in the end they gave in, despite his slight disability. He got a commission and was posted abroad, I think to North Africa, where he was killed soon after his arrival. I had a letter from his parents, and I have a photo of him leaning on his bicycle in Cambridge. He must have made me take it with his camera, since I never had one, and sent it to me. Or perhaps his parents did. But my mother never forgot him. And I now realise what a friend he would have been.

31 · Reactions

I KNEW NOTHING about this debate between my parents, John Butler, Bill Simpson and no doubt many others about their reactions to my deportation (as it was called) and internment. But if I had been asked I would obviously have been on the side of my father and John Butler. I never felt any bitterness, and nor did any of my friends in the camps. It was war. And this country, to which we now felt we belonged, clearly had its back to the wall. Our real worry was whether its resources and competence would be sufficient to enable it to survive. And we felt no confidence about either.

The camp at Huyton was so vast that I never became familiar with the communities, sections and sects which it contained. There must have been an external authority and an internal hierarchy, but I had no contact with them. I suppose I got depressed, since there is a void in my memory. I thought about my sweater, shirt and shorts, and the tennis shoes which seemed all right, and getting as much to eat and smoke as I could scrounge. There were various words for that, throughout the war, which disappeared later when we got into the age of consumer affluence. The only luxury was cigarettes, and occasionally chocolate. We were always hungry.

So I don't remember how I came to be included in some hundreds of others to be marched to a boat to sail to Douglas, on the Isle of Man, on 14th June 1940, Judy's seventheenth birthday, when Paris fell to Hitler. It was another perfect day, like nearly every day of that summer. But we all knew the news from France. We also knew that although the great majority of the British Army had escaped from Dunkirk, all their weapons and equipment had to be left behind. So we thought that the final stage of an inevitably lost war was about to begin. And we realised that we, a few thousand refugees from Germany and Austria, were not of the slightest significance. In fact we gave credit to the establishment, presumably the War Office, for thinking of sending us somewhere more or less permanent, for some purpose. To question what was happening to us seemed irrelevant and impertinent. So there were none of the personal feelings of individual unhappiness and awkwardness which had ruled me for years. They were only to come back later, when things got better and therefore more manageable, and when individual lives could again have a meaning.

Sailing on an internment ship from Liverpool to the Isle of Man on the day when Hitler danced in Paris and France surrendered felt like existing in a vacuum. I knew I was alive and felt perfectly well. And I knew that my parents and Judy were in London and that I had a lot of friends who were also on the ship and in the same position. So I did not feel alone. But I felt that I was nowhere, in a void. All plans and ambitions, and all perspectives of my previous life, had disappeared. I did not think about being unable to communicate with my family. They did not know where I was and we were now in different worlds. I only thought about food, how to get some cigarettes, and when it would get too cold for my tennis shorts.

But there was no bitterness about what was happening to me. In fact, throughout my internment I never met anyone who felt bitter against the British government. Our only reaction – like everyone else's – was to feel appalled that such a defeat, like a rout, could have come so quickly and easily. It showed a total failure in military intelligence and planning and suggested a high degree of incompetence, as in the first world war. We ourselves were only a small fragment of a vast picture of confusion and apparent collapse. But no one I met ever expressed any rancour.

Some time ago someone sent me a book entitled *The Internment of Aliens*. It was first published in 1940, which was obviously absurdly early, and was then republished in 1988, but with little sign of improvement or increased maturity. The blurb on the back, quoting a review in the *Observer*, says that it tells a story 'which made the British wince with shame.' But I never met anyone who winced, nor anyone who was really interested in discussing the rights and wrongs of the internment episode. However, someone obviously did wince, since the book opens with an extract from a speech made by a Major Cazalet, a Conservative, in the House of Commons on 22 August 1940, at the height of the Battle of Britain. He is quoted in Hansard as follows:

"No ordinary excuse, such as that there is a war on, and that officials are overworked, is sufficient to explain what has happened … Horrible tragedies, unnecessary and undeserved, lie at the door of somebody … Frankly, I shall not feel happy, either as an Englishman or as a supporter of this Government, until this bespattered page of our history has been cleaned up and rewritten."

That episode reflected exactly how my father saw the spirit of England. It was the country with the highest values of human decency. He must have gloried in the thought that a Conservative MP could say this in Parliament at a time of mortal national danger. But he would never have listened to any criticism of the government at such a time on points of detail, such as my internment. And I agreed with him. The only aspect on which I would have differed from my father, because he would not have understood it at all, being himself hugely impractical, concerned administrative competence. While there was no ill will, the bureaucracy of Whitehall was shown up at its worst and most incompetent, as it was in all aspects of government and administration until Churchill took charge of the war. The men who then governed England (there were no women), like those who governed India and the rest of the still existing Empire, were certainly decent and well-intentioned. But they were also totally insular and lacking in any form of international or other-cultural understanding, let alone imagination. They were so blinkered and obtuse that the result, in retrospect, can only be described as unbelievable ignorance in relation to anything beyond the Channel.

One must remember that in the thirties it was derogatory to refer to any man as clever, and that foreigners were regarded like Martians. And although tens of thousands of foreigners ultimately came to England during and after the war, this attitude did not really change. I saw it mostly with law students from Commonwealth countries in the fifties and sixties. They came here to be called to the Bar, and it was obvious that they would in due course play important roles in their home countries and that their memories of England would remain with them for ever. But nothing was done to ensure that these memories would be good. They were mostly lonely and homesick, because they could not afford to go home in the vacations. So, many were here for years. It is said that when Nkruma came to power in Ghana the only person from this country whom he invited to the official celebrations was his landlady from Kilburn, who had befriended him during the five years which he had spent here as a student for the Bar. No wonder he hated this country.

Coming back to the wholesale internment of 'enemy aliens' in 1940 and the brave speech of Major Cazalet, if and in so far as that page of English history is to be regarded as shameful, it has certainly never been cleaned up or rewritten, as he urged. There was never any inquiry into any of the Whitehall stupidities, probably stretching back for decades, which must have been lain at the root of the indiscriminate events of 12 May 1940 and the following months, and of all the mistakes which continued to be made for several more years. But the absence of any public post-mortem should not give rise to criticism. Anyone sufficiently competent to have conducted an inquiry during the war was obviously much better employed elsewhere. Afterwards, five or so years later, the waters of history had flowed under many bridges, and this country, together with the whole of Europe, was facing immense new problems.

Knowing England and English governmental processes, I expect that someone, some time after the war, raised the question in Whitehall, probably in 1946, whether some form of public enquiry should now be held. But he would also have known that the correct establishment answer would certainly be in the negative. Inevitably it was, if indeed the question was ever asked. But the point is that a negative answer was not only inevitable, but understandable in the circumstances, and in my view right. There had been so many far greater tragedies during the intervening years. A Civil Service investigation into this relatively minor wartime incident, unlikely to be repeated and only affecting a few thousand people, most of whom survived without permanent damage, would not have been appropriate at the time. It would have seemed fruitless and out of perspective. The war inevitably saw many histories of muddle and incompetence which remained unregurgitated. "*A la guerre comme à la guerre*," as my father would have said; war is war. Long-term history, as it has become in retrospect, may see the position differently. But there is no reason for bitterness with hindsight.

Only two further thoughts.

My father always used to say "perfidious Albion," but generally with a smile. Inevitably it is a French sentiment, which is attributed to Bossuet. Experience certainly bears out this epithet. English foreign policy, and much of its history, consists of expedient short-term compromises dressed up in the guise of principle. But what is always overlooked about these compromises is that the underlying attitude, which requires that they should be dressed up as principles and which provokes the sense of hypocrisy, invariably involves a feeling for fairness and decent behaviour. That was the point of Major Cazalet's rhetorical demand in the House of Commons. And its probable sequel after the war, in the form of some internal Home Office memorandum asking for views whether there should be some inquiry, would have been a reflection of the same spirit. That is the civilised aspect of England, and a few, if any, other countries would even bother to ask the questions. The hypocrisy, which is ultimately no more than pragmatic compromise and good sense in all the circumstances, lies in the predictable negative response to rhetorical appeals to principle. But the crucial point is the fact that such questions of principle are raised at all.

As I write this it occurs to me that presumably all the Cabinet and departmental papers concerning the history of the internment of aliens during the Second World War, and any post-war sequels, are now open for inspection. It would be interesting to know if there was in fact any echo of Major Cazalet's speech. I could find out, but I haven't got the time. My apologies to the powers that be, presumably the Home Office, if I'm wrong in thinking that nothing further ever happened.

The second post-script is that, amazingly, it was post-war Germany, of all the countries in the world, that made the greatest reparation for the unspeakable horrors which its government had perpetrated. German governments, beginning with Adenauer, made amends – at a significant level – for the misfortunes of all those who had been lucky enough to escape, including those who were interned in England. I clearly remember that during the sixties I thought that Germany was emerging as the most democratic and idealistic country of the world, even though I never got to like it. Later on we will come to that time, when my mother returned to Berlin to earn her living.

But that would be nearly twenty years later. Meanwhile our ship had left Liverpool on its way to the Isle of Man on a fine summer's day, with some hundreds of different kinds of 'enemy aliens'.

32 · The Isle of Man

ALTHOUGH DOUGLAS sparkled in the sun, we felt that we were finally going to prison. This was not a transit camp. This was for good, where we were going to spend the rest of the war. I would have felt less depressed if I had known that the next time I would see the island would be from a Wellington in Coastal Command four years later, from 5,000 feet at night, with its outline picked out in green dots on the radar screen in the cockpit. But meanwhile I felt that I was in a prison ship going to an island prison.

The front of Douglas, from the little I saw of it and remember, extends northwards from the landing pier in a long succession of terraced hotels and boarding houses intersected by narrow streets going uphill to the back of the town. All that I and my group were ever to see of it was one block about two-thirds of the way along, after we had been marched, about five abreast, from the pier. The block may have been about 150 yards wide and 75 yards deep, surrounded by a 12 foot fence of barbed wire on all sides. The wire took in the pavement of the promenade, as well as one of the pavements and half of the carriageway of each of the two side streets which formed the boundaries to the next blocks. But they were empty when we arrived. I am told that the holes which held the posts for the fence could still be seen fifty years later.

There were perhaps three or four hundred of us, of all ages and kinds, from boys to old men. One person I remember in particular, now that a lot of it comes back to me, was a young Cockney stable boy of 16 who hoped to be a jockey. He had no idea where he was or why, and felt a bit lost because he couldn't speak a single word of German. At the other extreme was the grandson of Kaiser Wilhelm, named Hohenzollern but who was known as Herr Lange, together with his aide de camp, Rüdiger von Etzdorf, who gave the number of a Panzer Regiment in Prague as his last address. He became a friend for a while later on. The Emperor's grandson would later marry a Guinness and ultimately commit suicide by drowning himself in the Rhein. But meanwhile they held a special position in this camp, I think No. 2, in Douglas.

The sleeping conditions were perfectly adequate. All the rooms had two or more beds with blankets, and people shared with their friends or those whom they had got to know. I shared with my cousin Klaus, Peter's younger brother. He was very depressed most of the time and pining away for his Peggy, saying over and over again that all would have been so different if he hadn't come up to Cambridge for that weekend, which had proved to be a disappointment anyway.

Since it was clear that this was not a transit camp like the others, we organised ourselves for an indefinite stay. A Camp Leader or Commandant was appointed by the Major in charge of the camp, another first world war veteran, after consulting some of the older inmates.

The Camp Commandant was Pastor Hildebrandt, a Lutheran priest with an impeccable anti-Nazi record as the disciple and assistant of the famous Pastor Niemöller. I think that he had also come from Cambridge, although I had never met him before. But he seemed to have taken a liking to me, and since my English was better than most, he asked me to be his assistant. This became a semi-official position, known to the military, and that is how I was later to be able to avoid being sent on one of the terrible passages to Canada or Australia. I can't remember much about my duties except to walk around the camp with him, look at things and talk to people, and then to interpret when he passed on complaints and suggestions to the Major.

We were more or less autonomous in our daily lives and saw little of the soldiers guarding us, except those with rifles patrolling up and down outside the barbed wire. We were to see more of them later on, when the overseas deportations started and patrols were sent in to search for people on the lists. Apart from organising the cooking and distribution of food, about which I remember nothing except that I was always hungry, the main preoccupation among the Cambridge contingent, and similar groups from elsewhere, was to set up a camp university, as it was called. There was a noticeboard and a large blackboard, and a number of the dons rapidly organised a weekly timetable of lectures comprising many subjects. I remember teaching English and French and listening to talks on many topics, some of which I could not understand at all, and also a few on Law. But most of the time I just walked around in my tennis shoes and shorts, talking to people and whistling endless tunes. Although I have never played an instrument, I have always had a great musical memory and the ability to recognise snatches from composers, symphonies and operas. So I used to go around whistling tunes which I knew and asking people to help me identify them. There must have been some sort of camp shop, because I have four or five penny notebooks in which I kept a bit of a diary, including all the names of the tunes that I whistled, as they were identified. Many years later these diaries, which I still have somewhere, were transcribed and put on microfilm by the Imperial War Museum, where they no doubt still are.

Fortunately for us, but not for England, where the Battle of Britain was at its height, the weather continued to be perfect. But it was often unbearably hot and airless in the overcrowded camp. At first our daily worries continued to be much the same as before, a great shortage of food and cigarettes, and no communication with the outside world. But as time went on things began to change. It appeared that somewhere in the camp there may have been a small nucleus of real Nazi supporters, although I never met one. Alarmist rumours began to circulate. As the expected invasion of England failed to materialise, there were apparently reliable reports that the Germans would invade Ireland, or had already done so, in order to take England from the rear, where there were no coastal defences, and that there would be no attempt to defend the Isle of Man. Many of the inmates who had already suffered terrible things again feared for their lives, and there were several suicides.

But the more immediate fear was not from the Germans but from the British authorities. It had been decided, allegedly for the protection of the internees themselves, that those who were well enough to travel should be deported to Canada, and to a lesser extent to Australia. By the time when this scheme came into effect the internment of so-called enemy aliens had become general, not only from the coastal Defence Areas. There were now thousands from London and the Midlands, and a considerable proportion of women and girls in separate camps in other parts of the island. Inevitably there were tragic mistakes and confusions and a great deal of avoidable organisational incompetence. I remember rows of internees being marched past our camp towards the pier to be shipped abroad, with members of their families in our camp, screaming at them in vain across the barbed wire, unable to make themselves heard, with the marchers unaware of their presence, since no one knew where anyone else was. Later on it became known that in some cases husbands had been shipped to Canada and wives to Australia, and other family members broken up. The passages and conditions on board the ships are said to have been terrible, and a number of them were torpedoed, notably the *Arandora Star*. At the other end, the Canadian and Australian authorities had clearly been insufficiently briefed, since all these contingents were regarded as prisoners of war on arrival and for a long time thereafter, and were treated accordingly.

My own life also began to change. Klaus and I had been joined by his old father, Otto Reichenheim, who had been swept up with the wave of internment in London and had arrived at our camp quite by chance. Klaus was meanwhile becoming more and more depressed. Some of the Reichenheims had emigrated from Germany to Brazil, and when it was announced that people who wished to emigrate would be considered for release, he decided that this was his only visible hope. His application was accepted and he left, asking me to give his love to Peggy, which I later did, for about two years. He has lived in Brazil ever since until his death a few years ago, first as a banker and financial adviser and then an antique dealer. When the International Union of Judges met in Rio in the late seventies, and I was asked to go as the English delegate, I visited him and his family in Sao Paolo. By then he was well-off and married with children. But he never felt happy in Brazil and always longed for Europe. His whole life was changed by an unlucky coincidence. If he had not been successful in persuading Peggy to go to Cambridge for that weekend in May 1940 he would not have been interned until much later, when alternative possibilities of release began to be announced, and he would probably never have emigrated to Brazil.

I was also in something of a dilemma, but luckier. My two great friends, Brian Grant and John Wilmers, as they became later, had been told that they would be deported to Canada. I was also on the list, but as the assistant to the Camp Commandant I was told that I could apply to stay behind. All three of us agonised about it. I hated to be separated from them, but I also knew that I wanted to stay.

So that is what happened. Brian presented me with a copy of a then fashionable, and now unreadable, novel – *Sparkenbroke* by Charles Morgan – and we all wrote pompously sentimental thoughts on the flyleaf to each other under the heading 'A parting gift and dedication by Konrad Goldschmidt and Hans Wilmersdoerfer,' dated 'Central Promenade Camp, Douglas, I.o.M., 3.7.1940.' I still have it and recently read again what we wrote, wincing through clenched teeth. But Brian's message was pointed, quoting from verses in the book:

'Who stays? A Fool. Who Knocks? A King.'

* * *

'Though in sweet April thou dost shine,
December waits for thee and thine.'

They suffered grim conditions on the crossing and during nine months of internment in Canada, where they were treated as were prisoners of war until things were finally explained and understood. Then they were released and sent home in relative comfort with the additional consolation of apologies from the Home Office for the mistakes which had been made. Later, when some "enemy aliens" were allowed to join the fighting forces and not only the Pioneer Corps, both volunteered (under their anglicised names) to join the Commandos. John Wilmers opted for a commission course and finished the war as a Captain attached to the SAS. Brian took the direct route as a Sergeant in a special Commando Troop and was blown up by a mine on a reconnaissance in Italy, shortly before the Battle of Cassino. The next time I was to see him was in a military hospital in Harpenden, about two years later, hopping about on one leg in Army pyjamas. But although he had many years of pain and discomfort with various artificial legs, he ended up being able to play squash and golf again, though never his beloved tennis. His greatest affliction was that the mine destroyed both his ear drums and affected his hearing for life. But he nevertheless managed to have a successful career at the Bar and later on as a highly popular circuit Judge. John Wilmers also went to the Bar and became a successful QC, but he died, sadly, of leukaemia in his early sixties. We all remained friends for life, but never talked about the war.

But I must go back to the Isle of Man in October 1940. By now I was sharing a room with Klaus' father Otto. The camp population had begun to hear about tribunals to decide who could safely be released, but it was clear that it would take many months, perhaps years, before the thousands of internees would come up for consideration. But meanwhile there was some relaxation; those over 60 were to be released, to Otto's great joy. He was a well-known gourmet who was to suffer greatly from the camp food, but had arrived with a suitcase full of black market goodies. All that now remained was the prize item, a small tin of chicken in aspic, which Klaus and I had seen him handle longingly many times. I was watching him handling it again now, sitting on his bed as he was packing, and I could read his thoughts. Should he eat it, or take it, or give it to me as a farewell present? I was holding my breath as he went on packing, putting the tin in and then taking it out again. At the end, as he was being led through the gate to be marched down to the pier, the unexpected happened. He shook my hand and pressed the tin into it, with a look which said that no one could do more for a fellow sufferer who had to be left behind.

I went back to my room, clutching the tin, but it was not yet the end of the story. It was a stormy October day, and when Otto's contingent got to the pier they were told that it was too rough for any boats to cross and that they would have to wait until the following day. Meanwhile they were taken back to their camps. I knew nothing of this and was sitting on my bed, still holding the tin, when the door flew open and Otto burst in.

"Have you eaten it already?" he shouted in his Teutonic English.

I shook my head and showed it to him.

"Then let us eat it now, this minute, before anything else happens," he said.

He opened the tin and in a few seconds we had spooned out the contents. On the following day he left in peace.

I then moved rooms to share with a man called Henry Seligman, a physicist of about 35 who was distantly related to Melanie Plesch, and whom I had often met at The Pavilion. He was an astonishingly exuberant and superficially carefree personality. We played endless games of poker for matches, which were then multiplied on paper, and I ended up by owing him several millions, which he never allowed me to forget. He was also due to be deported to Canada, but decided to try to save himself. By then there was a rule that anyone who was married or engaged would be taken off the lists for further consideration at a later stage. Henry was neither, but he had a girlfriend and he worked in the camp Post Office. He just needed a little time. When a search party came to look for him he hid under the bed on which I was lying, and I told them that he was at a lecture. He had meanwhile somehow manufactured a telegram from the girl agreeing to marry him, and when he was found on the next day or so he produced it as evidence of his engagement. They checked up with the girl, who was delighted to support his claim, since she greatly wanted to marry him. She was less delighted later, when he got out and explained that the engagement had only been a logistic necessity, for which he was very grateful to her.

In the end he was also sent to Canada, but as a VIP, one of the select band of nuclear scientists who included the traitor Fuchs. He and Henry and many others worked for several years on the atomic bomb, first in Canada and then at Aldermaston. After the war Henry had a distinguished career in nuclear physics and ended up as a Director of Euratom in Vienna, where Diana and I met him again and he lived happily into his eighties.

Apart from the lectures we also had some music in the camp. The Amadeus Quartet formed itself from three inmates, beginning as a trio. A well-known pianist, Alfred Blumen, gave a concert on a grand piano which was found in the foyer of one of the hotels. There was an audience of hundreds, listening to him playing Schumann, including my father's favourite *Davidsbündler*, and many of the older men were crying uncontrollably.

Some of the inmates whom I remember became famous later, as well as many more whom I did not meet at the time or cannot remember.

People like Professor Hermann Bondi, the famous mathematician, Sir Klaus Moser, later the Chairman of Covent Garden and much else, the famous molecular biologist Max Perutz, and countless others. I met some of them again at the reunion party organised by the Imperial War Museum in May 1990 to celebrate the 50th anniversary of the start of internment, as well as two old men who said that they had been among our guards on the Isle of Man. Bondi made a speech and I gave a press interview. He said that he had had to spend the whole war as an internee. As soon as he was released from the Isle of Man he was put back behind barbed wire in Canada and America with other ex-internees, because of the secrecy of their work. It culminated in the atomic bomb.

33 · Release

IT WAS NOW November 1940. The Battle of Britain was over, the Blitz was in full swing, and I was still on the Isle of Man, in my sixth month of internment. The weather had grown cold, but in September I had got some clothes from somewhere; I think that by then we were allowed to receive some parcels and mail, though everything was carefully searched and censored. My only hope of release was to wait and wait for a tribunal, unless I were to volunteer for the Pioneer Corps, which I was still hoping to avoid. Then I had some luck, and as so often I had to thank my mother for it. She had never for a minute given up trying to get me out, by ceaseless agitating and lobbying. In November she saw another chance. The sensation at that time, which took people's minds off the Blitz, was a new film called *The Mortal Storm*. It was based on a novel of the thirties by Phyllis Bottome, about the tribulations of an anti-Nazi family in Germany. The father loses his post at his university and is taken to a concentration camp, where he is beaten up; the children are forced to leave school; the mother is humiliated, etc., etc. But finally good triumphs over evil – although it hardly ever did in real life at that time. There is a thrilling escape over the Swiss border, and the book ends with the whole family happily on their way to England.

I have no idea whether this is a fair summary of the plot, since I can no longer find my copy of the book. But that was the gist of it, and the nation braved the air raids to see the film. It was triumphantly reviewed in the *Evening Standard* by Michael Foot, later to become the leader of the Labour Party.

One of the central characters was a boy of about eighteen, the son of the family, and this is where my mother saw her chance. She persuaded my father that they should write a joint letter to Frank Owen, then the editor of the *Evening Standard* and a great man. The letter said, in effect: "And what would have happened next? The boy would have been taken away from his family after all and put behind barbed wire into some internment camp, without his parents even knowing where he was. Just as happened to our son." My mother then added a brief biography of her offspring, which she was used to reeling off at the slightest provocation, and also a word or two about my father and the family history. Frank Owen did not publish the letter, but he did something much better. He sent it straight to Herbert Morrison, the Home Secretary, also a Socialist. And within a week I was out.

The first I heard about it was when I was fetched by two soldiers and taken to the Camp Commandant, wondering what I had done. He then told me that I was to be released because my former headmaster, George Riding, had applied to the Home Office to allow me to return to the school to teach Modern Languages, since he was now short of staff. This was news to me, but I realised that it wasn't the time to argue. So I gravely said that I would be willing to leave on these terms.

He then took me totally by surprise by asking whether there was anything that could be done to make things better in the camp. A great mass of thoughts and topics flashed through my head. I have not really tried to describe camp life as it was, and much of it has been sublimated, like hunger, endless queues for food out of buckets, limited washing and loo facilities since the water was mostly turned off, and the delays and censorship in all communications with the outside world. So I didn't know where to start or what to say, and all I could think of was a ping-pong table. The Major considered this gravely and finally nodded his assent; he thought it was a good idea.

That is my last memory of Douglas apart from being marched to the pier and escorted onto a ship. The crossing felt no different from the camp, but when we reached Liverpool it was a very odd feeling to be able to get off the ship and to go wherever I liked. Anywhere - I was suddenly completely free. But I had lost the habit and sat on a bench, wondering what to do. It was a November evening and I had been given a rail warrant to London. But the last train must have gone, because I also had a voucher for one night at the Adelphi Hotel, the best in Liverpool, as I discovered many years later at the Bar, and probably the only one that was open. It was all a bit like a dream. That Sunday in May, when we had been marched through the city in the summer heat, with the old people dragging their suitcases, seemed to belong to a different world. I thought of trying to find the route to Huyton or just wandering about, but then an air raid started. It was quite a fierce one, my first experience of bombs. I was surprisingly frightened and rushed into a shelter, and only went up to bed in my luxurious room in the early hours when it had stopped. The next morning I got on a train to London, just as though I was a normal person.

34 · Another interlude – 'fast-forward'

BEFORE FINISHING with my internment, which has had a great effect on me throughout my life, I must recall a sequel to my involvement with The Mortal Storm, the film which had brought about my release many months earlier than if I had had to go through the usual and highly inefficient release processes of the time. Of course I knew nothing about the history of my release until my parents told me when I got to London. I had thought that I really owed it to George Riding, though very surprised that he had such influence, because teaching was not an exempted occupation. When my parents then told me how it had happened I read the book and saw the film. Both seemed fairly corny and when the film was re-screened on TV recently it was almost embarrassingly bad and I could not bear to sit through it.

But ten years later, in about 1950, *The Mortal Storm* was to make a brief re-appearance in my life. I was a pupil in Chambers, and this was my first time of appearing in the House of Lords, though not yet on the record. I was merely sitting shyly, though in a wig and gown, beside my bulky master, John Megaw, who was the Junior to a fashionable libel Silk – I think that it may have been Valentine Holmes himself. The case was an impossibly brave libel action brought by a writer and critic, Arnot Robertson, against Metro-Goldwyn-Mayer. They had banned her from all their previews because she had slated one of their films. She had merely mentioned the title and written 'Bla, bla, bla.' My father would have approved. But MGM made an announcement that she would no longer be admitted to their press shows. She then bravely sued them on the ground that they had libelled her by presenting her as an incompetent critic. It was David against Goliath. But she won before Hilbery J. and a jury, who awarded her what were then huge damages. But then she lost in the Court of Appeal on the ground of a minor misdirection by the judge, with the result that a new trial was ordered which she could not possibly afford to fight. The misdirection only consisted of a few words which John Megaw had discovered in the long summing-up. By then the case was a *cause célèbre* and she got leave to appeal to the House of Lords, just when I arrived in Chambers. Of course, all my sympathies were with her, but we were on the side of the big battalions. My reason for remembering the case is that she got the great D N Pritt QC to do it for nothing in the House of Lords, and I shall never forget how he did it. He was a vast man, a brilliant lawyer and espouser of lost causes, and a dedicated Communist all his life. When my Chambers in 3 Essex Court were later to take over No. 4 as an annex, I moved into his old room and sent him the two things hanging on a wall which he had overlooked when he moved, a photograph of Lenin and a red flag with the hammer and sickle.

But John Pritt was just the man to come to the help of Arnot Robertson, a left-wing critic, fighting the might of MGM. I cannot remember the arguments. But part of his case involved the need to demonstrate that she was a serious writer and critic. So he read a number of her writings to their somnolent lordships, and one of them was her review of *The Mortal Storm*. And this is what I always remember. When the great, vast John Pritt read this review, which described the moving story of the film, he could suddenly no longer go on. He burst into tears and had to hand over to his Junior to finish reading.

I don't think that anyone present knew anything about my origins and background. Everyone was embarrassed. But I was also deeply moved. Not by this film or its part in my history. But by the fact that it had made this middle-aged woman, sitting on the other side of the Committee Room, write about it in such a way that the great John Pritt burst helplessly into tears. It is one of my memories about the wonders of this country, which happen only sometimes, on special occasions, but usually about things which really matter.

However, to my sorrow, we won again in the House of Lords. Arnot Robertson could not hold on to her verdict and award of damages. But there was never a re-trial, as the Lords had ordered. She committed suicide a few months later. But she was vindicated as a critic.

35 · The Blitz – back to Aldenham – the RAF

I REMEMBER NOTHING about getting back from Liverpool to my parents and Judy in London, or any feeling of euphoria. The Blitz was then at its height, and to live in London was depressing and sometimes frightening. I briefly got together with Pru, who had come down from Cambridge and had a flat near Westminster, and I remember standing with her on one of the bridges, Westminster or Waterloo, with hundreds of people watching the City in flames. The fires lit up the dome of St Pauls, which looked doomed, and everyone was amazed on the next morning when it was still there.

But London looked awful, unbelievable. The air raid shelters were full and thousands of people slept in the Tube stations, then getting up and going to work like zombies. A week after my release, the day before I was due to go to Aldenham, the house next to the Foyer Suisse got hit. We had not gone down to the basement as we should have done, and I woke up when I was thrown out of bed. My mother and Judy also survived unhurt, but we feared for our father because we could not get to his room, which seemed to have caved in. But somehow he emerged, looking white and surprisingly slight, the only time I remember ever having seen him in pyjamas and a dressing gown. He was covered in plaster and dirt, but unhurt and joking.

I was only too glad to go to Aldenham on the next morning, leaving my family and the inhabitants of the Foyer Suisse among the debris. Although they were more or less cleared up by the following night it soon became clear that the building was unsafe and would have to come down. So where were they all to go? Once again it was the apparently omnipotent Janos Plesch who found the answer. One of his patients, a Maharaja from what was to become Pakistan and a former High Commissioner to London, had a large house in Putney opposite the Common. It had something like twenty bedrooms and was empty. He was going back to India, and happy to sell or let it. Madame went to view it, the verdict was favourable and a deal was closed in a few days. Whether the money came from Madame or the Swiss Embassy I do not know. And so they all moved out to Putney, my father again in a small room, but my mother and Judy now having to share, as they did for the next five years.

The Putney 'foyer Suisse' lasted a year or so, but my mother had never got on with Madame. She was too boisterous for her Swiss reserve and sense of order. Madame was heard to say that she couldn't stand the way my mother came down the stairs. So they were asked to move again. There was a boarding house in Lytton Grove, half way down Putney Hill in a large garden, called Lytton Hall. It was run by a French woman who took to my father and agreed to take the family, again in two rooms, a double and a single. And there they lived until after the war, my father's last "home" for 7 years until his death. But all his rooms had been the same throughout his life when I knew him; small, a bed, a wash basin, a table, his typewriter, a gas ring, and all the rest of the space covered in books and papers. This one, as he pointed out, was in a house whose name gave him the pleasure of being associated with the author of *The Last Days of Pompeii* a century earlier.

I was lucky to be out in the country, in Hertfordshire, only about twenty miles from London, but how different at the end of 1940! Green fields and no air raids to speak of. It was strange to be a master at a school which I had only left a little over a year ago. I had a small room in School House, a double house consisting of about 120 'Odds' and 'Evens' in which I was to act as assistant house tutor. I taught French and German, and despite my objections George Riding also made me teach Spanish to seven boys as an additional School Cert subject, which I had only just passed myself. Our set book was an abbreviated version of *Don Quixote*; they had to do one paper on this and one 'unseen,' a translation from Spanish into English. We found Cervantes too difficult in Spanish, so we read the book in English. They all passed easily in their essays about the book, but all seven failed their unseen, and so none of them got through. Fortunately I had already left before the results came out. But I had not wanted to pretend that I could teach Spanish and had made them all take another subject as a fall-back. So no one suffered in the end, except Riding's statistics.

I did not enjoy Aldenham and found it difficult to get on with Riding, whom I now saw from another angle which was even less endearing. We had a number of blistering rows. He had put me in charge of ARP for School House and there was a terrible row about parties of boys in tin hats being taken up on the roofs or not having been taken up. To do so was strictly against school rules, but required by fire-fighting training regulations. I can't remember who argued in favour of what, but a door was slammed at the end. It was a nervous time for everyone, and it left me with a life-time of dislike, despite admiration, for teaching as a profession. Boarding schools, like universities, are riddled with politics, envy and frustrations. Only the junior matron cheered me up.

The mainspring of all our lives was the war. Rationing was severe. Coupons were not only needed for food and clothes, but of course also for petrol, which was almost unobtainable. The war was going badly, although the threat of invasion had been beaten off. But the air raids continued. Then there was a great event: Hitler attacked Russia. We all realised that this gave a new dimension to the war and that it would take the pressure off England, by then fighting on alone. I remember reading the news in a copy of *The Times* which was displayed daily on the school noticeboard. There was the first faint, long-term, feeling that there might be hope at the end. And I wanted to feel part of it, instead of being an enemy alien who had just been released from internment. Apart from Riding and a few of the old masters, no one knew about this, and I kept it as an anxious secret throughout.

My burning ambition was to get away from Aldenham as quickly as possible and somehow to join the RAF. And, amazingly, it happened. Without my knowledge, George Riding had written to another headmaster, John Wolfenden, who was temporarily the head of the Air Training Corps, the ATC, and in charge of entry for Air Crew recruits into the RAF. Many years later, in the sixties, the Wolfenden Report was to become a household name when it recommended legalising homosexuality between consenting adults. And somehow John Wolfenden, whom I never met, must have pulled strings for me.

The first I heard, and quite out of the blue, was when I got a letter to report to the Air Ministry, then somewhere in the Aldwych. I suppose I must have filled out some application form and given it to George Riding. I was briefly interviewed by three officers, but I was much too confused to notice their rank. In fact I really had no idea why I was there. They seemed to know all about me. Having confirmed that I wanted to be a pilot they said that they wanted to ask me just one question: if I were shot down and taken prisoner by the Germans, and they discovered my antecedents and about my father, would they treat me as a prisoner of war? I said that I had never thought about it, but that I supposed the answer had to be no. They had de-nationalised us, so that I was no longer German, even though I was still an enemy alien in England. But I had to accept that they would not be too interested in the legal niceties. All I could do was to beg them not to turn me down on that ground. They thanked me and said I would hear in due course.

And then I waited and waited and nearly despaired. But before I get to the happy end to this crisis and to the RAF I must come to the end of the story about my initial interview. That was nearly four years later, in September 1945.

My time had come to be demobbed, demobilised, among the first, because I had a scholarship to Cambridge. It involved a considerable rigmarole to get released to civvy life, but this part was only concerned with the paperwork. I had to go to one branch of the Air Ministry in London, collect a sealed envelope containing all my records, and take them to another branch. Since I went by taxi, I must have been given a voucher. What I remember is opening the envelope in the taxi as untraceably as I could. There was a lot of paper, but only time to look at the beginning. The first sheet was a record of my interview four years earlier and the resulting orders. The report said that I was an enemy alien, but was nevertheless accepted for pilot training in view of family circumstances. However, I was only to be permitted to fly as an instructor, or to tow targets, or to ferry aircraft. I was to be retained in the United Kingdom, and not to fly on any operations. And I could not be commissioned as an officer.

The restriction against operations was presumably because I would not have been treated as a prisoner of war if shot down. The prohibition against becoming an officer was presumably because an enemy alien could not take the oath of allegiance and hold the King's Commission. Both were entirely logical. But fortunately logic did not prevail at the end, although this piece of paper must have dogged my movements throughout the rest of the war.

36 · Air Crew Cadet

I WAITED AT Aldenham for many weeks, hearing nothing, and then filled in the time with two memorable holidays. It is very strange how one remembers things from fifty years ago so clearly, but cannot reconstruct the events of the last decade. The first was at Easter with Peggy, and Henry Seligman with Leslie, a girl he married later although they were to spend most of their lives apart. We rented two punts to go up the Thames, starting at Kingston. The punts had metal hoops which could be covered with an awning at night, and we were camping and cooking. The second holiday was in the early summer with John Butler, who was also waiting to be called up, in his case by the Army. We decided to hitchhike to the Lake District and stay in Youth Hostels. We met at Eros in Piccadilly Circus, took a tube to Hendon and started to try to hike. Our first lift was by a local parson who was doing his rounds near Pinner. But then we picked up a Buick which took us to Preston, an enormous stroke of luck, and by the evening we were in Windermere. We stayed two weeks, climbing Great Gable and getting lost in the fog on Helvellyn as night was falling, trying to rejoin three girls who were doing the rounds of the hostels before us. Meanwhile we walked and climbed, like I have never done since. Being 6'6" and refusing ever to give up any planned objective, it was difficult to keep up with John, and I suffered a certain amount. The great outdoors on foot have never been my milieu.

Then I went on waiting. My mother had found me a small room near their boarding house in Putney; depressing, but closer to Air Ministry than Hertfordshire. But there was no news and I began to fear that I would have to go back to Aldenham in September and face Riding again, this time with the Spanish results. But then one day the blessed letter came, needless to say already opened by my mother, who read it to me. It must have been about July 1941. I was to report as an Air Cadet to an RAF Reception Centre at Viceroy Court, NW1.

I couldn't believe it and thought that, despite the interview at Air Ministry, they must have failed to realise that I was still an enemy alien. But my mother said she was not at all surprised and seemed to claim the credit for it. None of us knew about George Riding or Wolfenden until much later.

Viceroy Court proved to be an unfinished block of what were to be luxury flats overlooking the north of Regents Park. The structure and the roof were there, and most of the internal walls and staircases as well, but little else. Each intake was about 60 cadets, and we were to be there for a month to be kitted out, medically examined and instructed in the ways of the Air Force. We each got a kit bag and a number, which we had to stencil on it, and then a uniform, boots, gym shoes, a webbing belt, black boot polish, Blanco for the belt and a button stick with a tin of Brasso. We handed in our civies and we were told we would get them back after the war. We slept on blankets on the floor. I shared a room with a huge Canadian. The first thing I heard him say, looking dreamily out at the sky lit up by searchlights, was: "My teeth are like stars, they come out at night." Why have I never forgotten this? He only stayed for a few days and disappeared; there was a constant coming and going, and no point yet in trying to get to know anyone well.

For all our meals we were marched to the Zoo, which was only a few hundred yards down the road. Most of it seemed to be closed, and the few desultory spectators watched us silently from a distance being fed at trestle tables, evidently more interesting to them than what remained of the animals. Our other activity was to be marched on every other day to some public baths near Marble Arch. But as we halted at traffic lights with buses nearby, the back of the column tended to melt away into the buses, and only the front half got to the baths. In fact I never got there, though what I did instead I cannot remember either. But we were always worried about the RAF police, who picked up stragglers. Our distinguishing mark and source of pride was a white triangular flash in our caps, worn at an angle like kepis, to show that we were destined for flight crew, the elite of the RAF. But there was always the danger of being chucked out altogether, or to be relegated to navigator or – worst of all – rear gunner.

After a month or so we finally came to the end of Viceroy Court, the Zoo and the marches down Baker Street towards the unknown baths near Marble Arch. About 50 of us were collected and told that we were to be posted together to an Initial Training Wing (ITW) at Stratford-on-Avon. I had never been there but knew of its fame as Shakespeare's birthplace.

We lived in Nissen huts at one end of this pretty town; the headquarters of the Wing was The Falcon Hotel in the centre. There followed two or three months of endless parades, drill, square-bashing, physical exercises, runs and iron discipline inside and outside our huts. We had to Blanco our belts, shine our boots, Brasso our buttons and make our beds to perfection, with everything laid out correctly and symmetrically to the nearest half inch. This was our idea of life in the Army, which we thought we had avoided, not of Air Crew, and we wondered if there was some mistake. But there was none; however illogical it seemed to us, it was all thought to be a necessary part of the training. I spent Christmas night, from midnight to 4 am, guarding The Falcon with a rifle and fixed bayonet, standing by the front door and marching round the back every three minutes. It was snowing and bitterly cold. But there were no Germans or ghosts, or signs of Shakespeare. Only cooking smells at the back which I finally traced in my memory to the attic of our unused garage in the Grunewald where Judy and I used to light fires and try to roast bits of food.

This was easily the worst of my time in the Air Force, though the only bad time. It included 'Jankers' or punishment fatigues, mopping up floors in the kitchens, peeling potatoes and cleaning latrines, as well as runs with full packs for breaches of discipline. But the end came, with a group photograph of the Wing, which I still have, remembering some of the 50 or so faces, though many were killed later on. There was a big red-head called Hornby, the only man I had ever met who could always beat me at ping-pong. He did his flying training in Canada, but I came across him again towards the end of the war. Then there was Girvan, whose name spoke his origin, a wonderful ugly little man with a brilliant mind. He had started university in Scotland, reading Philosophy, and he tried to explain it to me and to make me believe in a God at the same time. We whispered for hours at night in the hut, like soul mates, while everyone else was sleeping. I had always felt so confident about my atheism. But he was poking fun at it, because to him it was far too simplistic to provide an explanation of the universe and of our existence. He confused me and made me feel humble. I only knew him for a few weeks. Later I heard that he had been killed on operations.

After the group photograph had been taken and we had been ordered to give three cheers for the officer, we each collected an envelope with the all-important posting details for our flying training. About half were sent to the United States and Canada, some to South Africa and Rhodesia, and the rest were kept in the UK, including myself. My posting was to an Initial Flying School (IFS) at Anstey, a small grass aerodrome near Coventry.

37 · Wings

THE AIRCRAFT were all Tiger Moths with two open cockpits, one behind the other, no canopy, dual controls and a voice tube for communication. We were each given what became our most prized possession, a heavily padded leather flying jacket, and a leather helmet and goggles. Many years later I gave the jacket to my son Jo, who wore it for years; by then they were fashionable and expensive rarities. The seats were shaped like shallow metal buckets fitted to take our parachutes, on which every pilot sat, whatever he flew. But although I knew how to pack one and how to roll over on landing, after jumping from a tower with a fixed chute, I never had to use one.

The first flight, optimistically called Air Familiarisation, seemed like a disaster. My main recollection is that the ground was either right beside us on the wing tip or on top of us, but never sedately below, where it should have been. I was totally bewildered, frightened, and very nearly sick. That was no doubt the intention. But presumably I survived just well enough not to be kicked out.

And so we began to learn, with 20-minute trips and endless hours in classrooms. The theory of flight, navigation by dead-reckoning, Morse, aircraft recognition, elementary gunnery, and so on. It was harder work than at school or Cambridge. With all my changes of school I had never done any science. To this day I have never had a single hour's physics or chemistry, and only one hour of biology, which was devoted to the psychology of bees, a topic which subsequently played little part in my life. I also knew that I was bad at maths and had no aptitude for mechanical things. My classroom marks were barely average and I had only come out top in rifle and pistol shooting, which presumably carried little weight. So it all depended on the flying. If you were not ready to go solo in – I think – 14 hours, you were out. By that time you also had to be able to get yourself out of a spin and do a loop. But I didn't think that I was a particularly good pilot, and I had never driven a car. So it was touch and go. But then surprise and relief when my instructor suddenly got out after a reasonable landing and told me to go round on my own. I felt wonderful, did a straight take-off and an uneventful circuit and bump, as it was called, at 12 hours. It was as though a huge cloud had lifted and I had got through another barrier.

That was the crucial stage and I went on to the full course. In those

Tiger Moths 1941

relatively early days this involved some 96 hours of flying, including cross-country and the entire programme of aerobatics, for which the Tiger Moth was ideal. Slow rolls at the top of loops, without losing even a few feet of height, and easing out of double spins, were the most difficult. But gradually I felt entirely at home in the sky and became a fanatical flyer. At the end of the course I came out third, which surprised me greatly, particularly since I could still not understand how this yellow thing made of canvas and wire managed to get off the ground and stay up there. I could recite all the formulas and talk about airflow, lift, drag and stalls. But none of it meant anything to me. And it still doesn't.

The next posting was crucial, since it would tell us what sort of flying we would do, Bomber or Fighter Command, Coastal or Transport or Flying Training. We all hoped for fighters, but by that time the main call was for bombers and coastal. And the top four, including myself, were retained for Flying Training, to become instructors. Whether in my case this was due to having done well in the course or because of that interview at Air Ministry, I never discovered. Perhaps it was both.

There was a final parade and all who had passed were presented with two pairs of wings, one for the full-dress uniform and the other for our battle dress. There was a great farewell party and we were sent home on a week's leave before reporting at our next station.

Most of my leave was spent with Peggy, as had been all my 48-hour passes. She had become a despatch rider in the Wrens and was stationed at the Admiralty in Bath. To get together in wartime Britain was extremely difficult. We spent frustrating hours trying to phone each other and then to arrange to meet, in Bath, or near Coventry, or half way, or London. But trains were unreliable and frequently stopped by air raids. Hitch-hiking was often the only way, but in uniform it generally worked, and in the end we usually managed to meet, if only for a few hours, though most of our energy and interest went into the planning and preparations. But gradually the effort became too much. When the first Americans arrived, I was quietly replaced by one of their colonels. He had many advantages over me, being older than Peggy, far better off and easily accessible, with a jeep at his disposal. We had previously had it out, on the top deck of a bus going round Hyde Park Corner, that we were not going to get married. From then on it was only a question of time, with an amicable parting in sight, not a drama like others later on.

38 · Learning to teach flying

HAVING GOT my wings I was now a Sergeant Pilot and no longer a nonentity in the system. I had a reasonable rank and got more pay. So it was with a different outlook and far more confidence that I faced my next posting. This was to an Advanced Flying Course at Scone, just outside Perth, in Scotland.

I have never forgotten the day of my arrival. It was again one of the few memorable days of my life. At lunch, in the Sergeant's Mess, I recognised one of the heroes of Aldenham whose picture I had seen in innumerable team photographs. He was John Barrell, a former Captain of Football and Cricket, Captain of my House, and a legendary figure. He had left two terms before my arrival, but his fame lived after him throughout my time. To my amazement he recognised me too and said that he had seen me play in goal for the school. In fact he seemed to know all about me. He had been one week on the instructor's course, which he loved. He was about three years older than I, but we had so much in common, and we were now to be together for nearly three months at Scone, which he described as "a wizard station." So we arranged to have dinner together after he had done his next flight and I had settled in.

Unfortunately it was not the happiness of that short meeting which made the day so memorable. In the afternoon, when I had found a spare bed in John's hut and unpacked my kit bag, I got a message to go to see the CO, a Wing Commander. I had seen him on my arrival and wondered what he wanted. He said that he knew that John and I knew each other and was sorry to have to tell me that John was dead, killed in a flying accident an hour ago. He told me to come with him to his jeep and we drove up among the mountains for about an hour, following other vehicles, until we found the place. It was a narrow gorge near a summit. Squeezed in it, only about 10 yards below us, was what remained of a Tiger Moth and of two people in it. The wings had been torn off and the small yellow fuselage was wedged between two rocks. Two brown helmets could be seen, sticking out of a mass of blood covering two flying suits.

I never discovered for certain whether John or his instructor was in the front cockpit; not that it mattered. Or how it had happened. I only remember the silence. It was a beautiful, still summer evening with a glorious sunset as we drove down.

After that I remember virtually nothing of Scone except a red-haired, blue-eyed girl in the town called Susan, who worked on the station. She was still in her teens, and this was a very proper relationship, including high tea at her home with her parents. But we were shy, idealistic and juvenile and it ended in inevitably atrophy. Although we continued to write and I once travelled back to Perth from my next posting, it was obvious that we had nothing in common. I endured yet another high tea with her parents and fled south, feeling relieved and free.

When I passed out of the Advanced Instructors' Course, I really knew a lot about flying. I could spin from one side to the other and do a slow roll off the top of a loop without losing even a few feet of altitude. I could find my way across country, map reading mostly from roads and railway lines, and fly by instruments. By now I had done over 200 hours, plus a lot of instrument flying in simulators, then called Link trainers. Apart from Tiger Moths I was flying Magisters and Austers, which were hedge-hoppers used by the artillery for spotting, and I did a lot of low-level flying, which is the most dangerous, apart from bad weather. I also did a few hours on the more powerful rotor-engined Harvard trainers on a station somewhere near Reading. So I was ready to be let loose on new cadets.

39 · Flying Instructor back in Cambridge

MY POSTING, of all places, was to Cambridge. As everyone familiar with the town knows, there is a civilian-run aerodrome called Marshall's out on the Newmarket road. It has been family-owned for decades, and perhaps still is, though now it has a runway. During the war it was a well-known flying school with Tiger Moths and Magisters, and Austers later on. The nation paid dearly to the owners for every hour flown from its grassy bumps, and Marshall's made a fortune out of the war. That, at any rate, was what was said.

Over the next year or so I contributed about a thousand flying hours to these revenues. But when I came back to Cambridge after the war and wanted to do the 20 hours flying which were required for my A Licence, there was to be no help from the owners or the administration. I asked to do the hours on the basis of cost, paying for the petrol and depreciation. But they required the full private fee, which was far beyond me. So I never flew again after the war, except once, in the seventies, with John Droeger from San Francisco to Yosemite and back. He even let me do a landing, but it scared us both. And I found it strange, and almost frightening, to fly without sitting on a parachute.

All flying instructors at Marshall's were billeted in the town, and we cycled to and fro every day. I was lucky in my billet, but having a university connection may have helped. Peter and Edith Brighton lived in a terraced house on Parker's Piece, which they rented from Jesus College. For about 10 years it became more like a home to me than anywhere else, and they remained life-long friends. Both of them were in their forties, tiny and frail to look at, and neither could have existed outside a university. Edith was like a sprite. She loved people, talking, writing letters, and a constant flow of gatherings for coffee and sherry in her drawing room, which was like a salon for university gossip. Peter was the opposite, a geologist, a shy silent man who fared badly in all aspects of university politics. He was a member of Christ's, but was never made a Fellow. Throughout the years I knew him he was the curator of the Sedgwick Museum of Geology in Downing Street, about three minutes walk from the house, and his life was the classification, cataloguing and exhibition of tens of thousands of fossils. When he gave up his original research PhD, which held out much promise, to take on this job, there were literally hundreds of thousands of specimens stored in crates in this so-called museum which had been neglected for years. It was Peter's life work not only to create order from chaos, but to devise a new system for cataloguing which made the result comprehensible. Every morning and every afternoon, including weekends, he would slink off to the museum, puffing away at his endless cigarettes, saying very little when he was at home. Apart from his work his life was Edith, music of the Haydn and Mozart type, and Victorian novels, in particular Dickens and Trollope. For the rest of his life he was a spectator, amused by Edith's gregariousness, but not by people like me, though in the end we got used to each other. He smoked between 40 and 60 cigarettes every day throughout his life, but only suffered from emphysema in his late seventies and died when he was 85. Unfortunately it was only then that his tireless work received the recognition which university politics had always denied him, by a posthumous medal awarded triennially by the Royal Geographical Society to promising students, and naming a new Geology building after him.

But Edith lived to see this, into her 90's, on crutches in an old people's home on the outskirts of Cambridge. She was tiny and frail all her life, but the liveliest person I have ever known, a spirit of the best of university life. She did not reach my shoulder and seemed ageless, though she was in fact about 20 years older than I and became something like a mother figure for some years. And through me, she and her house became a centre for a lot of my friends, as well as for my sister Judy. Many of us went on phoning her regularly and going to see her when we could. She always told us all that she hoped to die as soon as possible. And when she did, a few years ago, there was a large party of her friends and followers at her funeral.

I must have spent about 18 months at Marshall's, from the summer of 1942 to the end of the following year. It was curious existence between the aerodrome, the town, and what was still functioning as a university. All three were remote from the war, which was happening in North Africa, Russia and the Pacific. Montgomery and the Eighth Army had turned the tide at Alamein. Moscow had not fallen, and it was clear that Stalingrad would be a turning point. In the Pacific, although the day of the loss of the *Prince of Wales* and *Repulse*, shortly after the fall of Singapore, was probably the blackest single day of the war, the Americans were now committed to the defeat of Japan. The attack on what Churchill called the Germans' soft underbelly, which could have been France but proved to be Italy, was imminent, and an ultimate invasion of France from England was bound to come. So the outcome was no longer in doubt, only the duration and the suffering and destruction meanwhile.

Although flying was by now almost like doing an office job, there was a danger in treating it merely as a routine. Every morning I would cycle out to Marshall's at 7.30, usually together with Eric Hall, another instructor whom I had met at Reading, and who was billeted with friends of the Brightons close by. He was enormous, a printer and businessman by training, and a prolific success with women, at any rate according to him. We would check in and inspect and test our Tigers, which would be tied down at one of the flight huts around the perimeter. In theory our preliminary duties included three pre-instruction test flights every week and practising emergency landings. We did this, but only in summer, early in the morning. The emergency landing field which was used for practice was about six minutes flight away towards Bedford, and it grew huge mushrooms in profusion, which were greatly welcomed by our hosts in town. We flew with baskets or paper bags which we filled and put into the spare cockpits behind us and then took them home at night. The crash landing or mushroom field, as it was called, was small and square, with high hedges, so that one had to do a steep sideslip through the morning mist or sun to get in, and then to take off diagonally to get out again. It was flying at its best.

I suppose that we flew about four or five hours every day, usually in periods of 20 minutes or half an hour; only the occasional cross-country would take an hour. This would be six days a week. We each had our own Tiger and our own pupils, and for some time we taught the full 96-hour course, with full aerobatics. But this soon became a luxury which the country could not afford and which was in any event unnecessary in Bomber Command, where most of our pilots went if they passed the course. So then it was cut down to about 40 hours, which became much more of a monotonous procession of new faces and endless take-offs and landings. We then also got courses of Army officers whom we taught to hedge-hop in Austers, but these were also only short courses. There was only one bad crash in my time, when Peter Brown, another instructor, and his flight engineer were killed on a test flight. It appears that a wing failed and they spun in.

At night I had a full social life in Cambridge, which was crowded with wartime science and medical students, injured servicemen, some of them married, and what remained of the university. The house on Parker's Piece became something like an open salon, ruled by Edith, whom I could supply with things from the NAAFI and Sergeant's Mess which were not obtainable on coupons. I had a local girlfriend who was studying to be a singer, and at weekends I usually went to London for my 48-hour passes to see my parents and Judy. But I never liked it. My mother always heaved a sigh of relief to have me safely "home," in digs around the corner on Putney Hill or with friends. But I felt far safer flying over East Anglia and the Midlands in a small open aeroplane, where I was in charge of my own fate, than listening for the cut-out of the engine of the V-1 rockets which had by then replaced the air raids.

And of course, the family was not happy. My mother still worked as a personal assistant to various people, at that time mostly for a refugee in textiles somewhere near Oxford Circus. Judy had got a job with the Hon. Mrs Gamage, collecting and distributing clothes and uniforms from dead and wounded servicemen. Despite all her qualifications, Judy could not get any job which was intellectually closer to the war. But Mrs Gamage was a splendid woman. Although her husband owned Gamage's, which was then a large department store in High Holborn, and she lived more or less permanently at Claridge's, she had a lot of understanding for our family circumstances. Her father had been Lord Hirst, formerly Hirsch, who had founded GEC. And when her only nephew was killed – she had no children – she told Judy to deal with his Air Force uniform and personal effects in the same way as any of the others.

Only my father could not get any paid work, although he was constantly writing. Among other possibilities he was besieging the World Service of the BBC to write for them and to broadcast to Germany. But this was never permitted. He was not popular with the small clique of refugees who ran that side of broadcasting. Their official excuse was that he was too well known, too implacable in his views, and that he would alienate listeners in Germany. He did write quite a lot, but it was never broadcast under his name, and not enough to earn much more than a pittance. Later on, towards the end of the war, he was allowed to write some broadcasts about the war and Germany to South America, for the consumption of the Germans who had settled there, which the BBC translated from French into Spanish and Portuguese. All or most of these BBC texts have since been collected and published as a dissertation by a professor of German at an American university as an esoteric part of my father's work and a wartime curiosity. But they brought in virtually nothing, and he must have felt mortified to have to be supported by his family.

My mother's and Judy's earnings only just paid for their board and lodging, a double room for my mother and her and my father's small room. I was far better off in the Air Force, where rationing was much less severe, and I could bring them food and also spend some of my money on them. I think I got about 24 shillings a day at that time, which included flying or 'danger' money. It would probably be about £12 today and was then more than I needed.

By then I was getting restless as a flying instructor. Like most of my friends, I had volunteered for operations as soon as I had completed a few months at Cambridge. But for over a year we were told that experienced instructors could not be spared. However, I was greatly cheered when I was called in by the C.O. and told that he had recommended me for a commission and that it should come through within a couple of months. That would make a great difference to one's daily life in the RAF. But then, one morning when I was about to take off on my first flight, I got a note to say that the recommendation had been turned down. I remember reading it and going to the tail wheel of my Tiger to be sick on the ground, out of sight. My C.O. said that he entirely failed to understand what could have happened. I knew, but I did not tell him.

However, I told my family, and Judy told Mrs Gamage. She was outraged and, typically, phoned an old friend of hers, Air Marshal Sir Philip Joubert de la Ferté, to give him his full title. I only knew him by name and from photographs in the papers; he had a great reputation for being different. The first I heard about it was when Mrs Gamage asked me to have tea with both of them at Claridge's on one of my 48-hour passes. She then left us alone and we talked for about an hour. There was no reference to my promotion or anything personal. He just asked me to describe all the courses and stations on which I had been and what I thought about the standard of flying training, and he told me a bit about how he thought the war was going. Then I saluted him when he was driven off in his car and went back to Putney.

Two weeks later I had a message from the station adjutant that my commission had been approved and would shortly come through. Nothing more was said. It had proved to be a similar episode to my release from internment. Luck, a bit of fortuitous indirect influence at the right time in the right quarter, and a piece of the old-boy network. It probably works in exactly the same way, or worse, in every other country. But I have only seen it in England and therefore think of it as typically English.

However, just when everything seemed wonderful after all, fate struck. On the following morning, in a moment of aberration, jubilation or absent-mindedness, I landed my Tiger 20 foot up in the air on a test flight. What I actually did was to level out far too high, stalled, and came down like a lift, breaking the undercarriage. I could not even taxi in; the wing tips were on the ground. I think I nearly cried because I knew what it meant. The report would have to go up to Command and there would be an automatic bar to promotion for at least six months while the accident would be investigated. I wrote my report to the C.O. and made no attempt at any excuse, since there was none. All I could say was that it was the first incident in what were by now about 1,000 hours of flying. He called me in to see him. I did not know him and cannot remember his name; it was only the third time we had spoken. But he may have known more about me than I realised. What he said was again typical of this country, though in a different way. He said that he had looked at the aircraft and the damage was not as bad as he had feared. He had given orders to 'tuck it into a corner in the hangar' for repair as part of its overhaul, and he therefore saw no need for any report to Group. I thanked him in three words, saluted and marched out, and afterwards was nearly sick again. A week later I was commissioned and moved into the Officers' Mess.

Edith Brighton, Cambridge, 1942

40 · Twin engines

THIS MUST have been around the beginning of 1944. If I looked at my Log Books I could trace every date and every flight. But, as one used to say in innumerable judgments many years later, the precise details do not matter. What happened, soon after I was commissioned, was that the last of my repeated applications for transfer to operations was unexpectedly granted. I was to convert to twin-engined aircraft, and at some stage, then or later, I learned that this was with a view to being transferred to Coastal Command. Why, I have no idea. Air Marshal Joubert had been, or was, in charge of it. My hope had been Fighter Command, night fighter Mosquitoes, and my fear had been bombers. I had never even thought of Coastal. It may have been a coincidence or it may have had something to do with Air Marshal Joubert. Or it may have been a logical extension of the original interview at Air Ministry, since I would not be flying over German occupied territory but only over the sea.

My first posting was to the most beautiful village in England, as it still proclaims, Castle Combe near Bath. It was a small aerodrome with one runway, and I was to convert to twins on Oxfords and an occasional Anson, also known as the flying motorcycle because of its awful noise. After Tigers, the flying was entirely different, like driving a bus after a small open racing car. The emphasis was not so much on the handling of the aircraft as on instrument flying, radio and the beginnings of radar, which were all new to me. For the first time there was also a lot of night flying, and one had to spend hours in Link trainers full of instruments which exactly reproduced the feeling and effect of being in the cockpit. It took about two weeks before I went solo by day, then two or three more weeks of instrument training and navigation before going solo at night. Then I was off on my own, peacefully practising cross-country courses over the south of England and the Midlands by day and night. It was lovely to be alone in the sky, with only the noise of the engines and the luminous instruments to think about. The only things I disliked were one-engined landings, cutting back one engine during the approach, particularly at night.

On the ground I was adopted in the village by a Lady Brakespear and her daughter with two young children, the wife of the local vicar who was away on service. They lived in a small manor house where they had spent all their lives, near the vicarage, and it became a sort of home from home for me, far better than the Mess and the Nissen huts up at the aerodrome. Lady Brakespear was terrified of the war and would dive under the enormous dining room table whenever there was a siren or any unusual aircraft noise. I got very friendly with her attractive daughter, and later on they invited Judy and my mother to stay. All of which I had totally forgotten until I met the daughter and her husband some years ago up in Suffolk. He had ended his career as Archdeacon of Ipswich and Diana worked out that he must have confirmed her when she was at school. They wrote to me out of the blue, having seen my name in the papers about some case or other, and asked me to visit them when I was next with Diana's sister and brother-in law nearby. It was only when she showed me a photograph of herself during the war that it all came back to me vaguely, including a Christmas which I had spent with them in Castle Combe later on after my return to Cambridge.

I don't know why I am mentioning all this when it is of no interest whatever, even to myself. But there is nothing else to say about that time. It was an interim period when I felt I belonged nowhere. Conversion courses from Training Command to twins, like the one at Castle Combe, were on an individual basis. I did not form part of any RAF training group, nor yet of a squadron, and there was no home base.

But the next posting was different. Squire's Gate, an aerodrome just outside Blackpool, was then the RAF's main school of navigation. They had an exacting course for pilots who were to be posted to Coastal Command. That was where I went next, for another two months or so. It involved no flying as a pilot, only as a navigator, on Ansons, and a great deal of radar, radio and dead reckoning on the ground. Instead of simulators which reproduced the flying controls in the cockpit there were cabins which reproduced the navigator's table and radio aids. The cabins were grouped above a large floor area painted blue and divided into squares, so that it looked like the sea viewed from an aircraft. Models of warships, U-boats and merchant shipping could be displayed on the floor, heading on different courses and showing a chalk wake behind them from which their speed could be estimated. With all this apparatus we had to practise long simulated reconnaissance flights over the Atlantic and North Sea, receiving and sending radio reports in Morse about what we saw and heard, and of what was made to happen through our earphones, or on the floor below us with models of ships. Some of these exercises lasted three hours and were totally exhausting. We also had special tests, not only in identifying aircraft but now also in ship recognition, having to learn to recognise the silhouettes of the main German and even Japanese warships, including some – to our fury – which had already been sunk but had not yet been taken off the syllabus.

Coastal Command 1944

For a month of two I became an expert at this, but it was never the same as flying as a pilot. Such flying as I had to do as a navigator/passenger, which was all at night, I did not enjoy. One trip, in particular, turned into a total mess and nearly cost me my life. The pilot happened to be someone whom I had taught at Cambridge. He had not been brilliant and had wound up flying Ansons at Squire's Gate on night navigation exercises for pilots who were due to join Coastal Command squadrons. But none of what happened was his fault. My job was to navigate on a triangular course over the Irish Sea, and I simply got lost. I was taking star sights through the astrodome to calculate our position, and at one point, according to my calculations, we were over Manchester, but at the same time I could see the sea below us. Then we got into cloud and when we came down, praying that the altimeter setting was right, we once glimpsed the lights of a city due west, which could only have been Dublin, where there was no blackout. So then we steered east to get back somewhere.

By then we were totally lost and probably both in a bit of a panic, though neither of us said anything. We were low on fuel and just looking for somewhere to get down as quickly as possible. But what I forgot all about, being a pilot and not a navigator, was Snowdon and the Welsh hills. We broke cloud at about 800 feet, which would be well below their crests, looking for lights. Then, suddenly, to our incredible relief, we saw a flare path straight ahead. We learned afterwards that it was pure luck that it was lit up for some test or exercise despite the blackout. With no time for radio messages or an exploratory circuit we went straight in. Although I was nervous, I was determined to leave the landing entirely to my ex-pupil and to say nothing, whatever happened. As it was, it was awful and we bounced along the runway like a kangaroo. But we were down, though with a fuel gauge showing nearly zero. We taxied to the tower, where there was little life: it was 2 am. We were told that we were at Valley, in Anglesey, and fortunately the duty officer was too sleepy to ask many questions. We asked him to send a message to Squire's Gate to tell them that we were all right to stop them reporting us as missing. Then we settled down in armchairs in the Mess, waiting for morning. Before we went to sleep the pilot apologised for his landing. I said that in the circumstances it had not been too bad. He said: "Then why did you shout: 'For Christ's sake, get the stick back.'?" I would have taken any oath that I had not opened my mouth, and I told him that I had been determined to say nothing. But he convinced me that I had, automatically, without realising what I was doing.

As wartime flying stories go, this one is very tame. I was merely lucky that it was to remain one of my major ones, and so it has always stayed clearly in my mind and I used to dream about it. If the flare path at Valley hadn't by chance been open, we would have crashed into the Welsh hills within a few minutes. And even with this miraculous survival I should have been chucked off the course. Our four hour flight was incompetent throughout, and by the end there was panic. We were just very, very lucky.

The next morning we refuelled and flew back to Squire's Gate. I don't remember anyone saying anything much about our report. No mention was made of the incident on my record, otherwise I would have had to have been told. So I tried to put it out of my mind. In the end I passed the course quite comfortably. I was promoted to Flying Officer and got a posting to join a crew to fly Wellingtons.

41 · Joining a Wellington crew

THE POSTING was to Silloth near Carlisle, an aerodrome by an estuary on the Irish Sea.. Within a few days of my arrival I was faced with a difficult choice and an unwelcome decision, even though it was flattering in a way. As Squire's Gate I had got to know a Wing Commander, Tom Taylor, a youngish ex-headmaster of a large prep school somewhere in the north. He had read Classics at Oxford in the thirties and then joined the Volunteer Reserve, so he had already got his wings and commission before the war. He had also converted from Training Command, where he had been a Station Commander. So we had quite a lot in common. He was converting to Wellingtons to take over the command of an operation squadron, No. 612, then based at Langham in Norfolk, on the Wash, flying anti-U-boat and E- boat patrols, mostly over the North Sea.

I had known that this was to be his posting, but what I had not foreseen was that he would ask me to join his crew as second pilot. Every Wellington crew consisted of a captain, second pilot, navigator and radio officer, engineer and two gunners, and I had naturally assumed that I would have my own crew. By then I had over 1500 flying hours, far more than most pilots when they joined squadrons. On the other hand, the offer was obviously difficult to refuse. In the end I followed the "establishment" line of not refusing, perhaps partly out of weakness, but mostly because it seemed safer not to oppose fate in wartime. He told me that I would pass out as a crew captain before joining the squadron as a Flight Lieutenant, and that it would only be for a while. So I accepted.

He picked the rest of the crew, a commissioned navigator and three sergeants. I only remember Mac, the big navigator who was about ten years older, already married, and living on Parsons Green, in Fulham, as I hope he still does, well into his eighties. He was an accountant whose hobby was refereeing football matches, for a time at the top level, and he spent a lot of his life with one of the major firms of solicitors, keeping an eye on me from a distance, as he once told me. When we moved to Fulham about ten years ago he wrote to me and we agreed to meet, but we still haven't got round to it.

We took delivery of our Wellington, a new one, which was surprising at that time of the war, and got to know it. The first stage was simply learning all our individual jobs. I had to do some dual flying with an

Wellington Crew 1944

instructor and pass out solo, first by day and then by night. Then we started flying a lot of exercises, nearly all at night. The aircraft was equipped with a Leigh light, a searchlight which could be lowered below the fuselage, designed to light up U-boats tracked at low level. But Leigh lights were being phased out and we began to practice with a new type of navigation and bomb release system operated by radar and designed to attack E- boats in the North Sea and Channel. These so-called *Eilboote* were powerful large motorboats, very fast and armed with rockets and machine guns, which the Germans were using out of Holland, Belgium and northern France to disrupt the sea lanes off the east coast of England and Scotland.

This radar navigation system seemed miraculous, though by now every civil airliner has had it for decades. The radar signals thrown back by whatever is below the aircraft produce blips on a screen in the cockpit, so that one can see what is below as though it were a map traced in green dots. That was how I saw the Isle of Man shaped perfectly, as in an atlas. Our first job was to master the navigational parts of this new device. Bomb release training was to be done after we joined the squadron.

The final passing out exercise was a five-hour triangular daylight flight with the main object of finding and photographing Rockall. This is a large square rock, about the size of four large houses above sea level, some 300 miles into the Atlantic and 400 miles south of Iceland. Its only inhabitants are thousands of sea birds, but there is now a dispute about its ownership between the UK and Iceland because it is thought that there might be some oil there. We took a huge wooden camera with an extension piece with us; it looked like an old pair of bellows but was official operational issue in Coastal Command. Taking the photograph was the job of 2P, as my job was known in the crew. So when Mac triumphantly found the rock, somewhat to our surprise, the bottom hatch was opened and 2P got hold of the camera and made sure it was working, as he had been taught. He was then lowered through the hatch, held by his legs, with the camera in his extended arms, and he clicked as we flew over Rockall, as slowly as possible, at a height of about 300 feet. Fortunately everything worked, including the hauling back of 2P. The photo was signed by all members of the crew as proof of success, and I still have a copy somewhere.

On the following day we were passed out and flew our Wellington down to Langham in Norfolk.

42 · 612 Squadron

JOINING 612 Squadron at Langham did not prove to be as much of a pleasure as I had hoped. It was good to feel that one would belong somewhere again, after months of courses, and that I would finally fly on operations, to use everything I had learned, although I had no false romantic ideas about bravery. The main point was clearly survival. We were by then in August or September 1944, just around D-Day, and the end of the war was becoming a reality for the first time. So the main point was to live to see it. But this was also reflected in the atmosphere in the squadron and the Officers' Mess. The idea of a new Wing Commander taking over at that stage, with a background of Training Command, was not popular, and he and his crew were not eagerly awaited by a station which had become greatly attached to its prior C.O. Moreover, Tom Taylor, when he appeared, proved not to be a typical RAF figure, which was what had drawn us together in the first place. And the squadron was undergoing changes in training and equipment as the war zones began to narrow. The U-Boats were no longer the menace which they had been for so many years, at any rate off the east coast, and Leigh lights were becoming obsolete. In addition, and apart from changes at the top, a number of crews had been broken up, and there was talk that ultimately the squadron itself might be disbanded. So the atmosphere was unsettled.

But Tom Taylor was admirable and pretended to notice nothing. He was determined that the squadron should become proficient with the new radar bomb against the E-boats whose sorties from Holland and Belgium were increasing, whenever the weather allowed, inflicting severe casualties on merchant shipping off the east coast. So we did a lot of practice bombing over the Wash, mostly with large bags of cement and later with bombs.

There was nothing special about the fragmentation bombs as such, which were designed to explode just before they hit the water, to cause maximum damage to the superstructure of any surface craft. What was new was the approach for attacks and the automatic release. We had to fly straight and level at a fixed speed at a height of 100 feet for a mile and then at 50 feet to track over the target. This is not a particularly pleasant experience, in a Wellington at night, even without anyone shooting at you. But if the approach was done perfectly, which would be shown on our radar screens, then the bombs would drop off automatically, without anyone pressing any buttons, and hit the target over which we were tracking. It was a brand-new device and revolutionary at the time.

However, the target, in the singular, proved to be the key word. The squadron practised and practised in daylight on a buoy anchored in the Wash, at first with bags of cement and then with explosives. The success rate was amazingly high; we could see our bombs land within feet of the buoy. But what had not been foreseen, and we did not yet know, was that the system would not work with the E-boats. It would have done if they had come out singly. But they always came out in pairs, or three or four in formation. And as the Wellingtons tracked over them, the bombs would be released perfectly, but to explode precisely in their geometrical middle, which was invariably too far from any single boat to do much damage. The multiplicity of radar contacts would pull the mechanism away from each single one and compromise in favour of the centre.

This problem was never solved during my time, and I can still not see how it could be solved in theory. However, it was a long time before this was known. What we knew was that we lost some aircraft even at that stage of the war, which was tragic. There was also a horrifying incident when a Flight Lieutenant navigator, one of the most popular men on the station, was so relieved to get back from a sortie in which they had been shot up and badly damaged, that he forgot everything as he jumped out onto the tarmac and walked straight into a propeller, to be decapitated in an instant.

Unusually, I had several letters from my father during the years when I was flying. Usually my mother was the letter writer, copiously. These letters recently came to light again when a German researcher found them in the Archive in Berlin and sent them to us. I had forgotten them, but now find them deeply moving, typed on his instantly recognisable old portable typewriter in an English which he called pidgin, not in German, in case they were censored by the RAF. He was clearly struggling and feeling lonely, but never even hinted at this. What comes through is his unrelenting courage in a ceaseless quest for outlets for his work and an undimmed determination to survive and to remain optimistic about everything. And then also, for the first time as it now seems to me on re-reading them, a deep affection of which I had never been conscious before. At this time I must have mentioned at home that I was a bit worried about Tom's flying. The problem was that, as the Wing Commander, he got less practice than other captains. My father wrote that he hoped that Tom would improve, and it now seems amazing to me that he could even have visualised what flying an aeroplane might be like, when he could never have imagined learning to drive a car. And then he ended, even more uncharacteristically for him, with something approaching a reluctant prayer: "Please help fate. By being as untemerarious as possible."

In the end, after all our training flights, our crew only flew five or six operations during that autumn and early winter. I don't know whether that was the average for this period or whether the Wing Co.'s crew flew less than others. They were all long dusk to dawn patrols over the North Sea along the coasts of northern France, Belgium and Holland, never higher than 200 feet in order to keep below the German radar. After briefing and takeoff there was always a reluctance to set course and to leave the peaceful beauty of the English coast just as darkness fell, and the coming night seemed endless. I was constantly looking at my watch, wishing the time forward and chewing gum or raisins to help the nerves. There were six of us in different places in the Wellington, with radio silence and little talk over the intercom and only the light of the instruments. Tom Taylor and I flew the aircraft in turn for an hour at a time, and all of us were hoping that nothing would happen before dawn. If anything went wrong at that height it would have been over in seconds, since there was virtually no chance of survival if one had to ditch. One the other hand, if we returned, there was a full English breakfast with eggs and bacon, which was only served after operations, and a 48-hour pass.

I only remember one of those nights in detail; I don't think anything eventful happened on any other. But this is again something I have never forgotten. Three German E-boats came out from Antwerp. We tracked them half way across the North Sea heading towards the English coast. So we finally had an attack, as we had practised so often. The long approach at 100 feet seemed endless and then we went down to 50 feet just before releasing our bombs. Throughout that time they fired at us with machine guns and rockets. How on earth they missed I shall never understand. But there was no time to be frightened or even really to understand what was happening. All that I remember distinctly was being in the middle of what seemed like a Christmas tree of slowly rising coloured lights. I knew that it was rocket fire all round us and that it could not have been as near as it looked, or we could not possibly have failed to be hit. But what I still cannot understand, and always forget to ask someone who does, is why the lights appeared to be going up slowly instead of whizzing past the cockpit windows. They floated past, evenly, in many colours, and apparently harmlessly. But they were rockets.

Tom and I heard Mac say: "Bombs away," and immediately afterwards we saw the explosion on the radar screen, in the geometrical centre of the triangle formed by the three E- boats. They scattered and turned away, and we went thankfully back up from 50 to 200 feet. We had both missed each other and now both went home. A good result, but still better for us, because they had failed to reach any of our shipping.

All that now remains of that night is a "poem" which I recently found in a notebook full of diary entries and fragments of those years, dated February 1945:

> "We have one life. Just one. There's nothing else beyond.
> Yet here am I at night, hung in a flimsy frame
> Of fabric, wood and metal in the whistling wind.
> The all-engulfing sea rolls endlessly below
> And red-hot searing steel is rushing up to meet us.
> What does it mean? What am I doing here?

We flew two more ops after that, on tenterhooks because the war was visibly in its last stages. But nothing more happened. And that proved to be the end of my flying career.

43 · The war in Europe ends

I AM NOT going to write much about what is usually called one's private life, and I have already left out a great deal. This account is intended to be factual, about things that happened, and only about feelings in so far as they were caused by events. So I will only mention in passing that much of the next nine months or so was taken up with Sally, a ravishing WAAF Signals Officer on the squadron. We became inseparable, and I took her to meet my parents and Judy. But I'm not going to write about her, only about events in which she figured.

Shortly after our last operational flight the squadron was grounded and we heard that it was to be disbanded. The war was drawing to an end. Hitler's final desperate offensive in the Ardennes was beaten back and the Allies were across the Rhine. Everything to do with the war suddenly appeared to be breaking up, and people were once again only really interested in their own fate. The air crews and ground personnel worried about the bridging of the time between the closing of the airfield and station at Langham and their ultimate release from the RAF. Different demobilisation categories were being mooted and there were many courses of lectures on rehabilitation to civvy street. The great fear was that the war in Europe would end long before the war in the Pacific, so that a posting to the Far East at that stage was to be avoided at all costs.

Although always anxious about my future, I remember that I was unusually unconcerned. I knew that university scholars were in a high priority demobilisation category, and I could not imagine that I would be posted to the Pacific at that stage. And so it proved. I was in touch with my family, as always, and they knew that I was at a loose end. Once again the news about me appears to have permeated via Judy and Mrs Gamage to Air Marshal Joubert, and I was summoned again. There may have been another tea at Claridge's. But I cannot remember the details because this time I was not really concerned. What I remember is that he said that I should go on a course to learn Russian, because a lot of interpreters would be needed in the chaos which would follow the end of the war in Europe. I said that I would love to learn Russian, but that there was no point, because I would be in the first category to be demobilised to return to Cambridge. He said: "Never mind. It will be useful and interesting, and no one knows what will happen. There is a good course at the London School of Slavonic Languages."

And so I readily agreed, in accordance with "establishment" precedent ('never volunteer, never refuse'), but perfectly happy anyway. What could be better than a posting to London while waiting to go back to Cambridge?

There were some intermediate postings, both for me and Sally, but I can remember little about them. I know that for a month I was Duty Officer on the Control Tower at a Coastal Command Station on Southampton Water looking across to the Fawley Refinery, and I now have a picture of it over the arch between the sitting and dining rooms in our house in Fulham, which I found by chance in a shop in Wilton. I also spent a week or two in a similar capacity at Felixstowe. In both cases I had to deal with civilian planes, seaplanes and – indirectly – ships, mostly by radio. But I remember nothing about these postings except that nothing went wrong, nor where Sally was at the time.

My next memory is the London School of Slavonic Languages, somewhere around Gower Street, and an intense course in Russian. I made one great friend, an Army officer called Patrick Roger. He had read Philosophy and Classics at Cambridge and had been sent there by the Army in similar circumstances. We both lived in digs, I cannot remember where, and we clearly had a lot in common. But, to my amazement, which I was tactless enough to make plain, he said that he thought of taking Holy Orders when he got out of the Army. This in spite of the fact that he was Scottish and a member of the Church of Scotland, which would not make for a fashionable way to promotion. However, he did what he said and went back to Cambridge to read Theology at Westcott College. Ultimately he became Bishop of Manchester, where I met him again on my first Circuit 27 years later, and finally Bishop of Oxford. But we never had as much in common as we did over about six months in 1945 in Gower Street.

For some time Sally and I remained inseparable. We both got some leave and decided to go to Land's End, or as near as we could. The trains were still as crowded and unreliable as ever, even though there were no more air raids except the V-2 bombs on London. We finally got to Penzance and that enchanting railway station which I was to see so often 20 years later. The nearest hotel to Land's End was at Cape Cornwall, near St Just, and we were there for a week, pretending to be married, which was essential in those times. We even somehow got to the Scillies and left the war far behind. But coming back to London brought it all back. We had to share a seat all the way, and the train was about ten hours late, arriving at four in the morning. We thought that we would have breakfast at Lyon's Corner House, which was supposedly open all night, but when we got to Piccadilly we found that there was no breakfast till seven. London was deserted. We walked into a hotel across the road to have a bath, because we were filthy after nearly 24 hours on the train. But there was no one about. So we walked upstairs and found a bathroom and came out at seven in time for breakfast. That was London in wartime.

The war was then nearly over. VE-Day was on 15 May 1945, more or less five years to the day from my internment in Cambridge. I was a Flight Lieutenant with wings and the Atlantic Star and other so-called campaign medals. But I was also still an enemy alien, though even I no longer gave this a lot of thought.

Sally and I spent VE-Day in the multitudes dancing, singing and drinking in and around Trafalgar Square. I still have some photographs of her, including a Dachshund which she must have acquired by then. I can't remember where either of us was living, but the Air Force still paid us. It was a wonderful time, a feeling of enormous release, joy and goodwill.

But I wished that I'd seen the liberation of Paris. It would have meant even more than VE-Day in Trafalgar Square. And the joy and goodwill did not last long. The aftermath of the war was in many ways more depressing than the war itself. It lacked the feeling of inspiration which had kept everyone going for five years.

44 · Demobilisation

MY DEMOBILISATION came through even before VJ-Day in September, the end of the war with Japan after the atomic bombs had been dropped on Hiroshima and then Nagasaki. There was no regret or remorse about this in the country at the time, only relief that it was over. And also, it has to be said, a feeling of retribution for the unspeakable cruelties inflicted by the Japanese on all allied servicemen and civilians who fell into their hands. There were equally no feelings of guilt when the pictures of the destroyed German cities began to appear. They coincided with those of Belsen and Dachau. Although only confirming what a lot of people knew already, the full horror then finally got through to everyone. The *Diary of Anne Frank* was an epoch-making book for the whole world, far more than *The Mortal Storm* for this country a few years earlier. The only reaction to the plight of Germany and Japan was an overwhelming sense that great evils had been stamped out in both the theatres of war.

Some years ago there was much argument about the erection of a statue for 'Bomber' Harris. Whether he deserved it as an individual is perhaps debatable. But, as a symbol of what the war was about, and how it was won to a large extent, the statue was obviously right and overdue, coming 46 years later. And all who ranted against it because of Dresden, etc. should have remembered Guernica, Rotterdam, Coventry and London, assuming that they had ever heard of what had happened to them.

But enough about the war. In fact, I have said very little about it, although the defeats and later victories, the constant fears and later relief, and the never-ending casualties and privations were at the centre of everyone's life for years. The real war, leaving out the "phony" first six months or so, only occupied five years of my life between the ages of 19 and 24. But it dominated the rest of my life and my generation still dates more or less everything from before and after the war.

However, back to Cambridge. The London School of Slavonic Languages closed for the summer holidays, but I never returned to complete the Russian course. I collected my envelope of service records from one branch of the Air Ministry to take to another, and opened it in the taxi, as already told. The actual demobbing was somewhere near Shepherds Bush or Olympia. I can't remember whether we got our old clothes back, but we each got a two-piece suit, some shoes, two shirts, two ties, some socks, a raincoat and a hat. I am fairly sure about most of those, but certainly the hat. I never wore it, but for some reason I had it with me on a ship to Norway two years later. I was supposed to sleep on deck, but a Norwegian steward let me sleep in a cabin. I had no money, so I gave him the hat, since clothes were still scarce. But he threw it straight overboard.

However, we did not hand in all our RAF outfits, whether we were meant to or not. I kept the leather flying jacket and helmet, which Jo got later on, and years later I came across my dress uniform and peaked hat. Above all, however, I kept the heavy, warm blue officer's greatcoat. It was of superb quality, unobtainable at the time, and I wore it for many winters.

Our demob'civvies' were so awful and scant that most of us were still in uniform when we reappeared in Cambridge in October 1945. It was a strange time. Nothing like the Cambridge of 1939, and nothing like what it would be again from the fifties onwards. The 'Backs' along the Cam were ploughed up or used as allotments and as parking places for tanks and armoured vehicles. There were no gardens; everything was planted with vegetables. Many of the returned undergraduates were married and in uniform, and the whole of life was dominated by rationing and shortages of food, petrol and clothes.

My first reaction, which persisted for several weeks or months, was that I missed the war. I missed getting paid every day, being told what to do and not having to worry about problems, plans, ambitions and the rat race which was rapidly breaking loose all around. But the war was over, and now we had to make our own lives again in competition with everyone else.

For my first year I was not living in College, so I went back to Edith and Peter Brighton in Park Terrace. Although they were not officially permitted to be used as Clare digs, we did more or less what we liked, and no one asked too many questions.

Before I could settle down in Cambridge one way or another there was the question of what was to become of Sally and me. We agonised over it. But at heart we knew that we had no long-term future. We were not ready to settle down and she did not really fit in with Cambridge and the law, or with me in peacetime. So we parted several times, but inconclusively. It was a complex time in my life, like others later. But in the end we managed to make the break. I later heard that she had married and emigrated to Australia. The rest is silence.

45 · Post-war Cambridge

THE FEELING that I wanted the war to go on, to avoid the responsibility of having to run my own life, quickly disappeared in the hurly-burly of Cambridge. I can't think of any other phrase though I have never used this one except to describe marriage as the deep peace of the double bed after the hurly-burly of the chaise longue. But it wasn't that sort of hurly-burly, or only to a small extent.

There were many overlapping circles of people and activities. The law and work, old and new friends, football and tennis, Girton and Newnham, and moving in between.

John Butler was back with the formal rank of Major and a DSO which he got as a Second Lieutenant for a mortar and machine-gun attack in Italy, having been recommended for a VC. But just as languid as ever, and deliberately contemptuous of the rat race around him. Throughout the years I have known him he has written moving and witty letters and poetry, full of originality and wit. That is what he wanted to do, to write. And he did write: accounts of his travels and life, some essays and I think some brief fiction. But none of it came alive like his personal letters and poems, because all of it was written for writing. He tried industry, Africa, farming and teaching, but none of it really interested him. And Pippa, who had some money and married him soon after the war, was only too glad to have him to herself at home, as far away from people and the rat race as possible. So they lived in the depths of Northumberland for years, exploring the countryside in long walks, and doing little else. Voltaire called it '*cultiver son jardin*'; we now call it opting out. Both were very content and would have hated a life like mine. Ultimately they emigrated to New Zealand, where John died a few years ago. But when I first knew him I thought that there was no limit to what he would do, and so it seemed during the war.

When he returned with his DSO he was back at Christ's reading English. So we had different groups of friends from different colleges and faculties. But a large inner group overlapped and remained friends for life. And at its centre was the Brighton household in Park Terrace, a salon ruled by Edith with coffee and sherry, tolerated by Peter for her sake.

All my Cambridge friends date from that time. The pre-war period of 1939-40 was too short, with people departing all the time and many not surviving, like Bill Simpson. So when I go to a Clare Reunion for my year, 1939, I know hardly anyone. 1945 was different, even though it was my second year and the first for many others. Ronnie Coubrough became a close friend from the start, also reading law and wanting to become a solicitor. He seemed so carefree and straight-forward when I first met him, and it was only months later that I began to know what he had been through as a prisoner of war in Burma, captured by a Japanese patrol in the jungle, at the age of 19. For a year his parents had no idea whether he was alive, and he then spent the rest of the war in one of the infamous camps near Rangoon. It was only when he had been at Clare for some time that his friends began to realise what he had endured. In the end he got over it all, but it had left its mark. He was my solicitor for most of my life and we were each other's best men at our weddings. But he thought that once was enough, so when I married Diana, his present was to make new wills for us immediately after the ceremony, pointing out that the old ones had been revoked by marriage.

Then there were Michael and Peggy Parkington, already married and both reading law. My first impression, which still remains the same, was that he was the cleverest man I have ever met, but not the easiest. The three of us were close friends for many years. But he and I had a fateful and final row when he was working at the Law Commission and I became its Chairman. The rights of that row were largely on his side, but the resulting estrangement lasted for more than a decade, until they both died, far too young.

Then there was Geoffrey Kirk. He became a Professor of Classics at Bristol and ultimately Regius Professor of Greek at Cambridge as one of the greatest experts on Homer, all more or less by default because he didn't like any of the jobs which were offered to him after the war. He was looking around in industry and business, for which he would have had considerable ability, and he would also have done extremely well in the law. But his university subjects were Greek and Latin, and so he accepted a Fellowship while he was looking around and waiting. And then the Classics took over his work, though not his heart. Later on we became godfathers of each other's daughters, whom we both neglected after the age of one.

Those were among the central figures, leaving out the girls, of whom none remained central. But on the periphery I also met scores of undergraduates reading law who would remain parallel to me for the rest of my professional life. Among the closest, for instance, were Peter and Mary Oliver, with whom I sat in lectures. She was enchanting and lived to see him reach the Court of Appeal, in the knowledge that he would go to the

Lords one day, as he has. But she died tragically young. I wrote an obituary for her in *The Times* unasked, and without Peter's knowledge. I have also written a precautionary one for Peter and about six others of my judicial friends. But fortunately, so far as I can think, only those of Kenneth Diplock, Eustace Roskill and Tony Lincoln have so far had to be used, and Tony's was only written when he was already dying. One of the greatest compliments I have had was from one of the Obituary Editors, who wrote that I 'really brought them back to life.' I replied that no writer of obituaries could ask for more, and could he please make a note to have it included in mine.

But these were all dots on a landscape, and I don't want to get involved in personalities. Moreover, I did not find Cambridge as happy or enjoyable as all this may sound. In fact I never really liked it. I spent far too much time there when I was young, including every weekend in term-time during my first five years at the Bar, doing supervisions for Clare and other colleges. All my different times at Cambridge seemed unsatisfactory in different ways. It was never a place of *jeunesse dorée* for me. It also never acquired the golden glow of an *alma mater*. And now that I am an Honorary Fellow of Clare it seems no different, on the occasions when I have gone up to College 'Feasts,' reunions, or – more interestingly – to talk to students. I thoroughly approved of Candy's and Tim's choice of Oxford. In spirit and in every other way it is more civilised and closer to London and the world. But when Cambridge University appealed for covenants I found that I responded instinctively by return, quite generously and uncharacteristically, because I recognised that I owe a great debt to Cambridge, as I felt I did to Aldenham. Not for what either did for me directly. But indirectly, simply due to having been there.

My first year back, 1945-6, was inevitably fairly drab. I had a lot of friends, but no money, although my scholarship and grants had been revived and I had managed to save a little from the Air Force. But life was still fairly grim, in some ways worse than during the war, when there was a cause and one knew that austerity – then a term of art – was necessary. There was no real student atmosphere. Many were married, some already with children, and all faced the need to make their lives in the post-war world and earn a living. There was a fear of exams and of failure. The everyday question, when meeting in the Whim for coffee or wherever, was: "How many hours have you done today?" The fewer hours others had done, the better one would feel about one's own work, particularly if lectures were included in the answer. It was a time when work and exams were everything. But I still had to drive myself to open my notes, and I went back to my bad habits of 1939 of saying that I would start on the half-hour, and then on the hour, and so on; but always not yet.

Nevertheless, I must have worked extremely hard, and apart from girlfriends, football and tennis, I thought of nothing else. My method of work was largely automatic, like a personal crammer. I never read widely or deeply. I worked in my room or, more often, in the Squire Law Library for fear of interruption. But although the study of law consists largely of the knowledge of decided cases, of the principles which they laid down and therefore also the facts of the disputes, I never read a single law report throughout my time at Cambridge, and I would not have known how to find them on the shelves. Everything I did was based on textbooks, lecture notes and what had already been filtered out in essays for supervisions. Every subject which I had to do, and every topic within it, was condensed into notes with numbered and lettered paragraphs, sub-paragraphs, and so on. Then, for revision, every note was further condensed, and for the final revision little remained other than the headings and sub-headings. In this way I knew the material almost by heart or by rote. That obviously gets you an easy pass. To do well, you need more, but it is only another technique which I have already described, of knowing what the examiner is looking for and producing it for him in a way that he may find interesting and attractive. And of course to do the necessary number of questions fully, devoting about the same length to each.

The exam technique is also quite a good recipe for advocacy, particularly for anticipating and dealing with the questions the judge is going to ask. You hold something back and then you give it to him in answer to his question. He then feels that his own perspicacity has elicited the point, and he will take it.

For Cambridge, at any rate, my system worked perfectly. Oxford would probably have required more. And Cambridge is easier because there is a Law Qualifying exam and a Part of the Tripos at the end of every year, not just one set of Finals after three years, which must be far worse. As it was, in Part I in 1946 I got a First in every subject and a "starred" First overall. In Part II the following year I slipped a bit and failed to get the star. But a Double First is the conventional optimum, and my mother was perfectly happy.

In the autumn of 1945 I played my last game of football, in the final Varsity Trials. I was in goal for the Possibles against the Probables, and that is how it turned out. I dived at someone's feet to momentary applause and went off with a broken wrist. But the goalkeeper at the other end was an undergraduate called Pinner, who later played as an amateur for England and also semi-professionally for Chelsea for a time. So the outcome would have been no different without the broken wrist, except that I would have gone on playing at College level. But there are better ways of spending scarce time. So – *à quelque chose malheur est bon.*

In the summer of 1947 I played a lot of tennis and in due course became Captain of Clare. However, I never had the time to take it really seriously. And when I took it up again at Queen's in London in my forties or fifties it was obviously too late, although I remember feeling that I could still have beaten myself at any earlier stage. I never had enough steadiness or practice for any kind of class. But it always reminded me of my mother, who adored it and ultimately died on a tennis court.

As I got to know people, and life began to get more normal, I spent time staying with friends in the summer of 1946, since a room in London was no attraction. But I remember few of the details. I stayed with Ronnie in Hadley Wood and with a girlfriend, June Hooper, at her home in Galloway. I also stayed with Damaris du Boulay at her family mansion in Hampshire. We had met somewhere during the war. She was a Wren officer and we collected each other as platonic curiosities who were very different from each other. I couldn't keep up with her at all; she was always taking taxis, which of course I never did. She insisted on my coming to stay at her home, and to meet her family, which I did without feeling particularly comfortable. But she had a small car which she let me drive for practice, which proved a great help later on. I could fly aeroplanes but I couldn't drive. There is one great difference even after you get used to not trying to pull the steering wheel backwards to go up in the air. This is in bends on the road. To turn an aeroplane you lower a wing and return the control column to central; otherwise the turn gets steeper and steeper. So going round bends in her car I was always turning the wheel back and shooting off to the middle or side of the road, until I got used to it.

Wayland Young, later Lord Kennet, also became a life-long friend dating from that time. He insisted on my coming to stay at his family's country house in Norfolk. He was Peter Scott's half-brother, whom I met later when one of his children and Candy (or was it Tim?) were born on the same day at a nursing home in Welbeck Street. Much later he gave one of his signed prints to Diana and me as a wedding present, organised by Wayland. But I did not enjoy country house weekends in Norfolk any more than in Hampshire. I had no proper clothes, no money and little conversation, since I avoided talking about myself as much as possible. And since the interest of the people who invited me was mostly in my background, these encounters never seemed much of a success to me. My main memories of Wayland's home are of having forgotten to bring any pyjamas and having to borrow his Lordship's, not being anything like as clever at word games and charades as the others, and getting knocked off a sailing dinghy on the Broads when something called the boom swung across and hit me in the middle.

46 · 1946

SOMEHOW I got through the summer of 1946 in this way. I hardly went home because a room cost money, and life with my parents was not cheerful. Judy had meanwhile won a scholarship to the Central School of Arts and Crafts. She was learning to draw and paint. For the first time, at the age of 23, she was beginning to feel happy, and she had gone off to Wales with a group of friends. My parents, on the other hand, were probably unhappier than they had ever been, even though the war was over and Nazidom had been crushed in a way which they must have dreamed about for years. Their financial situation was disastrous, only kept going by such semi-secretarial jobs as my mother could still get. But with the return of so many from the war, and her increasing age, this was becoming more and more difficult.

Judy remembers that at this point our mother got so desperate that she finally took the cyanide pill which Janos had given her years earlier against the possibility of a German invasion. But fortunately it didn't work. He may have given her a placebo, knowing of her ideas about suicide even before we came to England, or it may have lost its power over the years. We don't know the truth now and I knew nothing about it then. But I did know how deeply unhappy she was. My father was approaching 80 and earning nothing, though his spirit never flagged. He saw the end of the war as a new turning point in his life when his voice would again be heard. His sorrow was for my mother's unhappiness and her daily worries about money, when he could do nothing to help.

My mother's only comfort and hope were my successes. She related them to everyone she knew, with embellishments of the English scene and society in which she saw me move, or as she imagined it. She really lived through and for me. It must have been about then that I realised how close to the edge she lived. In 1942, for my 21st birthday, she had surprised me by giving me a pair of hairbrushes made of dark hardwood and engraved with my initials, which I still have. But she refused absolutely to tell me how she could have afforded them. They were probably not particularly expensive. But virtually all the family shopping in those days was done at Woolworth's, where sixpence was still the maximum price, though it bought a lot. She then told us, much later, that she had stolen them from Harrods and had saved up to have them engraved at a small shop off Putney High Street. I was horrified, but I think that Judy had known or suspected it anyway. And, knowing our mother, we were not surprised to hear that she regarded it as an achievement, as a brave and necessary act, and not something which was really wrong. She pointed out that they were wooden, not silver. I remember that the conversation ended with talk about a piano. This had been my mother's greatest wish ever since we had left Berlin. Judy and I begged her not to wheel one out of Harrods onto the Brompton Road with the excuse that she wanted to see what it looked like in daylight.

I expect that there were other episodes like the hairbrushes and find it hard to think about them. Not because of the shoplifting, of course, but because of what my mother must have gone through in those days. I had been able to send her a little occasional money when I was in the Air Force, but by now I needed every penny to survive at Cambridge.

To escape all this I went back early to Cambridge to work, as one could, because it was the only place where I felt secure. I was now in College, on H staircase in the Old Court, and life became quite enjoyable. There were lots of friends and a number of episodic girlfriends, and although I could not go skiing or on holidays like the others I was beginning to feel that I belonged. A great burst of confidence came with a letter from the Home Office to say that my naturalisation had come through. I had applied in 1944 when this part of the Home Office reopened. On 4 December 1946 I duly appeared before a Justice of the Peace, a doctor who was a friend of Edith Brighton, and took the Oath of Allegiance before her. This was the second time; I had already taken it once in 1941 before some Air Force officer, who would have had no idea that he was swearing in an enemy alien.

Later on, in 1947, my parents and Judy were also naturalised. It was amazing that we now all had passports after 13 years without them. In a rare burst of extravagance and joy my father sent me a telegram in Cambridge. 'Proud to be your countryman.'

47 · 1947

BY THE SUMMER of 1947 my life was changing. I was not 'enjoying' myself, a word which I have always disliked and never use. But my time was so crammed with things which I had to do, that I was happy. And that is the way in which I have been happy all my life.

It started with Part II of the Tripos and getting a Double First. Then I went to three May Balls running, Monday, Tuesday and Wednesday, without going to bed. How I managed to pay for them I cannot remember, but I think they were with different girls who paid for themselves. On the Monday, when Clare and Trinity have their ball, I had a date with Wayland for breakfast and punting to Grantchester. When we got to his rooms at 6.00 there was a girl asleep on his sofa. Not Anthea Sutherland of the night before, as I got to know her later, but Liz Young and later Kennet, as she was to be. Wayland put his finger on his lips and said: "I've swapped."

On the Tuesday or Wednesday morning of that week I passed my driving test, having had some more practice with the cars of friends, but never a lesson. This was necessary because John Butler, Ronnie Coubrough and I were planning a great holiday immediately afterwards. Ronnie, who had some money, had bought an ex-Army van for £100, christened 'the hearse,' and we decided to go on a camping tour for two months. The question was where. We opened a map of Europe and stuck in a pin. It landed in the middle of Enare or Inarji, a huge lake in northern Finland. So we decided that we would swim in it.

We took the hearse across to Gothenburg on a cargo ship; there were not yet any ferries. We then drove to Oslo and Bergen, and then along the great northern highway to Trondheim, Narvik, Tromsö and Hammerfest on the North Cape, about 400 miles beyond the Arctic Circle. We had two small tents and Army sleeping bags and slept out every night. But it was a hot summer and we soon stopped using the tents. There were a few memorable events. I drove the hearse into a ditch, but the others forgave me. At Abisko, on Lake Torneträsk near Narvik (about which I wrote a poem), the mosquitoes were terrible and only alleviated in my case, but not the others', by a Swedish girl about whom Ronnie still talks with bitterness, because he saw her first. Then, somewhere on the road and miles from anywhere there was a terrible sight of a huge cemetery in the wilderness, with thousands of graves of workers whom the Germans had brought from Yugoslavia and Greece during the war to build the highway to the North Cape. And then another one with hundreds of graves of Germans and Russians who died when the Russian armies invaded from the north before the German defeat.

But my most vivid and embarrassing memory was waking up one Sunday morning. The previous night it had been dark before we found a camping place behind some bushes off a side road. When I woke up in my sleeping bag there were three black figures bending over me. I looked around and realised that we were in a Swedish churchyard, in front of the porch of the church, on a Sunday morning, with the congregation just arriving, all severely dressed in black. It was like a scene out of an Ingmar Bergman film. I didn't know what to do. For one thing, I had no pyjama trousers. So I just looked at them and said good morning and that I was sorry. This seemed to satisfy them and they all drifted into the church. Ronnie and John were further away among some gravestones and less involved, roaring with laughter, and as soon as the church door closed we all jumped into the hearse without dressing and drove away. For me it was a worse awakening than when my face was licked by a cow, a most unpleasant rasping sensation even when one hasn't shaved.

We were the first tourists to reach Hammersfest since the war, and I have a long article in the local Norwegian paper about us. Then we drove south-east, through Lapland. But the main villages, Karasjok and Kautokeino, were deserted except for the very old and a few of the reindeer. All the rest of the population was high up in the snow, together with the herds. We crossed into Finland, drove to the shore of Lake Enare and duly swam in it; it was deep and bitterly cold. But my main memory of our time in northern Finland was lying in my sleeping bag in a huge birch forest somewhere between Ivalo and Rovaniemi. It is strange how these wonderful names have remained with me. At that time of the year it never got dark and we saw no aurora borealis until further south. But we were back below the Arctic Circle, where the sun sinks just below the horizon and rolls around it all night. So there was a blood- red sunset to the south of us travelling from west to east for many hours. And I remember lying there thinking that I would never see it again and would never come back. And of course I never did.

We then drove south to Tornio and Haparanda, at the top of the Baltic, and left the car to take a train down to Helsinki. The engine was fired by logs, it never did more than 20 mph, and it stopped every two or three hours at stations for food and to take on more fire-wood and water. In Helsinki we got to know some Finnish families who spoilt us, delighted to meet people from England after the long war, and we exchanged Christmas cards for years. The English were then highly popular everywhere, because everyone realised that Germany would certainly have won if it had not been for Churchill and England.

We went back north to Haparanda, picked up the car and drove down to Stockholm and then across to Oslo, where we made some long-term friends. A boy of about 15, Finn Sohol, carrying a tennis racket, picked us up when we were camping on a beach in Bygdoy. Later on he became the Norwegian champion and played for Norway in the Davis Cup. He was keen to practise his English and took us to his home nearby. That was an instant success on both sides. His parents loved the English, played bridge, had a tennis court, and also a daughter, Inger-Johanne. We transferred our sleeping bags to their garden and stayed nearly a week.

Thereafter I-J, as she was always called, became quite important in my life for a year or two. I went back to visit her in Norway once or twice, and then she came to live in England, to learn English and to work at her Embassy. But although we were very close, and she even came to share a flat in Ladbroke Gardens with Judy and me, we gradually went into a decline. I-J in Norway, like Sally in the Air Force, were different from how they seemed in England and in Cambridge. But she remained a life-long friend and many of my friends, in particular Edith Brighton. For years she didn't get married, and then, shortly before her wedding to an outstanding Norwegian Air Force officer, he was shot by a madman who called himself the King of Lapland. He had gone to find and arrest him and was shot as he got out of a small seaplane on a lake. It was a tragic national sensation in Norway, in particular for I-J. But she finally married in her forties, when I met her again on a visit to give a talk to the Law Faculty at Oslo University.

But all that came later. There was more travelling in 1947, now that I had a passport. First, there was the trip to Prague for the meeting of the *Institut de Droit International*, about which I have already written, when I met the Czech girl who gave me the 1933 photos from the Sonne in Küsnacht. Damaris came along as well, which I had forgotten until Judy told me. We all met up in Paris with a group of her friends.

It was strange to be back in a new Europe, and strange to see Michèle and her parents, Fernand and Maggie, after all these years. And wonderful to be back in Paris, which had survived the war without damage. The London Blitz was terrible. But the German occupation of Paris must have been worse, in a different way.

48 · Michèle

I MUST SAY something about Michèle Fizaine, because she was so much a French child of her time and then a product of the German occupation. But it was never a happy story. Throughout the war we thought about each other and wondered what would happen when we met again. But when we finally did, we had both changed. She had spent the whole of the war in Paris and had had a terrible time, as all Parisians did who hated the Germans. The only way to survive was to collaborate or to operate in the black market. By the time of the liberation Michèle was a tall, voluptuous blonde of about 21 and was determined to get out of the misery left by the war and to marry the first GI who asked her. This did not take long and she moved to New York, where she became a model. She then met a wealthy art dealer and collector, Daniel Wildenstein, and they were together for many years. She divorced her GI, came back to Paris and lived in an apartment in Neuilly which Daniel had bought for her. She never had to work again, but she was also never happy.

We had first met after the war when she came over to England with Daniel. But our much-anticipated meeting, after all these years of expectation, was clearly a disappointment for us both. She was too hard and rich and sure of herself, at least on the surface, and I had become too English and conventional, and therefore boring as well as poor. But it didn't always stay that way. I went to see her in Paris several times when work took me there, and one long weekend we seemed to fall desperately in love and it passed like a dream. I remember the most peculiar happening afterwards. I was due to meet Geoffrey Lewis, a partner in Herbert Smith and also a close friend, on the Sunday evening in the George V, for a conference with some French lawyers on the following day. But when we met in the hotel I found that I couldn't speak to him. I could not speak a single word of English, literally. Only French. I had been with Michèle for several days, back together in Paris, and I had reverted to my childhood. Geoffrey said nothing; he knew me quite well, and I think he sensed something of what had happened. So I went to my room and began to re-read the papers for the next day. Then everything fell into place again, we had dinner, and I reverted back to being an English barrister.

There were one or two more weekends with Michèle in Paris and in

Michèle Fizaine, about 1960.

her family country house near Pontoise. But it was never again the same. She travelled incessantly with Daniel and a number of jetset girl-friends, and got involved with pictures and antiques. But basically she was always lonely. Much later she got cancer. Although Julia and she never liked each other I never gave her up as a friend. When she was told that the doctors could do no more for her in Paris she came to London, and I tried to help her to get the best advice. But she was already in a bad state. She had always been very tall and later became quite large. But towards the end she was visibly wasting away. I helped as much as I could with doctors, but it was clear that there was no hope. After she went back to Paris she wrote me a last letter to say that she wanted to leave me her country house, where I had so often stayed. The flat had always been owned by Daniel Wildenstein. Fernand, her father, had then died long ago and Maggie was very old and lived in Lorraine. Michèle wrote that she had no one else to leave it to.

I heard nothing for some time, and then that she had died after her next operation and had been buried in the family grave in Lorraine. Needless to say, I also heard no more about the house. But for years she had been one of the greatest friends of my youth, a tragic misfit due to her childhood under the Germans in Paris throughout the war, and never happy again.

I have written about her because no one else ever will, and because I often felt that I had let her down. But at the end of the day one can only be one person in real life, however many others one would like to think of being, for oneself and others.

49 · Going to the Bar

I MUST GET ON to the next stages of my parents' lives, the final one for my father. But first I must fill in the background and my own life after Cambridge.

I have always felt as though nothing really noteworthy happened to me after the war, or at any rate after I went to the Bar. That is how it seems, however stupid it may sound. Perhaps everyone feels like that about their youth, even when there was nothing unusual about it. The events and their memories are more vivid, and one can face up to them because one was not yet responsible for one's life. So one is not judged in the same way as later.

Whatever may be the reason, the first twenty-eight years of my life were quite different, and much more personal to me, than the next fifty plus, and it is really about the first twenty-eight, and my parents, that I wanted to write. I have a horror of legal memoirs. One of Julia's ancestors in the 1870s was also a judge and I found his small vellum-bound volume in a glass bookcase at her parents' home, Wyck Cottage in Sussex. It had obviously been published privately, and was entitled *Legal Tea Leaves*. You can see what I mean. But those were no doubt memoirs for his colleagues and friends in the law and his legal posterity, which these certainly are not. My cousin Peter Rickham, about whom I wrote earlier, ended his memoirs with his 30th birthday and the beginning of his brilliant career. However, having got this far, I might as well sketch in the rest. But only as an account of events, not of a career or a list of cases; and leaving out all emotions. I have already written too much about some girlfriends, and about people who are still alive. And, unlike my cousin Peter, I do not believe that our children are in the least bit interested in our philosophy of life at any stage of our or their lives. His memoirs are interleaved with wise reflections and comments on the contemporary scene, most of which I skipped, as I told him.

So this will be mainly, if not entirely, a chronicle of events. As a lawyer would say: facts, not law. And even if I stopped writing about my own life, which I could and perhaps should, I must complete the story of my parents.

In the autumn of 1947 I had a number of choices. I was sounded out about Law Fellowships at Clare and King's, and the venerable Dr Daube, Reader in Roman Law, did his best to persuade me to devote my life to this burning topic, in which he said he could guarantee me a glittering future. I have always found it difficult to say no to offers. But fortunately I did to all of these, and later on I sometimes had nightmares that I might have become an academic lawyer. Although I knew practically nothing about it, my idea was to go to the Bar. To be a solicitor never occurred to me for a moment. I didn't want to be employed or to have partners, and it is only recently that the solicitors' profession is becoming as varied and exciting as the Bar.

Inevitably there were a number of people who helped me. If you had no money and no contacts you could not go the Bar, at any rate not then. But the Bar was then a small world, and if you had a good academic record, one or two words in the right direction were sufficient to get you in somewhere.

Old Professor Hollond, who held the chair in English law at Trinity, was a friend of Janos Plesch. He insisted on giving his lectures at 9 am, and mostly without the new teeth for which he was waiting, and I had therefore never met him. Now I was sent to see him and found him wrapped in a rug on a sofa in his rooms in Trinity. He said that Janos had saved his life, but that he was now dying. He went on saying this for a further 20 years into his nineties. He also said: "Young man, you must go and join Lincoln's Inn." So I said that I would, although I was not quite sure what or where it was, but I knew that one had to join something. In those days there was no Law Tutor at Clare or recruitment by the Inns, so one had to find out for oneself.

This proved to be a good idea so far as it went. On my next visit to London I found Lincoln's Inn and somehow raised the £70 to join as a student, which is all one paid for the rest of one's life. Now you pay a bit more, but the principle is the same. The Under Treasurer also suggested that I should fill in some forms applying for scholarships. I had more or less forgotten about this, but a few months later I was summoned to an interview. There were about 40 people in the waiting room and my heart sank, although I really had no expectations except for having no money. In due course I was called in before a large gathering presided over by Viscount Simonds, before whom I was to appear again in the House of Lords and Privy Council in later years. He asked me some questions about my exam results, which they all had on paper before them, and I was out in under a minute. Needless to say I thought I had no chance. But I got the Cassel, the top scholarship, which had presumably already been decided in advance, £300 a year for 3 years and extendable. Security. Another thanks to this country. The Bar was now a reality.

Then I also got help from Cambridge by offers to do supervisions of law students at Clare and King's, and I think one or two other colleges as well. This meant that I could easily keep myself, since I could stay with Edith and Peter. It also meant that I would have to cram for the Bar Finals on my own in Cambridge, without going to any lectures in London, where I had nowhere to stay, but that did not matter too much in those days. And there were not yet again any obligatory dinners in Hall for Bar students. Three of the four Inns were bombed and their Halls were destroyed. Lincoln's alone had escaped, and in those days it was said that that was the one which should have been hit, before Victorian beauty was rediscovered. So I worked for the Bar from Cambridge as best I could, and in those days the exams were nothing like as difficult as now. I took them at Easter and came second or third of the Seconds. There was no First; there rarely was in those days. But two years earlier Brian Grant had got a First, and a Certificate of Honour, still hopping about on one leg and crutches, bless him.

Next there was the question of finding a pupillage and Chambers. My uncle Nucki was a close friend of Sir John Foster, as he later became, an impressive figure and personality in the law, politics and socially. I was sent to see him in the House of Commons. He said that he would like to take me but couldn't, because he was taking Silk at Easter. However, he was either making an excuse or he failed to get it, until the following year. If I had gone to him in what became 2 Hare Court and now Blackstone Chambers my life at the Bar would have been entirely different. I would have been competing at short range with Mark Littman, who later became a close friend, in a general and far more fashionable practice than Essex Court, and I am not sure how good or comfortable I would have been in it.

So then I turned to Arnold McNair, already an elder statesman and later to be President of the International Court at the Hague and of Caius College, Cambridge. He knew me as an Old Aldenhamian, and I had already been to Prague as his assistant. He asked me what sort of practice I was interested in. I said that it should preferably be international, since I spoke languages. He said that in that case I must certainly go into the Chambers of his brother, William McNair, in 3 Essex Court, Middle Temple, because his practice involved shipping and required constant travel. Later on I discovered that apart from fishing regularly in Scotland, Willie had only once been out of England, when he was asked to go to Lisbon to advise on a scuttling case, which settled as soon as he arrived. But he spoke fluent Scottish.

Before I could take up this offer I got some more help in a remarkable way. When I was at Cambridge I noticed that I was getting deaf in one ear and went to see a well-known ENT specialist there, the father of a friend. He said that I was suffering from some blockage which had probably been due to flying with colds, the endless 'circuits and bumps' with their constant changes of pressure. He tried to blow it out, or something, but it seemed to make no difference. Then one day, when I rang Judy at home to see if there was any mail, she said that there was a letter from Air Ministry, or perhaps the Ministry of Pensions. I asked her to open it and she found a kind of silver button with some patriotic message around the rim, as was then worn by wounded ex-servicemen to encourage people to give up their seats for them on buses and the tube. There was obviously some mistake, but then she found a letter. This said that I had been awarded a gratuity of £150 for war injury and was classified as 10 per cent disabled due to partial deafness. It also said that I could appeal to be classified as disabled to the extent of 14 per cent or more, in which case I would quality for a pension.

I heard later on that the ENT specialist had written to Air Ministry and applied on my behalf without telling me. Needless to say, I was overjoyed with the £150, which I got a few weeks later. I had been greatly worried about the 100 guineas which one then had to pay to one's pupil master at the beginning to cover the year's pupillage. £150 was then a small fortune to me, and with it and the Cassell I knew that I could face the Bar. It was one of the most important financial events of my life.

Two Postscripts:

First, when I began to get deaf in the other ear a few years later, it became clear that the cause had nothing to do with flying. It was otosclerosis, probably hereditary, perhaps from that distant great-aunt Lucy in Paris with her ear trumpet. So the great ENT man had been wrong. But he had said that he wasn't sure, and perhaps he had merely given me the benefit of the doubt. I saw no need to trouble any government department with this news.

Secondly, I never had to pay a pupillage fee. John Megaw, a giant Ulsterman in 3 Essex Court, said that he would take me as a pupil on Arnold McNair's recommendation. We were both agonisingly shy with each other, but he was firm on two points. I must never call him Sir, and he refused to accept any pupillage fee.

So I was now finally set for the Bar. I was called in April 1948, by Lincoln's Inn, together with Tony Lincoln, at whose funeral I had to speak some years ago. We had met in Oxford arguing a moot against each other on behalf of the two university Law Societies. It was on a recent controversial case called *High Trees*, decided by a controversial young judge called Denning. Tony Lincoln duly won before the Oxford don who had set the moot, convinced that the case had been wrongly decided. All law dons usually think that all judges are wrong. This is part of their *métier* and stock-in-trade. (Apologies to any who may ever read this). But it would never have occurred to me that one day I would sit with Tom Denning in the Court of Appeal, and that he would become something of a friend and protector.

The final event was that of course I had to move to London. Judy and I decided to share a flat. We found one in an attic in Ladbroke Gardens near Notting Hill Gate full of broken furniture which we mostly piled up to the ceiling on a huge shelf covering the tank beside the bath. The flat could take three or four people, and many came and went, with Ronnie being the first. Judy had already earned some money decorating a restaurant near Victoria, and had had other jobs and teaching Art part-time. Then she met Tom, already a rising BBC author, who got her a job in the newly emerging world of TV in which he was to become famous. But meanwhile all that we knew was that between the two of us we could just afford the rent for Ladbroke Gardens. We were twenty-seven and twenty-five and it was our first home since the Grunewald, when we had been twelve to the day and getting on for ten.

I bought a double bed in the Portobello Road for £14. It had a lot of character and I managed to hold on to it as a spare into my second marriage, for about 30 years, before I was forced to let it go.

50 · My mother leaves

I MUST NOW GO BACK to my parents and to 1947.

My mother was sinking into ever greater despair. The world was changing for the better. People could travel again, though they could only take out £25. But she hadn't even got that, and she was now fifty. The labour market was awash with young people returning from the war, and new hope all around her. She applied in vain for a job with the British Control Commission in Germany. But she was now too old. So life would finally pass her by.

But then came what she saw as her miraculous salvation: employment by the Americans in Germany as an interpreter. At first in Frankfurt, and then an offer of glamorous promotion to the Nürnberg War Crimes trials, for which simultaneous interpreters were needed. She was obviously made for one of the jobs that were going there. The Americans were far more imaginative in their employment policy in post-war Germany than the British Civil Service, and also far more interested when they learned about her connection with my father. Once they had understood the position, there was never any doubt that she would get a job with them.

But this salvation for her was very hard on my father.

He could not have stopped her, and he never even tried. Her argument was money, to which there was no answer. The pay and allowances were munificent. Of course that was no argument that would have moved my father to accept a separation. But he knew that she desperately wanted to get away and had to get away. So he never tried to stop her, although it must have hurt him deeply.

She started in Nürnberg in the autumn of 1947. By her standards she had a wonderful time, although the city lay in ruins, as did the whole of Germany. But she was there as part of the Allied Forces, well paid in US dollars, and with access to the PX, the American Army stores which had everything, without any rationing. And literally anything was obtainable in Germany in return for the cartons of cigarettes and nylons which one could get quite cheaply from the PX. In addition, she found the work fascinating. At the trials she met a lot of interesting and important people, and with her name and background she soon became something of a celebrity.

So her life had changed at last, just when she had thought that it never would. The only shadow was my father. She wrote, phoned when she could, which was very difficult until much later, sent him lots of money, such as they had not seen for fifteen years, and also came back for short leaves once or twice. We must have been all together on 25 December 1947, his eightieth birthday, but I have no recollection of it. I only remember the laconic poem about his expected approaching death, which he then sent on printed thank-you cards to well-wishers, as he had done on his 50th, 60th and 70th birthdays. The poems survive him in his re-published works to this day.

Until Judy and I got our flat together when I came down from Cambridge, Judy had lived in digs in Putney round the corner, and she went to see him nearly every evening on her way back from art school. But after my mother had left he was mostly all alone, and he missed her terribly. There was some compensation. For the first time in eight years he could leave England and travel to his beloved France. He loathed to be kept by my mother, with money from Nürnberg, and worried about the Exchange Control Regulations when she provided the money abroad. But her job opened a window for him, for the last time. He went to Paris once more, back to the Fizaines, to the sun and to wine, after the kind of prison that London and the boarding houses in Putney had been for so long. My mother also arranged for him to travel on to Switzerland and to pay a brief secret visit across the frontier to the ruins of Nürnberg. But then he felt that he had to get back to his typewriter to put it all down, in the hope that there would be some official invitation back to Germany, with recognition of the role which he could still play.

During the summer of 1948 he was back in Putney, and mostly quite alone. Once or twice he came to visit Judy and me in our attic flat in Ladbroke Gardens, climbing all the stairs without any visible effort, and trying to understand how we lived. And when we could, we visited him in Putney, but not as often as we should have done, at any rate in my case. I was starting to do what I have done ever since. To work without ceasing, and usually without having to make any great effort to make myself do it. It simply became a way of life, and still is.

I remember one of the last occasions when I saw him. I had been sent to Kingston Magistrates Court to appear for the wife of a wealthy Greek shipowner who had been charged with some traffic offence. I remember nothing of what happened, but on the way back to the Temple I called in to see my father in his boarding house in Lytton Grove in Putney. He was typing in his room, as always, with manuscripts and books everywhere. I had given him all the books which I had got as prizes or somehow collected at school, English, French and German classics; and when I got them back after his death I found innumerable little red dots in the margin where he had marked passages and scribbled a few notes. It was a fine day and I dragged him out into the garden. He made me explain about my work and what my case had been about, and he was thrilled with it, or with the way I explained it. He then did something quite uncharacteristic, because he generally avoided social contacts. He took me round to introduce me to all the old people sitting in the garden and the entrance hall, saying: "This is my son. He defends people."

Soon afterwards, and the thought of it almost makes me believe in something, he got the call for which he had been waiting so long. It came from the British Council or some predecessor organisation connected with the Foreign Office. He was invited to visit the main cities in the Allied control zones in Germany to see what was happening to the new beginnings of the German theatre and to write about it. He was overjoyed. It was towards the end of September 1948, when he was coming up to eighty-one. He was to fly to Hamburg, his favourite German city, and he had never flown before.

I recently discovered an old notebook in which I had kept a very irregular diary over the years 1944 to 1950. It contains four closely written pages about the events of the next two weeks. I had not been aware of its existence when I wrote the first version of this book about nine years ago. Now I can be accurate about things which I had previously forgotten.

On the night before he was to fly I fetched him from Putney with his battered suitcase and typewriter, and the diary records that we took a No 14 bus to Knightsbridge and then changed to a No 52 which stopped by our flat in Ladbroke Gardens. He spent his last night in England in my bed, sleeping in his clothes, and Judy produced some breakfast before the taxi which had been ordered for 6.15 at his insistence. We arrived an hour too early at what was then Kensington High Street Air Terminal, and he relaxed for the first time, saying "Ich habs geschafft", (I've made it). He was in high spirits, and the diary says that he looked marvellous.

He adored the flight and scribbled some notes which have survived. Impressions of snowy clouds and vistas of blue sky beyond, all new to him from the air, and a line saying that hereafter one might see quite different celestial realms, but they would not be sunlit. When he landed in Hamburg in the afternoon there was a welcoming party. There were speeches and he was taken to his hotel, the Atlantic, which had survived the bombs and which he had known all his adult life. He then insisted on going to the theatre that night, which was *Romeo and Juliet* performed by the local company in the Stadttheater, and he overrode all objections, asking only that the taxi should go past the harbour on the way so that he could see it again, although heavily bombed. At the theatre a lot of people were introduced to him and it became a festive evening. But it must have all been too much for him. When he was taken back to his room in the hotel and had got into bed, he had a stroke. It paralysed the whole of one side and he fell on the floor, unable to breathe properly. He spent six hours crawling to the door. They found him there in the morning, unable to move anything on his right side and only able to speak with difficulty. Later on he said that his stroke had had nothing to do with the performance. "*Na, so schlecht war es doch nicht.*" It wasn't that bad!

51 · My father's death

JUDY AND I first heard about it after my mother had arrived in Hamburg from Nürnberg, and then few details. Telephoning was still difficult. But we understood that our father had been taken to a British military hospital because he had had a stroke and that he didn't want us to come to see him. He was not vain, but always fastidious and private, and my mother explained that he didn't want us to see him partially paralysed. So we wrote some 'Gute Besserung' letters and just waited for news. It was only later that we knew what had happened.

At first it seemed that he might get better, and he made my mother return to Nürnberg. But as soon as she went, he got much worse, helplessly paralysed on one side and unable to breathe without great pain. All he could do was speak with difficulty and scribble with his left hand. So my mother rushed back. He then knew that he would not recover and that he could not stay on drugs much longer. So he only had one insistent message for her, to help him to bring it to an end. He begged and commanded her, and told her that it was the last thing which she must do for him. "You are my mortal enemy if you don't".

My mother had never been opposed to suicide and thought that it was absurd that it was still a crime in England. But it was, and my father was in the British zone in a military hospital. This was a problem. But help was to come from a Scottish businessman and former journalist, temporarily a Major in the Army, who must remain nameless. His job was to supervise *Die Welt*, one of the few German papers which were again being published. He had known nothing of my father previously, except that he had been assigned to look after him during his stay. He then learned about him from the Germans and got to know him and my mother when my father was in hospital. So he began to understand. And my mother could be very persuasive and insistent. In the end he agreed to go and see a German doctor whom he knew. In the ruins of Hamburg, under Allied occupation, it was all still like wartime, and many things were possible. And the doctor, whom I should have liked to have known, agreed to help my father by providing some pills, 20 Luminal.

All this took nearly two weeks. A few people managed to see my father during this time, despite his objections. One was a well-known journalist from *Die Welt*, Willy Haas, who wrote about it all some years later and

Last picture of my father on landing in Hamburg, 1948.

said that my father had agreed that they should call each other '*Du.*' But Judy and I knew nothing.

A date was then agreed between my parents and the Scottish Major, and the pills were put into a folded envelope in my father's wallet, "to be taken in fives". To avoid suspicion, he insisted that my mother must again return to Nürnberg, knowing that she would be recalled again the following day. Then they had a final day together before she left.

And then it happened as arranged, during the night of 12 October 1948. The Major went to see my father in the evening, to try to dissuade him for the last time, and also to ensure that no last notes would be left lying around. My father was in good spirits, but quite unmovable. He said that he had to confess that whoever was paying the bill for the Atlantic would be cheated, because he had ordered the most expensive wine, but noticed too late that the waiter had brought a cheaper brand. At the end his last words were: "Lead on, Scotsman". He was found dead early in the morning

But he had left some notes, scribbled with his left hand on torn off bits of paper. They were found by the Scotsman in the morning and later given to my mother. The originals are in the Alfred Kerr Archiv in the Akademie der Künste in Berlin, but I have copies and more or less know them by heart. He wrote, apart from personal messages to the three of us and thanks to the Scottish Major, "my last and best friend":

'Midnight. When the nurse comes in the morning she will find me dead. I loved life greatly, but put an end to it when it became torment.'

And then on another piece in a closed envelope addressed to me:

"Dear son. Observations. The sexual drive remains, strangely, for weeks before one dies. There is still a strong impulse to pinch the nurses' bottoms. This is only mentioned to establish a fact, for science. Everything must be said which is true and worth knowing. It is a strange world. Don't speak about this to women . . . It may lessen your grief, but increase your knowledge. Sadly, that's how things are. Ultimately the world is incredibly comic, and this should at least be stated."

All the messages to us were of course in German. But there was also an open note in English on the table beside him, carefully prepared:

'I did it when the balance of my mind was disturbed.'

That was his way of seeking to protect me and my career against any possible consequences of my father having committed suicide, which was then still a crime. He had so much faith in England that he must have thought it would work.

But there were no consequences. My mother was again called back from Nürnberg. I don't know who signed the Death Certificate or how it was worded. But it was treated as death from natural causes.

It was only then that Judy and I heard, and only that he had died. When we arrived in Hamburg we gradually learned the details, and after a while my mother showed us the notes. A lot of people came to say how sorry they were and we got very friendly with the Scottish Major. There were newspaper articles about a great loss for the new Germany, 'just when he was about to come back.' They were annoying because they implied that my father might have returned to live in Germany, which he would never have done. It was a confusing week. And we saw him once more, lying slightly on his side behind a huge glass pane. He looked very small and white.

My father had given clear instructions about his funeral. As he had said all his life, there was to be no priest of any kind, no service, and no reference to religion. His only wish, if it was possible, was that the Second Movement of Beethoven's Seventh Symphony should be played, the one with the slow, gentle lament like a funeral march. And so it happened, but I don't remember how it was arranged. It was in the Musikhalle, a large hall in the city which had escaped bombing. When we were first taken to see it, Furtwaengler was rehearsing. Then it was filled with flowers. On the day there were about 250 people, the orchestra, and the small coffin on the stage, covered by a Union Jack, which would have made him laugh. I have the photographs somewhere. Then the Hamburg Philharmonic Orchestra, under its conductor Professor Karl Jochum, played the Beethoven beautifully. My diary says: "The forte was terrible to bear, a dreadful inevitability". And then I had to make a speech. I have a photograph of me standing on the stage, but I cannot remember much of what I said. My diary says that I spoke first in German and then in English. I must have said how much my father loved Germany and the German language all his life. But there would certainly have been no note of forgiveness, and I certainly said that he had had no intention of returning. But how happy he would have been to have heard his favourite piece of music. And perhaps he was.

I have been told that there is a tape or transcript of the speech in the Akademie, but I have never looked at it.

After the ceremony we took the coffin out to a crematorium in Ohlsdorf, a huge park on the outskirts of Hamburg which is the largest cemetery in Europe. We were driven around to choose a place. He is buried there under some trees, and he would not have wished for anything else. My mother and I arranged for a simple large stone with his name and dates, in a style of that time, which has evidently since acquired some artistic interest, though that was not the object. She joined him there 17 years later with a similar smaller stone at his feet. I have often been there. The cemetery is so vast, with roads for cars and buses, that I have always had great difficulty in finding the grave, even with a marked map. I have also seen many pictures of it in press cuttings which people have sent to us from Germany. And the Senate of the City of Hamburg has now taken over the care of the grave in perpetuity. I have been to Hamburg several times for legal conferences and always go to see it. Candy, Jo and Tim saw it in 1967, two years after my mother's death, when I was there with Julia, together with Judy and Tom and their children. The occasion was the opening of an exhibition about my father's life and works, the first of many in different cities over the next decades. And Diana, Lucy and Alexander saw it when we went on our disappointing holiday to Neuhaus on the Baltic.

* * *

Two postscripts.

Perhaps it is unnecessary to say so, but of course I agreed entirely with what my father did to end his life, and I am proud that he did it. He was entirely clear in his mind and he would have wanted nothing else. People may not be entitled to commit suicide in all circumstances, where others depend on them. But my father was absolutely right and it was typical of him. He died as he had lived. If the circumstances are similar, I hope that I will have the strength to do the same.

I therefore also agree with what my mother did, and of course she never had any doubts about it either. Whether Judy sees it in quite the same way I didn't know at the time. I thought that she would have agreed for his sake, but might have had some reservation about my mother's decisiveness. But 50 years on, having now read this to help me with my recollection, she tells me that she never disagreed. My mother's – perhaps surprising – pragmatism in the events is totally overshadowed by what our father wanted.

The final postscript is a kind of farewell written by my father himself, now for himself.

His critical writings, essays and prose generally remain untranslatable. He was also a lyrical poet and a volume of his poems has recently been republished as part of his collected works. Most of them are equally hard to translate. He also wrote some poetry in French, including a moving call to his beloved Maggie Fizaine during the dark years of the war, which appears in the same book. But there is one poem in it which is an adaptation from the English. He always said that his favourite English poem was Christina Rossetti's 'Song.' Many have said that his version has the same beauty in German. Here they both are, as a farewell.

Song

When I am dead, my dearest,
Sing no sad songs for me;
Plant thou no roses at my head,
Nor shady cypress tree:

Be the green grass above me
With showers and dewdrops wet;

And if thou wilt, remember,
And if thou wilt, forget.

I shall not see the shadows,
I shall not feel the rain;
I shall not hear the nightingale
Sing on, as if in pain;
And dreaming through the twilight
That doth not rise nor set,
Haply I may remember,
And haply may forget.

Sterbelied

(Nach Christina Rossetti)

Lass, wenn ich tot bin, Liebster,
Lass Du von Klagen ab.
Statt Rosen und Zypressen
Wächst Gras auf meinem Grab.
Ich schlafe still im Zwielichtschein,
In schwerer Dämmernis –
Und wenn Du willst, gedenke mein;
Und wenn Du willst, vergiss.

Ich fühle nicht den Regen.
Ich seh nicht, ob es tagt,
Ich höre nicht die Nachtigall,
Die in den Büschen klagt.
Vom Traum erweckt mich keiner;
Die Erdenwelt verblich;
Vielleicht gedenk ich Deiner –
Vielleicht vergass ich Dich.

52 · A postscript

JUDY HAS read all of this and made a lot of helpful comments and corrections, which I have followed. But she also feels, more generally, that while I have got my mother entirely right, in some ways I have not drawn a true picture of our father, nor of the balance between him and my grandfather, who were such enemies. I agree with what she says and summarise it here.

First, it would be a mistake to think that my father's dislike of my grandfather had anything to do with his opposition to my mother's marriage, which was in any event less intense than that of my grandmother. She saw it in entirely personal terms, an old man for her young daughter, whereas he saw it more acceptably in terms of what he called '*der grosse Kerr*.' But Judy points out that there were many unpleasant aspects of my grandfather's personality which were not known to us, though they were obviously known to our father and explain his dislike of him. My grandfather was in many ways an unprincipled man, and certainly a coarse one. He gave unflattering nicknames to all the Reichenheim children, and two of them became known for years as '*Klosettdeckel*' (lavatory lid) and '*Spucknapf*' (cuspidor). A joke, but a cruel one. And he certainly hired thugs to beat up his son-in-law. How did he know where to find them? And had he hired them before to beat up someone else?

That is how my father saw him. And after our grandfather had retired as Secretary of State, a year before the advent of Hitler, when he was still only sixty, he never did another stroke of work for the rest of his life or tried to help any member of his family. He was supported entirely by his son Nucki, and it was also Nucki who paid the expenses of our time in Nice. Our grandfather just became a kind of leisurely retired *flâneur*..

Our father was totally different. He was a fighter all his life and full of energy until the end. And despite his aesthetic discrimination, sometimes to the point of arrogance, he was never a recluse who lived in an ivory tower of culture and literature. As a young man he was very sociable, and he wrote about it. '*Jeden Abend in die Gesellschaft*,' etc., parties in society every night. When we were children in Berlin our parents went out almost every evening, and not only to the theatre. He was not as remote as I may have described him. He made us laugh all the time with endless stories. I still tell many of them today, mostly Jewish or

Home Office No. K. 22204

Certificate No. AZ 20732

HOME OFFICE
7 JAN 1947
REGISTERED

BRITISH NATIONALITY AND STATUS OF ALIENS ACT, 1914

CERTIFICATE OF NATURALIZATION

Whereas **Michael Robert Emanuel Kerr**

has applied to one of His Majesty's Principal Secretaries of State for a Certificate of Naturalization, alleging with respect to **him** self the particulars set out below, and has satisfied him that the conditions laid down in the above-mentioned Act for the grant of a Certificate of Naturalization are fulfilled in **his** case:

Now, therefore, in pursuance of the powers conferred on him by the said Act, the Secretary of State grants to the said

Michael Robert Emanuel Kerr

this Certificate of Naturalization, and declares that upon taking the Oath of Allegiance within the time and in the manner required by the regulations made in that behalf **he** shall, subject to the provisions of the said Act, be entitled to all political and other rights, powers and privileges, and be subject to all obligations, duties and liabilities, to which a natural-born British subject is entitled or subject, and have to all intents and purposes the status of a natural-born British subject.

In witness whereof I have hereto subscribed my name this **4th** day of **December 1946.**

Under Secretary of State.

HOME OFFICE,
LONDON.

PARTICULARS RELATING TO APPLICANT

Full Name	Michael Robert Emanuel KERR
Address	Lytton Hall, Lytton Grove, London, S.W.15
Trade or Occupation	Law Student
Place and date of birth	Berlin. 1st March 1921
Nationality	Of no nationality
Single, Married, etc.	Single
Name of wife or husband	- - -
Names and nationality of parents	Alfred and Julia KERR (Of no nationality)

(For Oath *see overleaf*)

Certificate of Naturalisation, 1946.

about operatic fiascos, like Lohengrin missing the swan (sings on an empty stage "When does the next swan go?") or William Tell missing the apple (Sorrrrrry). Or about the proverbial refugee, boasting of past grandeur, and typified by the dachshund meeting an alsatian at a lamppost in Golders Green and explaining that in Vienna he had been a St. Bernard.

Above all, Judy points out that we both failed to see at the time what a great fighter he was, perhaps because our mother never praised him to us. We failed to see and understand all that he was trying to do throughout our emigration to survive financially and to save his family. He never talked about his efforts. We now know that he was constantly trying to interest people in new ideas for broadcasts, books and films and writing articles on spec., however discouraging the results. Our mother was different. She was making her own efforts in her own way. But we always knew all about them. Every unsuccessful phone call and every disappointing reply to every letter, was discussed with us in detail, together with even greater hopes for some alternative plan. But nothing was said about our father.

What he was doing he kept to himself. When, 20 years later, we were shown his correspondence with the BBC it was a revelation to us. He never gave up, however discouraging the responses. Any notions of rest and leisure would have been alien to him. Even after the war he was still earning a little money from BBC work written in French and translated into Spanish and Portuguese for broadcasting to South America. He was then 78. At 79, he had a slight stroke, when our mother was already in Germany. Judy was with him at the time, but I had totally forgotten. He recovered and continued to work as before and was still earning a little money at the time of his death, aged nearly 81, determined never to give up.

And he always had style. Brevity. In one of his last letters to me in the RAF in 1945, in the English which he had by then learned, he wrote: 'I like very much to write in French, because French is marvellous as an epigrammatic language. And in this confused world of babbling and chattering, only what is epigrammatic will survive.'

53 · Beginnings at the Bar

MY FATHER'S death in 1948 was the end of an era for me. But I was now 27 and in any event at the beginning of a new stage of my life. It was going to be work and work and work, and secondly marriage and children. I probably made a mistake in the way I allowed work to dominate my life. That is why I feel that nothing really happened after this time. But whether or not it was all a mistake, there is nothing I could or would have done differently. It's the way I am. And it still is, although I saw the other day – which I had forgotten – that I had put in Who's Who under Leisure: 'A second lot of children – trying not to work.' But not trying very hard, and certainly not succeeding. So a lot of what follows inevitably involves aspects of work.

I have taken a vow not to write about my endless cases at the Bar and on the Bench, and I promise only to mention a few special ones. But everyone remembers their earliest briefs.

In my year of pupillage there were two. Virtually the whole of Chambers was involved in *Ibarra*, a case about a large part of the Spanish merchant fleet during the Civil War. The owners were pro-Franco and based in the south, but the ships were all in Communist-held ports, Santander, Bilbao, Barcelona and Valencia, and they were all seized by the Republicans for the war against Franco. The insurers refused to pay because there was an exception of 'Seizure by Spanish authorities'. Were the Republican anti-Franco forces, whatever they called themselves, 'authorities' in the parts of Spain which they held? My sympathies were entirely with them; I had got deeply involved in the Spanish Civil War and knew a lot about it. But that was neither here nor there; this was the first of countless battles throughout my working life between insured and insurers in large-scale scenarios. Witnesses were collected from all over the world to describe what went on. One side presented a picture of order, organisation, uniforms, discipline and authority. On the other side the evidence concentrated on the burning of monasteries and convents, the shooting and raping of women and children, mob rule and private vendettas. The difficulty was to provide a convincing general picture through eye witnesses. But after about six weeks in the Commercial Court and the fascinating description of a lot of Spanish history, the insurers settled, I think for about 50 per cent. My part in this was to sit behind John Megaw and Eustace Roskill, the

Juniors on my side, as a 'devil' in my new wig and gown. I was still a pupil. But I did a lot of research and work, mainly on the evidence, and at the end they each gave me 50 guineas, on top of the pupillage fee which John had already refused. So I was doubly launched.

The second case was my own first brief. It was in the Westminster County Court, but relatively prestigious. I was briefed by Slaughter & May to appear for Air France in a case brought against them by Lord (Sydney) Bernstein, Chairman of Granada, as he later became. He had booked to fly to Paris but arrived only 25 minutes before take-off, and was then refused permission to board, although the aircraft was still there. So he chartered a plane and sued Air France for the cost. A lot turned on the small print of his ticket, which required him to be there at least half an hour before take-off. But Air France tickets were then still issued in French and he said that he couldn't speak a word of French and didn't know that the ticket contained any conditions. After a discussion about his education I took him through the heading on the first page, '*Conditions du Contrat de Transport.*' He reluctantly agreed that he could just about follow that, and in the end he duly lost and the case got in the papers. To appear for Air France briefed by 'Slaughters' was a bit of a coup which helped my morale, and I got a lot of work from them later on.

There's quite a lot of magic in names in litigation, such as appearing for Air France. I remember on my first day as a judge getting a surprising number of phone calls from well-wishing brethren just before I went into court. They all congratulated me and then enquired casually how it had happened that my first case in the printed Cause List involved an action against the BBC. But when I told them that it was about a tea-lady who had slipped on an oily patch in the canteen and broken her leg, they calmed down.

I really must stop writing about such trivia, or this will become as ridiculous as Muriel's great-grandfather's *Legal Tea Leaves*. But, going back to my early years at the Bar, there were not many trivia, or indeed anything else, to write about. There was very little work for the youngest members of my Chambers. John Donaldson, later to succeed Lord Denning as Master of the Rolls, had a few regular Rent Act cases from a solicitor in Edmonton County Court, and I used to trail along enviously to see how it was done. But most mornings were spent in the ABC in Fleet Street discussing what we could do to persuade Albert, the senior Clerk in Chambers, to bring in some County Court work. However, he was then the *doyen* of Barristers' Clerks in the most successful set of commercial Chambers in the Temple, and not interested in small work.

So, despite occasional bits of encouragement, the next year was pretty bleak. I just kept myself going with my supervisions at Cambridge every weekend and also did some evening teaching in London. In the summer of 1949 I answered an advertisement to coach a boy at his home in Sussex for the Cambridge Entrance exam. He was the son of an old retired Admiral and an energetic mother, determined to push him. But there was little that I could do for him, though his tennis got better. Once it had become clear that nothing would get him into Cambridge we got on very well, and I had a month's pleasant keep and earned a little money.

But by then I felt that I was in a state of crisis. There was no work, though the names of John Donaldson and other young men in Chambers were appearing in the diary against the names of prestigious City firms. I was sharing a room with a new arrival, Michael Holman, with great family shipping connections, who got a brief for a summons in the Commercial Court on his first afternoon. Later on he became one of my closest friends, and for ten years or so we stood on the terraces to watch Chelsea and Fulham on alternate Saturdays. He then left the Bar to run the family business until he died quite young, having chain-smoked all this life. But at that time, with such competition, I simply couldn't see how I would ever get any work.

There was also a new worry of a different kind. The hearing in my left ear had got worse and I began to feel that the right ear was weakening too. This of course is fatal for a barrister, who must hear the mumblings of the judge and witnesses, and the whispers – which I could never hear at all – of his solicitor sitting behind. And worrying made it worse. You get very tense, knowing that you won't hear what someone is about to say, and then of course you don't hear it.

At that point, in the spring of 1950, there came a great temptation to which I nearly succumbed. Later on I was to have nightmares that I might have accepted, like the Fellowships at Cambridge. I was asked by Lord McNair to accompany him again to the next meeting of the prestigious *Institut du Droit International,* in Bath on this occasion, after its last meeting in Prague. One of the main participants was Edvard Hambro, a Norwegian who was then the Secretary-General of the International Court of Justice at the Hague. He said that they were looking for a Registrar and that I would be ideal for the job. The salary was munificent and tax free, and the job carried diplomatic status. This meant that I would immediately be able to buy a car free of tax and duty, for which the waiting time was normally a year, and for about half the price. And although I would have to live at the Hague for most of the year, the work load was not at all that heavy and there would be long holidays.

I liked Hambro and his friends and we got on to a wave of mutual enthusiasm. He said that I could think about it until June, and I said that I thought I would accept.

Back in the Temple I asked for advice. No one would take the responsibility of advising against it. There was a lull at the Bar as the wartime disputes were coming to an end. My head of Chambers, Willie McNair, strongly advised me to go, as well as Harry Phillimore, later to go to the Court of Appeal, for whom I was doing some devilling. He said that he owed his practice entirely to two advantages, neither of which applied to me: his father (or grandfather) had been a judge, so that he had "a good judicial name"; and with his hair having turned white in his mid-twenties, he inspired confidence in solicitors.

But I suppose I always knew that in the end I wouldn't go to live in the Hague to do what was largely an office job, however safe and well-paid. I finally had an excuse to decline when I was asked to go over for an interview on the day when I had a summons in the Commercial Court on a case from Crumps, my first from them. And I didn't see why I should subject myself to an interview, although Hambro phoned to say that it was only a formality. So instead I got myself enthusiastically involved in this case, the first in a series of what became a staple diet of spring potatoes and vegetables shipped from Cyprus which arrived rotten in the UK. Was it the fault of the seller/shipper or the shipowner, or was it 'inherent vice,' the fault of the potatoes themselves? This seemed interesting at the time, but later on cargo claims were to become the lowest class of work in my practice.

And then the break-through came later on that year. I was hanging around Chambers in August because everyone else was away. There was an urgent arbitration involving a lot of money. A Greek ship had been withdrawn by her owners from a charter for alleged non-payment of the monthly hire, because the freight market had jumped and they could make a great profit by getting out of the contract. But the charterers said that they had in fact paid the hire in time by means of a banker's draft before the notice of withdrawal had been given. It turned out that at the time of the notice, the draft was already in the bankers' 'clearing' in the City. So it was as good as cash and as good as paid, and we had no merits whatever. But the money hadn't reached us by the time of the notice, and when it reached us we sent it back. There was a two-day hearing against the Hon. Tom Roche QC before Ashton Roskill QC. I was only a year out of pupillage, but I won.

The news of this arbitration appeared to have got around in

September when people had got back from their holidays, because I suddenly got work. Much later on I heard that my instructing solicitor, old Noel Davies of Botterell & Roche, later to merge with Norton Rose, had written letters about me to a number of his friends in the City firms. So things suddenly changed. I had earned £120 in my first year and less in my second. Then £330 in my third. But in 1951-2, the following year, I earned over £1100. That was a real living. I was beginning to get more work than John Donaldson and becoming a promising young junior. Willie McNair had already taken Silk and would soon go to the Bench, and Alan Mocatta, Eustace Roskill and John Megaw were clearly going to take Silk in the next few years. So the future suddenly looked promising.

And there also appeared to be some hope for my hearing, although in the end it came to nothing at this stage. Otosclerosis causes the little horseshoe-shaped bones, the *stapes*, to overgrow with tissue which stops them vibrating. There was then a fairly new operation under a full anaesthetic designed to shake them loose, called a mobilisation. I had one in each ear, the first in London and the second in the Alder Hey Hospital in Liverpool, arranged by Peter Rickham, who was then its Registrar. At first, both operations appeared to work. I still remember how I could suddenly hear the London traffic when I came round on the operating table, and then the waves on the beaches in Cornwall when I came back from Liverpool. But ultimately neither operation worked for more than a few months..

To end this trivial chapter, two other bits of trivia which I remember from that time.

Lord Devlin, who was for some reason always one of my supporters, once introduced me to Cecil King, one of the lords of the press and then I think Chairman of the *Daily Mirror*. He asked me what sort of work I did, and I said mostly shipping. Since he seemed to expect more, I stammered out some illustrations and mentioned the word demurrage. Understandably he had never heard of it and asked what it was. It is now a byword for boring shipping work. But Pat Devlin explained with great fluency that it was a special type of claim for damages for detaining a ship at her loading or discharge port. Cecil King looked at me gravely from a great height and said: "Young man, I don't think we'll be serialising your memoirs." A prophecy which is likely to remain true.

The other bit of trivia is a little more colourful. I still think of it as a perfect piece of staccato communication. A well-known Greek shipowner, a regular client of Chambers, used to employ British crews for low pay on his old ships, and they disliked him intensely. One day he stormed into Chambers with his solicitor, furiously brandishing a telegram and demanding instant action. It was from one of his captains at sea in the Far East and I saw it in the Clerk's Room later. It said:

"Have won thirty thousand pounds in a football pool. Fuck you for a start. Insulting letter follows."

The Greek was outraged when he was told that there was no known legal remedy. I never heard the end, but I think that we lost the Greek and he lost his captain.

54 · Marriage, etc

I GOT MARRIED to Julia in 1952. At one point she said that we should call it off. I can still see her saying it, sitting on the narrow winding staircase inside the front door of the attic flat in Ladbroke Gardens. To have called it off would probably have been better for me in the long run, certainly for her, but less good for Candy, Jo and Tim. And the engraved invitations to 200 people had already gone out. Because of them – Candy, Jo and Tim – I am glad that we went ahead. As they know, they were born in 1954, 1956 and 1958. I am bound to admit that I remember little about Candy's birth at The Clinic in Welbeck Street except that Eustace and Elizabeth Roskill were there and took over the proceedings, since the then famous John Ledingham, who was officiating, was "their" doctor and they had sent us to him. Elizabeth then became Candy's godmother and I became godfather to one of their's, without much effect in either case. Jo was born in a fashionable nursing home in Wimbledon, and when I arrived to see him and Julia we had a furious row; I mean Julia and I. I said that we should put him down for some public schools, but she said that he would only go to a co-educational day school. I felt that his future was being ruined from the start by her philosophies, and she felt that the public school world of stupid men was already taking her son away from her. In the end we both got so furious that matron threw me out.

As for Tim's birth, I owe him an apology, and of course to Julia as well. I was just going to bed after a day in court when I was rung in Hasker Street to say that he had arrived. So, without really thinking about it, I said that I was delighted and would come and see Julia and him the next morning. As with so much else, I thought nothing of it at the time. But in retrospect I can see that I should have got dressed again and gone at once, as I have been reminded from time to time, to put it mildly. But not by Tim, who is now at least as busy at the Bar as I was, and has never mentioned the incident.

However, I have already said that I wouldn't write about my marriages or my children. They will remember all our holidays, some spectacular, and mostly happy. Camping in France, the Costa Brava, Corsica, and the trip to India, Bangkok, Singapore and Malaysia when I had a case in Singapore. One of the high points was the rat in Jo's bed in Aurangabad, where we had gone to see the caves at Ellora and Ajunta.

Julia, Candy, Jo and Tim, 1958.

When he had convinced us in the middle of the night that there was something in his bed, and we then saw the long tail disappearing under the sheets, I bravely picked it up. But the large black thing at the end climbed up its tail to bite me. So I threw it out of the window into the yard below. They will all remember how disappointed they were when there was nothing there in the morning, and the manager explained that the vultures would have got it at dawn. And then they will remember our journey around Malaysia in two cars with the Karthigesus and the trip on the cockroach-infested ship back from Penang to Singapore. And then the long Indonesian case against Desmond Ackner, with Bob MacCrindle, who was bound to win against one of us and didn't care which, sitting in the middle, trying, but failing, to keep the peace and explaining to the judge that his sole function was to maintain the dignity of the English Bar. But all this was lost on the judge. Afterwards Desmond and I had a terrible row in the Robing Room, in which we both accused each other of gross unprofessional conduct. But in due course we settled the case, mostly at my clients' expense, as I recollect they deserved on the merits. None of us can now remember what it was all about, but Desmond and I didn't speak for six months. But since then we more than made it up over the last forty years.

Above all, at that time, there was the cottage in Cornwall. Our London houses were fairly uninteresting. We had bought a short lease in 48 Hasker Street with the help of a loan of £2,000 from Julia's mother, Muriel. It was twee, but too small. Then we paid £6,500 for a longer lease in Campden Hill Road. Although the Town Hall had not yet been built opposite, I never liked the house, because I don't like houses on a slant on a hill. But then I managed to turn it into a long lease by getting an extension from the Phillimore Estate for a few thousand pounds, which they must have regretted later. So it became worth enough to enable us to move again. In 1961 we then bought 51 Bedford Gardens for £19,500 with a £3,000 mortgage. We were coming for a drink with the Sutherlands in thick fog to have dinner with the Spira's a few doors away, and walked up the steps of No. 51 by mistake. When we got to the door we could see that it was up for sale, and in the end we bought it. It is now worth well over a million. Julia still lives there and Candy, Jo and Tim now know it much better than I. I never really liked it, and I haven't been there for 35 years.

But Nanjulian, the thatched cottage between Sennen and St. Just, is something different, and I loved it all my life. I drove down to Cornwall one February with a Farm Holiday guide, trying to find something for the summer. Nanjulian was the last place I came to as it was getting dark. After I had met the farmer (who later shot himself by biting on his shotgun) I ran down to the sea and saw that fantastic rocky cove. And I knew at once that we had to go there, although there was only an outside loo at the top of the garden. Then, after some years of holiday renting, I persuaded the owner, Bernard, another farmer, to give us a lease, and we went there every year. Then Julia said that we must buy it and that she wanted it more than anything. She may remember the occasion in Switzerland, running from the car into a wood when I said that we could not afford it. So I agreed and have certainly never forgotten it. But she was quite right. It is in one of the remaining most beautiful places that I know, and it will be there for our children and theirs. When I left in 1976 the bathroom and indoor loo were nearly finished; I paid the last bill later on that year. But I have never seen it again, and probably never will.

Now this is verging on the maudlin and perhaps controversial. So I must again turn to something more important, at any rate to me, in what I am trying to write about: my mother.

55 · My mother in Germany

IN NÜRNBERG she had met a nice, comfortable man, even before my father died. He was called Walter, a German lawyer in his mid-fifties who had never qualified in England. He had worked at a bench in a factory throughout the war and was married with two grown-up daughters who lived at home with his wife in England. The Nürnberg trials were now his chance as well. My mother and he were drawn to each other because they wanted the same simple things for the remaining years of their lives. Affection and more, their own place to live, freedom from money worries, better food than they had had for years, and perhaps a car and being able to travel together. He had known about my father since he was a student, and he enjoyed the reflected aura of being seen as a couple with my mother, who was like a minor celebrity and much in demand. He was a very, very nice man, and they loved each other.

All the simple things that they wanted were now open to them because they were part of the Allied Forces, and enjoying them and making the best of their new lives was like a game. I remember taking Julia to meet my mother, and we all had a week on the Chiemsee near Munich. Later on I also took Julia and the children to see my mother and my grandmother Gertrud, who was then again living in some style in Garmisch-Partenkirchen, near her sister Lulu and her husband Victor von Leyden. She was once more *Frau Staatssekretär* and men took off their hats when they met her. This had nothing to do with the war, it was merely a continuation of the old order of things, as before. And my mother even succeeded in getting permission to take me up in the mountain lift to the entrance of the *Berghof,* Hitler's retreat in Berchtesgaden, which only remained open for visits by allied personnel for a few months.

My mother in Nürnberg, 1948.

It was all fascinating, but whenever I was with my mother and Walter I felt that I was in the company of the conquerors, the occupying power, who were above the local inhabitants, and that the sights and amenities were their property, to be used and shown off. It didn't stay like that, of course. But that was the atmosphere in the early years, and sometimes I found it embarrassing. But for them it was simply like a new world in which they had a privileged place. And of course I was delighted for my mother. She could get far more food and luxuries than we could get in England. And she was so pleased and proud to be able to show me how this new world worked. I felt that she deserved it all. And she was of course interested in much more than the material advantages of living as a visitor in post-war Germany. There were the beginnings of proposals to republish my father's works, particularly in East Germany, where he was seen as a political champion whose writings supported their anti-Fascist posture. And apart from being lionised as my father's widow, my mother was now also in demand in her own right. Several radio stations were showing interest in *The Chronoplan*, and later on there were to be some broadcast performances.

But then the War Crimes trials were coming to an end and new plans had to be made. My mother had to earn money, and the obvious next place was Berlin. But apart from her attachment to Walter, what she really always wanted was to live in England, with her children and grandchildren. She often used to say that anything else was unnatural and that in most parts of the world – she usually mentioned India and Pakistan – it was taken for granted that ageing parents lived with their children. But of course there was no question of that, though I never stopped feeling guilty about it, even after her death, and sometimes even now. Our lives were too full; we had to fight for ourselves; and she had to work in order to live. Moreover, although we had always been a very close family, there were inevitably some strains. Judy and she had had to live on top of each other for too long to find it easy to get along, and they were very different. I, on the other hand, was perhaps too much like my mother to find it easy to be with her for long. It was almost as though we were competing against each other, trying to trump each other's achievements. And she and Julia had nothing in common, though she adored the children, especially Jo with his passion for music.

But although I felt guilty about it all, and fully realised that I was failing her, the clinching point was that she had to earn her living. There was no way she could have done it in England, but it was relatively easy for her in Germany. And Walter was there. It was not only the obvious answer but the only one. And it was frankly a relief to us all; in my case –

and perhaps also Judy's – with a constant bad conscience. Admittedly, I have feebly suffered from bad consciences all my life, perhaps too much. Judy, who has had far greater difficulties in her youth, is more of a realist and can be surprisingly firm. But it was still hard for my mother to have to live away from her family.

She had no problems in getting a job in Berlin, because she was able to go straight to the top. The President of the Senate of West Berlin and later its Mayor was then Willy Brandt, who ultimately succeeded Adenauer as *Bundeskanzler*. He was an admirer of my father's works and delighted to meet my mother. He immediately appointed her as an assistant to the Senate, and mainly to himself, to look after important foreign visitors to Berlin. In effect, she took charge of all visiting VIPs as an interpreter and cicerone.

Berlin was then a centre of world attraction, the focal point in the Cold War. The wall was in the process of being built and the West was determined to show its solidarity with the surrounded outpost, West Berlin. So there was a succession of pilgrimages to it, from heads of states downwards. I have many pictures, letters and press cuttings about my mother's role in those years. Harold Wilson sent her an umbrella and Indira Ghandi wrote to her and invited her to India. There is a picture of her sitting behind President Kennedy, translating the famous speech as he gave it, all except the words: "*Ich bin ein Berliner*," which he said in German. And she knew all the German cabinet ministers from Bonn who regularly came to Berlin.

My mother had never had a time of greater success and fulfilment since her youth, and she was now old enough to appreciate it. Walter had also been able to transfer to Berlin and had found an excellent job in the organisation which administered compensation for the refugees and families of Nazi victims. He helped her with the legalities affecting our family and she got as much compensation as she could, for the seizure of all our assets, the ruin of my father's professional life, something for herself, and even £300 for Judy and me for interference with our education! What she got was not vast, but respectable. She never had any need for money worries again. But of course she worried about money all the time, because she couldn't help it after the years in Switzerland, France and England.

She and Walter did not live together, but they were inseparable. Each had a small flat close by. He could drive and they bought a car together, though my mother never learnt, and they travelled all over Europe, particularly to Italy, to Ravello above Amalfi, their favourite place. I went to see them there and in Ischia and Capri and other places; how, when or why I can't remember. I also visited her often in Berlin, and we went to Hamburg to arrange for the headstone on my father's grave.

My mother's other great preoccupation and success lay in what she achieved for my father's works and memory. She became friendly with Walter Huder, the Director of the recently created *Akademie der Künste.* He was enthusiastic and insistent about creating an Alfred-Kerr-Archiv, in which there would be a record of everything that could be traced about his life and work. So we sorted out a lot of our papers, and the old suitcases from the emigration, including the *blonde Koffer,* were dug out and sent to Berlin. There was a formal opening with many celebrities, to which I went, and many of the memorabilia, family photos, portraits and correspondence with the famous people of his time were shown in an exhibition. It toured Germany and I took my children to see it in Hamburg, and then opened it at the Goethe Institutes in London and Dublin. The two large photographs of my parents, which have always hung wherever I have lived since my mother's death, came from this exhibition.

I recently saw it revived in Berlin with Diana, some twenty years later. The Archiv is now complete, so far as one knows, and fully catalogued. It is strange to go there and see students poring over my father's papers, and to see drawers full of photographs of us as children and correspondence with our parents. For the record, and since the contents now obviously have a great collector's value, I should mention that Judy and I have concluded an agreement with the Senate of Berlin that the Archiv would remain on indefinite loan to the Akademie, and that our heirs can only take it back if it is no longer publicly available and properly displayed in memory of our father, or something on these lines. Effectively, therefore, it belongs to Berlin. I hope my children will see it one day.

My mother's other great achievement was to set in train the republication of my father's works. It started with odd volumes of selected collections, first briefly in the West and then increasingly in the East. My mother lived to see most of this stage of his revival. This then took the form of a new full-scale production by a publisher in Berlin, which is associated with the *Berliner Tagesspiegel.* It was administered by an editorial committee of scholars in different parts of Germany to bring out selections of his collected works in eight volumes, each dealing with different aspects of his writings, all of which have now appeared.

His name will clearly survive in German literature as a minor classic. It is strange, as has often happened to me, to go to German plays in Germany, or in translation in England, and to find an extract of his review of the first night set out in the programme. And due to Judy's efforts there was also already a plan for an annual Alfred Kerr prize for the most promising young actor or actress during the annual *Theaterwochen* in Berlin. A committee was to decide each year who is to make the choice and award the prize, and we were to be invited for the presentation. The plan was to finance it by sponsorship from the publishers and by our royalties from our father's works, which we did not draw.

That was the position about ten years ago, when I first wrote these memoirs. Since then something quite unexpected has happened, as told in the last chapter.

56 · A painful family reunion

IN THE DESCRIPTION of my mother's life in Berlin there was unfortunately something left out. It happened in 1955; when she and Walter had been there for about three years.

The story started when I was on holiday with Julia and Candy, then one and Jonathan (Jo) on the way, in a small hotel at the far eastern end of Majorca. I got a message late at night that my mother was very ill in Berlin, and it sounded like a heart attack. I think that it came from Walter, who must have got my address from Judy. So somehow I had to get to Berlin at once. But in those days that was not easy.

It was even difficult to get quickly to Palma at the other end of the island. There were no taxis or buses when I started, literally at dawn. Somehow I hitch-hiked to the airport, but that was where the problems really began. The only flights in and out of Majorca at that time were to Barcelona. I was told that they were all full, but somehow I got on the first flight. "*Mi madre* ... !" works wonders in Spain. But how to get from Barcelona to Berlin? I went to Lufthansa and explained in German; I told them that I had been a pilot (admittedly on the other side) and begged them to help me. In the end they put me on a jump seat in the cockpit on a flight to Frankfurt. The immediate post-war world was not yet fully bureaucratic. Then I caught a Pan-Am flight to Berlin and got there the same evening.

I knew that my mother was in hospital, but not where. I got a few names and locations from the information office and took a taxi. The first one, near where I knew she lived between the Grunewald and Dahlem, proved to be right. But when I said who I was and asked to see her, I was told, after some hesitation, that she had not had a heart attack. She had pneumonia, because she had taken a large overdose, and was in a coma.

They took me to her, but she was deeply unconscious. She remained unconscious for the whole of the next day. Judy had already been there for two days, and Walter came to the hospital; he seemed to be there all the time. He had found us a small hotel, and it was nice to be with Judy in Berlin. We had never spent so much time together since we were children, mostly because I am too busy, or feel I am, and we have different friends and interests. But with this crisis for our mother, and the two of us being back together in Berlin, it was a landmark for us. And yet, for many years, I had quite forgotten her part of that week in Berlin. In my mind it was all about my mother and me.

On the following day she began to move a bit and started to make moaning noises. She said several times, "Don't wake me," in English. And then, after many more hours, she suddenly opened her eyes. As I remember it now, we were both standing at the foot of her bed. She realised where she was and that we were there. Then she looked at me and said:

"You've come. But you were on your holiday and you needed it."

It wasn't tactful and I felt embarrassed in front of Judy, who had been there for three days. But it was typical. And then she collected herself and looked at Judy and said, "And you too." From that moment we knew she was going to live and be her old self again. But what we didn't know was why she had done it. There had been so many threats before - but surely, now things were better!

She went back to sleep; we went and had dinner with Walter; and he told us. He said it was all his fault and that he felt dreadful about it. He had been having an affair with his German secretary and my mother had found out. There had been scenes and he had promised to stop it, but he hadn't. Then she found out that it had started again, or had never stopped, and took all the sleeping pills which she had accumulated over the years. They were then precious, like nylons and cigarettes, and she had hoarded them. But fortunately her constitution had been too strong, although the doctors initially told Walter that she wouldn't come out of the coma.

We said that of course he mustn't blame himself at all. He said that he did, particularly since the affair meant nothing to him. It was really over, he was terribly fond of our mother, and when she got well everything would again be as before.

We knew that he meant it at the time, but I don't think we believed it. Not even I, who usually believe everything for the best.

There then followed some painful and embarrassing days with our mother. She cried a lot and was a bit like a child. At one point she said to me quite seriously: "Why doesn't he want me any more when I still want him so much?" Like a child that has been hurt. Her life had been so hard, but she had never before gone through anything complex like this. And now her new life, which she had built up with so much love and joy, was falling apart again.

But then she soon got better in every way; she was on antibiotics and had enormous mental resilience. Not merely innate optimism, but a kind of day-dreaming make-believe which always insists that everything will be fine. She was soon back to telling us all about her successes and friends, how she played in tennis tournaments in the American sector and duplicate bridge, and about all the people she knew. And where she and Walter had gone on their holidays, and would go again. Walter was marvellous with her and with us, and he really meant it. He felt terribly responsible. It can't be easy for a man to explain himself to the children of a woman who has nearly succeeded in killing herself because he went to bed with someone else. We kept telling him that he must live his own life and not blame himself. But he kept telling us that he loved our mother and that it would all be as before.

I talked to her a lot over the next two days. She wanted to hear all about my life and work and to paint it in the rosiest colours. She used to have a way of insisting on it by putting leading rhetorical questions like: "But you're very happy and successful, aren't you?" which always irritated me. So, as often before, and still more often after, I said that everything would become better and different for her. She must come to England, stay with us in London and Cornwall, and see a lot of the children. And I always meant it. Away from my own daily life it was easy to believe it, and to see things as she wanted to see them. I always had a great tenderness and affection for my mother. But not what she wanted, which was my time and involvement in her life, and her participation in mine. So long as her involvement posed no risk to my successes, which she craved even more than I, for she saw them as reflected glory for herself. This had always been one of the dreams of her life, as I always knew. So I always felt guilty about her.

My mother in Berlin 1963

But my memory of our parting was happy and full of hope. I think that she insisted that Judy and I should go to some party to which she had been looking forward. But Judy says this never happened, so I can't be sure about that evening. But what matters, and what I remember for certain, is that my mother did not really mind my leaving the next day, because she always felt that my life was important, though never Judy's. So it was with a great sense of selfish relief that I let Walter and Judy drive me to the airport on the next morning, back on my way to Majorca, with my mother's entire approval, leaving Judy to hold the fort and pick up the pieces.

It was a singular tripartite family reunion, typical of each of us and our different lives and of the way we were with each other. And Judy was always by far the strongest of us three. As an independent character, her own person, she comes out best and was repaid for all her unhappiness.

Judy and Tom (officially Nigel) Kneale were married in 1954, and happily still are. Both became famous writers, a legendary literary couple. Judy of children's books, about *Mog*, the cat, *The Tiger who came to Tea*, and an acclaimed children's family trilogy beginning with *When Hitler Stole Pink Rabbit*. Tom wrote all the *Quatermass* series and many other works for film and television, now constantly revived from the archives. They have a daughter Tacy and a son Matthew who also became a writer. Like his father Tom in his youth, Matthew won the Somerset Maugham Prize, and then went on to win the Whitbread Prize last year. A very happy, now elderly, couple, they live close by and we see them a lot.

57 · My mother's death

TO FINISH this part of the story, the lives of my parents, we go forward a decade, from 1955 to 1965.

My mother and Walter got together again, though I don't think it was ever the same. Anyway, it didn't last long. After my mother recovered they went back to their beloved Ravello. But poor Walter, by then already well into his sixties, fell very ill soon after their arrival and was diagnosed as having caught polio. Somehow my mother got him into a hospital in Rome. She said it was awful, because the nursing and feeding were expected to be done by the relatives. In desperation, she rang Walter's office in Berlin and asked them to ring his wife in London. And the next day, lo and behold, his secretary appeared in Rome, polite and efficient, with a wheelchair, and took over. She had obviously never been off the scene. But my mother now accepted it all as fate, and there was nothing else that even she could do or hope for. Walter was taken back to Berlin and looked after devotedly by his secretary. He never left his wheelchair again and took an overdose about a year later.

This must have been about 1960 and my mother was alone again and now also in her sixties. Somehow she carried on as before, still a small celebrity and a success in Berlin, but with more intervening trips to see her children and grandchildren in England, by then three on my side and two on Judy's. Her mother Gertrud, Omama, had died meanwhile, and she sorted out her papers and belongings. She also got herself appointed as an interpreter for a Conference in the Cameroons and travelled there on her own, bringing back trophies for the families. And she was proudly at the House of Lords when I took Silk in 1961 and often insisted on coming to hear me in court. In between she came and stayed near us in London or with us at Nanjulian in Cornwall in the holidays.

But basically she was in Berlin and therefore on her own. I had a constant nagging feeling of guilt whenever I thought about her, which was not dissipated by her letters, brave and cheerful on the surface, but always sad and lonely underneath.

On 3 October 1965, when she was sixty-seven, I had a phone call from Berlin. She had had a heart attack on the tennis court and had died in the ambulance. Judy and I rushed to Berlin. After going to the hospital and meeting the doctors (of which I have no recollection whatever) there was another week of meeting many of her friends and admirers and hearing so much about her. I even met the Americans with whom she had been playing doubles in some tournament when she collapsed. She had often said that she wouldn't mind dying on a tennis court.

We were told that the Senate of the city would take care of all the arrangements. All we did was to sort out her flat and her family belongings. It was a sad, sad business and I felt inconsolably guilty. We left everything behind and only packed up her mementoes and papers.

There followed a great funeral service in a church near her flat. It was all organised by the Senate; we did nothing. There were crowds of people and wreaths and flowers with German, English and American flags on her coffin from various ministries and delegations. I took off the flags and still have them. There was even an attempt to play a tape of some of the music of *The Chronoplan*, but the sound didn't work properly and one could really hear nothing. It was all very sad.

Then, or later, we flew to Hamburg with her ashes and buried her at the foot of our father's grave. There is a small headstone for her in the same style as his, and I have often been back to see them both.

She was a wonderful mother, and she was so proud to be able to leave us some money; as she had often told us she would. About £22,000 accumulated from her compensation from the German government and her salary, carefully saved up. A very large sum, after all her years of misery. If only she could have had some of it earlier, when just a few pounds would have been the world to her .

One strange postscript about something which I have never understood.

As soon as I got the phone call from Berlin I wondered if she would still have got a special long letter from me. I had written at last, two days before, to tell her that everything would be different, this time for good. That she should give up her job and come to live in England, which she could now afford to do. And that I could afford to help her. And that she would be with us all the time. She should give up Berlin and finally come home.

I hoped and hoped that she would have got the letter before she died. The chances were about 50:50. But when we got to the house where she had her flat it was the first thing I saw, unopened on a table in the hall.

I took it back, but I couldn't bring myself to open and re-read it when she had never known what I had written. I felt that it would have made all the difference to her if she had, and I couldn't face it.

So I left it unopened for over twenty years. But some years ago I came across it again. And as I was beginning to think of writing these memoirs, one day I steeled myself and opened it.

Exhibition for my father in Germany, 1970.

What I found was that I had written none of the things which I have described and which I was quite sure I had written. Nothing about the future or things changing for her. It was a perfectly ordinary letter about what I and the family had been doing and were planning to do in the next few weeks, and about a few of my cases. Just a routine letter.

They say that the mind can play tricks, but I could never believe it. Certainly not that it could happen to me. But this time it did. There was total certainty in my mind, when I got that phone call, of what I had written two days before. There was total certainty when I found the unopened letter on the next day; and total certainty remained for the next twenty years. But all of it was guilt and imagination and the workings of my subconscious. Which I never thought I had.

I have dreamt about my parents regularly for many years and still do. Quite regularly, every other week or even more often. I don't know whether this is unusual. But whatever one's age and life, we change after the death of our parents and start facing up to the long haul towards our own death. I never remember dreaming about them when they were alive.

58 · End of a Generation

AFTER MY mother's death on 3 October 1965 her two brothers, Diez and Nucki (Gert), were my only remaining direct relations of that generation. On my father's side there had never been any except his older sister Annchen and her only daughter Käthe in Silesia, of both of whom my father had been very fond. I only remember meeting Annchen once, when I was probably about nine. She was already a widow, and her husband, Dr. Ollendorf, must have died quite young. We spent one Christmas with her in the Riesengebirge in Wüstegiersdorf, and I remember tobogganing down a long road on the Grosser Kamm, a mountain that looked like a long comb. Since the war all this now lies in Poland, and Breslau is Wroclaw.

Käthe was also a doctor and briefly married to a man called Becher, who later became prominent as a Communist poet when the DDR emerged after the war. But their marriage was short, and Annchen and Käthe had emigrated to Israel in the mid-thirties. Annchen died soon after my father, but Käthe survived into the sixties. She had been a regular visitor in the Grunewald, but we never saw her again after we left, though we corresponded with her in Jerusalem. When I went out with Candy to wind up her estate in 1973 we learnt that she had become something of a mystic and healer who would accept no money and lived very poorly. But it turned out that she had received considerable sums for compensation from the German government. The money was in various bank accounts in Israel, but she had never touched it. There must have been about ten thousand pounds. But she had died intestate and a lot of it went in lawyers' fees because there was a last minute claim from some alleged Ollendorf relation in America who said that he was entitled to an equal share with us. But ultimately his family tree proved to be too remote or unsatisfactory, and our lawyers got permission from the Attorney-General (it went that high!) to release the remainder of the estate to us, less a donation to a fund for making the desert bloom, which we were glad to make at their suggestion because Käthe would have wanted it.

That only left my mother's brothers. Diez, who was a year younger than my mother and four years older than Nucki, had emigrated to Mexico and then the States and had always had a hard life, much of it on the poverty line. After an unhappy first marriage and a bad relationship with his only son, he had the good luck to meet Ruth, a gentle American widow with two daughters, who was much younger than he, but adored him. They married happily and lived in a house in Stamford, Connecticut. With his violin lessons and working in a factory making radio components, and her earnings as a commercial artist, they just survived, but only with the help of his rich younger brother to pay the mortgage.

Nucki had been born with the proverbial silver spoon in his mouth, and apart from one or two difficult years as a stockbroker in New York during the war he had never lost it. Even after the emigration he had been well-off when he lived in England, and after the war he became quite wealthy as a merchant banker, probably a sterling millionaire. During the bleak war years in New York he had met Gretchen. She was born in Hamburg and had been working on a liner which arrived in New York as war broke out; so she stayed there. When they met she worked as an assistant in an art gallery where he had gone to sell some of his pictures.

After the end of the war Nucki had become the personal assistant to McCloy, the US Secretary of State for War who more or less ran the American-Occupied Zone of Germany during the early post-war years. Gretchen and he then lived in Frankfurt, already in considerable style. He then joined a bank in Zürich and finally became a director of Warburgs, when they moved to London. I had been to see him from time to time in Frankfurt and Zürich, and he then took me up as a more or less constant weekend companion when they moved into a beautiful flat in Eaton Square. By then I was a successful QC, and success was the only thing which counted with Nucki. We used to go on regular walks around the Round Pond on Sundays, with me pushing a pram or dragging Archie, the whippet of those days, and him trying to control two idiotic miniature poodles, gloomily walking our awful dogs and discussing our lives. Then he quarrelled with Sigmund Warburg and moved away from England for tax reasons. He had bought a beautiful property in Marbella, a ranch-style house with a swimming pool and outhouses for guests, and became a partner in a small merchant bank in Frankfurt. But we remained in constant touch and I was going to meet him at Heathrow on the morning he died. We had spoken on the phone the day before, but on the next morning he had a massive heart attack when he was getting up in the Hessischer Hof in Frankfurt to catch his plane. Two weeks before he had had a perfectly satisfactory ECG ...

That was in 1970. Nucki died at the age of 67, the same as my mother five years earlier. They were physically alike, as I was to both of them.

Michael and Judy, Nice 1935.

PLATE X

My parents in England, 1936.

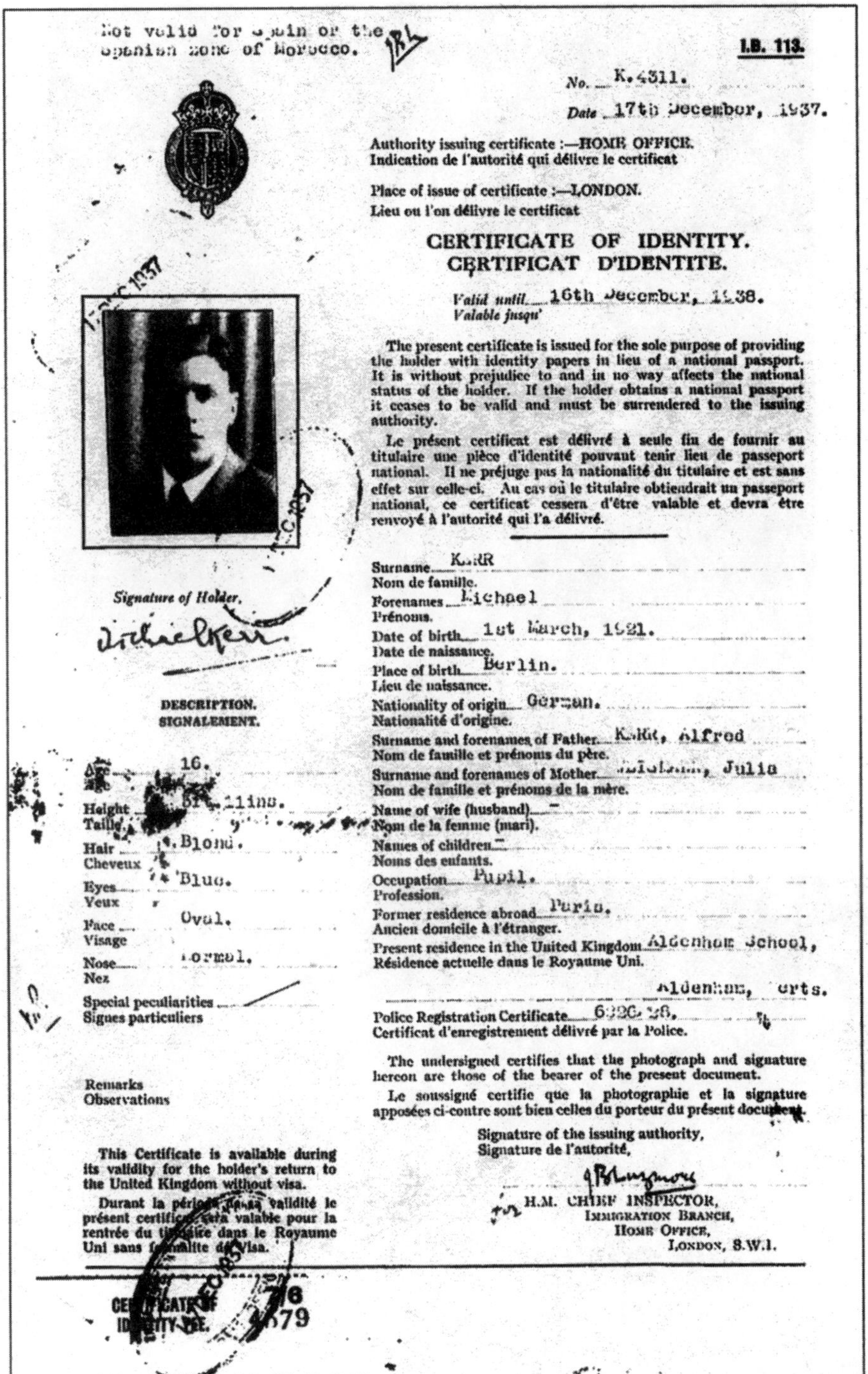

Not valid for Spain or the Spanish zone of Morocco.

I.B. 113.

No. K.4311.

Date 17th December, 1937.

Authority issuing certificate :—HOME OFFICE.
Indication de l'autorité qui délivre le certificat

Place of issue of certificate :—LONDON.
Lieu ou l'on délivre le certificat

CERTIFICATE OF IDENTITY.
CERTIFICAT D'IDENTITE.

Valid until 16th December, 1938.
Valable jusqu'

The present certificate is issued for the sole purpose of providing the holder with identity papers in lieu of a national passport. It is without prejudice to and in no way affects the national status of the holder. If the holder obtains a national passport it ceases to be valid and must be surrendered to the issuing authority.

Le présent certificat est délivré à seule fin de fournir au titulaire une pièce d'identité pouvant tenir lieu de passeport national. Il ne préjuge pas la nationalité du titulaire et est sans effet sur celle-ci. Au cas où le titulaire obtiendrait un passeport national, ce certificat cessera d'être valable et devra être renvoyé à l'autorité qui l'a délivré.

Signature of Holder.

Surname KERR
Nom de famille.
Forenames Michael
Prénoms.
Date of birth 1st March, 1921.
Date de naissance.
Place of birth Berlin.
Lieu de naissance.
Nationality of origin German.
Nationalité d'origine.
Surname and forenames of Father KERR, Alfred
Nom de famille et prénoms du père.
Surname and forenames of Mother [illegible], Julia
Nom de famille et prénoms de la mère.
Name of wife (husband) —
Nom de la femme (mari).
Names of children —
Noms des enfants.
Occupation Pupil.
Profession.
Former residence abroad Paris.
Ancien domicile à l'étranger.
Present residence in the United Kingdom Aldenham School, Aldenham, Herts.
Résidence actuelle dans le Royaume Uni.
Police Registration Certificate 6[illegible]
Certificat d'enregistrement délivré par la Police.

DESCRIPTION.
SIGNALEMENT.

Age 16.
Age
Height 5 ft. [illegible] ins.
Taille
Hair Blond.
Cheveux
Eyes Blue.
Yeux
Face Oval.
Visage
Nose Normal.
Nez
Special peculiarities —
Signes particuliers

Remarks
Observations

This Certificate is available during its validity for the holder's return to the United Kingdom without visa.

Durant la période de sa validité le présent certificat sera valable pour la rentrée du titulaire dans le Royaume Uni sans formalité de visa.

The undersigned certifies that the photograph and signature hereon are those of the bearer of the present document.

Le soussigné certifie que la photographie et la signature apposées ci-contre sont bien celles du porteur du présent document.

Signature of the issuing authority,
Signature de l'autorité,

for H.M. CHIEF INSPECTOR,
IMMIGRATION BRANCH,
HOME OFFICE,
LONDON, S.W.1.

CERTIFICATE OF IDENTITY FEE.

(S.O. 1414). [illegible] 5,000. 3/37. C.T. Gp. 689

Certificate of Identity, 1937 et seq.

PLATE XII

My father and Judy in Berlin, 1932.

Judy about 1941.

Michael in Nice, about 1935.

PLATE XIV

Judy and Tom (Nigel) Kneale's wedding, 1954.

Michael and Diana, Moscow, 1991.

PLATE XVI

Lucy, aged 17.

Alexander, aged 14.

But I was luckier. When I was 65 in 1986 my heart condition was discovered, more or less by chance, and I had a triple bypass. They could both have lived for many years if commonplace medical knowledge and practice in the sixties had been what they became a few years later. Diez died in his eighties, peaceful and happy, but poor, as he had been all his working life, with a last great disappointment about Gretchen's interpretation of the wishes expressed in his brother's will, which left him as poor as before.

Later on Gretchen was swindled out of her beautiful property in Marbella, which I still remember with wonder and envy. She had been planning to sell it and signed a disastrous Spanish contract at the suggestion of a plausible German couple, posing as estate agents, to whom she had shown the house on her last visit to Spain and who then called on her in Eaton Square one Sunday morning with a draft contract. The Spanish text differed crucially from the unofficial English and German translations which they had helpfully provided for her to read, since she knew no Spanish. In the Spanish, which she was told was the obligatory language for disposals of land in Spain, the peseta price was a small fraction of the agreed sterling price shown in the "translations", and it was expressed to be payable in instalments over some 9 years from completion. Having got her signature and the keys over a glass of champagne, exchanged for a small cash deposit and an impressive Spanish receipt together with a copy of the contract, they departed in amity. When the truth came out, sometime after they had taken possession, she pointed out that it had all been my fault, since I had been out playing tennis when she had rung for advice as to whether or not she should sign. Later on I was still more at fault, together with the famous Dr. Francis Mann of Herbert Smith, when we were unsuccessful in our efforts over several years, both acting *pro bono* assisted by another firm in Madrid, after the police had evinced a total lack of interest, in seeking to penetrate the jungle of Spanish property law and the Spanish civil courts with applications and affidavits to try to have the contract set aside and to evict the couple. But they countered successfully by instituting criminal proceedings against Gretchen for not providing the *escritura* for the registration of title following a sale of Spanish land, which was an offence under the criminal code. The result was that she was not able to go to Spain again in case she was arrested, pointing out that I had only made matters worse by interfering. She has never forgiven me for these and other failures, and we did not speak for years. I believe that the position was ultimately resolved by Gretchen receiving some small further compensation against delivery of the *escritura.* But she out lived the German woman, who was killed in a fiery car crash, though this did not help her with the loss of the house. Now 89, she still lives in Eaton Square, the sole survivor of that generation, with a great attachment to Diana, "the only member of my family who has ever been kind to her".

59 · The second half

THAT IS the end of the family story. The rest is mostly about the law, and less interesting to me than the story of my parents and my youth, which had originally been the sole theme and purpose of this book. In a way it is also about a different person - the more commonplace story of an English barrister and judge, then arbitrator, and finally - like Jaques' seventh age in As You Like It - an old man writing his memoirs.

But it is not really about a different person. There is no Jekyll and Hyde, but a mixture of two scenarios in one person side by side. The family story went to 1970, when I was already nearly 50, and contains within it more than 20 years of life in the law. And the same person continued, always aware of the familiar figures in his background of time. "Ghosts go along with us until the end". Although I had long ceased to be "foreign", and had certainly become more English than anything else, I also came to realise, more and more as I got older, that one never becomes entirely English, or at any rate never ceases to be a bit different. In the modern mixed world of today this is of no importance, or often a positive asset. But in yesterday's England a foreign origin was a crucial characteristic which could not be shaken off or ignored. Despite our naturalisations, Judy and I would never have been considered for any job in the Foreign or Diplomatic Service, and I used to worry whether the same might secretly apply to becoming a QC or a judge. In the end it didn't. But perhaps nearly: I was once told in *1972* that I was the first foreign-born High Court judge to have been appointed since the time when some Norman judges were brought over from France in the reign of Henry II ....

So I'll go on, and I'll even go back to where the law should have started. In Chapters 49 and 53 I've already written something about my beginnings. So I'll go back to the Bar of those times. But please remember: if an author has no talent as a writer, then his autobiography can only be as interesting or boring as his story. And few readers are fascinated by the law.

60 · The Junior Bar

IT IS OFTEN SAID that the Bar has affinities with the stage. But in modern times, if the comparison is between appearing in court and acting, this is romantic nonsense, even in cases before juries. Emotion and personal involvement are hindrances for barristers. What matters is the power of analysis: the ability to master and present a complex web of fact and law with clarity and maximum persuasion. Even experts in jury advocacy, such as George Carman in our times, always relied on simplicity and understatement in their addresses, never on rhetoric. I have always remembered the unkind, but no doubt necessary, advice of Lord Justice Scrutton to a young barrister in the Court of Appeal: "We are having some difficulty in following your submissions and wonder whether you might like to put them in some sort of order. Logical order would obviously be best, but this is clearly not to be hoped for. Alternatively you might consider a chronological presentation. But if this is also too much to ask, at least try alphabetical."

But something that junior barristers and actors certainly have in common is that both are individualists, working alone, with "clerks" or agents instead of partners or employers. And both are waiting for the phone to ring to produce work, parts in one case and briefs in the other. In between, actors "rest"; while barristers wait around in Chambers, reading The Times in the morning and the Standard in the afternoon, or – if they're lucky – "devilling" by working on someone else's papers and hoping to be paid a part of his fees. (Nowadays there would be a 30% chance of it being *her* fees, but not in the 1950's. Whenever the subject of a woman tenant was raised with Albert, the Senior Clerk, he said that the lavatory was unsuitable).

A much closer professional analogy is between doctors and surgeons on the one hand and solicitors and barristers on the other, general practitioners and specialists. Doctors and solicitors often become closely involved in the lives of their patients and clients, whereas it has been said that a barrister is like the surgeon who takes out the appendix without looking at the face. But the specialist sides of both professions are dependent on the other for work referral. And although a barrister's expertise cannot sensibly be compared with the skill of a surgeon, until recently only barristers had the right of audience in the higher courts, with wigs as their hallmark. Out of court they usually wore black jackets and striped trousers and hats, to take off to judges, with some silk top hats on the Chancery side. And they never carried any papers to or from court.

These generalisations are no longer true of the Bar of today. It is perhaps not surprising that suitably qualified solicitors can now appear in all courts, although appendices are still only removed by surgeons. But I am writing of the bar of 50 or more years ago when – for the first 4 years of my participation in this world – QC's were still KC's. In those times barristers and solicitors did not mix socially, and barristers never went to solicitors' offices. Even the senior partner of a City firm would expect – and be expected – to attend upon a newly called barrister for a conference in his Chambers. All other communications had to be channelled through the barrister's clerk. It took years before I dared to allow Albert to find out that I often rang solicitors about cases directly from my desk, and much longer before I could persuade him to put calls through to me personally, since it was "not done" to speak to solicitors directly.

Working conditions and practices were also unrecognisable. 3 Essex Court (as it then still was) in the Temple was one of the leading commercial sets of Chambers in the country throughout the fifties, with 3 QC's and about 9 Juniors and a vast international practice (though this adjective was never used.) But we operated with 2 clerks, 1 boy to carry the books and papers to court, and a part-time typist. A lot of the work was sent out in manuscript, and any necessary copies were made with carbon paper or later – as science progressed – with curious " roneo" winding devices. But such technical processes, like other secretarial tasks, were usually left to the solicitors, as were all calculations: "I am advising on the figures in principle, but would be grateful if my instructing solicitors would be good enough to perform the necessary computations".

The end products of all this for the barristers were payments of fees which were invariably expressed in guineas, plus a clerk's fee also expressed in guineas. Thus, a Junior's brief for arguing a Summons in the Commercial Court might be marked, say, 12 and 2, which would be £12.12.0 plus £2.2.0, nominally for the clerk, but in practice Albert would charge a flat 10% of the total of £14.14.0 and round it off to £1.10.0. It was a breach of the etiquette of the Bar – and later of a Rule of the Bar Council – for a barrister to go into court without a "marked brief". This was the frontispiece for the papers sent by the solicitors for the hearing, tied with red ribbon, or white in the case of Treasury or other government briefs, which stated the court, the names of the parties, the barrister and the instructing solicitor(s) and, most importantly, the agreed fee for appearing. The brief fee covered all necessary preparation and the first day of the hearing and would have been negotiated by Albert after he had looked at the papers. Hourly rates were unknown.

Fees depended on Albert's assessment of the complexity and importance of the case and the standing of the barrister in question. When he discussed fees on the phone, or with the "managing clerks" (or "west clerks" in the case of firms located in the City, from where they had to come west to the Inns of Court) who brought the papers into Chambers, he would often look reflectively up at the sky before saying, gravely: "The proper fee is ... £X", as though it was written up there. Then agreement would be reached and he would mark the brief. I have watched him do this many times, sometimes looking up anxiously as well, if it was my case. If the hearing was due to last longer than the first day, daily "refreshers" also had to be negotiated by him in advance.

Juniors, ie any barristers of any age or seniority who were not Silks, appeared alone, unless they were "led". But Silks could only appear with a Junior, sitting behind them, who would then be entitled to two-thirds of the leader's fee, both on the brief and the refreshers. The fees for drafting pleadings or advisory work, such as Opinions and Advices on Evidence, were also negotiated in advance in the same way. For Albert these procedures were like laws carved in Mosaic tablets. He was one of the elders among barristers' clerks, who had spent his whole life in the Temple since he was a boy, universally respected, highly successful, and ultimately a legend... for a time...like so many others, before and since....

This was the new world in which I arrived in 1948, hoping to make a living and ultimately a career. I knew nothing about it before my first day in Chambers. Although I had read the necessary law, I do not remember that there was then any literature describing life at the Bar. I remember John Megaw, my pupilmaster, endlessly telling me not to call him "Sir"and being horrified when I asked if it would help if I brought a typewriter (my father's old one) into Chambers. But he showed me where I could buy stiff white cardboard collars, cheap, presentable, disposable, and conveniently exchangeable for the stiff evening dress collars and bands worn in court, without having to change shirts. I wore them for years and wonder if they are still made.

For some time it all felt as new and strange as arriving at Aldenham from France in 1936. But then I got to like it; and gradually, as work began to flow in over the years, with a total fascination. It was a small world, but it felt like a large elite in which people knew each other and shared the highest standards of loyalty, friendship and trust in an exhilarating working atmosphere. We were "fighting" cases and we were "against" each other, but always with a common bond, which was not the law or the administration of justice, but simply membership of the Bar. Every day was new, every case was different, and every disputed or doubtful issue of law or fact somehow turned itself into an interesting intellectual challenge. But there was also a lot of heartache. We were all operating in a system of intense, but always politely veiled, competition, even with our closest friends in Chambers. I remember agonising about the briefs which others got from coveted solicitors, or – worse – from solicitors who might be in the process of leaving me for them. And we were all watching Albert, for signs of hope, approval, or – fearsome thought – displeasure. He used to come to watch us in court. But, being "on our feet", addressing the Bench, we never knew he was there.

The choice of counsel by firms of solicitors in those times depended much more on the managing clerks, or "west clerks", than on the partners. Solicitors' litigation departments (which also dealt with arbitrations in exactly the same way) were run by the managing clerks. There were no litigation partners, because litigation was effectively conducted directly by the instructed barristers, and the fees involved would not warrant partners' time. The clerks had no legal qualifications, but they knew the barristers' clerks and the courts, where they would usually represent the instructing solicitors by sitting or standing behind counsel. Even for trials, the main hearings, the partners in charge of the cases would rarely come into court, or only for a short time to make contact with the clients, and virtually never for the procedural "interlocutory" hearings. But that was where the young barristers would be cutting their teeth, on applications and summonses in pending cases in the Commercial Court or the "Beargarden" for other Queen's Bench work, and where they would be judged by the solicitors' managing clerks and then recommended – or not – to the partners. Senior managing clerks therefore wielded great power over the Bar, such as Jack Smeaton of Slaughter & May, who reminded me for decades that I had owed my "Slaughters" practice entirely to him, as I no doubt did. He also always said that in his time "he had 'made' every judge who had ever been appointed out of the Temple", though the Lord Chancellor might also have claimed a part of the credit.

It took me about five years to come through the system. Three years to reach the point of knowing that it would work, that one would survive, and another two, with a lot of teaching in the evenings and at weekends, to achieve a platform of financial security. But when work began to flow in, the paper work was unremitting. The first thing on Monday mornings would be to pick out the sets of papers to be done over the following weekend, which could wait until then, the first available time. Others would be earmarked for the evenings, because the days were usually fragmented with conferences (or "consultations" if with a Silk) or being in court. But even the evenings were also often taken up by having to stay in Chambers with the Law Reports to prepare for the next day's hearing. There was no photocopying for hearings, and the books could not be carried home. And some Silks, in particular Alan Mocatta, the Head of Chambers, would always want to stay until 9.30 or 10 if we were in court, rehearsing the arguments for the following day, even the order in which they should be presented, and continually revising his notes. He even used to make me feel guilty if I then slunk off home.

And gradually I also got into the same habits, against my better judgment, redrafting my notes every night for the next day's hearing. This was a form of insurance, although I knew that it was unnecessary or perhaps even a mistake, because one was invariably thrown off one's stride, and therefore off one's notes, by counsel on the other side or by the judge, and often both.

My main field of work was still in shipping and came from all the specialist City firms who are still around, though now much bigger and international, such as Holman Fenwick & Willan, Ince, Crumps, Richards Butler, Clyde, Sinclair Roche, etc. Much of it was on behalf of the P&I Clubs, the shipowners' defence associations, but which also included time charterers, and Robin Troughton, the senior partner of HF&W, became a particularly great friend, ending with my speaking at his Memorial Service. The more general work came from all over, but my "specials" were Slaughter & May, and Coward Chance as they then still were, who instructed me regularly in the Privy Council, several times as the Junior to the legendary Garfield Barwick, probably the greatest Australian advocate for many generations, with whom I stayed in touch and last saw with Diana in Sydney when he was 90. Then Francis Mann began to appear, mainly after he had joined Herbert Smith, which was then a firm of about 6 partners, and then some of the others followed, such as Geoffrey Lewis, and ultimately both became life-long friends.

As regards the senior Bar, my "leaders" were mostly from my Chambers or other commercial Silks, including Sir Robert Aske, a dear old ex-Solicitor Baronet from Hull, though the H tended to be silent. It was said that when he was arguing a damage to cargo case, no one was sure whether his complaint was that the weevils had been eating or heating the maize in the hold. But in wider fields there were also cases with a further leader on top, some of them now legendary names, when I felt that I was so far removed from having a speaking part that I hardly knew what was going on. I have two main recollections, both "establishment" cases.

The first was my first arbitration, a word which I had never heard mentioned at Cambridge and which was then an unknown process to me, and probably to most recent graduates of those days. It arose out of the nationalisation of the railways and airlines by the Attlee government after the war, headed by the Chairman of the British Transport Commission and the Minister for Civil Aviation. In about 1953 the two incumbents, Lord Hurcomb and (later Sir) Lennox Boyd, had a great personal and mutual dislike for each other. This erupted into an open feud when the Railways man found the shares of Channel Island Airways Ltd. in one of the safes which he had taken over, because they had previously been owned by Southern Railways Ltd. So he demanded that the Aviation man, or rather his department, should buy them at their market value, which was claimed to be a very high sum. This was indignantly refused. When the departmental accountants were then brought in to look at the figures on a "without prejudice" basis, the two sides were unbridgeably far apart. The resulting row then reached Cabinet level and the two departments were ordered to go to arbitration, before the most eminent accountant of the day, to determine the price which a willing buyer would have paid, and a willing seller would have accepted, for all the shares of Channel Island Airways on the date when civil aviation was nationalised.

This exercise was then put in hand, with months of preparation by two teams of solicitors, accountants and barristers. The Silks at the top of the teams were Sir Milner Holland and Sir Andrew Clark (though their knighthoods may have come later), and I remember Milner reflecting at the beginning of the first consultation that he had spent his working life procuring or resisting the transfer of money from one pocket to another and that it made no difference to him that on this occasion they were both in the same suit. I was the fourth or fifth of his team, with a "noting brief" and at least one Junior and another QC on top, and we were on the side of the hypothetical seller. But, as the weeks passed – quite amusingly and profitably – and the accountants and experts increasingly disagreed, it became abundantly clear that no hypothetical buyer and seller would ever both have been "willing" at the same time and price. I remember that the other side staged a major upset of all our figures when they announced that the company had been about to transfer its operations from Croydon to Heathrow, which was then in its early stages, and that the resulting costs would obviously have reduced the price of the shares. But we countered when Milner entirely destroyed their cabin crew costing projections by announcing that "we would have used girls, like the Americans", stewardesses instead of stewards, then unheard of on this side of the Atlantic, who would have cost less and attracted more passengers. And so it went on and on, for weeks of evidence and speeches, until it finally stopped. Some months later the arbitrator produced a figure, but I can neither remember it nor greatly cared at the time. Except to wonder about its relation to the total costs of the exercise, for the taxpayer.

The second case was on an important point of what we would now call public law, but which I have also forgotten. Our team, led by Hartley Shawcross, went to Walter Monckton's Chambers for a discussion to see if we could settle. When it then became clear that the case would have to fight, Monckton said: "Who shall we get to try this? What about Pat Devlin?" This was immediately accepted by Hartley. Whereupon Monckton picked up the phone, asked to be put through to the Attorney General, Manningham-Buller, and explained the situation. The AG said that we could have Pat Devlin and that we should agree dates with his Clerk. Unfortunately I have no memory of what then happened to the case afterwards. But whenever I have mentioned this incident in discussions with foreign lawyers, as an illustration of how the English system can sometimes work swiftly and informally, they have always been profoundly shocked and declared that such a thing would be unimaginable and wholly unconstitutional in their countries. The difference is that we (at least at the Bar) trust judges absolutely to be independent and impartial, and that we can therefore allow ourselves the luxury of "horses for courses" instead of having to choose them by lot for every case.

My time as a Junior covered about 12 years and other isolated memories of a few wonderful moments still remain. I remember flying to Naples to take evidence on commission before the British Consul, in an improbable case involving a fraudulent sale of millions of wartime ex-Army packets of NAAFI razorblades, sitting in the front of the plane, drinking champagne, on a perfect May morning, with the spring snow sparkling on the sunlit Alps as far as one could see, and thinking that the world was perfect. And then down the Italian coast and over the square rock just off Ischia around which I had swum with Candy on a family holiday. But, as usual, the feeling did not last. As we started our descent I remembered the three greatly senior Chancery opponents in the case who had appeared at different stages from time to time, memorably called Drabble, Droop and Squibb, some of whom would also now be on their way to Naples, and my euphoria evaporated. And one other wonderful moment, when Albert solemnly and ceremoniously brought in a brief marked £1,250 guineas and put it on my desk. It was a quantum leap in my career, and I had to go out and take a walk around Essex Court, wondering if that was the biggest Junior brief delivered in the Temple on that day.

Finally about this stage of the Bar, there is the inevitable topic of pupils. Juniors of (I think) more than 5 years call, but not Silks, could and were expected to take pupils and were entitled to charge them £100 guineas a year, and some Juniors had more pupils than work. But in good Chambers there was usually a tradition to remit pupillage fees, and I don't think we ever charged any. John Megaw certainly remitted mine, and during my years as a Junior I had about 15 pupils but never charged one. Then, as now, the forensic Mecca was for a pupil to be offered a tenancy in Chambers. But the numbers involved were then a small fraction of today, and the problems of getting tenancies correspondingly smaller, though already traumatic in some cases.

My pupils included Bob MacCrindle (for one term, when Eustace Roskill bequeathed him to me on taking Silk) who never wanted to go on the Bench and spent most of his highly remunerative working life with an American firm in Paris, and among the judiciary, three later Law Lords, Tony Lloyd, Michael Mustill, and John Hobhouse and, as cherished "grandsons" in the Lords, Mark Saville and Nicholas Phillips, now the Master of the Rolls. In the Court of Appeal there was Tony Evans, and Tony Colman in the Commercial Court. In the real world of politics there was Paddy Mayhew, MP, later Attorney-General and Northern Ireland Secretary and now also in the House of Lords. Of the others I remember quite a few, but not all. At one point I tried to reconstruct the full list of all my pupils, but now I cannot find it. So apologies to all the others, including (once again) to the Assistant Attorney General for Sri Lanka, whom I met (again) in Colombo in the eighties and who had to remind me, with the utmost courtesy, of his short pupillage with me in the fifties. I said "old men forget", but that I seemed to have started early. And I have been apologising to semi-familiar faces and names ever since.

61 · Silk

IN EARLY 1961 Albert Smith, the senior Clerk, had told me that John Donaldson, later to succeed Lord Denning as Master of the Rolls, was applying for Silk. This came as a total surprise. John hadn't told me. But in those days one only had to write to those who were senior on the same Circuit, to warn them, so that they would have a chance to apply if they wanted to. That tradition stopped soon afterwards. John was a member of the South-Eastern, whereas I had been sent up on the Northern, because Liverpool and Manchester were ports that might generate some shipping work. This proved to be an illusion. I only ever got one case on Circuit, in Manchester about textiles. But I had had to go up and dine on the Northern Circuit mess a few times before I could join. This was soon after I was called, and no one knew me. When they asked me if I intended to practise on the Circuit and I said no, I couldn't make out if they were relieved or offended or both. But I have always been loyal to the Northern and spent most of my time there when I had to go on Circuit as a Judge. And they gave me a dinner when I went on the Bench, and another one when I got to the Court of Appeal.

When I heard the news that John Donaldson was applying for silk, I was amazed. Admittedly, he was more than a year senior to me, but at that stage I had more work. So I got a bit cross and suddenly thought that I would apply as well. And Albert didn't see why I shouldn't. It was a simple thing to do in those days. Merely a short letter with one's date of call and Chambers address, two judges as references, and a statement that one had the honour of applying to be appointed one of Her Majesty's Counsel (learned in the Law, to complete the official formula). No forms to fill in, no declarations of income, and no payment as now (£335 on application and a further £150 if granted).

We were now in late February 1961. The list of the successful applicants is published on Maundy Thursday, just before Easter. Nowadays one has to apply by the previous November, but a few weeks notice was then sufficient.

I didn't really mind very much whether I got it or not. To take Silk involved quite a risk to one's practice, and I felt sure that I would get it the following year anyway. But things did not turn out so simply.

One day, about two weeks before Easter, I was summoned out of a conference in my room to see Sir George Coldstream, the Permanent

Secretary in the Lord Chancellor's Department, in John Donaldson's room downstairs. He said that he had just seen John and would say exactly the same to me as he had said to him. This was that the Lord Chancellor, then Lord Kilmuir, had much pleasure in recommending me for Silk. And that, obviously, no conditions could be attached to this recommendation. But nevertheless ... There followed a complex sentence which I used to remember verbatim and which somehow combined the expression of a wish, and a denial of any possible reservation or condition, with a mandatory request, or something of that kind. The velvet glove, but the Whitehall fist inside. The point was to inform me that a policy decision had been taken by the Lord Chancellor that henceforth there should be no more than two QCs in any set of Chambers. We already had two, Alan Mocatta and Eustace Roskill; John Megaw having meanwhile gone first on the Bench. So if John Donaldson and I got Silk, Chambers and we were being asked, or told, to split. George Coldstream told me that there was no need to give an answer there and then, but added that the recommended list of Silks "did not go forward to the Palace for another two days." Which spoke for itself. He also said that he was on his way to give the same news to a number of other Chambers.

Naturally I replied that I was honoured by the recommendation and that I would accept that we would have to split. He said that John Donaldson had said exactly the same. It was all very smooth and quick, and what my father would have called perfidious Albion at its worst.

This idiotic policy stemmed from the Attorney-General, Manningham-Buller, later to become Lord Dilhorne as Lord Chancellor, who had long been jealous of a few highly successful specialist sets of Chambers when he had practised at the Bar. It was as stupid and ill considered a piece of policy as can be imagined, rash and quite impractical, and it survived for less than a year. But during that time it caused a lot of misery and changed a few lives.

John and I duly got Silk, and in 3 Essex Court we then had some weeks of agonising discussions and cabals, like C P Snow's unforgettable *The Masters*. Who was to go, with whom, where, and with what Clerk? Some Chambers simply had no way of solving these problems because there was virtually no available spare accommodation in the Inns and not yet any question of Chambers outside. And for some reason there were also not yet any Chambers in Gray's Inn. Above all, however, there was the quandary that no senior practitioner could bear to be parted from his Clerk. In one case a new Silk simply had nowhere to go and had to apply for the County Court Bench. But we fortunately started with two advantages. We had an annexe next door in 4 Essex Court, so that we could simply reshuffle rooms and declare both sets to be independent, like bits of the Balkans. Secondly, the senior and junior Clerks, Albert and John, were father and son and were to some extent already pooling their fees anyway.

But the big problem was of course who would stay and who would go with – presumably – John Donaldson and me; facing a dismal prospect of a new set of Chambers with two brand-new Silks. Whereupon Alan and Eustace, the two sitting Silks, surprised us all by announcing that we should split vertically. This was magnanimous and a vast relief, and particularly unselfish of Eustace, since it followed that, inevitably, the choices would be made in order of seniority. This meant that Alan would stay and Eustace would have to go, since everyone naturally assumed that staying was better than going. 3 Essex Court was a magic name and number, whereas No. 4 was unknown, smaller, and much less comfortable. And a consideration of overriding importance was that Albert, the senior Clerk and a star of the Temple, would obviously stay, and that No. 4 would have to make do with his son John. So John Donaldson, the next senior, elected to stay with Alan, and I had to go. But further down it was a question of personal loyalties. Bob MacCrindle, who had been Eustace's and my pupil and never feared anything, had no doubt about coming with us, as well as Michael Mustill, also my pupil. But Tony Lloyd, whose pupillage with me had overlapped with Michael's, said that, sadly, he would have to stay in No. 3.

But as soon as all this had been worked out, with much agonising, and rooms had been claimed and allocated, everything changed again. Alan Mocatta went on the Bench before Eustace could even move out. So he obviously had to stay and I became the head of No. 4. Later on No. 4 became at least as prestigious as No. 3 ever was. But in 1961 it was unknown. And then the situation got even more absurd because the following term, in January 1962, Eustace also went on the Bench. So John Donaldson became head of No. 3. We were back to two Silks and need never have split at all. And within another six months or so this silly and unworkable policy of having no more than two Silks in one set of Chambers was simply dropped, having caused a great deal of unnecessary anguish.

The other unexpected event was that for several years No. 4 did better than No. 3, and it was said that Albert's covenants in favour of John somehow had to be reversed.

I was now in a new group of Silks and one of the youngest heads of Chambers. The 1961 list had contained thirty-three names, at that time the longest in history, and included many of my life-long friends. It was made up in order of seniority, and I was the last but one. Apart from John Donaldson, and in no particular order, there were Mark Littman,

Henry Brandon, Desmond Ackner, Roger Parker, Tasker Watkins, Ted Eveleigh, Michael Wheeler, Jeremy Hutchinson and many others who would all do very well.

At the swearing-in ceremony Dilhorne told us that although we were now "Her Majesty's Counsel," we were all on our own and could expect no help from the Lord Chancellor's Department if our practice failed. On the other hand, and although it was part of the oath that we had just taken that we would take no fee for advising the Crown and would not appear against it, he said that there was obviously no rule which precluded us from appearing for the defence in criminal cases or against government departments in civil disputes, and that the government would pay brief fees just like any other client. Another classic instance of my father's perfidious Albion. First we are told that we could in effect forswear our oath. Secondly, it was quite untrue to tell us that government departments paid the same fees as private clients. It was then usually nearer half. So virtually the entire solemn ceremony was a pack of traditional white lies.

But the greatest piece of archaic nonsense of this kind is encountered on the Bench, at any rate throughout my time in the High Court. On every occasion when Parliament is dissolved, every judge of the High Court and Court of Appeal gets a rolled piece of parchment, with red tassels and the embossed royal seal, called a "Writ of Attendance at Parliament" in decorative script. It recites that "Whereas by the advice and assent of Our Council for certain arduous and urgent affairs concerning Us the State and defence of Our United Kingdom and the Church We have ordered a certain Parliament to be holden at Our City of Westminster on the .... next ensuing and there to treat and have conference with the Prelates Great Men and Peers of Our Realm", Then it goes on to the business bit: "We strictly enjoining COMMAND you that (waiving all excuses) you be at the said day and place personally present with Us and with the rest of Our Council to treat and give your advice upon the affairs aforesaid. And this in no wise do you omit".

When you get this you can put it straight into the waste paper basket or preserve it for your more credulous grandchildren. It has no other obvious use. If you were to obey the order and present yourself in Westminster you would be turned away because you hadn't got a ticket. And someone would want to know why you were not sitting in court and working. But in my days this piece of parchment was sent out every time, faithfully and regularly, by the Lord Chancellor's Department, with the Queen's command, addressing every judge by name and rank as "Our trusty and well beloved . . . Greeting". It seemed churlish to ignore it and not to obey. But to ignore it was the real command of the government to HM's judges, clearly demonstrating that our constitutional monarchy has been stripped of all executive power, as we learn at school. . . .

But back to 1961. Although everything now seemed set fair, there was a recurrence of an old anxiety. I was now really becoming deaf. It was beginning to be noticed and I worried about it constantly, which made it worse. I couldn't hear the mutterings of judges and witnesses in court and, above all, the whispers of my solicitors to tell me what they'd said. But just when I wondered what on earth I would do, there was another *deus ex machina* salvation. I went sent to see the doyen of ear surgeons, Sir Terence Cawthorne. For years until his death I used to remember him in my prayers, in so far as I had any. He was a great character, appointed to Her Majesty, who drove himself around in a bright blue Rolls Royce, which I often saw and always saluted. He said that there was a new operation under a microscope which had come over from America called a stapedectomy. Instead of 'mobilising' the little bones by shaking them loose, they are simply cut out and replaced by a direct link which can vibrate freely. At first it was a piece of wire, later it became plastic. It even had the advantage over nature, so far as I understand, that they wouldn't readily overgrow again, being inorganic. He did this on my left ear and I found that I could hear almost perfectly. It was one of the greatest moments of my life to notice that the noise of the traffic going up Campden Hill Road really worried me. Then, when the right ear failed a year or so later, I went back to him, shortly before his death. But he held out his hands and said that they shook too much for operations under a microscope. So it was done by someone else in about 1964, when it had become a standard operation.

Since then I have had wire in my left ear and plastic in my right. By the eighties it got worse again and I should have got a hearing aid. But I was always too busy and just about managed on the Bench, relying on knowing what people were going to say before they said it. I remember trying an industrial injury case about deafness when Counsel said that I could probably not imagine what it was like to be deaf. He looked bewildered when I said that I had got into the habit of not even listening to the radio without trying to lip-read. As Diana would say – "followed by sycophantic laughter in court". Since I 'retired' in 1989 I've got two small hearing aids, of which I only need one, and have no more problems.

What life in this generation has revealed for all of us who are part of it, more than for any other generation in the world's history, are the staggering advances of science, and - on the personal level - medicine. If I had lived at any earlier time I would not only be long dead, but deaf as well.

62 · Some Highlights

THE FIRST years as a Silk are the best of the Bar, provided that one's practice holds up. To be liberated from drafting, particularly pleadings and – worst of all – " Further and Better Particulars", and to have a Junior to talk to and help with the research, and sometimes do a first draft of Opinions and Advices on Evidence, opens up a new plateau of the legal world. You suddenly find yourself in control of cases and enjoying them, instead of being swamped in trying to keep up.

Mine were at first dominated by shipping, an industry which was probably much more important and certainly far less regulated than now, and amazingly fruitful in international disputes of all kinds. The Greek shipowner millionaires, each from their original beloved island, were a major clientele of City firms and Chambers. Most of them had worked hard to make their money, first as Officers and then Masters and finally as Owners of American ex-"Liberty" ships, built for "Lease-Lend" during the war, and then converted and used as tramps under flags of convenience world-wide in the great explosion of post-war trade. But when they became successful they would not only have penthouses in Mayfair, Manhattan and Athens, offices in Piraeus, and yachts in Cannes, but also a lot of disputes, not just for the money, but always "principle" and sometimes "honour". One big problem was that their ships were ageing and deteriorating, sometimes to a value below the amount for which they had been insured. One of the older Silks in Chambers once said that Greek owners would not necessarily regard it as immoral to cheat on their insurers, but that they were rightly shocked at the way we treat our grandmothers.

I got to know many of them, and the first – struck by some disaster to the crankshaft on one of his ships which Lloyds had failed to understand, but which was explained to me when I visited the engine room during a night stop in Antwerp – produced an unexpectedly wonderful invitation, of course via the solicitors, for my (first) honeymoon, on his line from Genoa to Piraeus, and then – without his help – to Mykonos, a small fishing village hardly known in 1952. There were others later, in particular Niarchos, though at first he appeared on the other side. He had ordered the world's fastest yacht, powered by three of the then new Viscount turbo aero-engines, from Vosper Thorneycroft. But she would not do the thirtyfive or whatever knots which he said had been guaranteed. The reason, which was common ground, to use a mixed metaphor, was that the design had failed to make allowance for the effect of the inevitable salt deposits on the propeller blades, which had never been a problem for Viscounts in the air. But there was a big dispute about what speed had been guaranteed. Why? Because the record of the "contract" was what had been scribbled, literally on the back of an envelope, when Niarchos and the chairman of Vospers had been queuing for a chairlift when they were skiing in St. Moritz. This was the only part I found a bit surprising, since I was doing a lot of skiing at the time: Would Niarchos really have queued?

When this had settled, Niarchos came back with something quite different, an unsuccessful bid for a Rembrandt at the first of the resumed Christies auctions, at the Dorchester. His agent, Mr Agnew, had signalled the top bid by duly folding his arms, which had previously been agreed as a secret code for bidding, but which the auctioneer had unfortunately forgotten in the excitement of the day and had therefore ignored. When the portrait of Rembrandt's son was then knocked down to someone else, after he had given several vain hints to Agnew to raise his hand and bid, there was a protest by Agnew and a threat to read out the agreed correspondence. This was successful to the extent of compelling a fresh auction, but one in which Niarchos was outbid.The portrait of Rembrandt's son is now famously in America, and we were (rightly) unsuccessful in our claim for breach of contract against Christies. But I think that we must have got something out of it, because the case never went to court or arbitration, and no Greek shipowner ever settled for nothing.

A few cases were pure law, particularly on topics like banking and the dreaded bills of exchange and bills of sale, which were Dickensian. But most involved strongly disputed, and often fascinating and sometimes highly technical, questions of fact before any law would be relevant. When the *Atlantic Duchess,* a large tanker, blew up at her discharging terminal at Milford Haven, was the cause that her cargo of crude oil had been unlawfully "spiked" with butane in liquid form, or was this a permitted and customary method of transportation? This simple question took me to the Sun Oil company in Philadelphia, who were reputed to be doing this regularly. After a helpful meeting with some of the directors there was a teetotal lunch with the Quaker Board at the High Table in the hall or canteen, flavoured with assurances from my charming hosts that this was the most puritan city in the United States. I still remember that this statement acquired a new perspective in the evening when my instructing solicitor and I were confronted by a stark naked girl

MK at Swearing in

dancing on a table in the bar next to our hotel, booked by the company. But the case also produced a sight of Niagara and of the St Patrick's day parade in New York, which, together with leaning skyscrapers, my family had to endure as early home videos for years.

The difficult shipping cases, and occasionally heart-rending, were the "scuttlers", in which ships were lost and the insurers denied liability on the ground that they had been "wilfully cast away with the privity of the owners", having been (perfectly legally) overinsured. In a number of cases this was no doubt true, particularly during the depression between the wars. But I also happen to believe that most of the self-made traditional Greek shipowners were proud men of the highest personal integrity and that some of them (not all) were unjustly accused and condemned of "privity" in a deliberate loss. I will never forget the owner of the *"Tropaiophoros"* who came to see Alan Mocatta and me in tears after we had lost in the Commercial Court. He said that he would accept having lost the case on the ground that we had failed to prove a loss by an insured peril, but not that he had been privy to scuttling the ship. We told him that an appeal was hopeless and that his P&I " Club" would not support one. But he insisted to go on at his own cost, saying that he had a son at Oxford who would always believe that he had done it if he did not appeal. So we had to go ahead, with the moral support of other Greek owners who withdrew their ships from this Club because it would (quite understandably) not support a hopeless appeal. The hearing was due to last two weeks, but the Court of Appeal, presided over by Fred Sellers, fully understood our motive and predicament and made it very clear, already on the third day, that it would be pointless to go on. So we stopped. The owner was heartbroken and died within six months. But at least he had shown to his family and friends that, for him, the decision had been a great injustice. And where the truth lay, we will never know.

Although by no means my favourite field, one of the great advantages of a shipping practice is that it gains from international crises and slumps and booms, since these always occur and directly impinge on the freight market. The grain elevator strikes on the west coast of Canada and the USA in the late 50's immobilised hundreds of government chartered ships in ports from Vancouver to Seattle and beyond, which produced a long trip to take evidence, flying on the newly introduced polar route from Amsterdam in high-level bunks via Greenland and unforgettably watching an arctic fox sniff the wheels of the Liberator. The hearings in Vancouver were followed by a holiday in San Francisco and Mexico and ultimately by my first trip to the House of Lords as a Silk in the case. Later on, the staggering accumulations of ships at different times in Calcutta and Lagos, waiting for a berth and claiming demurrage for lost time (I used to think of Proust's *"A la recherche du temps perdu"*) produced a lot of work, fortunately without my having to go there.

And the closures of the Suez Canal in 1956 and again in 1967 paid for my first children's education, first school and then university. Many ships were caught in the Canal and were claimed, and disputed, to have become "constructive total losses" under their owners' insurance policies. Others had to be diverted around the Cape, with their charterparties being claimed, and disputed, to have become "frustrated" by the additional time and distance. And what was the nature of these Middle East conflicts in the context of long-term time charters, concluded by their owners in more peaceful and less profitable times, with their suddenly crucial cancellation clauses beginning "in the event of war"? I remember a pleasant, lengthy and interesting arbitration, debating the nature of war and the events of the Arab/Israel conflict in 1967 with experts in public international law, while the ship in question was safely anchored off Rio de Janeiro. Could the owners cancel? The never-ending ups and downs of the world freight market, particularly for tankers after oil crises, when owners and charterers had opposing interests to break or retain their time charters, and flocked to their lawyers, were always a staple diet of Chambers work, and no doubt still are.

But although the bread and butter was always all in London, the most exhilarating disputes involved travelling. Taking evidence for cases pending in London or arguing in courts and arbitrations abroad. An alleged all-correct football pool coupon, which went astray in the offices of West Indian Airways in Georgetown, Guyana, and then missed the BOAC "Clipper" from Port-of Spain to Heathrow and was duly disqualified when it arrived late in Liverpool, took me to the Federal Court of Appeal of those times in the Caribbean and enabled me to present the first and (I am told) only Silk's "red bag" to a Junior in that former colony. The heat and humidity in court seemed overpowering, and I noticed that my opponent's black silk gown was turning green with some sort of fungus at the cuffs. But on the occasions when the ceiling fans were working all loose papers tended to become airborne and wafted over the bench.

Then, together with Geoffrey Lewis of Herbert Smith, we had to advise the government of the Sudan and to address the cabinet in Kharthoum (soon to be liquidated or in hiding after the first of the coups) as to how they should handle a bitter dispute with their contractors on the vast Wadi Halfa Dam resettlement scheme, which took us (with Michael Mustill) to a game park on the Ethiopian border and then on an unforgettable ride to Cairo on a Kitchener-like wooden train with huge open cookpots on the platforms between the carriages. And later there was the extraordinary dispute about the large oil pipelines assembled and laid across the shallow mud flats of the Shatt-el-Arab, carefully aligned with the direction of the incoming tide, but which were then constantly broken because, for some mysterious reason, the rising waters always divided as the tide moved in and only built up along one side of each line, until it buckled and ultimately fractured. When I went to meet the Texan contractor tycoon again, always wearing his Stetson, at his next site in Durban, where there was to be a demonstration of a similar project to be filmed for his insurers, I said that I had never heard of anything like it since the miracle of the Red Sea parting for the tribes of Israel. He said that he had already told his American lawyers that that was exactly what had been happening. and that he had given them the reference in the Old Testament to pass on to the insurers.

But my favourite destination was always the Far East, Singapore and

Hong Kong, with short breaks en route in between or beyond to India, Kashmir, Sri Lanka, Thailand, Malaysia and Taiwan, some of them with Julia and the children. Together with, or rather usually against, Bob MacCrindle, I spent weeks, if not months, in Singapore, with local lawyers who became life-long friends, like Karthi and his family, Murray Brash and Dennis Lee. In one form or another the cases usually involved alleged Indonesian shipping or currency frauds in the Singapore and Malaysian trade, claimed to have been perpetrated by Chinese businessmen on their slower Malay colleagues, for which we would then seek to exact retribution by suing in the courts of Singapore after trying to get the evidence in Indonesia, Malaysia or Thailand, and once with Dennis Lee as far away as Egypt and the Lebanon. On one occasion Bob MacCrindle and I got ourselves called as life members of the Bar of Hong Kong, which was then still possible. But in my case the Bench supervened, and I never made any use of it.

One final point, by way of comparison with the eighties and nineties. Although I was overworked throughout most of my 24 years at the Bar, I unfortunately never became what is nowadays known as a "fat cat". The archaic privilege of being able to take all one's outstanding fees free of tax into retirement from the Bar, on ceasing to work or going on the Bench or elsewhere such as the City, was abolished in the mid-sixties, shortly after having thinned the elderly ranks in anticipation. (Though one or two returned later after a respectable interval). But it never helped me. And the fifties, sixties and seventies were mostly the decades of legendary high taxation, over 90% if one had a private income, though I was spared that. And there were also no comparable rights of putting aside large chunks of one's earned income to accumulate a pension, which is now the financial hallmark of all successful barristers and the main reason why many can still afford to go on the Bench, with young children and (now) 20 years of work before their judicial pension as against 15 in my time. Things only changed with the advent of Maggie Thatcher in 1979 and then John Major. The present Blair/Brown combination never went back to the bad old days, apart from a few tax increases by stealth. But in the result I was never able to collect more than a very small pension from the Bar of the sixties and early seventies, in annual single premium policies of a few hundred pounds or less over about 7 years. This is something which has dogged me all my working life, and provided the excuse for my never having been able to shake off entirely the feelings of financial insecurity, or worse, of my childhood and youth.

But enough of that, though – as my father used to say – everything must be said that is true.....

53 · Towards the end of the Bar

As I was getting more senior as a QC, travelling became more of a rarity. But I remember two unusual trips in Europe, both with solicitors and clients. The first was a fact-finding mission trying to trace a number of allegedly priceless ex-Rothschild paintings which the Nazis were said to have looted and hidden in a salt mine in Austria. I have long forgotten whether we found any facts, but certainly no paintings, though the salt mine was fascinating, particularly in retrospect after we had got out again. The other was a luxurious trip to Hoffman LaRoche in Basle to talk to the management about their marketing practices concerning Valium, which were attracting the attentions of the English Restrictive Practices Court and the Commission in Brussels. I only remember a sumptuous lunch and a discussion with their chairman, telling him that I was constantly trying to extract Valium prescriptions from my reluctant doctor. Whereupon he took me into the factory building next door and told me to cup my hands under a stream of Valiums shooting into a funnel and to stuff my pockets with them. That is all I remember taking back to London. The anticipated litigation then went off until after I had gone on the Bench, when I think it went all the way to the Lords. But the next few months were more relaxed and the nights much better.

Apart from occasional short trips, all my working time was now spent in London, in the courts or in arbitrations, and endlessly writing opinions and advising in consultations, as conferences with Silks are called. But nothing really changed, except that I gradually stopped offering cigarettes to solicitors and clients and felt that I had to ask for permission to smoke, as I did for another 20 years until my triple bypass operation. I would never have believed that smoking at home and at work would become virtually banished in my lifetime, and often wondered which I would hate giving up more, tobacco or alcohol.

I must have seemed like a workhorse in blinkers, which I largely was. Apart from travels, my working environment throughout my life has been tiny, a north-south axis of less than a mile, from the Temple to the Law Courts and Lincoln's Inn and then to the Law Commission beyond Gray's Inn, for the first 33 years, and then back again to the Law Courts and my old Chambers in the Temple, and finally back with Chambers to Lincoln's Inn Fields, for the next 20. That is where I have spent nearly all of my working time over the last 53 years, 24 at the Bar, 17 on the

Bench and the last 12 as an arbitrator. All of it on this small axis of what I call "legal London". I don't really know the City, because its denizens generally came to the Temple. And I hate having to go to the West End (and all shopping).

But in my working life there was never anything like a routine; I never had a partner or employer; and I found most of the work at the Bar endlessly fascinating. Reading new sets of papers, forming and expressing views on strategy, tactics and the probable outcome, often where other views had gone before, in cases which really mattered to the people concerned, cross-examining witnesses to get the points across to the judge whatever the witness might say, arguing the merits in court, watching the way the judges were going, and then – moderately often – being proved right in the end, or having to despair about the obtuseness of judges and witnesses. And of course the prevailing atmosphere was usually tense, with an undercurrent of anxiety that things might go wrong, which one later tends to sublimate and forget. *Faute de mieux*, because I cannot think of anything I could do better, I would probably do it all over again.

Of all my years in the law, those at the Bar were by far the hardest. In term time I used to work most evenings and parts of every weekend. In long cases with witnesses, each day's transcript of the evidence would be delivered at home in Kensington at about 10pm so that I could prepare the next day's cross-examination. As my first children will remember, I mostly had dinner at my desk, and I kept myself going with Coca Cola and listening to classical music in the background. From 1961 to 1972 I was also Head of Chambers and had to take most of the administrative decisions, such as fixing rents and interviewing staff and pupils, and then chairing occasional Chambers meetings to decide who should be taken on as a tenant. Work was like a treadmill over which I seemed to have no control. My main relaxation, though only much later, was playing tennis again, for which I had found no time since the war. For several years I played regularly at Queens, with Mark Littman, dear Walter Gruber (who sadly died) and other regulars, until trouble with my neck and back made me give up again. And before that skiing, though only discovered at 33 and only fairly fluent, became an important part of life for every winter, until I had to give it up about 30 years later. Even now I regularly dream about skiing and wake up thinking I can do it again. Skiing, tennis, music, the cottage in Cornwall and holidays with the children, sometimes combined with working trips abroad, were the breaks in what was otherwise ceaseless work. I never took long holidays, and after the end of the summer term on 31 July the beginning of August was always a time of collapse.

As I was getting more senior at the Bar I also got involved in more public activities, though I never tried for them. Eustace Roskill was the Chairman of Hampshire Quarter Sessions, as the criminal courts in the counties outside London were called in the days before Beeching introduced the Crown Court. He said that John Donaldson and I should get some criminal experience as an investment, to give us a better chance of appointment to the Bench, since our practices were so specialised. So we were appointed Deputy Chairmen. I had never addressed a jury in my life and had never even seen one until I had to do my first summing up to one in a burglary case in Winchester, then sitting in the Castle, with the Bench halfway up the wall under the huge Round Table ascribed to King Arthur. But I only did it for about a month each year and always remained slightly uncomfortable trying crime. Many of the cases at that level were not very serious. They were mostly local burglaries, and I remember Julia and the children coming down to watch one in which the main stolen exhibit was a stuffed crocodile. Or rather, I don't remember, but the children always remind me.

Then I was asked to go on the Council of 'Justice,' and went to a number of meetings over two years or so, but never with great interest. My heart was never in systematic law reform, because in those days it never worked, and this became a bit of an impediment ten years later when I became chairman of the Law Commission.

But I was interested in the professional aspects of the Bar. When Desmond Ackner was chairman of the Bar Council he co-opted me onto it and I served on the Executive Committee for about two years and then on the Senate. I also became chairman of the Bar's International Relations Committee, which introduced the new rules allowing foreign lawyers to approach barristers direct for advice, without going through solicitors, and allowing partnerships abroad, which I drafted. Both these changes involved hostility and some retaliation from the equivalent Law Society committee, which was then run by George Goddard and Blanche Lucas, and which had large funds and paid time at the disposal of its members, in comparison with the scant resources of the Bar. Both sides of the profession were then preparing for our entry into the Common Market and seeking to promote themselves among foreign lawyers. I remember a huge row when we succeeded in forcing the withdrawal of a particularly misleading Law Society pamphlet, by threatening to go to Lord Denning, the Master of the Rolls who was in charge of the Law Society. This purported to explain the English legal scene to foreigners by avoiding any reference to the Bar until the last page, where it said: "Although solicitors do not presently have a right of audience in the higher courts, as Officers of the Court it is their duty, with the assistance of members of the Bar, to draw the attention of the judges to the relevant authorities and statutes". On further consideration even the Law Society accepted that this might be considered a somewhat one-sided and incomplete description of the system, and the pamphlet was duly pulped. Then later, as time went on, these rivalries began to shrink and George and Blanche became close friends, though both are now long gone.

Meanwhile my practice was also changing. I often sat as an arbitrator and was less often in court. But the main change was that over a period of weeks, or even months, I would only be involved in one big case, advising and preparing for the hearing, and more or less forswearing all other work meanwhile. In these long cases one becomes a total expert on the topic in issue for a time, working and thinking in blinkers, acquiring sufficient understanding to explain the issues to the judge and to cross-examine the other side's experts with the assistance of your own. Then, as soon as it is over, you forget all about it. And why does this system work? For one simple reason: that the judge is no expert and knows even less than you have yourself by then absorbed, with the result that all the experts on both sides are forced into producing child's guides for everyone in court.

For me these long cases removed one of the most important attractions of the Bar, which is the variety. No barrister ever quite loses a momentary feeling of interest and anticipation on untying the red tape on a newly delivered brief, though admittedly this nearly always fades as soon as one begins to read. But there is also the variety of constantly working on different cases, and on different stages of cases, over short periods of days or even hours. I remember many instances of preparing for consultations to advise, particularly on evidence, discovery, witness statements and experts. In heavy cases I might spend up to two or three days doing this and making notes or dictating. Then there would be a long meeting with the solicitors, perhaps all day, when all would be reviewed and agreed and they would take lots of notes. And then the magic moment – when the solicitors would go away, with all the files and with months and months of work to do, while I could forget about the case entirely, which might anyway settle and never come back, free as a bird from all its drudgery.

These pleasant aspects ceased when life became more dominated by heavy cases with numerous ring files, though never in the same numbers as are now routine. Photocopying had by then come in, but it was not yet a forensic (and profit-making) activity in its own right, as it has since become. Skeleton Arguments and restrictions on discovery, orality and the citation of authorities (from books, not photostats) were not yet in force, though judicial and administrative feelers for reform were beginning to be put out. But commercial trials were still receiving what Derry Irvine once called " the Rolls Royce treatment" when we talked at some function before he became Lord Chancellor, which he then wished to retain for those who wanted it. It involved full discovery and full and detailed oral argument with unrestricted reading of the relevant documents, and then the authorities cited from rows and often shelves of books brought over by the clerks for counsel, and identified from lists supplied to the court and handed up to the Bench by the court ushers. Apart from the pleadings, there was no pre-reading by the judges. The pace was infinitely slower than nowadays, and both counsel and the judges had much more time to think. But there was no way that the old ways could survive the present practices of mass litigation and documentation. The Woolf reforms of civil procedure were certainly necessary in principle, even though in some respects the right working formulas have not yet been found.

I only remember a few of the heavy cases, all long in preparation and mostly long in court, which dominated large parts of the sixties.

The ownership of the trademark 'Bayer,' with its curved pharmaceutical cross, gave rise to a world-wide dispute between a German and an American company, whose roots went back to before the first world war due to the intervention of the Custodian of Enemy Property in the twenties, whose yellowing files remained part of the complex legal position after yet another world war. Outwardly it seemed that the essence of the dispute was whether the name should be pronounced 'Byer' as in Germany or 'Bear' as in the USA. I was on the American side. When we finally got to court, the other side's opening speeches took over a month, after which it was agreed that there should be an adjournment for negotiations. So I went off skiing, with Nicholas Phillips and Christopher Staughton, and when I got back the case had settled. I think that the parties merged or one took over the other, and since the general pronunciation nowadays is "Byer" and not "Bear", it seems that we were taken over.

Zeiss was an even heavier dispute, this time between East and West Germany. Did all the assets of Zeiss, and the name, belong to Zeiss Jena or to Zeiss Heidenheim? It all really turned on the recognition and existence of a separate state in East Germany, independent from Russia. The business and all its factories had always been in Jena, but when the Russian armies were moving across Poland, the senior management transplanted itself and all the movable machinery in convoys of trains to Heidenheim in the West and proclaimed that "Zeiss" was there. Jena countered by suing for the name and all the assets. Mark Littman led me, as a second Silk, for the West in the Lords, having won in the Court of Appeal by stopping the action on the surprising ground that because East Germany had not been recognised by HMG, neither it nor its institutions had any legal existence. A typical Francis Mann argument and a tribute to Mark's advocacy, but to my mind clearly unrealistic. The Lords thought so too, and we rightly failed to stop the action. Mark then left the Bar for the Steel Corporation and I went on alone, instructed by dear Francis Mann. We won the next two skirmishes up to the Court of Appeal in preparation for the main hearing, when there began to be talks of settlement. I was strongly in favour of settling, but Francis was strongly against it and said it would never work. We went to Heidenheim and both addressed the Board, who decided to settle. I heard that the settlement agreement was typed out on one sheet of paper with two copies, which each side put into its safe. Its contents were highly secret but totally simple, and there has never been any problem since. I got a pair of Heidenheim opera glasses as a memento, which I later gave to Alexander. But I noticed that the large microscopes which were used for my ear operations had all been made in Jena, whereas Heidenheim specialised in cameras, which never interested me. So I had more sympathy with our opponents, whose business it really was. Jena also had their own football team, which I followed from a distance

Before Zeiss there had been the first battle in the Thalidomide tragedy in which I was not on the side of the angels. I was for the manufacturers, and Desmond Ackner for the unfortunate children. It was a desperately worrying case. The drug had only been made under licence in England. All the research had been done in Germany, and that was where most of the evidence was. The first problem was that the Germans wanted to fight the issue of causation by contending that the drug had not in fact caused the deformities. But they gave in when I told them that no reputable expert would appear on their side if they tried to dispute the unchallengeable. So then the issue was negligence: should the effect on pregnant women, who took thalidomide between certain early weeks, have been discovered in the course of the manufacturers' research and tests? The drug had of course been tested on every conceivable animal, with no ill effects. But never on *pregnant* animals. However, we knew, as did the experts on the other side, that at that time no pharmaceutical manufacturers in the world had developed tests on pregnant animals. It was simply not something which had occurred to anyone as being necessary. I spent weeks reading books and experts' reports, which I couldn't really understand, about biology, medicine, genes, enzymes and teratogenic causes, in preparation for the cross-examination of the other side's experts. It was a nightmare. There were 74 children in the litigation, but we were only going to fight one as a test case. Then the word settlement was mentioned and ultimately Desmond and I agreed on a formula whereby we would pay 35%, I think it was, of whatever might be the appropriate damages in each case. What the other side had probably not realised was that although it was known throughout the industry that no one had by then carried out tests on pregnant animals, we would have had the greatest difficulty in proving it. The actual proof was only to be found within the big pharmaceutical companies, our competitors, and none of them would have helped us by proclaiming, in effect, that they would equally have failed to recognise the danger. But the other side may not have known this and offered to settle. The test case was then fought on quantum alone, and that unfortunate child was awarded a pitiful sum. My side and their insurers were delighted.

We would gladly have paid more than 35%, and perhaps Desmond would have taken less. We have never discussed it since. But anyway, our battle only proved to be the beginning of a much greater war. When the low settlement percentage for the 74 cases was announced, more than 300 other claimants appeared on the scene and there was a public outcry, championed by the *Sunday Times*. Everything then went back into the melting pot and I was glad to be out of all aspects of thalidomide. The *Sunday Times* case, on the issue whether its newspaper campaign had brought unlawful pressure on a party to settle a piece of litigation, went all the way to the House of Lords and then to the European Court of Human Rights in Strasbourg. Ultimately the *Sunday Times* won in Strasbourg, a vast trust was established, and some years later all the children who could establish causation got reasonable settlements, including the original 74.

Then I was one of a tribunal of three which sat for six months on a governmental public enquiry into the collapse of a large motor insurance company, Vehicle & General, leaving tens of thousands of motorists uninsured and without any remedy. The question was whether the Department of Trade, which controlled insurance companies, should have spotted that the company's premium structures and marketing practices were bound to lead to insolvency. Lord Justice Arthur James presided, and the other members were Sydney Templeman and myself. We ultimately held that there had been negligence by an Under Secretary in the Department, an unprecedented conclusion in any Whitehall context. For many years our names were highly unpopular with all the Civil Service mandarins who knew the ins and outs of the notorious V & G enquiry and said that, as outsiders, we had no understanding of the workings and problems of Whitehall and of the service. But it was the right result all the same, and important, *pour décourager les autres*.

My last big case before going on the Bench dealt with the insolvency of Rolls Royce and the privatisation and hiving-off of its motor business from the aero engines. But I never saw the end of it, because the Bench intervened. Like most heavy cases it settled, and I have always believed that settlements are generally in the interests of both parties, even though they may be unable to see it for themselves. I think that all my friends with similar practices had the same philosophy, and it would never have occurred to any of us to want to prolong cases to earn more "refreshers", of which some barristers have sometimes been justifiably accused. But this philosophy also has its dangers. Lay clients, and often in particular the solicitors, hate being pressurised into settlements when they believe, however mistakenly, that they are "in the right". They want their day in court, and if they don't get it, some of them, usually the managers, not the Board, will never get over the conviction that they have been sold down the river by the lawyers. Some years ago I was alone in a lift in a hotel in Dubai with a man who appeared to be glowering at me. When I asked whether we had met before, he mentioned the name of a case which rang a faint bell of 25 years ago. I asked him what had happened, and he said: "You made us settle", glowering some more, and walked out.

We are now at the beginning of 1972 and I was getting as exhausted at the Bar as I am at this moment, and you probably too. So let's have a new chapter. But first one final case before getting to the Bench, my favourite case of all that I remember.

It concerned an American opera singer, James McCracken, a tenor. He had studied singing with a GI's grant after the war and had worked his way up as a recognised soloist to the Met. On the way he had married a mezzo, Sandra Warfield, and then they toured the world with their small daughter Lucy, singing at many opera houses on the international circuit. Finally his great chance came when Del Monaco had an accident and couldn't sing Otello at Covent Garden. Jimmy's performance brought him success and world acclaim overnight, together with the offer of a recording contract from EMI. They had planned to record Otello with Del Monaco and were now deeply worried that someone else might sign up McCracken for it. So they offered him a contract to record four operas over the next three years, to be mutually agreed but excluding Otello, provided that he made no recordings with anyone else during that time. The terms were generous and he was only too glad to accept. But apart from some desultory correspondence over a year or so, nothing happened, and it seemed that EMI had no intention of fulfilling this contract. So he had sued them, little knowing what he was taking on.

The contract was badly drafted and governed by Swiss law, though I don't remember why. EMI took every point to frighten him off, and their resources were without limit. They said that by Swiss law the contract was not binding because it did not specify the operas to be recorded, that he had failed to get in touch with them about the choice of the recordings, and that he and/or his reputation were in any event not good enough to justify a major recording venture. This, they claimed, provided a defence under Swiss law, incredible though it seemed. They filed affidavits from Swiss lawyers and tried to force him to put up security for costs because he was not resident in England. They held all the cards for endless procedural attrition.

We had many conferences in my room with his solicitor over the months which followed, whenever he sang in England, to which he always brought Sandra and Lucy, because they always toured together. But, as the first flush of enthusiasm and the calendar of his engagements at Covent Garden diminished, the case became more and more of a burden, and then a potential disaster for him, and his singing began to suffer.

We finally reached the stage of the first hearing, a week ahead, when EMI were pressing for security for their costs of the action if it was to go on. I was pessimistic about this hearing, and I also knew that even if we were going to survive it, it was going to be the first of many, which would become increasingly long and difficult and bleed him white, when he had already spent thousands on the case. We would also have to instruct some Swiss lawyers on our side. With three days to go, we had fixed an all-day conference to finalise the statement of his evidence. And then, just when I had given up all hope, EMI caved in. They paid £30,000 into court in satisfaction of his claim, an enormous sum in those days. If we accepted it, they would also have to pay his costs to date.

Jimmy McCracken arrived the next morning with his solicitor, Sandra and Lucy as usual, but looking desperately tired and worried, because he now realised what a tiger he had got by the tail. When they had sat down I had one of the happiest moments of my time at the Bar. I said that we could do one of two things that morning and that the decision was his. We could finish drafting his statement for the hearing next week, for which he would have to fly back from New York and miss a performance at the Met, though that would only be the beginning of a battle which could last for years. Alternatively we could all walk across Fleet Street into the Law Courts and pick up a cheque for £30,000, knowing that his costs to date would be paid as well and that everything would be over. There was a silence, and I had to explain it a bit more. When they under-

Michael in the High Court

stood, Sandra burst into tears and clung to Lucy, and Jimmy, who was built like a bear, waltzed me round the room, singing, but also crying. When I realised that he was singing from the duet at the end of the second act of Fidelio I got out of control as well, and the solicitor and I left the family in a tearful huddle.

Later on, we walked across Fleet Street, picked up the cheque, had a cup of coffee, and then a great party and dinner after his performance at Covent Garden that night. Afterwards, for many years he sent me a copy of every one of his recordings, and I saw him once more, back-stage, in Zürich. Then his voice gradually went, and he died, relatively young. But he left me a memory of himself, and of a case that meant more to me than any other.

64 · The Bench?

I NEVER HAD any problem about making decisions for my clients at the Bar or for litigants as a judge on the Bench. But for most of my life I have had great difficulty in making decisions about my own affairs. That has changed, now that time is short, but then it seemed endless. I had agonised about staying on as an academic lawyer at Cambridge and then much longer about whether or not to go to the International Court at The Hague. However, all that was nothing in comparison with my agonising about whether or not to go on the Bench. Whether I could bear to be a judge, or whether I should avoid it to do something more active. And, if I did something else, from which there could be no way back, whether I might not regret it and miss the law for the rest of my life. The only aspect about which I had no worries, surprisingly as I look back, was that I might not be asked. This had been the traditional agony and sometimes tragedy among the Bar for centuries, and it remained true for the first decade after the war. There were some great disappointments among people I knew and in some of which I shared, including the anguish caused by the questionable preferment of a younger brother. But my favourite memory is the unforgettable reaction of a dear old man, throwing the Times across the room in disgust with the words: "If they were going to appoint a clot, why not me?"

By the sixties, however, the times and the volume of litigation had changed. Although elevation (as it is called) to the Bench was then a much greater event than now, since there were far fewer judges, there were also far fewer overworked QC's at – or near – the top of the Bar. So I was fairly confident that sooner or later I would be asked, always assuming, as even I by then did, that I would no longer be haunted by a foreign origin. But what I could not decide about was whether I really wanted it.

So I agonised volubly, consulted everyone, and knew by the end of the sixties that I had become a great bore to all my friends about it. My gut feeling was that I would probably come to want the Bench in the end, but like St. Augustin with his desire for chastity, 'please, but not yet.'

I had one memorable false alarm in 1970 when I was called to see the Lord Chancellor in the Wilson government, Lord Gardiner. The occasion had all the hallmarks of the classic summons, and I didn't want it. Sitting opposite him in that enormous room in the House of Lords overlooking the river, it took me several minutes before I realised that my prepared excuses would not be needed. He was asking me to carry out a confidential investigation into some allegations of corruption against Alf Robens, the chairman of the Coal Board, whose daughter was engaged to marry the son of the chairman of the largest suppliers of mining equipment. A dismissed, highly-placed employee had claimed that there had been improper favouritism in the award of contracts. I accepted the job with pleasure and relief, and telephoned Julia from a phone box outside that all was well. Then I went to see Harold Lever, the Minister of State responsible, whom I already knew, to get some details. He was sitting in his beautiful office in Millbank, the Headquarters of the Labour Party, surrounded by his own Impressionists on the walls. We agreed that I would read all the documents and interview the witnesses and come back in about two weeks. But by then the Heath government had taken over, Harold Lever had gone, and I ultimately reported back to Hailsham, not Gardiner, that the allegations were entirely baseless. For a long time the investigation and its outcome were kept secret, but ultimately it all leaked out and my report was laid before Parliament. As Alf Robens, a great character of total integrity, had said when I had questioned him after cross-checking all the other evidence, "I can't control to whom the lass takes a fancy".

About nine months later, however, towards the end of 1970, the real summons came from Hailsham. I was still quite unsure what I wanted to do and it was not an easy interview, although I knew him quite well. I made excuses about children and schools and about being in the middle of a huge case – it may have been *Zeiss* – which I couldn't leave, and – being too honest – also said something about possibly going into the City. This was received by him and the Permanent Secretary, Denis Dobson, with raised eyebrows verging upon horror. It was the time when Henry (Harry) Fisher had recently resigned from the High Court Bench to go to the City, because he was "bored", an unprecedented slap in the face of the judiciary of England and Wales then and since, for which he was 'sent to Coventry' for some time by many of his former colleagues and friends. In the end, to my relief and contrary to what I had been told and feared ("you never get a second chance") my temporising excuses were accepted. It was left on the basis that I would let Denis Dobson know within about eighteen months. In those days High Court appointments were far fewer than now, and Hailsham indicated that there would be no need for a decision before then, because he could fill the present vacancy and anticipated no others during the next year or so. The appointment went to my old friend Desmond Ackner, who had always reminded me about the importance of "seniority" in the judicial ladder, and who may also have been right on this occasion.

I then knew that I had about a year, and that was when my real state of indecision began. At that time the Bench seemed like a closed monastic institution, the proverbial ivory tower. Wigs and gowns and stiff collars every day in the High Court; and on Circuit living in judges' lodgings, dinners with High Sheriffs, and changing into a dinner jacket, at least for the butler, and having grace said at dinner, every night. And although I would be nominated to the Commercial Court as my primary sphere of work, I would have to try every kind of case, including quite a lot of crime, And above all there was the question of money. I was earning about £38,000 a year, near the top of the Bar, and I think that a judge's salary was then £11,500. True, there was a reasonable pension after 15 years, half one's terminal salary index-linked, but that was too far off to be of any relevance. So my hesitation was justified. But there was also the carefully calculated bait of the traditional knighthood, the security of the job and the pension, and the then prevalent knowledge that anyone who refused would never be asked again. Although this has changed since, it was still true then. And above all, there was the knowledge that the Bench was the natural summit of the whole of one's working life.

I remember a long lunch with Geoffrey Lewis of Herbert Smith, ostensibly to report on a possible merger with another firm which I had been asked to try to "broke" and which came to nothing, when we bared our souls about aspirations for our working lives after 50. I told him how I envied him for not having to make any decisions, because he had partners and security until retirement and beyond. And he said how lucky I was to have a choice of a change of career at this stage of life and to be able to transfer into working in the public sector. We were both idealists, up to a point, but I thought that he could afford it better than I.

So, although my indecision became something of a joke to all those who knew, I still think there were good grounds for it at the time. One of the main attractions of the City was that I would be able to use my languages and travel. I wanted to become cosmopolitan again, and I was coming through the long stage of wanting to be intensely English, which finally disappeared when my friends' children read Judy's *When Hitler Stole Pink Rabbit* at school and people realised that I was Max. I have often found on my travels that I was quite famous as Max, for having "bathed worms" trying to fish in a Swiss lake, and as the son of my father; but not for being an English judge.

However, back to the facts. I consulted a lot of people. My uncle Nucki sent me to Sigmund Warburg, who said that he would do something for me which he claimed never to have done before, to give me an open option to come in as a partner (they were then not yet called directors) whenever I liked. That had been in 1968. But I knew too much about the internal tensions within the firm from Nucki, and nothing would have induced me to go there. As it turned out, he and Sigmund quarrelled bitterly during the following year and Nucki left, supported by the regrets and affections of most of the management, and died in the autumn of 1970.

The really serious proposal was to go to Kleinwort Benson. They knew about me, and I became very friendly with Martin Jacomb. There was a dinner with the chairman and some of the directors and a lot of serious talk, including terms and figures. But then I suddenly shied away. It began with something the chairman said, about how envious one of their competitors would be when they heard that I had called on the chairman of some Italian bank in Milan on behalf of Kleinworts. Commercial QCs were then thinner on the ground. I suddenly realised that a lot of the job would involve window-dressing and, effectively, selling. The rest would be aeroplanes, hotels, constant meetings and – above all – negotiations, at which I have never been any good. I don't have the patience. I want to get things decided and get on, and I am not interested in money, let alone fractions of percentages. But Martin Jacomb was very good. As soon as he realised that I was hesitating, all the persuasion stopped and he suggested that we should call it off. I was embarrassed about the wasted time and trouble, but he told me to forget all about it, which I did.

So then I was really heading for the Bench, because apart from the City there was no other alternative. It was out of the question for me to go on working at this rate or to become a solicitor. And an old Silk can be a sad sight. As Geoffrey Lewis still remembers, I told him in confidence that I would go north, not east. To the Law Courts, not the City.

But ultimately it was Mark Littman, who is not a sad sight and knows everyone, who was responsible for a near last-minute *volte-face*. Mark had talked about me to Jacob Rothschild, and I went to have lunch with him. He was very persuasive and we got on very well. It was left on the basis that Stanley Berwin, one of his partners who was a solicitor, would take me out to dinner and tell me all about the firm and the work.

We had dinner at the Savoy and it was a really memorable evening. I liked Stanley enormously and we became great friends. He left Rothschilds about a year later and then founded Berwin Leighton, and later S J Berwin on his own. Then he collapsed and died a few years later, evidently due to overwork.

He said that he had been given the job of persuading me to join

Rothschilds. But as the evening went on it took a different turn. I began to sense that he himself wasn't really happy there. When we parted he said that he would be indiscreet and that, if he were I, he would definitely stay in the law. I, on the other hand, had become attracted to the idea of joining the bank.

The final act was another lunch with Jacob. I felt uneasy because Stanley wasn't there, and I may already have known that he was going to leave. It soon became more of a friendly debate about the pros and cons than the beginning of a honeymoon. He struck a wrong note when he belittled life on the Bench and gloried in the excitement of the City. At the end he produced his clincher. He said:

"Think of yourself on your deathbed after a boring life as a judge. That's when you will certainly wish you had been in the action in the City."

It was also the clincher for me, but the other way. I knew by then that every excitement and achievement in the City was a 7-day wonder, whereas the Bench was something which endured. Looked at in that way, there was really no comparison. So I told him that on my deathbed the choice would be obvious and that I might as well make it straight away. We parted amicably, but no more.

I could write a short treatise about the problems of a transition from the Bar to the City, about the many failures and the few successes. I would have been a failure and unhappy, as were Harry Fisher and Hubert Monroe. Others were successful and happy, like Gordon Richardson, who became Governor of the Bank of England, Martin Jacomb and Philip Shelbourne. You need to have money in your blood. But that was certainly not my scene. Diana has always said that any bank that employed me would go bust.

I remember the next events precisely, when I got back from the lunch at Rothschilds. It was in February 1972. I went to my room in Chambers and wrote a one-sentence letter to Denis Dobson, the Permanent Secretary at the Lord Chancellor's Department: 'I thought that I should let you know that I have decided against the City.' I got a stamp from the Clerk's Room and walked to the letter-box in Essex Court because I didn't want anyone to see to whom I was writing. When I got back to my room the phone was ringing. It was Denis Dobson. Before he could say anything I said that I had just posted a letter to him. He said, "What does it say?"

"That I am not going to the City."

He said: "Thank God."

It was a time when a number of Silks had gone to the City and had, or would have, refused the Bench, mainly because of the pay. Against constant objections by the Treasury, the Lord Chancellor's Department wanted to see the salaries increased, because they feared refusals and a general lowering of the standards. My rejection of the system at that time would have been the most notable event of its kind since Harry Fisher's resignation.

Denis Dobson's next words were: "When can you come and see him?" His lord and master; still Hailsham, still during his first period of office.

I suggested the following week. But he said that I was to come on the following day.

However, one hurdle still remained, which I knew I would have to face when I saw Hailsham again. It was the last and most powerful siren's call which I had to resist. We had just agreed to join the Common Market as from 1 January 1973 and I knew that we would have to provide a British judge and Avocat-Général for the European Court in Luxembourg. One would come from Scotland, our supposedly "civil law" jurisdiction, Jack Mackenzie-Stuart QC, who spoke French, as well as his wife. I knew the other: with my French and German and commercial background I would certainly be asked to go as the first British judge. But I didn't want to live and work in Luxembourg, arguing in French in committees about the drafts of judgments to be given by a Bench of ten judges about Common Market issues. Despite the compensations of a large tax-free salary and a Mercedes and driver.

So I was not surprised when, just before I was called into Hailsham's great room again, Denis Dobson said: "Oh, and by the way, he's going to ask you to go to Luxembourg." I said that I had feared this but couldn't accept. He said, as he opened the door, "You just tell him."

So I went in. By then I knew Hailsham quite well. I had become a Bencher of Lincoln's Inn in 1968, as he was, and we were on Christian name terms, which was obligatory among fellow Benchers. We started by agreeing that I would finish my present case and that I would be appointed in April, immediately after Easter. But then it came: "And by the way, would you go to Luxembourg for us next January as the UK judge?" I remember the next bit verbatim. I said: "Quintin, I'm sorry, I feared you might ask me and I am honoured. But I really can't. I have small children at school and it would be like exile."

And then he did something which would have delighted my father as typically English. He put his arm around my shoulder and said: "My boy, that's what I thought you'd say. Abroad is all right for the hols. But not for living."

Then he went on. "But who shall we send? After all, we can't send two from Scotland." He asked me whether I knew "what the screw is?" I had looked it up, together with all the terms of the appointment, and told him. He whistled and said that he would have to think again, but that there should be no difficulty in finding someone at that salary, and we parted on the best of terms. Before leaving I just made sure that he would appoint me to the Commercial Court and said that I wasn't too keen on doing too much Circuit. He said that of course he would, and that if I was getting too much Circuit I should let him know. That, of course, was just a phrase which was meaningless except to be nice. But it was something, and I went away perfectly happy. I knew where I was. I had security and would never again have to make any decisions about my work. Or so I thought.

However, I was not to escape the Common Market entirely. An important part of the negotiations for our accession was to re-negotiate the terms of the original so-called Brussels Judgments Convention for the mutual enforcement and recognition of judgments, and the allocation of national jurisdictions in various circumstances, throughout the Common Market, by producing a revised text for our Accession Convention which would be acceptable to the UK, Eire and Denmark, the three new members. For the work of the English Bar in Europe, the new text would be of the greatest importance. In the summer of 1972 Hailsham asked me to chair the Inter-Departmental Committee set up to monitor the negotiations with the other nine countries, which were to be in the hands of representatives of the Lord Chancellor's department and the Foreign Office. It was a Committee of about thirty Civil Servants including Scotland, Northern Ireland and all the government departments concerned. We also had to decide upon the internal reforms within the UK which would result from our accession, and there were also the beginnings of consequential negotiations within the Commonwealth and with the United States. I had to chair and monitor all this work, much of it in my spare time, with many trips to Brussels led by Karl Newman of the Lord Chancellor's Department, after he and my old friend Henry Brandon had dealt with the Admiralty law points, which had gone surprisingly well. But the jurisdictional and commercial issues proved to be far more intractable, and at one point I even had a season ticket for the Brussels underground.

I didn't like Brussels and I hated the negotiating meetings because we were nearly always in a minority, the odd man out. The Irish had similar problems to our's, but they were often not there. And although the Dutch and Danes were usually sympathetic, because they knew far more about the English legal system than the others, the French, Belgian,

Luxembourg and Italian votes were always solidly on the other side, and generally supported by the Germans. It was a difficult and frustrating time. I also saw something of the work of the Commission in Brussels and made several visits to the Court in Luxembourg. I stayed with Jean-Pierre and Sylvia Warner, who had meanwhile become the Avocat-General with Jack Mackenzie-Stuart as our judge. But I had no regrets, except the occasional twinge about their Mercedes' with drivers, large virtually tax-free salaries, and paid forensic travels. Luxembourg life seemed to revolve entirely around diplomatic-type cocktail parties and being driven to the airport whenever one could get away. I told J-P that I thought that if I had gone there, I would have become an alcoholic and shacked up with a local countess. But he saw it differently, explaining how important the work was. And no doubt he was right. But not for me.

Ultimately it took about seven years before the work of the Inter-Departmental Committee was entirely finished and it was formally dissolved. The text of the Accession Convention had finally been agreed and enacted by statute. Of the endless negotiations only one aspect remains in my mind. One of our primary concerns was to preserve the pre-eminent international role of the Commercial Court in London and the much used right of foreign parties to agree upon it as their chosen jurisdiction, even when the dispute had no connection with England. But this was highly unpopular abroad and in practice largely curtailed by the wording of the original Convention. There were many papers and discussions about the changes on which we tried to insist, with no success in sight. But in the end we got what we wanted, by one vote, with the help of Ireland, Holland and Denmark, against strong opposition from France, Belgium and above all – in this case – Germany, on a day when Luxembourg was fortunately absent. But the key factor was that on a Friday afternoon, the day of the crucial session, by the time of the final vote the Italian delegation had caught an early flight home. We won by 4 to 3. That was the origin of the present version of Article 17 of the Brussels Convention, which has become one of the cornerstones of the Treaty for the UK. I was told later that for some months Belgium had refused to ratify the new text because of the objections of the Antwerp Bar that this would have the effect of continuing to channel too much maritime work to London.

But all this is going ahead. When my appointment to the Bench was published I received a summons to have an audience with the Queen. Every High Court judge has a private investiture at which he is knighted, and then a private audience, a ten minute chat with Her alone. In my case it was to be at Windsor. The Queen was returning from the Gold

Cup at Cheltenham and was due on a state visit to de Gaulle on the following day. I was told that I had to come alone, in morning dress, and that it would be usual to rent a limousine. But I only rented the clothes from Moss Bros and drove Julia in our Volvo. Ultimately she was allowed to wait with the officials in an ante-chamber. In due course, after Leslie Boreham had come out before me, announcing that "She loves Suffolk", two doors were flung open by footmen in breeches. I went in, and when the doors closed I knelt down on one knee as instructed. The Queen was standing by the far fireplace, holding an intimidatingly tall sword. When she touched me lightly on both shoulders I thought that it must have weighed a lot less than it looked. But instead of saying "Arise, Sir Michael," she said: "So you're the new boy!" I protested slightly, saying that I'd been asked nearly two years earlier to go on the Bench. But she merely said, "Well, come and have a chat anyway."

It was easy to talk to her. She spoke about the deterioration in our way of life, and I remember being amazed when she said that "traffic-wise" conditions were awful. On the motorway, even when the road is clear and some speeding is allowed, "one gets overtaken by Fords and things." At the end she said that she often wondered, as her Nanny used to say, "whether one day it won't all end in tears." Then she pressed a button, the doors opened, and I walked out backwards.

Some years later, and I don't know why, I was invited to one of the small lunches at Buckingham Palace with the Queen and Prince Philip, and I sat next to her. I said that I had always remembered her Nanny's phrase, and how true it seemed. This was bad manners; since one is not supposed to initiate topics. But it didn't matter. She smiled vaguely and obviously had no idea what I was talking about.

65 · Life as a Judge

FROM THE moment I went on the Bench in April 1972 I knew I had made the right decision, the only possible decision as it seemed in retrospect. I never had the slightest regret or doubt for a single moment afterwards. I didn't miss the Bar. On the contrary, I was relieved to be out of the arena and above the fight. I no longer wanted to be partisan, fighting for one side. The horizon had become much wider and seemed far more important. My new creed, instead of fighting for one side, was to provide a service for both sides which should convey to them a sense of balance and justice, even though one side nearly always had to win and the other to lose. In every case my purpose was to make it clear to the litigants, and anyone who knew the facts or read the judgment at the end, why I had to decide the dispute as I did, and why I felt that there was no other way in which it could properly be decided In addition, I wanted to make the parties and the witnesses feel at ease and relaxed in court, because I had often noticed that anyone who had ever been in a court had an indelible memory of what the judge said and how he behaved. Finally, a judge has an additional responsibility to the law and to the administration of justice which transcends, and may occasionally even conflict with, his or her duties to the parties. Occasionally one therefore has to do something which neither side wants, usually because of a lack of jurisdiction, which also has to be explained to them. All of this was a new scenario, a different dimension from the Bar, which I have endlessly tried to urge upon others who hesitated like me and asked what they should do. But it does not suit everyone, and a few of my contemporary judges, including a present Law Lord, and quite a number from later generations, never got over their longing for the Bar, and disliked the Bench until they grew older, indifferent and used to it.

The daily routine in the Law Courts did not worry me at all. I had a comfortable room and a succession of Clerks, mostly ex-police officers, who could type, so that I was able to dictate my judgments into a dictaphone and revise as many drafts as were needed. Computers and word processors did not yet exist. It also didn't worry me that on nearly every day one had to sit in fancy dress half way up the wall, as somebody described it. I got so used to the wig and gown that I didn't notice them any more; only the stiff collar and bands were a nuisance because one had to change shirts. Diana always tells the story of when we came down to breakfast at a hotel in Melbourne, on a visit organised by the Australian Bar, where all the waiters and waitresses wore chef's hats and butcher's aprons. I couldn't make out what they were supposed to be and said, irritably, that I could never bear to have a job in which I would have to wear something ridiculous. She collapsed in laughter, pointing out "my daily poncing about in a wig and dressing gown." But by then I was unconscious of robes and even preferred the routine of prescribed impersonality in dress to having to think about what to wear. Now, a generation later, I feel differently and would abolish wigs altogether.

So the Law Courts in London were not a problem. But I didn't like going on Circuit, because the atmosphere in Judges' Lodgings was formal and lonely, with an undercurrent of ceremonial, dominated by whoever was the senior judge and by the butler and cook, usually a married couple. Most judges loved it, and the great majority of their wives, because it was – and no doubt is – a tradition that wives may not come down to breakfast, but must have it in bed. ("Wives " are singled out because in those days there was no woman High Court judge except one in the Family Division). But some of the wives on Circuit were worse for protocol and ceremonial than their judges. They were conscious of their husbands' seniority, which rules everything in Lodgings, and tended to remind others of it in a way which suggested – falsely – that their husbands were too immersed in their judicial responsibilities to trouble with the pettiness of formal traditions, and therefore above them. I have seen tussles about who goes first through a door into dinner, and have often heard of the famous debate between two judicial wives as to whether pouring out the coffee after dinner is the junior judge's wife's duty or the senior judge's wife's privilege. The lovely Helen Eveleigh, sadly missed, once burst into tears when she came back from the local Museum of Drains, or whatever it was, there being nothing else to do, and – without thinking – asked the butler for some late tea. Whereupon the senior judge, a bachelor, shouted at her from the upstairs landing, where he was wrestling with his collar while changing for dinner, that she had no right to ask for tea without his permission. Some judges disapproved of wives in Lodgings altogether; and the senior judge always had to be asked before one could invite them. Whoever was the senior judge also ordered the wines, chose the menus, and his Clerk did the budget and the accounts. He set the tone. In the evenings one changed into a dinner jacket even when alone. It was expected by the butler who represented the continuity of the Judges' Lodgings, and it would soon get around if one didn't, thereby letting the side down. After all, the Judge is the senior local representative of Her Majesty, as I was reminded countless times.

My first Circuit was in Manchester, and fortunately I was alone. But I started badly. I arrived in the late afternoon and sat down in the drawing room to write an urgent letter which had to catch the post. I vaguely saw the shadowy black figure of the butler approaching and heard him say: "Can I draw your lordship's bath?"

Without thinking or looking up I heard myself reply, verbatim: "Would you mind drawing one of the other ones, because I'm just going to have one." It was only his mystified silence which made me look up and realise what he had meant. It took a long time for both of us to recover from this.

Another, more senior, judge came later on for a week, and I remember our silent walks around a nearby cemetery and various dinners with the High Sheriff and local worthies. Every morning the judge or judges were collected by the High Sheriff, complete with sword, to travel in the limousine to the rear entrance of the courts in the centre of the city, convoyed by police motorcyclists in front and behind. On one occasion, on the first day of an Assize, I had to represent H.M. at the opening service in a cathedral, entering to the sound of trumpets, and sitting alone in the front pew in a long-bottomed wig and a scarlet robe edged with ermine. (Later on it became rabbit, and then nylon.) And there was never any question of going out to a cinema, let alone a pub, in the evening. One might be recognised or run into witnesses or members of a jury, and anyway, it just wasn't done.

In this way Circuit is quite different from London, where you can meet judges on any bus or tube going to the courts or driving themselves to work. On Circuit the security of the individual Judges is the direct responsibility of the local Chief Constable and High Sheriff, so that one never manages to feel anonymous and alone.

But one day, towards the end of my first Circuit in Manchester, I decided to have a look around the city, which I hardly knew. The case list was short and I changed into my civvies and went out the back way to walk around, telling no one. But within five minutes I was lost. Then I saw an imposing edifice with columns and steps leading up to the entrance. So I asked a policeman what it was. He told me it was the Crown Court, where I had been sitting every day for more than a month. But I had never seen the front of the building.

However, Circuit was not all bad. Many judges and their wives were highly congenial and a pleasure to be with. The Lodgings were extremely comfortable, some with table tennis and billiard tables, staffed by a highly competent cook and butler, and the food was usually excellent. The messing allowances to which we were entitled, or whatever they were called, were unexpectedly generous. Even with wine and entertainment, which were – surprisingly – allowed for by the Treasury and included in the budget, there was always a small credit balance at the end of every Circuit. So I soon found that there was no problem about having to go out of London too much, which I had dreaded. The Circuit sittings were chosen at the Queen's Bench Judges' meeting at the beginning of every term, and the right to choose by seniority, which had existed since time immemorial, had just been abolished. All our names were now put on a paper wheel which moved by a third of a rotation each term. If one wanted to get on the Western or South-Eastern Circuits, or to Oxford, which were the favourites, one had to be near the top. But if one wanted to stay in London one could nearly always swap with someone, because most judges liked going on Circuit. The living conditions were usually far better than at home, and one could even make a small profit. And one could get away from wives if one wanted, and/or please them by inviting them. An ideal set-up.

Admittedly, I have heard that nowadays Lodgings are not what they used to be. Not surprisingly, costs are being cut. There have always been scare stories of the closure of Lodgings and of High Court Judges being put into hotels. But in the end the Treasury has always drawn back in the face of the resulting judicial fury. Nevertheless, standards have begun to slip. A leaked copy of a memo from the Lord Chancellor's Department to Circuit Administrators, which I have seen, announced an end to the replacement of grape scissors for Judges' Lodgings. This appeared to some to signal the thin end of the wedge. But a retiring judge promptly reacted by setting up a trust fund, to nip this iniquity in the bud. Judges' Lodgings will ultimately not survive, but they are meanwhile assured of the necessary replacement of worn-out grape scissors, whatever else may be plotted against them.

Apart from disliking the atmosphere in Lodgings I also didn't like the work on Circuit, which was nearly all crime. I tried murders, a large number of manslaughters, which are much more difficult than murders, many robberies and endless burglaries. Also three memorable rapes. Having seen the records of the accused, who had all been convicted of rape or indecent assault before, and the evidence, including those parts which – on various technical grounds – would not be admissible, there was no doubt in my mind in any of the cases that the defendants were guilty. But all were acquitted. The defence in each case was that the girl had consented, and in each the case the facts presented a scenario which made consent a credible possibility. One victim was a prostitute, one a lonely hitch-hiker, and the third had let herself be picked up in a bar to be driven home late at night after a hen-party with her girlfriends to celebrate her wedding on the following day. She said that she had been raped in lay-byes at both ends of the Mersey Tunnel on her way home. Her mother described how she had arrived home in total distress, dishevelled, in floods of tears and with her clothes torn. The defence said that if this were true, which they did not accept, then the girl had done it to herself on purpose to explain to her boyfriend, who was staying with the family on the night before the wedding, why she had got home so late. They said that she had had a final fling, pretending to have been attacked. I knew that every word was a lie, and I couldn't see how any jury could think anything else. But they evidently did.

In those days the defence had come to realise that it was a good idea to keep women on juries instead of using their permissible 'challenges' to get rid of them. I could see from the expressions of the women that they had no sympathy for the girls. They were saying to themselves that the girls had simply been asking for what they got. Since I felt that I knew for certain, in each case after hearing the evidence and watching the girls under cross-examination, that they had been raped, with a hand round their throat or a knife, real or pretended, in their side, I hated to have to watch them suffering in the witness box with their families and boyfriends in court, often in tears. In one case the jury came back with a question: "Suppose we believe that the girl did not consent to intercourse but consented to oral sex. What should we do?" I thought that it was a strange question, and tried to imagine their version of the scenario. But I told them that if they thought that she had freely consented to anything, then they must acquit the man. And they did, in all three cases, perhaps because none of the girls said that they could remember having screamed. I tried to explain to the jury that no one would want to scream under the threat of being knifed or strangled. But they evidently thought that this was not a good enough reason for silence in the face of the loss of one's virtue.

After the worst of the three cases I was being driven away in my official limousine, I think in Preston, with a police escort, feeling sickened at the outcome. At a traffic light we were overtaken by a Jaguar, with the defendant sitting in the passenger seat, being driven by his brother who had also been in court and whom I knew also to have a criminal record. The defendant saw me in the limo in my robes, roared with laughter, made a nose at me, and both drove off in high spirits.

I apologise for all these trivia. I am constantly trying to guard against 'Legal Tea Leaves.' But it's not easy. And as with life generally, the oldest memories are clearest. The recent years seem little more than a constant rush.

I suppose that I must have spent about a total of 18 months on Circuit between 1972 and 1978, when I went to the Law Commission. But nearly all the rest of my work was in the Commercial Court in London. By chance I never sat at the Old Bailey and never had those famous lunches in robes and wigs with the Sheriffs. But they would not have been my scene, and I would not have enhanced the role of Her Majesty's 'red' judge among the ceremonial of the Corporation of the City of London. When I was in London I was always in the Law Courts in the Strand and always tried commercial cases unless the list collapsed, in which case I had to do ordinary civil work, mostly personal injuries known as 'plaintiffs falling off ladders.' And lunch was always at Lincoln's Inn, a mixture of a club and a canteen, simple, quick and pleasant. Although I was happy to be asked to join the Garrick and did so, I refused several invitations to join City Livery Companies, which were also not my scene.

I suppose that altogether, if you add up six years in the High Court and then about eight years in the Court of Appeal, I must have heard many hundreds of cases. When I retired in 1989 Diana gave me a 'Lexis' computer print-out of all the reported cases in which my name appears as counsel or judge. It's several yards long, though there must be many duplications. But I have never looked through it. It bores me to chew over the past, even though I want to put down the main events in these memoirs, more or less for the record. I only think about a few cases which were important to me. And all of those which were memorable, except the giant appeal in the Tin Council dispute, when there were over thirty barristers in court on many days for more than two months, were concerned with people, not just companies and money.

One such landmark case was about a Greek ship, *The Michael*, which had been scuttled, deliberately sunk by her Third Engineer, a previously convicted scuttler. The issue was whether her owner had been "privy" to the scuttling, in which case the insurers would not be liable. If not, they would be. Even though the *Michael* was worth much less than her insurance money, which was in any event commonplace and perfectly legal, I felt quite sure, after seeing him in the witness box and under intense cross-examination for over a week, that this young inexperienced Greek shipowner had not been involved in the scuttling of his first ship in a conspiracy with a professional scuttler, the third engineer, who had been engaged through routine channels and had in fact opened the valves to the engine room. I felt sure that the engineer had done this, as he had on other ships in the past, in the expectation of a reward from a grateful owner. I suspect that many of the lawyers involved, perhaps on both sides, were highly sceptical, and even Michael Mustill, for the owner, was surprised to win the case against the odds, though he said that he had always been sure that his man had been innocent. As with so much else, we shall never know.

Another similar battle against the odds, but where the truth became clear, was when a small Norwegian shipowner took on the great tycoon Armand Hammer and accused him and his minions of having forced him to cancel two long-term time charters by fraud and duress, in effect blackmail and lies about the alleged insolvency of his off-shore chartering company, and ultimately won. On that occasion, after several weeks of evidence, there was no real room for doubt. As Francis Mann would have said: "It was obviously all a *terrrible frraud.*" My only claim to any credit was to have made sure, against all resistance from one side, that all the evidence leading to the truth came out.

Commercial judges have few downright human experiences in their work and all judges must be careful not to get involved with the lives of the people in the cases before them. I once had a litigant in person on a Friday afternoon, sitting alone in the Court of Appeal, who argued for more than an hour that he should have leave to appeal against an order which had awarded the custody of his nine-year-old daughter to his wife, from whom he was separated. He said that she was not a fit person to look after the girl and that she would hurt her, physically and emotionally. But since there was no conceivable reason for the Court of Appeal being able to reverse the decision of the judge at first instance, who had heard the evidence of both parents and of welfare officers, merely on the basis of the father's disagreement with it, this was really a hopeless application. So I refused him leave. He looked at me for a long time, then turned round and walked out. On the Monday morning the case was back before me. The man had gone straight from court to his wife's flat and stabbed her to death. I was asked to make some order for the welfare of the daughter, who now had no mother and a father in prison, awaiting a life sentence. All I could do, which was a formality, was to put the girl in care of the local authority. And to wonder whether I could have done anything else, on the Friday afternoon.

But I won't go on with such reminiscences, though I obviously could, more or less endlessly and with increasing tedium. Instead, suffer while I say briefly something about the sort of judge I was, since I have no illusions about it. I'll be frank and short.

The plus side is that I really had a very high reputation and a lot of affection among those who appeared before me, many of them frequently, and many of them now old friends. The English Bar, particularly among the specialists, is quite small, and in retrospect parts of it appear like an extended family spanning several generations. But I will never be remembered as anything approaching a great judge. And although large numbers of my judgments appear in the reports, very few will survive as quotations. The reason is that I was always wary of trying to lay down general principles in quotable pontific paragraphs, preferably numbered. Several of those who ultimately did better than I – going up to the Lords – used to approach cases in this way, but I hardly ever did. My first priority was always to sort out the facts, to get to the truth by working out what had really happened and why. The main part of all my judgments was always an analysis of the facts. I wanted everyone who heard or read them, on either side of the case or merely as an interested spectator, to feel that the story had really been understood and that the truth had come out. Then, in most cases, there would be a second part about the law. I have a lot of aptitude for legal analysis and I would never shy away from it. I took pains to explain the consequences of the facts and the logic of the outcome by going into the law quite deeply and rarely taking short cuts. So the law is always there in the judgments, and sometimes quite original and penetrating. But it is often not free-standing, and only rarely will there by any general pronouncements of principle, which I distrusted. As a judge I was a trier of cases, a pragmatist rather than a jurist.

A final word about being reversed on appeal. One is always asked whether one minds. I have probably been reversed less often than many others, but everyone always says that. What I can say is that in the great majority of cases where I was reversed by the Court of Appeal, I agreed with the outcome. This is not because I could see some fallacy in my judgment when I re-read it. It is because cases often appear quite different on appeal. The loser starts and has the last word. And, above all, the Court of Appeal starts where the case at first instance finished. It starts with a judgment that has pulled everything together and enables the case to be seen in the round from the beginning. In the court below, the facts and the law come out piecemeal, through documents, witnesses and speeches by Counsel. One's mind goes to and fro, and most of the time one is simply trying to follow and keep up. And then, when the talking finally stops, one has to produce a judgment which tries to pull everything together and expresses what one thinks at that point, one's most recent thoughts. But that is the point from which the Court of Appeal starts, and it can stand back, working out the right solution with an overview of the whole case from the beginning, and an existing judgment to serve as a working template.

And so, if the answer on appeal is different, as it often is, I have found that it is usually better. I can remember a few notable exceptions when I have had the (sometimes dubious) support of academic writers, but generally one gets to recognise the passages on appeal starting "With all due respect to the learned judge..." and – usually – to accept what follows. The most memorable occasion when I was graced with this formula, which may even have been a record, was when I was reversed by 3/nil in the Court of Appeal and then by 5/nil in the House of Lords. It involved a respectable difference of opinion as to whether the threatened conduct of a shipowner was sufficiently bad to amount to a repudiation of a number of highly valuable long-term time charters, as all my Lords thought, with me in a more understanding and lenient minority of one. However, there was a single precious grain of comfort. As you can see in the report of the leading speech of Lord Wilberforce in the House of Lords, the operative passage begins with the memorable words "With *genuine* respect for the judgment of Mr Justice Kerr . . .". (Emphasis willingly supplied).

All of this is only another fragment in a host of forensic trivia. In the long run none of it matters. But it takes a long time to discover this for oneself. *Tout passe, tout casse, tout lasse.* The law may have made me boring, but it has never given me any sense of self-importance. Nor any belief in the intrinsic importance of anything mundane or materialistic. My motto expresses my philosophy of life exactly. I have a motto, because Lincoln's Inn asks that any Bencher entitled to a coat of arms should get a "shield" (as it's called) and to have it put up in the Great Hall at the Inn's expense. So, having been knighted in 1972 and being told to go to the College of Heralds before it got more expensive, I visited this improbable setup and negotiated the composition of a coat of arms for about £400, a fraction of what it costs now. The result can be seen in Lincoln's Inn, half way down the west side. I wanted grass and tennis balls, and I got a green surface and three white "roundels", which were permitted. I also got two wings for flying, a pen in memory of my father, and a pair of scales and a book in honour of the law. But then there was a fight about the motto, which was considered unsuitably irreverent, although respectable classical Latin. I had found it in a dictionary of quotations, the concluding words in Plinius the Elder's account of a recipe for an antidote to poison. After some unconvincing ingredients which I have forgotten, there it is at the end, "additio salis grano", which has become "cum grano salis" in general parlance. With a pinch of salt. My motto, for which heraldic permission was ultimately granted. It may not say everything to encompass a philosophy of life. But it says a lot.

But enough of the law and suchlike for the time being, and a brief turn to more personal matters.

66 · Separation

WE ARE by now into the second half of the seventies. The important event of that time, which I am not going to write about in any detail, was the final breakdown of my marriage to Julia in 1977. It had been coming a long time. Our lives together had really become unbearable, at least for me, though my departure was not due to any real fault on her side. The phrase of the times was irretrievable breakdown due to incompatibility, or something like that. So, although I had nowhere to go, I felt sure that I must leave.

It was the hardest and bravest decision of my life. Julia and I had innumerable friends, most of whom no doubt saw us an ideal couple. No High Court judge had previously ever been divorced on the Bench. All my conventionalism came out and haunted and harassed me. I dreaded people finding out that I was no longer living in Bedford Gardens, and looked at everyone in the courts and at lunch in Lincoln's Inn, wondering who knew and who didn't, and how amazed they would be if they did. I only told my closest friends and my Clerk. Later on, of course, I realised that other people's lives, even on the Bench, were also not at all as they seemed. But by then times had changed, amazingly quickly, with similar situations becoming openly known and commonplace, as they are today. But not in the judicial seventies. For over a year I felt like a secret leper, who would be an outcast if people knew. That is a problem created by living and working in a relatively small collegiate community like the law. Particularly in the law of those days.

I left on a Saturday evening at the beginning of September 1977. I didn't have to be in court until 1 October and thought that I had ample time to find somewhere to live. I knew that if I didn't go that weekend I never would. I remember two things said by the children. Candy was on holiday in Turkey, but I talked to Jo and Tim through most of the night. Jo said, and Tim agreed, that of course their mother and I hadn't got on for many years, and that I was quite right to go. But why hadn't I gone much earlier, to give her a better chance to meet someone else? When I said that it was because of them, they were unconvinced. And why should they have understood? As La Rochefoucauld said, "*Nous avons tous assez de force pour supporter les maux d'autrui.*" Everyone has the strength to bear the misfortunes of others, and children hardly notice them anyway. And even when they are grown up, they cannot see how vulnerable they would have been earlier on, if their lives had not remained so sheltered.

The other memorable thing was said by all three of the children in different ways. "How could your and our mother's marriage have been so unhappy, as you say, when we had such a happy childhood?" This really surprised me, because I then thought that they had seen and felt the problems and rows at every point. But it also cheered me up. It seemed that my children had been and were happy. Or at least indifferent to what I had decided I must do.

I was going out to dinner that evening with Tony Lincoln to Panos Gratsos' house in Harrow, a Greek shipowners' family who had become great friends. Julia was in Cornwall with Belinda, a friend whom we had met through Michael Mustill and who was staying with us. I phoned Tony and asked if I could bring some suitcases and stay with him and his father for a bit in Paultons Square, and he said of course. Then I rang Julia and told her. There was only a brief scene on the phone. When Tony came to pick me up in the evening she and Belinda arrived back from Cornwall, which I had hoped to avoid. A lot of bitter, inconclusive things were said on both sides, with poor Tony vainly trying to mediate. Finally we put my cases in his car and left.

I never went back. For about six months I lived in Robin McEwan's attic flat at the top of Tony's house in Paultons Square. Then the McEwans needed it and I spent a few weeks in Mark and Marguerite Littman's spare room in Chester Square. Then Marguerite persuaded George Weidenfeld to let me stay in the small flat above his on Chelsea Embankment. I had met him several times and he was a great admirer of my father. So I lived there for about six months. The wardrobe was full of evening dresses. I went to many of his parties downstairs but always felt awkward and alone. It was a time when I only felt at ease when I was working, preferably in court. So far as I remember I had surprisingly little contact with my sister Judy about my problems of finding somewhere to live and reorganising my life. I knew that she had no regrets whatever about the break-up of my marriage, which she knew to be unhappy. But she had known too much unhappiness in her own life to want to be involved in any way. She always prefers to draw a protective fence around herself and Tom, which I can understand.

Around Christmas of that year I might have gone back. But Julia wrote the wrong letters, and there was also some unpleasant correspondence with Joe, her father, which did not help. So fortunately nothing came of it. It wouldn't have worked if it had been tried.

The Weidenfeld flat came to an end when the inhabitant above me let his or her bath overflow and the ceiling came down when I was in bed. It was almost like the bomb in Russell Square. I went on camping there for a week or two. Then I found a lovely flat on the third floor of 11 Bolton Gardens. Rathi Karthigesu, known to all who have ever been on the Singapore circuit, helped me to find it and with furnishing it. I also got some furniture from a remarkable old great-aunt, Estrid. She was the widow of Peter, one of my grandmother's half-brothers. She was Danish and had studied in Copenhagen under a man called Neurode who had invented a method of exercising physically handicapped babies from birth. She was also an ardent converted Catholic and had her surgery in a house which formed part of a convent in Southgate. Not having a real home, I used to go to see her a lot. Although she was beginning to go blind and approaching eighty, she went out to Calcutta to work with Mother Theresa. But she didn't get on with her. When I once told her that no two saints had probably ever got on in the history of the world, she hissed at me like a snake: "That woman is no saint!" I expect that the feeling was saintly mutual, but I liked being with her. She still looked marvellous and had a fantastic sense of humour. When she went blind I used to read Judy's books to her. But then she got very old.

One day, when I was sitting in court, my Clerk brought in a note to say that Estrid had fallen and broken her hip and was lying on the floor in her house. She was refusing all help and said that she would not allow anyone to move her except the doctor who had looked after Tim about ten years earlier, when a bus had stood on his foot near Victoria and he had been taken to Westminster Hospital. She had heard about this from me some years before. I asked counsel to stop for a minute and wrote a note for my Clerk to phone through, saying that I couldn't remember the name of the doctor of ten years ago when Tim had still been at school, and that if she didn't let herself be moved I would never speak to her again. But if she did, I would come that evening.

It worked, but she never walked again and had to give up her house and surgery. She moved to a convent near Copenhagen where I saw her once more. But I persuaded the Mother Superior in Southgate to pay £8,000 for Estrid's loss of the house adjoining the convent, which was to have been her's for life. Estrid had a German son and a daughter in their fifties from a previous marriage, whom I knew. They were grateful for the money, and when they came to clear out their mother's house they gave me a sofa, a refectory table, some chairs and two Danish wooden beds, as well as some bookshelves. That solved most of the furnishing problems for Bolton Gardens. From Bedford Gardens I had only been able to take my Ladbroke Gardens double bed and one Bentwood rocking chair, together with some books and records. I also had very little money. Maintenance and lawyers fees have pursued me for over 25 years, and both are still current. I never set foot in the house again. After I left, Belinda moved in permanently, and there is now also a teenage son and some lodgers.

Julia and I concluded a Separation Agreement which Ronnie Coubrough, one of my oldest friends, negotiated for me. But she made it clear that she would never agree to a divorce and that I would have to wait for the statutory five years, which would not expire until the autumn of 1982. That was hard to forgive at the time, especially after Diana and I had met in 1979. But Diana, who has always been wonderful, agreed to wait. So it's forgiven now, and largely forgotten.

67 · The Law Commission

IN THE SPRING of 1978 Sam Cooke, also a High Court Judge and an old friend, died suddenly , when he was the Chairman of the Law Commission. This had been created by Gerald Gardiner, the new Labour Lord Chancellor in 1966, as a kind of department to deal with systematic law reform in England, Wales and Northern Ireland. There was also a smaller one for Scotland. It was said that Gardiner had only accepted his appointment on condition that the Law Commissions would be set up and that capital punishment would be abolished. And both came to pass. The first English chairman had been Lord Scarman, and I always referred to his time as the years of the prophet. The grand design had then been to codify as much of English law as possible, in particular the whole of the law of contract, and various far-reaching programmes had been drawn up. So the concept was Utopian. Leslie Scarman and Sam Cooke had each done six years as chairman. The legal and political community had come to respect, and sometimes to admire, the Law Commission as an idealistic concept which was needed in principle. But it was also felt that it could and would do little in practice. And on the whole this had been true throughout its history. So no one who was at the centre of things, on the Bench or at the Bar, wanted to go there, including myself. But as soon as I saw that Sam Cooke had died, I knew what was to come. I had the academic qualifications and was regarded as something of an intellectual. So I could smell the inevitability at once.

And two weeks later the call duly came. I was to see the Lord Chancellor, by then Elwyn-Jones, known to all as Elwyn. He was there between Quintin Hailsham's two terms of office, interspersed by the forgettable Labour government under Callaghan.

I felt that I needed help and went to see Tom Denning at 1 o'clock when the courts rose. We often walked over to Lincoln's Inn together for lunch, and as soon as I looked into his room he said: "Come along, I know why you've come. You are to see Elwyn at 4.30. He wants you to go to the Law Commission." When he saw my face, which pretended surprise and shock, he went on in his Hampshire burr, which he always put on when he was being folksy:

"I said to him: 'Michael won't want to do this job. He shouldn't be taken out of the Commercial Court. He's too valuable. And he certainly doesn't want to go there for five years."

That was the official term for the chairman, though Leslie Scarman and Sam Cooke had each done six.

Tom Denning went on: "So he said: 'I know. I'm only going to ask him to do three."

And then he stopped walking and said: "So now you know. Whatever figure he starts with, he'll come down to three. On that basis you might as well take it. It might even help you to come to the Court of Appeal a bit sooner."

Then we went in to lunch and talked of other things, probably his favourite topic: how much QCs earned nowadays, and how much they had on their briefs in the Court of Appeal.

After that I was no longer worried about seeing Elwyn, and it was always fun to talk to him. He was a brilliant after-dinner speaker who used to sing rugger songs during his speeches and always mentioned that he had defended the last man to be hanged in Swansea jail.

When I went to see him at 4.30 he said: "I don't suppose you know why I asked to see you."

I said: "I have no idea. But ever since I saw about poor Sam Cooke's death I looked every day in *The Times* in the hope that you had appointed his successor."

He laughed and said: "So you do know. I know it's not very popular, but you are the right man to do it. And I am only going to ask you to do it for four years, and ..."

He could see my eyebrows go up and so he went on: "Or let's say three. And then the Court of Appeal."

He could see that my eyebrows had gone down and that there was no more opposition. It was a replay of the old establishment axiom: never refuse, never volunteer. And I could see quite a few advantages. I was being singled out, and it would make an interesting change to run something and to learn about the workings of Whitehall and government.

Elwyn then went on to explain that of course he could not bind his successor about the Court of Appeal. But he said that most Lord Chancellors in recent times, whatever their politics, had been gentlemen and had honoured their predecessor's word. I said that that was fine, but if he should – unfortunately – no longer be there, how would his successor know what he had said? He looked amazed.

"Because an official will write it in your pink file. Do you mean you have never seen your pink file?"

I told him I had never even heard of such a thing and I was sure that none of my friends had either. Perhaps it was another nice bit of perfidious Albion. But he pressed a button and Wilfrid Bourne – then the

Permanent Secretary – came in with a buff or grey file, certainly not pink. Elwyn repeated briefly what had been said, that I would do three years as Chairman of the Law Commission with a view to going to the Court of Appeal afterwards, and Wilfrid wrote it down with a slight scowl. He did not believe in statements about the future, which could become embarrassing, let alone those recorded in the presence of the incumbent.

Then Elwyn spoke about the importance of the job and his strong commitment to the work of the Commission. He said that his door was always open and that I should not hesitate to come to him with any problems or if I felt that there were any administrative obstacles in the way of any suggested reforms. This equally failed to provoke any burst of enthusiasm from Wilfrid. But we all knew that it didn't mean much and was only said to be nice. It was common knowledge that the Law Commission had always had the greatest difficulty in getting parliamentary time for its proposals, and only a few of them had reached the Statute Book. That was the real trouble. But on the whole the record of Labour had been, and was likely to be, better than the Conservatives. The Law Commission had been a Labour creation. The Tories had generally done little more than pay lip service to it. And within a few months they would be back in power, with Maggie Thatcher and Quintin Hailsham for the second time. But we didn't know that then. Nor would it have made any real difference to law reform if Labour had stayed in power.

The Law Commission was in a large building in John Street, off Theobalds Road, a block behind Gray's Inn. Apart from the chairman there were four commissioners. In my time they were a QC, a solicitor and two Oxford dons. All were first-class, and each had his own specialist territories. In addition there were about twenty-eight other full-time lawyers; the total staff was about fifty. My Clerk, Chris Beardsmore, had come with me to deal with my personal affairs as before and because I was entitled to go on sitting in the Commercial Court, which I did from time to time. For the first time I also had my own secretary, a spinster lady who had worked in the Civil Service for over forty years. We were predictably shy with each other.

The first day started badly. I was taken all round the building and introduced to everyone. When I got back to my room I found that my new secretary, Eileen, had already put a typed note on my desk:

'Sir.

The Arthur Murray School of Dancing has telephoned to say that your Lordship's lesson for tomorrow has had to be cancelled.'

I immediately recognised the style of an old friend, Anthony Nathan. He knew that I was starting that morning and had probably planned it for weeks. The timing was perfect, from his point of view. From mine it was less amusing. By lunchtime it was all round the building that the new chairman took dancing lessons. I had a few strong words with Anthony on the phone and didn't speak to him for several months. But I leaked it round the building that one of my former acquaintances was a maverick psychotic practical joker. It was my first ever public relations exercise, and as time passed I got better at it.

I had not looked forward to going to the Law Commission, but – as often happens – once done, it became quite enjoyable. It was a total change from trying cases. I was on my own, and for the first time in my life I ran an organisation. Most of the work consisted of meetings and reading other people's drafts; in those days the chairman did no drafting himself. We were dealing with various areas of the law, from crime to landlord and tenant and enduring powers of attorney, which actually resulted in a statute, the only one for which my term of office might claim credit. I was learning a great deal, but about relatively very little, because everything had to be considered in such detail. Later on I was to find that I learned far more, and was able to achieve more, by sitting in the Court of Appeal.

There are three major problems about the work of the Law Commission. The first is inevitable under the UK system of legislation: any changes in the law must be right, not only for the great majority of cases or for 99% of the cases, but entirely right for every possible foreseeable situation. That is a consequence of the English tradition that all statutes have to be drafted in minute detail, attempting to cover everything which can be foreseen. The Continental technique is quite different, by framing laws in general terms and statements of principle. But our parliamentary draftsmen and our administrative and legal traditions will not permit this. We had six parliamentary draftsmen from 36, Whitehall seconded to the Commission, and there were many battles with them. Although I was fortunate with the allocations in my time, I soon came to realise why they were called prima donnas.

The second problem should be avoidable. In my view it is one of this country's great weaknesses, like our ineffective and over-elaborate planning procedures. Because there is so much legislation and all of it is so detailed, and because every topic is regarded as political and liable to create divisions along party lines, even if only for tactical reasons, parliamentary time in the Commons is infinitely precious to whatever government is in power. Ministers fight over it, and the Lord Chancellor has no clout at all. Moreover, there are no votes in law reform. So most of the Bills which had been drafted by the Law Commission after vast amounts of work, Working Papers, and wide consultations, were gathering dust on Whitehall shelves because of insufficient political interest, and therefore no parliamentary time.

The third, which has greatly changed in recent times, was simply lack of interest among judges and practising lawyers. Law reform was only interesting to academics, and judges were not interested in their writings. One was not even allowed to cite them in court unless they were dead, and when one tried, some judges would object, pointing out that, "fortunately Professor X is still with us". There was a lot of sympathy with the legendary judge, faced with a proposal for law reform which had been long debated in the Lords, who is supposed to have exclaimed: "Reform? Reform? Aren't things bad enough already?"

These were the frustrations of my life at the Commission. I spoke and wrote against the obstacles to the Commission and arranged meetings in the House of Commons with MPs from all the three main parties. I also complained to Hailsham, who was by then again in office. But all I got was sympathy and vague assurances from civil servants, though a bit more from Hailsham. I had written to him to say that the least that the relevant government departments could do was to tell us why they were doing nothing, and what objections they had against our proposals. He was a classical scholar and replied with a long letter, saying that on this point he agreed entirely with me 'echoing the cry of Ajax before the walls of Troy.' There followed a hand-written insertion in ancient Greek. Which is what it was to me. But not to Tony Lloyd, my former pupil and later to go to the House of Lords. He explained that the reference was to one of the occasions when the Greeks were winning an interlocutory skirmish at the foot of the walls of Troy, so that a faction of the pro-Trojan gods had to intervene to save Hector and his friends. They laid a blanket of fog over the Greek side of the battlefield, causing Ajax to cry out: "Slay me if you must, but slay me in daylight."

This was endearing and typical of Quintin. I put a photocopy of the letter on the Law Commission file and kept the original as a memento, together with a few others from him, Maggie Thatcher, etc. and many from Denning. But while the cry of Ajax warmed my heart, it did nothing for the Law Commission or its chairman.

Professionally, the Law Commission was also unsatisfactory in other respects. There were internecine civil service politics, staff and funding problems, and the sad death of the QC Commissioner in my time. I was eager for my three years to be over.

But there were also compensations. I was my own master and in a special position where I could be spared for other jobs, though mostly those which others did not want. So I became the English representative on the *Union Internationale des Magistrats*, an obscure and virtually unknown would- be worldwide organisation of judges with an extraordinary history. It was started by some senior Italian judges in the fifties when the Treaty of Rome was concluded, and a number of countries soon joined through their Ministries of Justice. Then it was noticed that the UK was not participating. It is at this point that I believe that an Italian founder judge, possibly over here as a tourist or for a conference, consulted the *Yellow Pages*. At any rate, what the organisation hit upon in this country was the *Magistrates' Association*, a titular reflection of its own French name. The Association was delighted to be invited to join, and it took nearly a decade of happy annual meetings before the *Union* discovered that its English member in fact included no judges, and that the English judiciary therefore still remained unrepresented and without any knowledge of the *Union*. When we then joined the Common Market on 1 January 1973, there was a formal *demarche* about this situation to the Lord Chancellor and something had to be done. One problem was that, unlike most or all Continental countries, we have no association or other collective body for judges, let alone anything in the nature of a trade union, apart from an Association of Circuit Judges which was formed later . So there had to be, or at any rate soon was, some fudged solution. This took the form of the unpublished and unpublicised "appointment", by the Lord Chancellor's Department, of a High Court Judge to go to the *Union's* meetings , but also leaving the Magistrates Association *in situ* as well, to enjoy the seniority and respect among the world's judiciary which it had by then deservedly achieved.

I cannot remember from which judge I took over in 1979, but among the scant papers which I received from him there was one memo from the Lord Chancellor's Department which stuck in my mind. This was to the effect that costs were to be limited to the utmost and that this was not an organisation for which HMG would be happy to host one of its annual meetings. Since the venue for the next meeting was invariably the first agenda item at each of the *Union's* annual meetings, I found it increasingly embarrassing to keep my head down and doodle while this item was being discussed, trying not to notice the silent but pointed looks in the direction of the UK judge. But fortunately some more ambitious and hospitable jurisdiction always intervened before the silence became intolerable. On the last occasion I remember a feeling of enormous relief on being rescued by Portugal, then eager to be noticed as a future candidate for the EU.

I went to several of the *Union's* annual meetings, though I remember little of the matters which were discussed. Apart from routine resolutions which we would regard as self-evident, extolling judicial independence and impartiality, most of the topics were of a trade union nature such as pay, pensions, court hours and secretarial and other assistance. These would have been hard to fit into the English scene, though it was also hard to find reasons to explain why we always appeared to be different. The main reasons, that in the UK the judiciary is not a professional career and is not structured as an organisation, that we only have less than a hundred High Court judges altogether, who were all former practitioners, instead of many thousands in the nature of civil servants, and that we have no Ministry of Justice, were rarely perceived as presenting any intelligible constitutional system, and were never accepted as any explanation for any relevant difference between us and the judiciary of civil law countries. At that point of the discussion one would usually politely give up and say that we obviously still had a lot to learn from other jurisdictions.

The only meeting of the *Union Internationale des Magistrats* which I can clearly remember was one in Rio de Janeiro in July 1980. I combined this with a visit to my cousin Klaus Reichenheim and his family in Sao Paulo, with memories of the Isle of Man in 1940. But despite the hospitality of the Brazilian judges it was not a very enjoyable trip, and I was glad when I went straight from the Copacabana beach in Rio to Ithaka in the Greek Adriatic, the island of Odysseus. It was an improbable steerage journey via Rome and Athens, after trading in my First Class ticket, to join Tony Lincoln who was staying with Panos and Beatrice Gratsos at their beautiful house on Panos' native island. With his wiry chiselled looks, brilliant mind and love of sailing, I always thought that Panos Gratsos must have been an Ithacaan descendant of the great Odysseus. Then, on the way home, I stopped off at a small *pensione* on the Giudecca in Venice to call on the august tribunal of an improbable international arbitration which was quartered in the Cipriani Hotel across the water, Harry Fisher, Pat Neill and Mark Littman, together with consorts. Each morning these were left at the pool for a few hours while their spouses, copiously surrounded by ring files, were collected by *motorscafi* to be taken to the hotel on the Lido which provided the official venue for the arbitration. It was to take more than a decade on the Bench before I also acquired an arbitral practice, much of it in far off places. But nothing to rival this Venetian scenario.

On another occasion, I think the following August of 1981, I was sent to represent the Lord Chancellor at a Commonwealth Law Conference in Lagos, because neither he nor any of the other senior judiciary were able to go. When I got there I could see that there were still some local problems. Although met by a resplendent huge figure in full indigenous dress, who presented me with his card at the steps of the plane introducing him as "Chief .... of Lincoln's Inn", it soon became apparent that things were still somewhat insecure. With our escort, we hurtled over potholes towards the city, through an army and then a police checkpoint without stopping, but with the explanation that neither had been "real" soldiers or police and that one had to keep going, fast. On arrival at the Conference hotel we were then met by a blackout which paralysed the lifts for some hours. It was also bad luck that it hardly stopped raining all week and that the access to the Conference Centre turned into a sea of deep mud. After I had given the Lord Chancellor's 'Keynote Address' towards the end of the Conference which I had written in London, probably about the harmonisation of commercial law in the Commonwealth, I couldn't wait to go home again. Indeed, the main subject of conversation throughout the week had been the unreliability of airline seat confirmations, and there were worrying tales about not getting on a flight unless one had influence. It was said that, even after checking in and getting a boarding card, another card with the same seat number might be in the process of being auctioned somewhere near the front of the queue. So it was a great relief to get back to the quiet peace of the Law Commission. But I was glad of the experience and made some lasting friends, who tell me how different and much better everything is now.

There have been about five or six chairmen (including Mary Arden) of the Law Commission since my time, and in recent years it has become much more noticed and successful. Times have changed, and there is now considerable media interest in piece-meal law reform on newsworthy legal topics which are thrown up by court cases with an unsatisfactory outcome. And no doubt this increase in public interest is also at last attracting more government support. The original concept of general, systematic law reform, with massive new programmes being issued from time to time, had always been a somewhat tedious and unrealistically long-term project for which it was difficult to generate any real interest, let alone enthusiasm.

The only piece of law reform in which I became directly involved was achieved entirely unsystematically some years later. I was in the Court of Appeal, but also President of the Chartered Institute of Arbitrators and of the newly refashioned London Court of International Arbitration, the LCIA, in both cases working with Bertie Vigrass as Director General, when he received an invitation for us to visit the Pacific Rim for conferences and seminars to spread the arbitral gospel as then seen from our shores. This was in the mid-eighties, when interest in international arbitration, as an alternative or even replacement for litigation, was sweeping the commercial world, and most countries were modernising their arbitration laws in order to offer themselves as attractive venues for international arbitrations. New Zealand's arbitration law was then still entirely unmodernised, as well as Singapore's, whereas Australia and Hongkong had produced somewhat improved variations of our recently enacted 1979 Arbitration Act, which had itself only been a half-hearted compromising advance. On the other hand, there was now also an entirely new solution on offer, the UNCITRAL Model Law, which was beginning to attract attention from jurisdictions looking for radical reform of their laws. Its chief exponent, Gerold Herrmann, then Secretary General of Uncitral and later to become a close friend, was therefore going to speak at each venue on the opposite side in favour of the Model Law, whereas I was to defend the common law approach. We were to start in Auckland, then move on to Sydney and Melbourne, because in Australia it is usually diplomatic to visit both, and end up in Hongkong. It was the summer vacation, and Diana was coming too.

We decided to start with a week's holiday in Hawaii, and before we left I spoke to an old friend in Vancouver, Brian Smith QC, then Attorney-General of British Columbia. He was interested in what we were doing, because he hoped to develop Vancouver as a neutral commercial centre between the USA and Japan. So he decided to come along to listen. He picked us up in the airport lounge in Honolulu and immediately managed to get us upgraded to his class for the flight to Auckland. Then, after a week of listening to me and Dr Uncitral, as we all called Gerold, he got sufficiently interested to ring his office to discover that the BC law of arbitration, like that of New Zealand, was governed by a statute which was about to reach its centenary and hopelessly out of date. So we had some long discussions about what might be done. He said that his party had a substantial majority in the legislature and that on a topic of law reform of this nature there would be no difficulty. We finally reached a conclusion on the flight to Sydney. I said that if I were in his position, and despite the existing Commonwealth patterns which I was trying to defend on our tour, I would go straight for the Model Law. This had then not been applied to any part of Canada. He was sitting across the aisle from me and we were writing and passing notes of which I still have copies. His last one was: "Right. I agree. First out of the chute".

This was in August, and by the middle of September he had set up a

Working Party to produce a draft Bill and commentary for consultation. Meanwhile, however, the other Provinces were taking notice of what was going on in BC, and several decided to join the bandwagon. Ultimately, I think it was shortly before Christmas, there was a day on which Ontario and BC both enacted an adaptation of the Model Law, but Ontario just won on the 3 hours time difference. The remaining Provinces and the Federal Government soon followed. So Canada adopted the Model Law.

That was law reform as it should happen, at least on topics of "lawyers' law" in which politics should play no part. It gave me far more satisfaction than three years at the Law Commission, and I was proud to go out for the opening of the Vancouver International Arbitration Centre in the following year. Canada would no doubt have come round to adopting the Model Law sooner or later anyway. But this made it much sooner, and it also helped to propagate the Model Law in other jurisdictions throughout the world. It marked the beginning of a new era of dispute resolution techniques, in which I was ultimately to become deeply involved as a practitioner.

68 · Diana

MEETING DIANA when I was nearly 57 transformed my life. For the first time it seemed to acquire a sense of purpose and strength of its own, separately from my working existence. I became quietly happy, secure in the knowledge that we were together and that she felt the same, and I never felt alone again.

And yet our origins could not have been more different. According to Diana, her ancestors were Vikings who had come across the North Sea and settled in East Anglia. Her maiden name was Sneezum, thought to be derived from Snettishham, pronounced Snesham, in Norfolk, though she was born in Ipswich in Suffolk. She had read Law and German for her degree and spent studying and working time in France and Germany, so that she was fluent in both languages. When we met, she was a litigation partner in Theodore Goddard, a firm from which I used to get a fair amount of work some 20 years earlier. Perhaps we belonged together like my father and Inge von Thormaehlen, his blond first wife from Pomerania, who died of the Spanish flu in 1918 and who may also have been a Viking.

We met on 29 January (which became a memorable date) 1979 at a British-German Jurists' Association Conference in Bonn. She was on the committee and I was to be the speaker. Our first encounter was at the airport of Cologne when the buses did not materialise, and she put me in a taxi together with Ted Eveleigh, then the President of the Association. I had already known her by sight, having seen her in court in one or two cases, with long blond hair down her back, but by then happily shorter. The attraction was immediate, and her knowledge of languages was a staggering plus.

We talked a lot in Ted Eveleigh's room after a party the first evening, when I drank a lot of whisky and broke a glass table top. The next day we went for a walk around Bonn, and talked a lot more at the Conference dinner and then at a lunch in the residence of the British Ambassador. It all seemed so natural and unforced on both sides. The final omen was that she had a flat off Kensington Church Street and that I was close by in Bolton Gardens. I remember thinking that if she had lived in Hampstead nothing would have come of it. But as soon as I got back to my flat from Heathrow I rang her and suggested that we should go out to dinner although it was already late. From then we became more or less inseparable. And as I am writing this we still are, over 22 years later.

The decision whether or not to get married was of course not easy, particularly for her. Twenty-eight years is a big difference and nearly a repetition of my parents' story. Her family were no doubt concerned and perhaps unenthusiastic, though they always showed the opposite. But we never really discussed it as a question of policy, and there were no dramatic decisions. It was all unspoken and just did itself. And with the production of Lucy and then Alexander I must have atoned for a lot. For once I don't feel guilty. I'm not going to write about emotions. But I think we've both been very happy.

Our flats were only about a mile apart, which made life easier, although we were both working hard. But we spent all our holidays together. Italy, Jamaica and Klosters are the main ones I remember. And when Diana's lease expired, she decided to try to buy a cottage in the country. We rented an agricultural labourer's cottage on the same estate as Tony Lincoln, in Upper Woodford near Salisbury, and looked around at weekends for about nine months. Finally we found Church Cottage at Winterbourne Stoke near Stonehenge in Wiltshire, about 300 years old, which we bought on 29 January 1982 for a (now) incredible £50,000 against the advice of an expensive local surveyor. His report condemned everything except the view, but concluded that one couldn't

Our cottage in Wiltshire

just live there and look out of the window. Yet we do, and the cottage has been a delight for us ever since. At first the village was wary of us, and we must have seemed an odd couple. But gradually they thawed. Even Mrs Henstridge, who had looked after the cottage for decades, accepted us and became a firm friend. Some years later, when the only stairs, which were like a ladder, became a bit unmanageable, we built an extension with a proper staircase and more room upstairs, and about 5 years ago another large extension downstairs with a breakfast room and a playroom for the children. The views are wonderful, across open fields and woodlands south towards Salisbury, with the "river" Till and a wooden bridge a few yards away, and a Norman church between us and the village, with the list of the incumbents going back to 1338. The garden adjoins an extension of the churchyard towards the top of the hill. This will provide as good a place for me hereafter as any, and better than most. And perhaps the cottage will then stay in the family and not be sold.

In November 1982, after more than the required five years, I finally got my divorce. The financial negotiations were bitter and long and I prefer to forget about them. Except my gratitude to Ronnie Coubrough, who was my solicitor, after we had been each other's best men at our weddings. But there was little that he could do. I went through one of the worst times of my life.

But Diana helped me through it all. She quickly became a close friend of my sister Judy and her Tom, and then my children Candy, Jo and Tim got to like and trust her totally. My friends understandably find her much more attractive and interesting than me, because she is a far nicer person.

On 29 January 1983 Diana and I got married, four years to the day on which we had met and one year to the day on which we had bought Church Cottage. It was a large wedding at Geraldine and Tony Pennington's house in Suffolk, her sister and brother-in-law. Mark Littman was best man. There was a blessing in church, and on the night before about ten of my friends, organised by Mark and Tony Lincoln, hired a mini bus and gave me a bachelor party at a restaurant nearby. It was a great occasion and can properly be described as unforgettable, except that I have inevitably forgotten a great deal about it. For our honeymoon we went skiing in Cortina and on to Venice, which happened to be carnival time and seemed an inspired combination.

After the wedding Diana gave up her flat and moved into my flat in Bolton Gardens. Then, when Lucy was due to arrive about eighteen months later, we bought 10 Kelso Place in the summer of 1984, above

Diana and I get married in Suffolk, 1983.

the tube between High Street Kensington and Gloucester Road, but we got used to the glasses vibrating. I was doing the *Times* crossword in the room in Portland Hospital where Lucy was being born, and had just done a clue to which the answer was 'Adonis,' when the doctor – to my surprise – pronounced her to be a girl. But it was what I had really wanted, so long as Diana could have a son as well. Then Alexander arrived, by caesarian at the Wellington Hospital, in 1987. Since it was August and we could choose the day, we picked the 12th, but I hope he'll never shoot. He was coated in white all over when he came out, a much quicker process than Lucy. My parking meter – far away – had not run out before Diana and he were safely and happily settled. And I was so delighted that we had a boy, as well as Lucy.

Then Kelso Place gradually became too small. The property slump appeared to accentuate the noise of the tube underneath, and it became increasingly difficult to sell. But then we were again lucky. We found 10 Peterborough Villas in Fulham and managed to buy it, probably paying too much, although we realised that it was a dream house as soon as we walked in. But the luck was that someone actually wanted to buy Kelso Place just at that time, at quite a reasonable price, and in the end we managed to exchange contracts for both properties on the same day and to complete on the same day three weeks later, in June 1991, an improbable achievement in the usual jungle of conveyancing. Our overpriced house has now more than doubled in value, like everything else.

Diana and I have now been married for 18 years and have known each other for over 22. It has been a time of great happiness. But it has also been a time crowded with events and unrelenting pressure. Both Diana's parents sadly died; her mother never knew either of our children. We have both had serious back operations and I have had a triple bypass, small operations on both knees, and recently a slight heart attack when Church Cottage was nearly flooded in December 2000 and I tried to cope with a pump and sandbags during the night. Diana is still working part-time And we seem to have travelled incessantly, on holidays but also mainly in connection with my work. Of the places I remember,

Diana in New York, 1984.

Lucy and Alexander in 1993 when part of this book was started.

we've been to Hong Kong, Thailand, Australia, New Zealand, Hawaii, America, Canada, Morocco, Moscow, Bermuda with the children, and many places in Europe. But most of that came later. First, with apologies for this personal interlude, we must go back to the end of the Law Commission in 1981.

69 · The Court of Appeal

THE GOVERNMENT changed in 1979, but Quintin was as good as Elwyn's word. When I had done three years at the Law Commission I got the next vacancy in the Court of Appeal. Throughout my time in the law there have been virtually no instances of party politics influencing judicial appointments. The most is that I felt at the time that two imaginative choices made by Elwyn Jones as a Labour Lord Chancellor – Morris Finer and Peter Pain for the High Court – would have been missed by Hailsham if the Conservatives had been in power. There were also one or two reputed instances of alleged broken promises after the end of Labour in 1979, but they were on personal or policy grounds, and no one suggested that they had anything to do with party politics.

There was some small ceremony, possibly another swearing in, by the Lord Chancellor for which one had to wear one's new gold robe. When I appeared in it, Quintin whistled (again) and said; "That must have set you back a bit". He was amazed to hear that it was government property, formerly worn by Henry Brandon who had gone to the Lords. But the full-bottomed wig, breeches, silk and wool stockings and court shoes were mine, with their silver buckles now promoted by a coating of gold paint, inventively and economically purchased for the occasion in Chancery Lane and applied by Chris Beardsmore, who was still my clerk.

Another ceremony came a few weeks later, to be made a member of HM's Privy Council. This involved, after one practice session, kneeling before HM in Buckingham Palace and kissing her hand, but imperatively without making contact, and then retreating backwards in a gradually rising motion. After taking a further oath of allegiance as a PC, collectively with other incumbents of the day, I left as The Rt Hon Lord Justice, having previously been merely The Hon Mr Justice. But although the oath involves some undertaking to give advice whenever called upon, I have never heard that anything further follows from this honour. I think that I was once asked to be ready to sign any necessary state documents when HM was abroad and I was sitting during part of the Long Vacation. But in the event the state seems to have managed without me.

There were only 18 Lords Justices when I came to the Court in 1981, and Tom Denning was still the Master of the Rolls. Of all my time at the

Court of Appeal, 1981. Swearing in with Jo, Tim and Candy.

Bar and on the Bench, the most interesting and enjoyable were undoubtedly the 8 years in the Court of Appeal. It has a collegiate atmosphere; there was no one in my time who was disliked or with whom one did not like sitting; and most of the work was interesting and well argued. We sat in threes for High Court appeals, generally in twos for appeals from the County Court or procedural matters, and with a Family Division judge for appeals involving children and financial disputes on separation and divorce. There were few cases involving the sexual abuse of children, which now abound, and the word "abuse" had not yet become part of everyday language. The work which I did not enjoy were criminal appeals, when one sat as presider with two Queen's Bench High Court judges. I never felt really comfortable with crime and gave it up when I became a regular presider. I also often disliked appeals in family cases. In the great majority we would naturally have to uphold the judge below who had seen the parties, the witnesses, and sometimes even the children. Save in exceptional circumstances there is no fresh evidence on appeal, so that everything turns on arguments based on the transcript of the hearing below. Immigration appeals were also frustrating if they were hopeless, often brought solely in order to delay the final outcome by months or even years and sometimes by counsel who must have realised their hopelessness perfectly well if they were not incompetent.

But some of them clearly were. These were still the early beginnings of the emergence of the "ethnic" Bar, with recently qualified barristers from recent immigrant families, briefed by solicitors from the same communities, being called on to argue appeals, with a sufficient command of written English to have passed the Bar exams, but not to articulate legal submissions in court. One often had to help by formulating their arguments for them in order to make it clear to them and their clients that their cases had been fully understood, before having to give judgments dismissing appeals that should never have been brought. The standard of advocacy has improved since, but not the delay in dealing with immigration and (now) asylum appeals.

Generally I felt that the outcome of cases in the great majority of appeals was in line with "the merits". That was the current phrase to describe the just result which should follow in any case from the facts and the situation of the parties, without regard to any conflicting impact from the law. One certainly always had the merits in mind throughout and did one's best to avoid an unfair outcome as the result of mandatory legal rules. But the constraints which are popularly believed to be imposed on judges by the doctrine of binding precedent are largely mythical. Prior decisions are often more likely to help in achieving a just result than to hinder, and if an odd decision really gets in the way of the merits, one can usually find sufficient grounds for treating it as distinguishable. In my early days at the Bar, as an inexperienced and partisan barrister, relying unduly on what I considered to be binding authorities, I had suffered many disappointments about judgments which, at the time, appeared to me to disregard precedent, but which, later on, I recognised as having been absolutely right.

My main anxiety was about appeals in which I suspected that the process had gone wrong at first instance, but in which the Court of Appeal was by its nature powerless to intervene. Sometimes one suspected the competence of the lawyers, sometimes the limited vision of the judge in his findings of fact, and often the inability of a party to get its grievances across to them so that the case was fully understood. But then the consolation would be: "Why should I know better? Remember, most of the background usually doesn't come out, so that the court only gets a partial picture anyway. There may be much more to it than you know."

The press and television, but not radio to the same extent, were a constant source of irritation, and sometimes near despair. Judgments make great simplistic news, and any would-be reporter, however ignorant or uneducated, seemed free to pontificate about them. The angle always had to be sensationalistic or at least titillatingly newsworthy in some way, and where the outcome was regarded as disappointing, it would be criticised with no attempt to refer to the judge's reasons for deciding as he did. With a few outstanding exceptions, such as Joshua Rosenberg and Marcel Berlins, commentators usually discussed judgments as though judges were free to decide whatever they liked, without regard to the evidence or the legal aspects of the case. There is no news value in explanations or in expressing satisfaction with anything or anyone. I have never yet seen a television commentator, spouting on the traffic island in front of the Law Courts in the Strand, who would say: "This was really quite a sensible judgment." And even if they cannot find too much wrong, they will still find some reason for ending on a note of doom as to what the morrow may bring. It is a disease of our time and part of a seemingly unending "dumbing-down" process of all intellectual values by the media (also only recently a word in common use).

But back to the Court of Appeal. Its work is of every possible kind. It encompasses every aspect of public and private life. One learns a vast amount and one can also do a great deal of good. I felt that I was doing more for the law in my judgments than I could ever do as Chairman of the Law Commission. But of course, not all the work was pleasant, in particular fights over children. There were many of them, where one's hands were tied, or where it was simply impossible to find any 'right' answer, because all were inevitably bound to be unsatisfactory, or even tragic, for one of the parties.

But despite all its variety, the Court of Appeal was inexorable, like a treadmill. Although every day in court was intellectually challenging, the pace was reminiscent of the pressure of the Bar and far harder than the work of a judge of first instance. A treadmill is a machine which you have to keep going by incessant pedalling. But, once it is fully in motion, it also has the characteristic that you can no longer get off. That is how it seemed. The pressure did not come from listening to cases in court but from the accumulation of judgments in past cases waiting to be given which hung over one like a cloud. Sitting in court and listening to counsel often seemed a waste of time, because one knew what the outcome would be once the talking would stop. One wanted the case to end, to give a quick judgment there and then, as we did whenever we could, to get back to one's room to dictate drafts of outstanding judgments and to correct the transcripts of earlier ones. Catching up and then reading into next week's cases took endless evenings and weekends, with committee meetings, after-dinner speeches and other extra-mural *pro bono* activities in between. None of these aspects were ever referred

Court of Appeal

to by the commentators in the media when pontificating endlessly about short daily court sittings and lengthy vacations.

In comparison with the John Donaldson era as Master of the Rolls, which followed from 1983 onwards, the Court of Appeal under Tom Denning had been run in a very *laissez faire* manner. His main direct concern had been to select the appeals which he wanted to hear and to select the people with whom he wanted to sit to hear them. The rest of the administration he left to his Clerk and the Clerks of the other presiders. Unbelievably as it now seems, there was no Registrar, with his present large department and staff, virtually no central listing organisation, and no 'skeleton arguments' which had to be filed in advance of every appeal to shorten the oral hearings. All that came later, under the pressure of ever increasing case loads. But then, as the court became more streamlined and efficient, so it became even more of a treadmill.

I sat a great deal with Tom Denning between my arrival in 1981 and his retirement two years later, and Peter Oliver and I sat with him every day during his last two or three months at his request. It was a highly interesting time, but occasionally also haphazard, because one often had no idea which way Tom was going. He tended to dominate the court and the proceedings so much that one had to stand up for oneself and insist on some control, or one would be swept along with him against one's better judgment. So far as I remember I often had to dissent from him, at least in part, as happened to most of us from time to time. He also worked his court extremely hard. I remember one occasion when he had to go to a funeral in the afternoon, to which Peter and I had been looking forward to give us an opportunity to draw breath and catch up a bit. But just before lunch he said: "Oh, I didn't want you boys to sit around with nothing to do. So I've fixed you up with a case for a two-man court".

Tom Denning had hoped to carry on for a few more years and to round off some of the remarkable statistics of his life. In 1984 he would have been 85 and 40 years on the Bench, and in 1987 he would have celebrated his quarter century as Master of the Rolls. But some indiscretion intervened, a remark about a jury which was regarded as having been "racist" or something of the kind, which more or less forced him to retire. When he did, he was the last so-called life tenant, who had been appointed before 1959 when there was not yet any age limit for High Court judges. After 1959 all had to retire at 75, and by now the limit has come down still further. I was sitting with him together with Peter Oliver on his last day when Hailsham joined us to pronounce his public farewell to a packed court. Even the public galleries had been opened for the occasion, having been closed for decades for fear of terrorists. And although Quintin and he had never liked each other much, the peroration was generous, describing him in the first sentence as a 'legend in his own time.'

Which he certainly was, and remained in the popular image, living to reach his 100th birthday in his beloved house in Whitchurch. I had presided over his 90th, together with Princess Margaret as our Royal Bencher, in the Great Hall in Lincoln's Inn in 1989, when his speech was as brilliant and entertaining as ever. And my last contact with him was a long overdue letter of legal news 10 years later, which he received and had read to him by his old Clerk, Peter Post, during the last week of his life, and which produced a lively "thank you and still with it" response via Peter.

Tom Denning will always remain a legendary figure as a reformer and innovator. But not as a forensic technician. In my years in the Court of Appeal after his retirement I noticed more and more how the persuasiveness of his judgments waned under critical analysis and how his preeminent influence soon diminished. He was surprisingly rarely cited and often with little effect. But this should not diminish his memory as the last great master of the common law. He took giant strides forward which then became accepted as part of the fabric. But having been accepted, and then having to be tested against a fast-moving jurisprudential scenario, his generalised *avant-garde* pronouncements began to appear too simplistic. Of the great judicial figures of these times, it is the analytical precision of Diplock, and not the imaginative inventiveness of Denning, which will provide the sounder and more enduring doctrinal basis for the future. But this in itself is also something of an over-simplification. It ignores the enormous conceptual strides which our law took under Tom Denning's beguiling persuasiveness, despite intense criticisms and resistance at every step. In the end, however, he took us forward too far with too many generalisations, sometimes against our better judgment or without us having realised it. Diplock then pulled back the reins and sought to impose a regime of analytical strictness upon this galloping horse, though sometimes his logic was too arid and inflexible to be workable in cases which he had not foreseen. Both tried to impose themselves and their styles on the system in opposing ways and, if they could, to rule us by binding pronouncements from their graves. But in vain, as always. And sometimes it was then left to Richard Wilberforce, who never sought to impose his views on anyone, to provide a kind of synthesis between these two extremes and to exercise a longer influence.

And who will come out best in the views of future generations?

Perhaps none of them to any really striking extent like the giants of a simpler past. Tom Denning thought of himself as a second Lord Mansfield. This may well be the popular, but not the jurisprudential, judgment of the future. He will always be remembered popularly for his fearless drive for change and simplification of the law, but not by lawyers for the analytical content of his judgments. The social and political requirements which the law now has to meet are too demanding, and are changing far too rapidly, to admit of the personality cults of former times. So, *vanitas vanitorum*. The waters close. Indeed, the common law itself is shrinking in the face of the demands of ever increasing statute law and regulations, and above all of administrative law by judicial review. This phrase was virtually non-existent when I went on the Bench and was more or less invented and developed by Tom Denning, without the rest of us noticing at the time, until it had come here to stay as the most important of all modern judicial functions. But now farewell to him! In this age, which is so over-dominated by the media, his was the first human face among all the figures of the judiciary which came to be recognised by the general public and which is still outstanding to this day above anyone else. But not among the lawyers, though this must take nothing away from Tom as a legend in his own time. The reason is that the new face of the *corpus* and content of the law, unlike the cherished simpler philosophy of the ancient common law which he so greatly revered, is hostile to any form of personalisation, individuality of approach, and old-fashioned jurisprudence.

My most striking recollection of Tom Denning at work will always be my first appearance before him in the Court of Appeal as a Junior as long ago as 1957. A wealthy widow, a Mrs Adler, who owned a small department store in Regent Street, had been a first class passenger on a luxury cruise of the P&O liner *Himalaya* when it was blown off the quay by an unexpected evening squall while moored at Trieste. Mrs Adler was unfortunately on the gangplank, on her way to a night club, when it gave way, and she was seriously injured. But her ticket exonerated the P&O from all liability and barred any claims against them. So she was advised to sue the Master, Captain Dickson, personally for negligence, and I was briefed to appear for him, financed by the P&O, for whom this was an important test case. The perceived wisdom and doctrine at that time, based on a weighty dictum of Lord Justice Scrutton in the twenties, was the umbrella principle, whereby any provision in a contract made with an employer also protected his employees while acting in the course of their employment and in furtherance of the performance of the contract. I had lost below on the evidence as to whether the vessel had been properly moored, partly because one of the ropes had been tied round a lamppost on the quay when no more bollards were said to have been available, and during the legal argument in the Court of Appeal, which had gone quite well, Tom Denning had given no indication of what he thought of this umbrella doctrine. But I knew that it was dead and buried when I heard the first sentence of his judgment and tied up the papers of my brief, ready to leave: "Mrs Adler, a widow, who keeps a shop, was minded to take a cruise". It can now be read in the Law Reports. Since then, personal actions against employees in negligence have become commonplace, and their intricacies – and the possible ways of overcoming them – have unleashed new chapters of jurisprudence.

In the autumn of 1982 the Court of Appeal gave a great farewell dinner to Tom Denning. It was a difficult time for me. With Julia I was between decree nisi and absolute. Diana and I were going to get married as soon as we could. But meanwhile I wanted to take her to Tom's farewell dinner. I had to ask permission from Joe Stephenson, the senior Lord Justice who was organising it. To oil the legal wheels I said that Diana was a solicitor and a litigation partner in Theodore Goddard. He looked at me wide-eyed."But surely, that can't do you any good now!" He was only half serious. But such is the work-providing power of solicitors for the Bar, although traditionally always the second profession, that even senior judges remain subconsciously under its influence. And so Diana made her entry into the Court of Appeal, still in time to get to know Tom Denning.

With his departure, it must be said, the court changed greatly for the better under John Donaldson as MR. Not in its working atmosphere, but certainly from the point of view of efficiency. Everything was now geared to increasing the turnover without diminishing the quality. John Donaldson was not the popular choice, and if he had proposed any measures which threatened our independence of thought or time for reflection, there would have been a rebellion. But, of course, he never did. Although administration was his forte, he was far too good a judge to forget what really mattered. But working time can be made compressible and lengthened at the same time, so that the throughput of appeals can be considerably increased without a reduction in quality. It just means working far harder, faster and longer hours. And that is what happened.

The effort is not in hearing appeals. On the contrary, that is often the easiest part. In many, perhaps most, cases one has a pretty good idea from reading the papers in advance what the outcome is going to be, although quite often there are changes of mind. Usually no more than a few words were exchanged as we went into court, with someone saying that such and such an answer seems pretty obvious, or that the judge below clearly got it right, or sometimes wrong. But it then often happened that by lunchtime we all came round, as the result of the argument and points which had not come through in the papers. And there would then be an equally brief and desultory conversation on our way out to lunch, except to the opposite effect as in the morning. And usually no one would even bother to point out how radically our minds had been changed by the oral argument and presentation.

But listening to cases is the least arduous part of the job. The real pressure is usually before 10.00 or 10.30 in the morning, and after 4.15 in the afternoon, with phone calls, meetings, appointments and – above all – judgments to write. This is particularly so for the 'presider,' who sits in the middle and is largely responsible for organising the list of his court. One listens to counsel, wishing he (or increasingly she) would stop talking so that one can give judgment and have some time of the day left over. One worries whether it will be possible to start tomorrow's case on time and, above all, about the judgment or judgments of last week or the week before which still have to be written. One cannot remember clearly what they were about, but a black cloud of overdue unwritten judgments is a permanent feature of work in the Court of Appeal.

The daily pace is so fast, and so totally unlike what the ordinary person would think, that sometimes it almost defies description. In my time the court was sitting in about eight divisions, usually of three, and changing composition about every three weeks. Going into court first thing in the morning and again after lunch was often like a mad rush, with troikas in wigs and gowns almost running along the red-carpeted corridors to their courts, throwing instructions at their Clerks over their shoulders, trying to keep up with what the others were saying, and shouting at members of other troikas, hurrying in the opposite direction, to try to arrange a meeting to discuss some case which was still awaiting judgment. The pressure was such that it was fairly unusual to meet in the presider's room to discuss methodically what should be done with a case in which the argument had just concluded. Usually there would be no more than a few words outside court, often inconclusive. Someone would then be asked, or volunteer, to write a first draft of a judgment and to circulate it. Many would then say: "I won't know what I really think until I start writing."

Those, of course, were the difficult cases in which judgment was reserved. Whenever possible we gave judgment at once, as soon as the talking stopped, or overnight from notes. But in at least a third of the cases that was not feasible. Reserved judgments would then be dictated or written, typed, circulated and often rewritten, before being 'handed down.' Unbelievably, when I first went to the Court of Appeal, all reserved judgments were still read out aloud, an archaic survival for the supposed benefit of any members of the general public who might be present. Then John Donaldson changed the system, though in the Criminal Division it remained as before.

After a year of John Donaldon's long overdue efficiency drive the pace speeded up so much that it became too much. I remember circulating a note threatening to publish 'A Day in the Life of Denisovich L.J.,' although I doubt whether Solzhenitsyn was Court of Appeal reading. It was decided to do more pre-reading, to do away with the lengthy opening of cases and reading from authorities, and to require the delivery of "skeleton arguments" in advance. For this I claim some credit, in particular for the name, but I am sure that John Donaldson as MR would claim the original copyright for a word which has now passed into the legal language throughout the English-speaking forensic world. But one innovation I did introduce, and it is the only one for which I might be remembered. This was to hold a 'tea party' for members of the Court of Appeal, for about 20 minutes, every three weeks. Amazingly enough, there was then no library or common room where the LJs ever met, apart from squeezing into the MR's room for business meetings once a term. But a place was found, originally at the end of a corridor among some aspidistras, where seven tea pots in woollen cosies, knitted by the messengers, were put out with plates of fruit cake and biscuits. It is a tradition which has gone on in better venues, supplying a basic need – one would think – for informal meetings in any community from time to time. But unheard of in the first 80 years of the modern Court of Appeal.

Despite the extreme pressures and the unavoidable treadmill effect, I loved the work, particularly during the five years or so when I was presiding. The Court of Appeal is an intellectual pinnacle, a daily series of Socratic debates in a collegiate atmosphere of all-round cordiality, particularly when there are good counsel engaged in the case and it raises an interesting issue of law. With daily quick lunches at our Inns, always with a cross-section of colleagues and acquaintances as at a club, our weekly 'reading days' (which I vainly tried to re-christen 'writing days', for that is what they were) and working weekends, but interspersed with longish vacations, it was a hypnotically pleasant and rewarding existence.

But all this was only the underlying everyday routine. On top of it were many '*pro bono*' functions, some more pleasant than others, but all involving extra work. I became the first Chairman of the so-called Supreme Court Procedure Committee, President of the Chartered

BUCKINGHAM PALACE

20th November, 1991.

Sir,

I have the honour to inform you that The Queen has been graciously pleased to grant to you Unrestricted Permission to wear the insignia of the Commander's Cross of the Order of Merit of the Federal Republic of Germany, which has been conferred upon you by His Excellency Dr. Richard von Weizsacker, GCB, President of the Federal Republic of Germany, in recognition of your services.

I have the honour to be, Sir,
Your obedient Servant,

Kenneth Scott.

The Right Honourable Sir Michael Kerr.

An unexpected encomium.

Institute of Arbitrators, and then also of the London Court of International Arbitration, which took a great deal of my time and life later on, as well as President of the British-German Jurists Association through which Diana and I had met. Then there were many more or less compulsory after-dinner speeches, which are surprisingly hard work. I have notes of about a hundred of them, all of them jotted down just before changing into a black tie. I could never do them in advance. Then there were other functions, such as being Chairman of the Centre for Commercial Law Studies at Queen Mary College and on the Council of Management of the British Institute of International and Commercial Studies and the Institute of Advanced Legal Studies, both of which covered many years. And for 25 years I helped to organise the annual 'F.A. Mann lectures,' first in honour of Francis, and then in his memory.

But there were also compensations in the form of numerous invitations to many parts of the world, and since the next chapter is headed "Disappointments", I might as well mention the main ones which I remember. I once gave a 'keynote address' to the Australian Bar from the pulpit of Hobart Cathedral in Tasmania and was elected a Life Member of the American Bar Association, the Canadian Bar Association and the American Law Institute. I have spoken at conferences as far apart as Tokyo, Auckland, Northern Queensland, Chicago, New York, Rio de Janeiro, Vancouver, Amman, Nairobi, San Francisco, Beijing, Shanghai, Sydney, Melbourne, Kuwait, Moscow, Quebec, Singapore and the Lebanon, and many others in Europe, but how or why I can hardly remember, though many of them were in connection with arbitration after I had retired from the court. For decades Diana and I have been surrounded by friends and acquaintances whom we regularly meet at legal occasions here and abroad, but all of whom usually lead equally hectic lives. To me the general atmosphere of this large legal community was once epitomised by John Donaldson, when he introduced me to speak at some dinner, but it could have applied to many among us: "We've known each other for decades. He knows there is nothing I wouldn't do for him, and I know there is nothing he wouldn't do for me. And so we've gone through life, doing nothing for each other!"

70 · Disappointments

I WAS LIVING on a high, so I knew that I must be riding for a fall. The first signs were physical. Apart from my deafness I had never had any problems with my health, and when I was young I hardly knew the meaning of the word tired. But in 1984 I suddenly had problems with my back. The pain was not due to a disc, for which Diana had been operated a year earlier, but a narrowing of the spinal column, with severe pain in the right sciatic nerve. Unfortunately the cause was diagnosed too late to save the nerve in the right foot, which has always been left with a slight drop in consequence. This in turn upset the weight on the knees and caused arthritis and a lot of pain in walking. So I suddenly became old, or at least obviously elderly, which was something quite new and unsettling. Having always been the youngest in any situation or gathering, things suddenly changed. By now it is fairly exceptional for me not to be the oldest, though some comfort to be still there at all, with young children, and still involved with what is going on. But that is another epoch later on, after John Butler's memorable phrase in a letter shortly before his death: "The 70's are all downhill". The problems started unexpectedly before then, and the nadir, the lowest point for me, came in 1986, when I was 65.

To write about past professional events, when – happily – the others involved are still alive, is inevitably difficult. But we are now more than 15 years on, and – again happily – all of them were and still are friends, and there is nothing bad to be said about any of them. And to write about past disappointments, instead of achievements, may be a welcome mark of autobiographical frankness. So I will write it all just as it happened.

There only remained one thing which could still be achieved in my work and career: the House of Lords. There was clearly nothing outside the law, and within it, that was the only possible remaining promotion. So, like being Captain of Football at Aldenham, it was something about which I thought nearly every day; and not only I. In 1985 it was known that three places would have to be filled by the following Christmas. Two of them were thought to be more or less automatic; Peter Oliver on the Chancery side and on the QB side Desmond Ackner, a great all-rounder, including crime and personal injuries as well as commercial law. There remained one other position on the QB side, and I think that most people assumed that it was going to be me. But some wiser ones thought of Robert Goff, academically a much more profound lawyer, and – or but – 10 years younger.

I must have thought, hopefully, that would work in my favour and was not really worried. But in the end I don't think it really played a part. Robert had a far better jurisprudential pedigree as a former Oxford don and the author of a brilliant ground-breaking textbook. And all this was in addition to having much the same commercial/international experience that I had. Nevertheless, I knew that I had a lot of support, and the odds certainly seemed to be in my favour.

It was a very tense time for all of us, just before Christmas 1985. Peter Oliver and I were looking forward to going up together, having run in parallel since our Cambridge days, and we knew that it would be decided before Christmas. We had a daily code at lunch at Lincoln's Inn, an imperceptible shake of the head, to show that we had not heard. But one day, to my anguish, he gave a slight nod. I had heard nothing. So I knew there and then that it was the end.

When the announcements came out there was a great show of incredulity, sympathy and some expressions of injustice, 'favouring Oxford over Cambridge,' etc, which were quite unjustified. It was all well meant, but really wrong. I had probably only had the conventional middle-of-the-roaders on my side, not the more original thinkers. I recognised at the time how much more an academic and more scholarly lawyer could contribute to the House of Lords than a purely pragmatic one like me. So I have never felt the slightest sense of grievance at the choice. Since then, over the years, I have heard many flattering echoes of the discussions which had gone on behind the scenes at the time, but nothing to make me feel aggrieved, only – for once – unlucky.

It was nevertheless a bit of a gloomy Christmas, and life suddenly seemed very flat. So I decided to try to ski again, one of the passions of my life which I had not tried since my back operation the previous year. I had only taken it up in my mid-30s, but had then gone every year for 25 years and became reasonably fluent. It still seems to me the best sport in the world. Since Diana had to stay at home with Lucy, who was only just over a year, I had to go alone and went back to Klosters, where I had been for many years and had lots of friends. But the spirit and confidence were no longer there, although I actually took an instructor, the first for decades. Then, on the second day, almost inevitably, I pulled a ligament in deepish snow. So that was also the end of that, and of a brand-new set of bindings.

The return to London was premature, painful and depressing. It was not yet term time, which would take my mind off things by the daily round of work and sitting in court. Mark Littman came over to Kelso Place for the evening. We sat on and on after dinner and discussed our lives, something which we had never done at length before. For some reason he was also feeling low. I remember us eating and drinking far too much, ending up with brandy, and becoming fairly drunk, untypical of us both.

There followed a terrible night for me with a lot of vomiting, though no pain of any kind. By the time our doctor, Peter Wheeler, arrived in the morning, urgently summoned by Diana after I had vainly tried to cancel him, I was ready to get up and go out. But he said he didn't like the look of me and sent me to a cardiologist, Howard Swanton. It was that which saved my life and the certainty of sharing the fate of my mother and Nucki at just about the same age. The tests immediately revealed two blockages, one of 100 per cent and one of 90 per cent on the upper left side of my heart. It was only because I had an unusually strong right lower artery, which had taken over all the work, that I never felt any pain and that the heart muscle remained undamaged. But, as Peter Wheeler said later, a few more months and I would certainly "have snuffed it."

So everything suddenly became very urgent. In early February 1986 my Chambers were for some reason giving me a dinner, together with others who had recently gone on the Bench. But although I tried to argue with the doctors, I had to spend that day on the operating table to have a triple bypass.

It all happened so quickly that I can't really remember being frightened. I remember getting a phone call on arrival from my old friend, John Wilmers, going back to the days of the Isle of Man but now a successful QC, who had just been told that he suffered from leukaemia. He had also just arrived in hospital but was full of optimism; "they know what it is and can control it." But he died within a week.

The doctors and nurses in the old private wing of the Middlesex were wonderful. During the afternoon before the operation they showed Diana and me around, so that it would feel familiar to me. There was only one awful looking old woman in the recovery room, where you are taken after intensive care. I drew their attention to the fact that she seemed to have been dead for several days. But they assured me that she was doing extremely well and that I would look just the same on the following morning.

I actually remember quite a lot about that night after coming to and finding that I was still alive, but in a strange disembodied way. I could see what was going on around me, but it felt like dreaming a sort of nightmare, and sometimes there seemed to be a lot of pain. But after two days I was thankfully back in my room, looking at diagrams of what the inside of my heart had looked like before, and what it looked like now. I kept them and recently showed them again to Howard Swanton after a mild heart attack 16 years later on. At that time the doctors were so pleased with me that they asked me to talk to other patients who were waiting for their operations and were frightened. I remember one well-known man, a captain of industry, still quite young and a whizz kid in the motor world. He was terrified, and nothing I could say would make him believe that he could survive. Whether he knew, as I did, that he had a blocked aorta, which was far worse than my blockages, I didn't know. We talked and talked and shook hands and I wished him luck. But he died on the table.

I was in hospital for about 2½ weeks. There followed about five grey and gloomy months. I was made to walk every day and dragged myself round and round the Round Pond in Kensington Gardens, with a stick, every morning and afternoon, back and forth from Kelso Place. I had never felt so old or so weak. But gradually things got better and in June the three of us went to St Lucia for a lovely recuperative holiday. Lucy, now nearly 2, adored it, always running around naked, fetching ice with me in a bucket for our room and talking to a huge parrot en route, chained to his perch. I had a horrible scar on my chest which has never faded and sometimes frightens young children in swimming pools.

But gradually everything came back to life and back to normal. I went to see Geoffrey Lane, the Lord Chief Justice, and my own boss, John Donaldson, the MR, and said that I was ready to return to work. All I asked was to give up presiding over crime. I had never been very comfortable in it and there had been a lot of changes to youth custody, community service and other aspects of sentencing during my six months' absence. Otherwise all was soon exactly as before, except that I felt physically older and frailer.

One postscript to this episode. I had smoked all my life since the internment camps. Usually 20 to 30 cigarettes a day; sometimes small cigars which were supposed to be better for one, and occasionally even a pipe. I always lit a cigarette as soon as I got out of court. But since then I have never smoked, not a single cigarette, and hardly missed it. Why? Because this is an operation which really changes your metabolism. You no longer feel that your body is the same as before, though of course in many ways better.

I realise that all this is intensely boring. But an autobiography is about oneself And one is what one is. No more. So what can you expect?

71 · A new profession

IN JANUARY 1989 I was due to become Treasurer of Lincoln's Inn. It is the ultimate accolade of one's life in the Inn and also quite a lot of fun socially. But for a year it involves a great deal of administrative work, committees, weekends with students, visits to the provinces and universities, Chapel on many Sundays and a vast series of receptions and dinners.

So I thought that this was a good time to retire from the Court of Appeal. There was nowhere further for me to go, and I had done 17 years on the Bench when only 15 were needed for a full pension. Being (only) 68 I could have gone on for another 7 years, since the age limit was then still 75. If I had gone to the Lords I would have stayed on. But I saw no point in another 7 years in the Court of Appeal and wanted to do other things. I wasn't going to let the treadmill grind me right down. At that time it was unusual to retire early and unpopular with the establishment. To get full value out of a judge, he should go on as long as possible, as most wanted to do anyway. But for once I had some plans of my own instead of letting the future run itself, and decided to buck the trend.

I had somehow become well known throughout the world of arbitration, both here and internationally, although on the Bench I had only been allowed to do a few as a Commercial Court Judge, with the fees going to the Treasury. But I had become President of the Chartered Institute of Arbitrators, written many articles about the subject, spoken at innumerable Conferences, and had then become the first President of the London Court of International Arbitration, the LCIA, in 1985. Together with its Registrar and first Executive Director, Bertie Vigrass, and mostly due to him, we had begun to build up the LCIA into something which had a world-wide reputation and was beginning to compete with other arbitral institutions on the global market, notably the International Chamber of Commerce (ICC). It was also a crucial time for the development of English international arbitration generally. But the early stages were extremely difficult. The beginnings of the modern LCIA had involved fierce arbitral politics and great unpleasantness in having to defend Bertie against unjustified personal attacks. Above all, the LCIA suffered from a chronic and continuous shortage of money. Unlike similar institutions in other countries, we received no help from the government or any outside source. For several years Bertie ran the organisation more or less single-handed on a shoestring, without pay, from a desk in someone else's office. It was only due to the subscriptions from members of the "Users' Councils" in different parts of the world, his invention, that we survived the early stages. Now, more than 16 years on, the LCIA is flourishing and paying its way from the fees earned by its casework, quite apart from the subscriptions paid by over a thousand members throughout the world. But in 1989 the position was still grim, and also generally for the future of English arbitration on the international market.

For that is what it was and is, a forensic market. As a byproduct of the complex network of modern global commerce, there has emerged a competitive network of arbitral centres and institutions throughout the world, with all major trading countries vying with each other to provide convenient, popular and legally effective venues for international arbitrations within their jurisdictions. London had always been a natural centre, but our statutes and common law practices were not yet foreign user-friendly. It required the advent and success of the LCIA, and above all the passing of the Arbitration Act 1996, to secure the future.

In the legal world these developments produced endless discussions over many years and are still going on. But I shall of course resist their temptation here. Volumes sufficient to fill a large library have already been written about arbitration and about the differences between it and litigation, and I have contributed a good deal to this (boring) literature. In the old days, when I was still on the Bench, I had confidently preferred litigation, and – if my publisher permits – I will annex at the end the somewhat legendary account of *"The Macao Sardine Case"*. This illustrates my early irreverent views and was even celebrated in a painting presented to me by the LCIA for my 80th birthday. But these views have changed with the years and with the realisation that, for many reasons, arbitration is really indispensable to international trade. Arbitration awards are as legally binding as judgments, and internationally far more easily enforceable than the judgments of national courts, at any rate outside western Europe. International litigation in the courts appears to have greatly diminished and suddenly seems parochial and formalistic in comparison, except for remedies which transcend the powers of arbitrators. Indeed, I now think that the future will tend towards mediation, and still further away from the sharp, but increasingly blunt, end of the courts.

I have always liked the story of the judge whose tombstone read : "He died part-heard". But by 1989, if this was to happen to me, I wanted it to be as an arbitrator. Although I like describing the process as "rent a judge", a successful arbitrator in fact requires different and additional qualities from those of a judge. Total integrity and impartiality for both go without saying (although a pragmatic old judge once said to me, on my first Circuit: "My boy, always remember to steer a middle course between impartiality and common sense partiality"). But the fundamental difference is that an arbitrator is someone who has been chosen by or on behalf of the parties, something like an *homme de confiance,* whereas a judge is simply imposed on them by the state. And whereas a judge comes with all the necessary apparatus provided by the state – court buildings, registrars, listing officers, transcription facilities, etc, – arbitrations are conducted by correspondence and then heard in conference rooms or hotels, and all the necessary facilities and dates must be agreed with the parties or ordered by the tribunal. To an arbitrator, the parties and their representatives are therefore something in the nature of clients, and their satisfaction with the process, and confidence in it, are aspects which must constantly be borne in mind. I had always felt that this was also part of the function of a judge. Although people may only be in court once in their lives, they never forget how the judge behaved. But with an arbitrator these aspects inevitably have a different and more important dimension. After all, he or she is setting out to acquire a professional practice as, in effect, a rented judge, and to make a living and a career from being chosen for appointment. Success depends on one's reputation for experience, soundness and fairness, and – perhaps above all – on a dependable manner and absence of any eccentricity or arrogance. Everything hangs on the quality of the arbitrator, or chairman if there are three, with each party appointing their own choice and the two choosing the third, which is the most common pattern. Since there are virtually no ways of appealing the decision of an arbitrator and few procedures for resisting the enforcement of an arbitral award, a single bad choice can have devastatingly serious consequences for at least one of the parties. In many ways an arbitrator's life is again like that of a barrister, waiting for the phone to ring. But while barristers can combine both functions, as many senior ones do, a former judge can only act as an arbitrator or expert, and may not do any other work ordinarily done by barristers. It is a delicate profession.

By 1989 I was ready for this world and more than ready to try to make a living at it. I became Treasurer of Lincoln's Inn in January and planned to retire from the Bench at Easter. My first function after my inauguration had been Tom Denning's ninetieth birthday, at which I had to preside, sitting between him and Princess Margaret, our Royal Bencher.

Lord Denning's 90th birthday with Princess Margaret and Lady Denning at Lincoln's Inn, 1989.

Many other functions followed during the year, including my two 'Grand Nights,' when you can invite anyone you want, and I was sitting next to Maggie Thatcher at dinner and Peter Ustinov at dessert. But meanwhile there had been a final hiccup about my retirement. James MacKay, the Lord Chancellor and by then a friend, called me in February and asked me to lead the British delegation at a diplomatic conference in April to hammer out a multilateral treaty on salvage at sea. I knew very little about the topic and asked to be excused, since I wanted to retire. But he persevered, so of course I gave in. However, I thought that I might as well get paid on a full-time basis while doing it, and postponed my retirement till June.

There was then an almost emotional farewell in the Master of the Rolls' court, with John Donaldson presiding and very funny speeches by Pat Mayhew, then the Attorney General and a former pupil, and others. Lucy was there, in the front row with Diana, pulling faces at me. I have an official transcript of the occasion, presented to me by the shorthand writers, and see that I thanked everyone for "a moving interlocutory memorial service". Since then there have been several more on other occasions. (But none as memorable as the earlier farewell to Ted Eveleigh in the Court of Appeal. When all the eulogies had finally stopped and it was his turn, he did what many have done in the Court of

Appeal at the end of a first judgment given by someone else. He looked up, appearing surprised and slightly lost, and said: "I agree and have nothing to add").

Then I finally left the courts and returned to Chambers. As is customary, my name had never been taken down from the top of the door of 4 Essex Court, of which I had been the first head of Chambers for about 11 years from 1961. The then head, Tony Diamond, one of the original tenants, and the senior Clerk, David Grief, both asked me to come back as a full-time arbitrator. At that time this was something unprecedented for a retired Lord Justice. But I could see nothing against it, even though Francis Mann greatly disapproved. He thought that it was *infra dig* and possibly unconstitutional. But I refused to share this view, which had nothing behind it except an old-fashioned restrictive attitude to former judges. Lord Wilberforce had become an arbitrator on his retirement from the House of Lords before me, though he had not joined any Chambers. I was also swayed by the fact that most of the senior members of my old Chambers, then totalling about forty when we had been six at the beginning, had been close friends for many years, such as Gordon Pollock, Lucy's godfather, Stewart Boyd, Ros Higgins and Johnny Veeder, among others. So why not? Since then, countless other judges have retired and done the same, and other old pupils and friends, Michael Mustill, Tony Evans and Tony Diamond, have returned to Chambers from the Bench – to sharpen the competition!

Chambers gave me a small room and full secretarial back-up, with typing, fax and everything. In return I paid them the same percentage of my receipts as all other members of Chambers, together with the same Clerk's fees. We were all very happy with the arrangement. A few years later Chambers moved into three – now five – buildings as "Essex Court Chambers" at 24 Lincoln's Fields, with about 70 inmates, where I have a room on the top floor overlooking the gardens and Lincoln's Inn. For some years I also went on sitting in the Court of Appeal as the first of the supernumeraries (also known as "mothballs" and "retreads") for odd weeks when asked or when my time table permitted, and also sometimes in the Privy Council. But I was almost relieved when all sittings had to stop when I became 75 in 1996. Then there was another minor interlocutory memorial service in court.

Since then I have never missed the courts. On the contrary I have always been glad to be no longer there. The nature and scope of the work has changed out of recognition, with far more public law, litigants in person, judges reading in their rooms out of court, and only fewer, much shorter – and hurried? – oral hearings. The Woolf Civil Procedure reforms have not reduced the judicial resources which are needed, nor the costs of litigation. They have merely shifted the costs "up front", so as to deter people from litigating. To that extent they have achieved their aim, but by a "sidewind", as we used to say. In the result, there is much less civil litigation, but more judges and inevitably further depersonalisation of the judiciary. Many of my friends, who are now successful barristers at the top of their profession, but who had seen the Bench as their ultimate vocation when they were young, now prefer to remain with the fleshpots of the Bar and to retire early. Accumulations of savings and pension have made this possible since the Thatcher era, which to this extent has been left virtually untouched by new Labour.

Chambers have brought me a lot of work over the last 12 years or so, but I have also brought in at least as much from my own contacts, and often it has been a mixture of both. For most of this period I have been as pressed with work as at the Bar, and felt that I was living in a similar but greatly updated atmosphere, close to my son Tim, who got Silk in the Spring of 2000, exactly 40 years to the day after his father. I also finally got to learn to operate a word processor, on which I am typing this book.

How many arbitrations – and recently also mediations – I have done during this time I have no idea. I could of course look them up in Chambers, but why? They have involved a lot of travelling, in addition to endless Conferences. I remember the hearings outside Europe more for their locations, such as Beijing, New York, Lahore, Cairns, Dubai, Hong Kong, Qatar and Singapore, and for the people with whom I was sitting, than for anything else. Some were relatively short, while others went on for years, with long adjournments for the parties between bouts of activity. And by way of public work, I have been chairman of the Appeal Committee of the Takeover Panel for 12 years and also held appointments to hear disciplinary appeals for other City regulators and the Institute of Chartered Accountants. So the variety has been enormous.

Of all the cases during these years only three have really stayed in my memory, and only the first of them could be described as an arbitration. This was in Hong Kong, where I had to decide a dispute between the government and the Harbour Tunnel Company as to whether the tolls payable for driving through the old Harbour Tunnel should be increased or stay as they were – and always had been since its construction. It was a long accountancy battle which left the tolls as they were, but demonstrated once again that anything can be done with figures.

The second was the longest, most difficult, but also the most interesting job I have ever had to do, and for a long time I wished I had never taken it on. Bob Ayling, an old friend, then Chief Legal Adviser to

Tim on taking Silk, with Nicola, 2001.

British Airways, later to become Chief Executive, asked me to do a "safety audit" of BA and to report my findings and recommendations to the Board. Such exercises were fairly common in the early 90's, after we had experienced the King's Cross and Zeebrugge disasters, and many large organisations were reviewing their safety structures and systems. The question was how, if there were to be some disaster followed by a public enquiry, BA would acquit itself and emerge as regards its safety record. It was not a far-fetched idea, and the day on which I first went to see Lord King, the Chairman, he still looked pale from the anguish of the previous day, when a BA 747 coming in from Kuwait in bad visibility had narrowly missed one of the airport hotel towers while mistaking the M4 motorway for a runway, before making a fraught emergency landing.

Having been a pilot, once upon a time, I have always been fascinated by aviation, and I had also edited a book and done a good deal of work in this field. So I accepted with enthusiasm, but soon began to have doubts. The job seemed impossibly big. I worked inseparably with an Assistant in BA's Legal Department, Caroline Boone, who was wonderful and supposedly knew it all, and I also had a car and driver and an office at Heathrow, with secretarial help when I needed it. But to understand the complexities of an organisation as vast as BA, and of its manifold operations, let alone to be able to analyse and – if necessary – criticise them, appeared for a long time to be an impossible task.

Ultimately, it took over 6 months, most of which I spent at Heathrow. The taxying of aircraft and other ground operations were excluded, as well as airport and aircraft security and air traffic control, which was not BA's responsibility. But everything else within BA's control was included, from the ordering and taking delivery of new aircraft; training aircrew, engineers and operational staff; daily flight operations and aircraft maintenance; crisis management; the vetting of foreign airports for operational safety; monitoring the records of routine flight recorders (which BA had, although not legally required); incident reporting from abroad; and – perhaps above all – the effectiveness of the co-operation between the different departments and personnel. The question was of course not whether the various technical operations were in themselves *actually* safe, e.g. the prescribed landing speed, or permitted flight hours between maintenance checks, of a 737, or the safe rotation hours for aircrew. The question was whether the *system* of seeking to ensure human safety was not only of the highest standard, as it undoubtedly was, but – above all – how it would be likely to be judged if BA had to face the full investigation of a public inquiry after a (theoretical) disaster. Could the pursuit and attainment of the highest standards of safety throughout the structure of BA be *demonstrated* and survive a critical, and probably hostile, investigation?

Many of the early weeks were spent simply in trying to understand how BA functioned. After interviewing the heads of the various departments, some of who became friends, and beginning to follow a multitude of organisational charts, it became a regular daily programme for us to attend the important routine meetings of Flight Crew, Engineering, Operations and Safety, which – as far as I remember – were the main departments with which I was involved, and – above all – the periodic joint meetings between them, together with their training and other sub-committees. Then, and in between, there were the direct experiences and observations of what went on. Some days were spent in the hangars, aircrew simulators and cabin crew training mock-ups and swimming pools. Then in the cockpits of aeroplanes on scheduled flights. The relationship between flight crew on the one hand, and management and cabin crew on the other, was one of the main points of controversy and discussion. The most memorable cockpit experiences were on Concorde to New York, the oldest of the planes in regular service, with an antiquated flight deck but still wonderful; a 757 flight to Geneva, and a 747 to Hong Kong – where I was going on a case – with an unforgettable landing at Kai Tak, the old airport on Kowloon, viewed from up front. Then there were visits to Gatwick, BALPA, the pilots's union, the CIA (Civil Aviation Authority), and others whom I don't remember, together with the reading of thousands of pages of miscellaneous documents and the taking of sheaves of notes. The end result was a report of more than 250 pages, with more than 50 recommendations, of what should be done: not to improve safety as such, to which the commitment was absolute, but to enhance its demonstrability in the face of any investigation and possible challenge. After a discussion with the Board, all this was evidently accepted. Some years later, long after the exercise had passed into the public domain, Bob Ayling invited me to the opening of Compass House on the perimeter of Heathrow, to house Flight Crew, Cabin Crew and Operations under one roof, which was one of the main products of this long exercise. But no doubt much has again changed since.

The third job that I remember was for Lloyd's. In the early 90's Lloyd's, in the form of many of its leading Syndicates, was assailed by claims from their members, the "names", for negligent underwriting. Many of the claims were on account of disastrous "long tail" reinsurance risks which had been written in the post-war decades for American insurers and had then been forgotten or buried, to result in vast losses in the 80's due to an epidemic of asbestosis and pollution claims. The main ones were due to the more recent folly and greed of the edifice of "spiral" underwriting of catastrophe reinsurance risks, which first became exposed by the tragic loss of the Piper Alpha North Sea oil platform and then by hurricanes and other insurance disasters. Lloyd's had valiantly tried to settle and get rid of all these claims by putting £900 million on the table and setting up a legal and financial Panel to advise on its equitable distribution among the names. I chaired the Legal Panel together with two QC's, Stewart Boyd and Stephen Tomlinson, and for about four months we worked full time and held numerous hearings, under great pressure, to seek to analyse the degree of culpability or otherwise of more than 120 "syndicate years" to claims for negligent underwriting. At the end, exhausted, we produced a comprehensive – and deeply boring – report which was circulated to all the names. But, whatever may have been its value, the whole exercise came to naught. The £900 million proved to be far too little to persuade the names to give up their claims, and the war in the courts went on.

Since then, all these events have been buried by the course of time and are hardly remembered. After some years Lloyd's more than doubled their offer of £900 million and set up *Equitas* to get a settlement with most of the names, though some skirmishes are still going on and fresh troubles are already brewing. And Hong Kong's newly developed harbour tunnel has largely eclipsed the old one and its ancient tolls. *Tout passe*, and in this febrile lawyers' world surprisingly quickly. All that now remains for me, of 12 years of awards, reports and expert opinions, and all the tensions and bitter disputes which gave rise to them, are piles of papers in the cupboards in my room, gathering dust in oblivion. Which someone will some day have to clear out.

But, at least, these piles are no longer growing, or hardly. A "DOB" (date of birth) in 1921, introducing a venerable and now static CV, is unhelpful to attract new business.

72 · A Resurrection

BUT ALL has not been decline and impending doom.

What I find interesting about life are not just the events, whether landmarks or blips, but the perspective as a whole. I have always felt that a life should have a shape, a pattern, like a symphony. That is why I often view events in terms of "on retourne toujours" and "the wheel has come full circle", as mentioned many times in this book. My father's miraculous return to Germany and the manner of his death, after a last night in a German theatre ending over 15 years of exile, almost made me a believer in some higher power.

There has now been a further happening for him, over 100 years since the event, and more than 50 years after his death.

When I wrote the first version of this book in the early nineties about 10 years ago, my father's memory and works were as described at the end of Chapter 55. His collected works were again being reprinted, which was in itself unusual for a writer whose main reputation had been as a dramatic critic, writing reviews of first night performances in the following morning's papers during the twenties. Much of the content was inevitably ephemeral, with *"Eintagsfliegen"*, flies which only live for a day, like the products of most legal disputes, as the title of one of the five volumes of his *"Die Welt im Drama"*, So, although a further reprint after 70 years was a considerable tribute to his reputation, in the nature of things it was not a publication on a large scale and only resulted in what one might call a posthumous *succès d'estime.*

But in 1997 something happened which was close to a literary *coup de foudre.* The leading editor of the republished works, Dr. Gunter Ruhle, planning to write a biography, had gone to look for material in Breslau and stumbled across a frail collection of old copies of the *Breslauer Zeitung* in the archives of the city university. They had survived from the end of the last century, printed in archaic script and difficult to salvage and decypher. He discovered that from 1895 to 1900, after he had moved to Berlin in his twenties, my father had written a regular column for his former local paper under the heading *"Berliner Briefe"*.

The articles were commentaries and chronicles of social, cultural and political news and events, with each piece dated like a diary entry. They discussed and described the affairs and topics of the day , in a style of consummate light prose, diffused with gentle satire, sometimes acerbic, but also expressing strong opinions with precarious socialist leanings, on the controversial issues of the times. The topics were mostly about life in the capital, ranging from reviews of plays and accounts of receptions, parties, political and civic events, scandals and court cases to tongue-in-cheek and sometimes *lèse-majesté* descriptions of Prussian imperial and governmental occasions, but with politeness towards Wilhelm II and veneration for Bismarck. He had met him when Bismarck was 80 and found him immensely impressive "although his hand was shaking on the crook of his cane and his two giant dogs were worrying him about the legs"

And sometimes, when my father was away from Berlin, there were also echos of his travels abroad, from Venice, Florence, Vienna, Paris and London.

When these articles were republished in book form in 1997 they became something of a sensation and instant bestsellers. They were like treasure trove, a lost literary phenomenon which had been miraculously rediscovered after a hundred years of total oblivion. This was at the time when the capital of Germany was being transferred from Bonn back to Berlin, and interest in Berlin, but without much affection in the rest of Germany, was again at its height. To the delight of the reviewers and readers alike, the contents confirmed that nothing at all had changed. The flavour of these pieces, though much is lost in translation, can perhaps be seen from the oft quoted first sentence of the first, dated 1 January 1895, in which west Berlin is described as "this provincial town, inhabited by all those who know something, are something and have something, and imagine that they know, are and have three times as much . . ."

There were 196 articles, spread from 1 January 1895 to 25 November 1900 at intervals of about 10 days. They were resurrected in two large and heavily annotated volumes, first in successive hardback editions and then also in paperback. There were endless reviews in the press and on television, readings on radio, talking book cassettes, and Judy and I even received CDs of the first volume entitled *"Wo liegt Berlin?"* Where is it? A well-known reviewer on television told his audience to buy "this book of the year, of the decade and the century". None of this could have been imagined by our father when he died in 1948.

The contents are amazingly readable and vivid, although describing six years of life in a foreign world of a century ago. But there are also occasional glimpses of more familiar scenes, even to an English reader. In two pieces written in September 1896, after participating in the Second World Socialist Congress staged in the Crystal Palace in August, my father describes the next three holiday weeks under the heading *"Berlin und London"*. The subtitle is "Berlin is a nice place". This was his landlady's amiable comment when she had asked him where he came from. Whether she actually had any idea of where or what Berlin was is tactfully left open, but he agrees with her: "Berlin is a nice, pretty little place". In comparison with London, the colossal *"Themsestadt"*, which has "forty to fifty *Friedrichstrassen*", the Oxford Street of Berlin, "where you can be driven around by a cabby for an hour without getting out of the crowds". There follow pages about the London metropolis of the mid 1890s, where he walked in Oxford Street every evening among spanking fleets of crowded horse buses unlike anything in small provincial Berlin, culminating in an accolade to the recently constructed Holborn Viaduct, "a street built in the air, with thousands of carriages, houses, people, stones and shops, and other streets crossing underneath, a *Friedrichstrasse* on pillars . . .". Everything about London is infinitely more imposing. But Berlin is cleaner ("maritime cities always smell") and there are better theatres, since *Kunst,* art in the sense of culture, is *"auf dem Hund"* over here, literally gone to the dogs. And, if asked to choose, he would prefer to live in Berlin: "Sirius . . . may be bigger than the sun, but it is not Sirius that ripens our grapes". He could hardly have foreseen that forty years later he would no longer have the choice between Berlin and London.

When I listened to the readings from these books, mostly in the car to and from our cottage in Wiltshire, it is the dates of the extracts which often produced the strongest impressions, like a time warp. I suddenly heard a description of what he did on a day exactly a hundred years ago, like 31 December 1899, to which I listened when both of us were celebrating the beginning of a new different century. And I sat up in the car when I heard his description of the events in Berlin on 28 August 1898, when I knew, but he did not, that his future wife was born on that day.

For Judy and me, apart from sentiment and some emotion, even after this distance in time, the newly discovered *"Berliner Briefe"* have also had practical consequences. We had already decided some years ago that we would not repatriate any royalties from our father's works, which had always been very small, but would try to use them for something in his memory in Germany. Now the royalties suddenly jumped to six figures in sterling. So we set up an Alfred-Kerr-Stiftung in Berlin, which will administer the annual drama prize which had been hoped for and planned long ago. Each year a German doyen of the stage will choose the most promising young actor or actress to emerge from the *Theaterwochen*, the annual Berlin theatre festival, and present a monetary

My parents' graves in Hamburg.

prize provided as to half by the Stiftung and half by the *Tagesspiegel,* a leading daily newspaper. We were invited to the first presentation some years ago, and Judy went again the following year. The inauguration was an emotional occasion. There was a large crowd of people, surprisingly many of them young, with moving speeches, including one from Judy, and even some tears from the older participants. His life and work in Germany had been taken away from him. But now it was being given back. The wheel had come full circle. *On retourne toujours.* And a few months ago, a member of my Chambers happened to see Chekhov's "Seagull" in Edinburgh and showed me the programme which mentioned that the leading actress had won the Alfred Kerr Prize in 1999.

Only one further thought. What would our parents have made of all this? We do not know whether our mother even knew about the past existence of these journalistic products of her husband's youth, published ephemerally more than twenty years before they had met. And neither my sister nor I had ever heard of them. Perhaps even our father had forgotten them. But he would certainly have been amused, though slightly sceptically, by their resurrection — except for one insufferable aspect. He would never have forgiven the reviewers who said that these were the best pieces he ever wrote.

Epilogue

I WROTE a first draft of the then final chapter "A New Profession" at Karachi airport on 1 March 1993, my 72nd birthday, waiting for a flight home after an arbitration "view" of a plant in Lahore. On re-reading this draft now, I am amazed at having survived so much longer. But mainly I wonder at all that has happened since, in less than a decade. I am now writing this a few months after the 11th September 2001, Lucy's 17th birthday, the fateful day of the attacks on both towers of the World Trade Centre in New York and the Pentagon in Washington, and the crash of a fourth hijacked aircraft.

To some extent there is nothing new under the sky. What changes are the objectives, methods, scale and the ferocity of human acts. Multiple concerted hijackings of aircraft have happened before. On 6 September 1970 the PFLP, the Palestine Liberation Front, hijacked four airliners on flights to New York, two American, one Swiss and one Israeli, as a protest against western support for Israel and Egypt's softening policy. One of these hijacks, of an El Al 707 at Heathrow, was unsuccessful, and the conspirators, including an Arab woman of the hour, Leila Khaled, were arrested. One of the other three aircraft, a Panam 747, was flown to Beirut and then to Cairo, where it was blown up on the ground after the passengers and crew had been evacuated. The remaining two, together with a BOAC VC10 hijacked in the Middle East on a flight to London three days later, in revenge for the failure at Heathrow, were flown to Dawson's Field, a small airstrip in Jordan. All the male passengers were taken hostage, and after a breakdown in negotiations all three aircraft were simultaneously blown up. After some undisclosed bargain with the hijackers the hostages were ultimately released.

I was then still at the Bar, and later on I was asked to arbitrate the resulting issues for the Lloyd's aviation market. The various submissions for the insurers and reinsurers were presented in the Council Room of the old Lloyd's building, led by Tony Lloyd and Mark Saville on each side, both former pupils in Chambers and later both Law Lords. Was there a total loss of each of the four aircraft when it was hijacked and successfully taken over, or only when the aircraft was blown up? Depending on this, and for the purposes of the limits of each of the relevant policies and the reinsurance layers, did the "ultimate net loss" under the policies "arise out of one event", or was it "a series of occurrences arising out of one event"? Or were there four events? Or two, one in Cairo and one at Dawson's Field? I had forgotten the outcome until I was recently shown a copy of my Award, dated 29 March 1972, a week before I went on the Bench. Similar questions then arose nearly 20 years later in the litigation which followed the seizure by the Iraqis of 15 aircraft of the Kuwaiti Airlines fleet at Kuwait Airport in 1990 and flying them to Baghdad, just before the beginning of the Gulf war, when the *Dawson's Field* Award was resurrected and cited in the courts. Similar questions have already arisen again in connection with the four hijackings on 11 September 2001, and I hear that the *Dawson's Field* Award, now 30 years old, is again being disinterred.

But that is the only similarity of the terrible events of that day with all earlier history. Everything else is different. In 1970, and even to a large extent in 1990, there was respect for human life. But the events of 11 September 2001, when aircraft carrying innocent passengers and crews were used as missiles to kill thousands of other innocent people, were cataclysmic. They will change the face and history of the world.

How they will be changed, no one can yet say as I am writing this. Except that we can be sure that the world will become still more dangerous, and that all our lives will become even more insecure. But this should not be surprising. To quote our local vicar at St Peter's church, Winterbourne Stoke, as related by Diana when she returned to our cottage: "Surely it must have been obvious to everyone that the world could not go on as it was. It was spiralling out of control". I have often thought this. The human race will one day destroy itself and this beautiful planet as we know it. Mankind now has the means to do so, and nothing will stop it, since it has never been able to control or enforce any self-denying ordinance upon itself. The terrible events of 11 09 01 may merely mark the beginning of a long and fearful ending.

Hopefully – as we now unfortunately say – not. But meanwhile it certainly marks the end of this book. I am grateful that it has covered so much time. All my life, and even when I wrote the first draft, I felt sure that I would never see the year 2000. Now I have. With my family in a crushing crowd on the Embankment under the millenium fireworks. And that was already more than two years ago. Now I should like to say *"Pourrvou que ça dourre"*, as Napoleon's mother Letitia constantly said in her Corsican accent on hearing of her son's triumphs, *"Pourvu que ça dure"*, so long as it lasts.

This is no longer to be expected for me. Although I am told that at my age prostate and bone cancer are containable by medication and some radiotherapy, the outlook is clearly not promising. In fact, it is something of a paradoxical joke to be told that, being 81, there is a reasonable chance that something other than cancer is likely to provide the *terminus ad quem*. My father scribbled that he had loved life very much, but put an end to it when it became torment. I now know how he felt.

All my life people have told me how much I look like my mother, but she never got to this stage and now the person looking back from the mirror to me is my father. But since so much of my life is due to the script of Letitia's life, which my father wrote and Korda bought for the most important £1000 of my existence, which saved us from the holocaust and brought us to England, we might as well end the story here with those words: *Pourvu que ça dure.*

With the hope, and crossed fingers, that it may all still last a little longer, apart from the pain. To see Lucy and Alexander grow up a bit more, and to be with Diana. And to see Winterbourne Stoke get its bypass, which was planned more than twenty years ago when we first bought the cottage. But that would be asking too much. There are no other ambitions left – except never to become a burden to anyone.

So what impressions remain?

A vast tapestry of colours, currents, people and episodes, mostly forgotten, with no central theme except one's own efforts to achieve optimum survival. Always being run by the pressure of events; never in free control of one's life. But at the same time struggling to leave some impression of lasting memory and value. Immortal longings, but on a steadily shrinking scale. A late love of children, nature and the countryside. Many regrets, mainly about my mother's life, wishing that she could have seen and shared in a little more of mine. And the constant realisation of how little any of it means or matters, except for a few loved spirits. And that the waters close inexorably.

All of which is of course commonplace.

I used to think that I wouldn't mind dying so much if I could have a paper in my coffin every day. But now I feel that it would make me despair of the world even more and to fear even more for the lifetime of my children and their generation. But again, that has been commonplace throughout history. Every generation hopes and fears for the next. But this must be a uniquely perilous one, embodying the starkest contrasts. Starvation, war, disease and crime throughout most of the world, and insane "consumerism" and dumb "pop" culture for the rest.

But then also a positive ending. An immutable belief that the vast majority of individual human beings are good, often wonderful. But likely to become stupid, dangerous and even evil when they act, or react, collectively.

This is again a cliché. But finally a last echo of my father. The title of one of his books was the cry of Goethe's Faust:

"Es sei wie es wolle	*"Happen what may*
Es war doch so schön"	*It was all so beautiful"*

And so it was. The last word is gratitude.

Annexe

The *Macao Sardine Case* is a forensic fable which was conceived for an International Bar Association meeting in New York in the mid-eighties when the comparative pros and cons of litigation and arbitration were a perennial topic of discussion. I was then still in the Court of Appeal and doubtful of the constant eulogies in favour of arbitrations. After it had appeared in several journals, the piece was translated and published in Germany and – I think – Sweden, and it has been cited in a number of learned footnotes, bestowing on it a measure of undeserved authenticity.

This painting in memory of it was presented to me at an LCIA Symposium at Tylney Hall in May 2001.

ARBITRATION v LITIGATION: THE MACAO SARDINE CASE[1]

THE RT HON LORD JUSTICE KERR

At the meeting in New York of the International Bar Association in September 1986 one of the 'plenary' themes was *Alternative Methods of Resolving International Commercial Disputes.* Inevitably, the main subject was arbitration. But by way of a change from this terminable conference topic I was asked to speak on the question: 'Is litigation so bad after all?' When one considers the qualities and great popularity of the Commercial Court in London, and no doubt of similar courts in other venues, as well as many good points in favour of litigation generally – if it is well administered - the answer is obviously: 'Not at all'. To justify this, one only has to consider some of the advantages of litigation; such as the possibility of consolidating related disputes by the 'third party' procedure before one tribunal; the certainty of a consistent approach by the application of the same legal principles to different disputes raising similar issues; the control exercisable by the parties over the proper progress and conduct of the proceedings within a prescribed framework by means of a known and enforceable procedure; the availability of a neutral professionally qualified tribunal with the single objective of deciding cases according to law; and the existence of rights of appeal, if necessary, to reverse decisions which are plainly wrong. I therefore had no difficulty in submitting that in many situations there was a great deal to be said in favour of litigation, and that arbitration clauses could prove highly disadvantageous and unsatisfactory; to put it mildly. At the end of the talk, I gave a brief summary of the famous *Macao Sardine Case* as an illustration of my allotted theme. There was no time for a full account of what I could remember about it; but I have now tried to piece it together.

I first heard of this legendary dispute nearly 30 years ago, but I have never seen it reported. If any reader is able to trace some official record, possibly in the archives of NPSMMB, the North Pacific Sardine Manufacture and Marketing Board, I would be very grateful.

[1] This article first appeared in (1987) 3 *Arbitration International* 79. (Not a few commentators believed the Macao Sardine Case to be too awful not to be true; and it is the subject of scholarly study in at least one well-known yearbook).

Meanwhile this is how I remember the facts and issues, with apologies for all erroneous and unintended similarities with past or present companies, organisations, courts, systems of law, etc. (if in fact they were not involved; though many were). I am deliberately mentioning none of the names of the parties and individuals concerned.

An old-established company in Macao had been in the business of producing and marketing tins of sardines for many years, when it ran into financial difficulties. Fortunately tin was relatively cheap even then, from Malaysia and elsewhere. The company also had its own inexpensive local labour force, as well as the necessary machinery and moulds in its factory for the manufacture of the tins. But sardines and oil had become unexpectedly expensive. The company's immediate problem was an order by a Taiwanese customer under a long-term contract for 400 tons FOB. i.e., about 280,000 tins of sardines. Since the Taiwanese and the Macao company were both members of NPSMMA, the North Pacific Sardine Manufacture and Marketing Association, any default was liable to be disastrous. On the other hand, fulfillment was financially impossible. After much deliberation, and only with great reluctance, the company decided that it had no alternative but to fill the tins with mud, of comparable specific gravity. Since its factory in Macao was situated close to a large estuary on the China Sea, there was no shortage of mud, and the collection and canning of the necessary quantities presented no problem.

When the tins had been sealed and checked in the usual manner and packed in the company's cases, the consignment was shipped on a tramp steamer plying in the Pacific, which had been nominated by the Taiwanese customers pursuant to the contract. The bill of lading was issued to the order of the buyers and duly negotiated against their documentary credit established in Hong Kong. The company's immediate cash-flow problems were spectacularly eased, and it viewed the future with a measure of confidence, since the sardine market appeared to be hardening.

Nothing of note happened for some four and a half years. The consignment was sold and resold many times on a steadily rising market. It became a recognised stand-by 'spot' parcel throughout South-East Asia and the Pacific. It was usually sold afloat and rarely unloaded. All the contracts of sale and resale were on the standard PRP form (FOB) of the Pacific Rim Produce Association, and therefore subject to Hong Kong law and the jurisdiction of the Commercial Court in Hong Kong. There was hardly enough room for the countless endorsements on the relatively few bills of lading which covered it as time passed, and many traders' names appeared repeatedly in an ever lengthening string.

Unfortunately matters went wrong about four and a half years later. An earthquake in the Philippines produced a sudden food shortage. Together with other staple commodities, this parcel was hurriedly bought 'spot' from its then Japanese owners by a Government Trading Agency in the Philippines and was ultimately taken into stock by a chain of supermarkets based in Manila. Then all hell broke loose[2].

We are not concerned with the recriminations, investigations and press scandals which followed, nor with the disastrous slump of the Pacific sardine market which claimed many victims over the next six months or so, including a number of tragic suicides. The accounts which I recollect only dealt with the claims down the lengthy string which had been built up over the years. Unfortunately there was no provision in the contracts for settlements between first seller and last buyer, as in other commodity contracts which have since been introduced. But means of dealing with the resulting problems were nevertheless found, once the initial confusion had abated. There were many negotiated settlements, and the original string of over 100 parties was also substantially reduced by the discovery of several large 'circles'. These were simply settled out by the payment of differences. However, a large number of buyers had no option but to sue their sellers.

Fortunately this presented no problem in the Commercial Court of Hong Kong. Since all the contracts incorporated the law of Hong Kong, every plaintiff buyer obtained leave to serve his seller out of the jurisdiction if the seller did not carry on business in Hong Kong. So no-one was beyond the reach of the jurisdiction of the court. The original claim in the action by the Philippine buyers against their Japanese sellers became the basis of all the remaining claims down the string, all in the same action under the 'third party' procedure, or as the result of purely formal applications for consolidation down the line of the main action. The claims themselves were also relatively quite straightforward. On the issue of liability, each buyer simply put in a formal affidavit for summary judgment on the ground that there was no defence, subject to damages being assessed. Each buyer pleaded that at the time of delivery the consignment had not been reasonably fit for the intended purpose, viz, human consumption, and that it had therefore been unmerchantable. As regards quantum, each buyer claimed the market value at the time of delivery. Since the market had risen throughout, this was in each case higher than the price paid. In addition there were various alternative claims, e.g., the difference between (i) the value at the time of delivery or

[2] Milton, *Paradise Lost*, Book VI, line 117.

(ii) the price paid for 400 tons, or 280,000 tins, of sardines in oil and (a) 400 tons of mud or (b) 280,000 tins of mud of the same weight. Plus, in all cases, interest and costs. Later on, by a series of purely formal amendments, each statement of claim simply followed the claims put forward in the one preceding it in the string, and claimed an indemnity in damages and costs.

The defences were a little more varied, but not in substance. None of them made any admissions as to anything. All pleaded *force majeure,* and some added Act of God. One seller applied for leave to amend in order to plead a defence of custom of the trade, citing an alleged similar incident in 1909. But this was refused and saved the need for corresponding amendments all the way up.

By the standards of the Hong Kong Commercial Court this was not a really complex piece of litigation. Despite the 'circle' settlements in account and many negotiated settlements, there remained 47 plaintiffs and defendants and 46 claims; but all in one action. After a well-attended hearing for directions before the Commercial Judge who was in charge of the case, it was agreed that two Commercial Silks should be brought out from London to argue the issues on behalf of all buyers and sellers respectively in principle. Their submissions were concise, and the hearing took little more than a day. The judge had no difficulty in concluding that there was no defence to any of the claims on liability. On quantum he held, first, that since the probability or serious possibility of a resale had been foreseeable in each case, the proper award was that each plaintiff buyer was entitled to an indemnity in damages and costs from his seller. Secondly, on the quantification of the damages, the judge briefly heard the evidence of two expert witnesses and concluded that the consignment was worthless. He therefore considered it unnecessary to deal with any of the various alternatives pleaded in the statements of claim. The tins could not be salvaged for their metal content, since the smell of the mud soon became overpowering, and the cost of disposing of it exceeded the scrap value of the metal. He therefore accepted that the Philippine Supermarket had been justified in dumping the bulk of the consignment in the port of Manila. But he rejected their additional claim for the handling costs involved. The Supermarket's accounts, disclosed on discovery, showed retail sales of about 2,000 tins to the earthquake victims before their complaints about the contents were accepted as justified and the consignment was taken out of stock. But no refunds were made to the customers, and the Supermarket was unable to prove that the cost of dumping exceeded the profit from these sales. The judge accordingly held that both should be disregarded. In the result, each buyer simply recovered damages from his seller equal to the market value of the consignment at the date of delivery, i.e., the transfer of the contractual documents, in the normal way.

In addition, each buyer was awarded interest based on commercial rates current at the various dates of delivery, and his costs. The consequential figures were left to be agreed, as they increased up the string by reason of the indemnity awards, or to be mentioned to the court in default of agreement. But working out figures is a national pastime in Hong Kong, and the drafting of the necessary orders presented no problem. The time from the issue of the original writ until the completion of the litigation, to the satisfaction of all but one of the parties, was a little under 18 months.

The resulting 46 judgments stretched from the Manila Supermarket to the Taiwanese customers of the Macao factory; i.e., from the last to the first buyers in the string. Unfortunately for the Taiwanese, they could not join the Macao manufacturers as defendants as well. Their long-term NPSMM contract was subject to arbitration under the terms of the standard North Pacific Sardine Manufacture and Marketing form. This had been negotiated and revised over many years by representatives of the manufacturing and trading interests involved in the Pacific sardine trade, and the resulting standard arbitration clause was incorporated in all long-term contracts with manufacturers as a matter of course. Since the original purchase was pursuant to an international contract between two foreign parties, which was subject to the Geneva Protocol or perhaps already to the New York Convention, an application by the Taiwanese to join the Macao company as defendants in Hong Kong was emphatically rejected by the Commercial Court and the Court of Appeal, and a further appeal to the Privy Council was rightly not pursued. The Taiwanese were also advised that litigation in Macao was certain to prove unfruitful, on many grounds. But they were forced to meet a judgment exceeding US $500,000 due to the accumulation of damages and costs stemming from more than 100 transactions. Accordingly, the sole hope of the Taiwanese to recoup their heavy loss lay by way of arbitration against the Macao Manufacturers.

I do not think that any report or discussion of the various aspects of the ensuing arbitration was ever published; even unofficially. As one knows, important arbitrations are rarely documented. But accounts of the subsequent events were current some decades ago. What follows are the salient features which I can remember.

The headquarters of the North Pacific Sardine Manufacture and Marketing Organisation was at that time in Seoul. Under the rules incorporated by the NSPMM arbitration clause, all arbitrations were to be administered by the South Korean Chamber of Commerce in Seoul, but no arbitral venue was prescribed. The arbitration clause required that each of the parties was to appoint an arbitrator and for the two arbitrators to appoint a Chairman. In default of agreement between them the Chairman was to be appointed by the President of the Sardine M. & M. Board in Seoul.

The first two years after the Taiwanese demand for arbitration were taken up with the preliminaries to these appointments. The Taiwanese were fairly rapid in appointing a well-known sardine broker carrying on business in Taipei. The respondents were much more deliberate in their choice, but they finally appointed the Portuguese 'in-house' Chief Legal Adviser to a leading casino in Macao. There was then a period of about nine months of wrangling correspondence between the two arbitrators about the choice of Chairman. But while this was still proceeding, with the continuous rejection – after lengthy consideration – of all names successively suggested by the Taiwanese, the Macao company discovered that clients of the Taipei broker's company had figured twice in the string of purchasers and sellers of this consignment. The company accordingly instituted proceedings in Macao, Seoul and Taiwan to have the sardine broker removed. In their submissions they went even further, insisting that in view of the widespread dealings in this parcel all over the Pacific for four and a half years, none of the members of the arbitral tribunal should have any present connection with the sardine trade. After some months of further correspondence between both parties and Seoul, the Taiwanese accepted defeat and replaced the sardine broker by the Deputy-Director of the National Aquarium in Taipei.

Meanwhile it was becoming clear that the Portuguese lawyer from Macao was never likely to agree to any Chairman proposed to him. After direct, but fruitless, appeals to both parties, the President of the Board accordingly decided, with great reluctance, that he would have to make a nomination. Since the Chairman of the tribunal would obviously require full security for the payment of his fees, and after taking account of the heavy administrative costs already incurred, the Chamber of Commerce in Seoul called on both parties to make a substantial deposit in addition to the registration and other fees already paid by the Taiwanese. After some months of total silence from Macao, the Taiwanese were finally compelled to make the required deposit on behalf of both parties. They also had to pay for the translation of all the voluminous files of documents into Korean. Up to then, these had only existed officially in the original English, with translations into Chinese and Portuguese;

although – being advised by a multi-national firm of lawyers established in Tokyo – the Taiwanese had also been supplied with one set of documents in Japanese. But now that the Chamber of Commerce in Seoul was requesting the President of the Board to appoint the Chairman of the tribunal, a Korean translation was obviously needed.

When the translation was available and the Chamber of Commerce had studied the documents for some six months or so, the President of the Board wasted little time. He appointed one of his predecessors, a former President of the North Pacific Sardine M. & M. Board, originally English, who had spent all his working life in the sardine trade in Hong Kong and was now living in retirement in Brunei. He accepted the appointment once he had received adequate assurances from Seoul about his fees and expenses. Having then digested the documents within a few months, he asserted his authority and rapidly secured the agreement of his co-arbitrators to a number of important administrative decisions. In particular, it was agreed that a further substantial payment on account of the fees and expenses of the tribunal should be made by the parties to Seoul, that the arbitration should be held in Bali, and that all necessary secretarial assistance should be recruited locally.

The Macao company paid nothing to Seoul. But it evidently made some payments directly to its local arbitrator, the Portuguese lawyer, since he participated actively over the next 18 months or so. As I recollect, the fifth year of the arbitration was one of great activity. The tribunal met several times at the Bali Inter-Continental and twice at the Hilton. It considered submissions, both in writing and oral, on the applicable law, procedural as well as substantive, from several teams of lawyers. When it became clear that they were unagreed on a number of fundamental preliminary issues, the Chairman, as well as the Deputy-Director of the National Aquarium, felt that the tribunal needed independent legal advice. They accordingly appointed a Singapore lawyer known to the Chairman to advise the tribunal. This provoked strong objections from the Taiwanese. But Seoul overruled these, and in the end the Taiwanese were compelled to fund a further large deposit, on behalf of both parties, to cover the fees and costs of the Singapore lawyer.

With his assistance, and advice which he procured at one point from counsel in London, the 'Terms of Reference', as required under the SNSPMM Rules, were finally drafted. But the Respondents and the Macao lawyer felt unable to sign these, since they still had reservations about the applicable law, both procedural and substantive. Faced with this impasse, the Chairman of the tribunal, armed with an Opinion –

albeit somewhat tentative – from the Singapore lawyer, claimed that he could overrule the Respondents' arbitrator. This provoked the strongest objections, under reserve of all rights, from all the lawyers advising the Macao company. Nevertheless, without their participation, there were then protracted discussions as to whether the Chairman, or the Secretary-General of the Chamber of Commerce in Seoul, could sign the Terms of Reference on behalf of the Respondents. Ultimately the Chairman signed the English version, the Secretary-General signed the Korean version, and the Macao arbitrator recorded his dissent with both at the end of the Portuguese version. The Chinese version was evidently overlooked by everyone, although equally official. For some reason which remains a mystery, no point appears ever to have been taken about this omission.

There then followed further lengthy discussions about a date for the hearing which would be convenient to all concerned. A period of three weeks in the winter of the seventh year was ultimately set aside for this purpose. Shortly before this, however, the arbitrator from Macao announced that he was obliged to retire due to ill health. Unfortunately this came too late for many of the participants, and their companions, who had already arrived and checked into their hotels in advance of the hearing, in order to spend some days in re-reading the papers.

When all concerned had again departed from Bali a week or two later, without having been able to resolve the consequent impasse, the Taiwanese and their lawyers expressed great dissatisfaction at the last-minute resignation of the Macao arbitrator, and little regard for the state of his health. They wrote to Seoul, to the members of the tribunal and to a leading Fisheries trade journal in Taipeh that he had retired on the instructions of, and in collusion with, the Macao Respondents. This was strongly refuted by them and him, and proceedings for libel were threatened. But none took place; partly because everyone could see that the Taiwanese allegations were obviously true, and mainly because there were many respectable precedents of similar misfortunes having befallen arbitrators appointed by respondents on other occasions.

The preparations for a hearing obviously had to await the appointment of a successor arbitrator on the Macao side before they could start again. Taipei appeared to be temporarily discouraged, and there were also many months of total silence from Macao.

But finally the Taiwanese rallied, after they had received favourable advice from Washington, London and Tokyo. A flurry of letters of protest and threats of litigation brought matters back to life. But despite great pressure from Seoul, as well as from the Chairman in Brunei of what remained of the tribunal, Macao did nothing for another 18 months, apart from pointing out that the President of the respondent company had died and that his family was observing a period of mourning. In the end this became unacceptable to the Chairman in Brunei, who was getting old and a little infirm, and had been unable to draw any fees for more than a year. He insisted, in many letters translated by the South Korean Chamber of Commerce into Portuguese and Chinese, that the Macao respondents should immediately appoint a successor to their arbitrator. They finally decided to do so, though wholly contrary to the advice of their lawyers. The reason for their change of mind was that the sardine market was bullish, and they were doing well. They could again afford to be concerned about their reputation. They therefore succumbed gracefully to the combined pressure from Seoul and Brunei, and appointed a former Professor of Commercial Law at the University of Oporto, then living in retirement in the Algarve.

Having read himself into the case within nine months, and upon receipt of a large sum – inevitably provided by the Taiwanese – to cover his interim fees and expenses, he became extremely active in 'progressing' the arbitration. Within the next year he flew no less than five times to Bali (First Class) for meetings of the tribunal, on two occasions with the teams of lawyers representing the parties. But he expressed dissatisfaction with some of the preliminary procedural and substantive conclusions which his predecessor had ultimately felt obliged to accept *de bene esse*. So matters went backwards rather than forward, and the turn-over in secretarial assistance became a constant preoccupation of the tribunal.

Meanwhile every letter and submission was copied to Seoul for information, translation, and incorporation into the official dossier of the arbitration. This attracted the attention of a newly elected President of the South Korean Chamber of Commerce who felt that he must assert his authority. By a series of registered letters, in four languages, he required matters to be 'progressed towards a soon final award'. He also wrote privately to the Chairman of the Macao company, pointing out that its reputation in the trade might suffer if it came to be thought that it was deliberately dragging out the arbitration. In the end Macao accepted a trenchant joint proposal from the Presidents of the Chamber and the Board in Seoul that both party-appointed arbitrators should resign and leave it to the ageing Chairman in Brunei to make a final award on his own. The Deputy-Director of the National Aquarium in Taipei agreed at once. But unfortunately the Professor of Law from Oporto felt unable to do so. He had become interested in the problem of the proper procedural law applicable to the hearings in Bali, and threatened to apply to the Commercial Court in Jakarta for a declaration that a binding award required to be signed by three arbitrators. However after some months of correspondence, and two further trips to the Far East, he was persuaded to withdraw his objections and retire, upon payment of a very large *solatium* – *as* he insisted it should be called for tax purposes – which the Taiwanese were prevailed upon to fund via Seoul.

The arbitration was then in its eleventh year and the Chairman in Brunei now the Sole arbitrator, was urged to proceed with all speed. There were secret fears about his health in Taipei and Seoul, though not in Macao. He decided that he had had enough of lawyers, particularly since the problem had always appeared to him to be perfectly simple and purely commercial. Some years earlier the Macao company had raised a new defence. This had not impressed any of the lawyers, but – as the Chairman pointed out – they had not spent all their working lives in the trade. The amended defence was that the consignment had been fully fit for the intended purpose viz sale and resale, and that it had therefore been perfectly merchantable.

Within a span of little more than a year the Chairman dealt with this problem and all other peripheral issues in a lengthy award published in the four official languages, as well as in Japanese. With the aid of the records of the Hong Kong action, which he had analysed during a lengthy stay at the Mandarin in Hong Kong, he reviewed the details of all sales and resales over the period of four and a half years during the preceding decade. He had also absorbed some legal learning from the Professor of Commercial Law from Oporto, who had recently become a keen supporter of the doctrine of the *lex mercatoria* in international arbitrations, largely because his French was much better than his English. The Chairman of the tribunal drew upon this learning in pointing out that the concept of 'merchantability', itself directly evocative of the *lex mercatoria*, was indubitably derived, forensically and etymologically, from the concept of the 'marketability of the goods in question, i.e., their capacity (*vel non*) of being sold and re-sold in the course of trade. As to this, the evidence of more than 100 sales during the four and a half years of the life of the consignment spoke for itself.

The award went on to point out that the Hong Kong judge had himself relied upon the foreseeability of resales for the purposes of his decision on quantum. The Chairman then drew on his own experience, pointing out that he was entitled to do so, by adding that he had never previously heard of a traded parcel of tins of sardines being landed and opened anywhere in the Pacific. He concluded by indicating that it was not his fault if the right point had not been taken by any of the defence lawyers in the Hong Kong action, and expressed his suspicion that the judge – albeit referred to as 'commercial – had probably never been directly involved with the sardine trade, as carried on in practice. He therefore made an award – published separately from his lengthy reasons – dismissing the claim of the Taiwanese, with an order that they pay all the costs of the arbitration and of the Macao company.

Following the publication of the award and the receipt of a very large sum, the Chairman's health appears to have improved. Although this was his first experience of arbitration, he received frequent appointments thereafter, particularly in commodity cases and on behalf of respondents; but not again as Chairman.

For several years the Taiwanese sought to have the award set aside by the courts of a number of countries; South Korea, Taiwan, Macao and even Indonesia. They were encouraged to do so by the Professor of Law from Oporto, whom they had by then retained for this purpose. He evidently overlooked or failed to disclose to them that the claim was by then time-barred over and over again, so that no purpose could in any event have been served by any judgment setting aside the award. But this was academic, since none of these countries had any procedure for appealing an arbitration award on a point of law. Such a procedure was of course available in Hong Kong, but the courts had no jurisdiction over the parties or the award. The only jurisdiction which was ultimately willing to consider the merits of the award was – surprisingly – the Admiralty and Fisheries Court of Macao. The surprise abated when it became known that the Macao company had unexpectedly withdrawn its opposition to the assumption of jurisdiction by the court, which included a cousin of its President. After a lengthy examination of all aspects of the litigation and arbitration, the court made a declaration that the award was perfectly correct; with costs against the Taiwanese.

That was the end of the matter. But where does it leave my allotted theme for the I B A Conference? The investigation of *all* the issues by means of the arbitration was clearly far more thorough than the Hong Kong action, which seems somewhat superficial in retrospect. Admittedly, the action disposed of 46 claims quite rapidly, relatively inexpensively, and by means of a flexible procedure adapted to the occasion. But the ultimate test of a legal process must be the forensic quality of the reasoning and final decision. Speed, low cost and procedural informality are not everything; a truism constantly pointed out by supporters of arbitration and frequently forgotten by advocates of commercial litigation.

This has to be accepted. Nevertheless, some lingering doubts remain about the outcome of this arbitration. There is of course no standard work on the legal principles applicable under the *lex mercatoria,* for the obvious reason that these do not exist; though some say they are none the worse for that. But I know of no text-book on the law of sale of goods – including, as I am told, the main ones published in South Korea Taiwan and Macao – which supports the conclusion reached in the arbitration; nor one which faults the outcome of the Hong Kong action, except possibly on quantum. So it is perhaps fair to say that it remains an open question whether the action or the arbitration produced a better forensic answer.

My task, however, is not to choose between them. For present purposes it is sufficient to conclude, as I respectfully do, that – occasionally – litigation is – arguably – not so bad after all!